ALEXI KAYE CAMⁱ

Alexi Kaye Campbell's pi.   .e *Pride* (Royal Court,
London, 2008; Lucille Lorte.   ., New York, 2010; Crucible
Theatre, Sheffield, 2011; Trafaɪɡar Studios, 2013); *Apologia* (Bush
Theatre, London, 2009; Trafalgar Studios, 2017); *The Faith Machine*
(Royal Court, London, 2011); *Bracken Moor* (Shared Experience at
the Tricycle Theatre, London, 2013) and *Sunset at the Villa Thalia*
(National Theatre, London, 2016).

The Pride received the Critics' Circle Award for Most Promising
Playwright and the John Whiting Award for Best New Play.
The production was also awarded the Laurence Olivier Award for
Outstanding Achievement in an Affiliate Theatre.

Alexi's work for film includes *Woman in Gold* (BBC Films and
Origin Pictures, 2015).

ALEXI KAYE CAMPBELL

Plays: One

The Pride
Apologia
The Faith Machine
Bracken Moor
Sunset at the Villa Thalia

with an Introduction by the author

NICK HERN BOOKS
London
www.nickhernbooks.co.uk

A Nick Hern Book

Alexi Kaye Campbell Plays: One first published in Great Britain as a paperback original in 2017 by Nick Hern Books Limited, The Glasshouse, 49a Goldhawk Road, London W12 8QP

Cover image: Bertie Carvel and JJ Feild in *The Pride* at the Royal Court Theatre, London, 2008; photographed by Stephen Cummiskey

Designed and typeset by Nick Hern Books, London
Printed in the UK by CPI Group (UK) Ltd

A CIP catalogue record for this book is available from the British Library

ISBN   978 1 84842 692 4

Contents

Introduction

I started writing plays through frustration. I had been an actor for almost twenty years and even though for the most part I had loved my job, I reached a point where I began to feel powerless and creatively thwarted. I had always written – my mother insists that I was penning reams of dialogue at the age of six – but I had found it difficult to *complete* anything. My drawers were full of half-finished plays, scraps of scenes, plot summaries.

And then one day, in between acting jobs, I finished something. It was a black comedy called *Death in Whitbridge*. It was messy but it was a *finished play*. Even then I was aware of the significance of the moment. Galvanised by what felt at the time like a substantial victory against the forces of procrastination, I sent the play out to a handful of theatres and awaited responses.

When those responses came, they were encouraging but non-committal. It was the producer Matthew Byam Shaw who most liked the play and organised a reading of it. The reading went well but afterwards, in his office, he told me that the large cast made it impossible to produce. 'Write a play with fewer actors in it,' he advised me and then added: 'But whatever you do, keep writing.' Something about the conviction with which he uttered these words encouraged me to do just that. I started writing my next play, *The Pride*, almost immediately.

Again I sent it out and again I received encouraging replies – but more importantly Anthony Clark offered me a production at Hampstead Theatre. I was about to accept the offer when my partner Dominic Cooke read the play. At the time, he was the artistic director at the Royal Court. He admired the play, but for obvious reasons was reluctant to offer me a production. It was Ruth Little, the then literary manager of the theatre who championed *The Pride* and put it into the script meeting under a pseudonym so as not to prejudice the response. The reaction was positive. After some soul-searching and discussions with the theatre's board and staff, Dominic decided, very bravely, to programme it in the Theatre Upstairs.

Jamie Lloyd directed a luminous production of it, and the play went on to be produced in New York and then in many countries across the world. I have watched it being performed in Sweden and Germany, Italy and Japan, and every time I have been humbled by the love and dedication of its actors.

Josie Rourke had commissioned me to write a play for the Bush before *The Pride* had even been programmed. In this way, Josie was the first person who decided to put her money – or at least the Bush's money – where her mouth was as far as my writing potential was concerned. I wrote her a first draft of *Apologia* and I thought it was a mess. Josie read it and asked to meet me. I expected she was going to advise me to stick to the acting. Instead, she told me that she was going to programme it. I reeled. I realised of course that the play needed a huge amount of rewriting, but Josie's faith in it was overwhelming. I knew I then had to honour that faith with a lot of hard work, which is what I proceeded to do. After substantial rewrites and some great pointers from Josie, I delivered the rehearsal draft and she directed an exquisite production with beautifully detailed performances from the actors she cast.

Meanwhile, following the success of *The Pride* I received a commission from the Royal Court. I set off to write a play for the main stage and knew that the space demanded something more ambitious in scale. I turned to a subject I had always been excited by, the legacy of Christianity and its role in the development of humanism. The play was *The Faith Machine* and I wanted Jamie to direct it because I felt he would have an instinctive grasp of its tone and how to make the play's epic qualities immediate and approachable. I was right – once again I marvelled at the result.

Bracken Moor was a commission for Shared Experience. I had worked with the company as an actor and had a real affinity with Polly Teale, one of the company's artistic directors. I wrote a play that I felt would suit Polly's passions – the play's sensibility, its metaphysical dimensions, its world of suppressed emotions, were all tailored to suit. Again, I was spoilt by a riveting production and an exceptional cast. I will never forget Helen Schlesinger's performance as the mother crippled by grief after the death of her son – it is quite simply one of the finest performances by an actor that I have ever seen on stage, and that it should be in a play that I had written filled me with pride.

Nick Hytner had commissioned me to write a play for the National Theatre after he had seen *Apologia*. Daunted by the task of writing a play for a theatre of which I had always been slightly in awe, it took me a very long time to write it and unfortunately I was able to deliver *Sunset at the Villa Thalia* only after Nick had programmed his last season. The new team under Rufus Norris did a reading of it and its flaws were evident, but with Ben Power and Simon Godwin's astute dramaturgical advice I did a major rewrite and the play was programmed in the Dorfman Theatre. I was thrilled by Simon Godwin's production and by all the performances, led by Ben Miles' thrillingly accurate portrayal of charismatic but tortured Harvey.

Looking back now I realise quite how spoilt I've been to have had the first incarnations of all these plays brought into being by some of the most extraordinary directors, designers and actors working in this country – and for that I will always be profoundly grateful.

And I have many unforgettable memories of these first ten years of my life as a playwright from overseas as well: watching Robyn Nevin bring a wounded, angry heart to her performance as Kristin at the Melbourne Theatre Company. Stepping out of the Lucille Lortel Theatre after watching Joe Mantello's haunting production of *The Pride* and realising that we were just one block away from The Stonewall Inn. Sitting in an auditorium in Tokyo, dazzled by the stark poetry of a production of *Apologia* at the Bungakuza Theatre Company.

But more than anything else as I now consider these five plays as they are about to be published together for the first time, I am reminded more than ever of what it was that drove me to work in the theatre in the first place: a curiosity about how personal lives are connected to a larger social and historical context, and an urgent need to try and figure out something of why we behave in the strange ways that we often do. Discussions about form will always continue, theatrical fashions will come and go. But for me, both as actor and writer, the theatre will always be one thing above all else – a place where we can question and explore what it means to be alive and how we live with each other.

Alexi Kaye Campbell
July 2017

THE PRIDE

The Pride was first performed at the Jerwood Theatre Upstairs at the Royal Court Theatre, London, on 21 November 2008, with the following cast:

PHILIP	JJ Feild
OLIVER	Bertie Carvel
SYLVIA	Lyndsey Marshal
THE MAN / PETER / THE DOCTOR	Tim Steed

Director	Jamie Lloyd
Designer	Soutra Gilmour
Lighting Designer	Jon Clark
Music and Sound Designers	Ben and Max Ringham

The Pride received its American premiere at the Lucille Lortel Theatre, produced by MCC Theater, on 27 January 2010, with the following cast:

PHILIP	Hugh Dancy
OLIVER	Ben Whishaw
SYLVIA	Andrea Riseborough
THE MAN / PETER / THE DOCTOR	Adam James

Director	Joe Mantello
Designer	David Zinn
Lighting Designer	Paul Gallo
Sound Designer	Jill B.C. DuBoff

The Pride was revived at the Trafalgar Studios, London, on 8 August 2013, with the following cast:

PHILIP   Harry Hadden-Paton
OLIVER   Al Weaver
SYLVIA   Hayley Atwell
THE MAN / PETER /   Mathew Horne
THE DOCTOR

Director   Jamie Lloyd
Designer   Soutra Gilmour
Lighting Designer   Jon Clark
Sound and Music   Ben and Max Ringham
Associate Director   Edward Stambollouian
Voice Coach   Charmian Hoare
Fight Director   Kate Waters

Author's Note

The main challenge in any production of this play is to handle effectively the constant scene and costume changes between the two different eras it is set in. How the director and designer deal with this challenge is up to them. Here, though, are a couple of thoughts.

When the play begins we should feel as if we are watching a 1950's drawing-room play. Only as the play progresses does this world slowly start to disintegrate and break up. The furniture and walls gradually disappear until we find ourselves in the multi-locational second half.

One idea is to make a virtue of the costume changes – perhaps they take place somewhere on stage and are partly visible to the audience. Something more stylised. This might help the transitions between scenes become easier and more fluid.

The most important quality is one of confluence. The two different periods should meld into each other. They are distinct from each other in appearance but they know each other in spirit: a young woman standing next to her elder self. Different clothes, different hairstyles, different textures of skin… but the eyes are the same. The past is a ghost in the present just as the present is a ghost of prescience in the past.

Characters

1958
OLIVER, *mid-thirties*
PHILIP, *mid-thirties*
SYLVIA, *mid-thirties*
THE DOCTOR, *late thirties*

2008
OLIVER, *mid-thirties*
PHILIP, *mid-thirties*
SYLVIA, *mid-thirties*
THE MAN
PETER

OLIVER, PHILIP *and* SYLVIA *are to be played by the same actors in both periods. One actor plays the* DOCTOR, *the* MAN *and* PETER.

ACT ONE

1958

PHILIP *and* SYLVIA*'s apartment in London. It is modest but tasteful. Lots of books, a sofa and armchairs, a few pictures on the wall.*

PHILIP *is standing by the front door. He is dressed for a night out.* OLIVER *has just arrived.*

OLIVER. Philip.

PHILIP. Oliver.

OLIVER. Yes.

PHILIP. At last.

OLIVER. Yes.

PHILIP. I've heard so many things.

OLIVER. Have you?

PHILIP. So many things about you.

OLIVER. Gosh.

PHILIP. All good.

OLIVER. That's a relief.

PHILIP. Sylvia's always talking about you.

OLIVER. Is she?

PHILIP. I'm beginning to get rather jealous.

OLIVER. No need, I'm sure.

PHILIP. She thinks you're a genius.

OLIVER. There are many things I am, but a genius is definitely not one of them.

PHILIP. Extraordinary is what she calls you.

OLIVER. Does she?

PHILIP. Out of the ordinary.

A slight pause.

Let me take your coat.

OLIVER. Thank you.

OLIVER *takes off his coat and hands it to* PHILIP, *who hangs it up carefully.*

PHILIP. I'm afraid the lady is running a little late. Applying the face paint, I believe. That ancient ritual.

OLIVER. I'm early.

PHILIP. Not at all. You're right on time.

OLIVER. I walked. I thought it would take me slightly longer.

PHILIP. It's a lovely evening.

OLIVER. Well, no rain in any case.

PHILIP. All the way from Maida Vale?

OLIVER. Yes, Maida Vale.

PHILIP. Across the park, eh?

OLIVER. Yes.

PHILIP. That's a long walk.

OLIVER. I enjoyed it.

PHILIP. It's the season for it.

OLIVER. Everything in full bloom.

PHILIP. Lovely.

A slight pause.

What can I get you to drink?

OLIVER. A Scotch?

PHILIP. Ice and water?

OLIVER. Perfect.

PHILIP. I think I'll have the same.

PHILIP *walks over to a small drinks table and pours them a couple of drinks.*

She thinks your stories are wonderful.

OLIVER. She's certainly captured the spirit of the thing.

PHILIP. She seems to care. About the book, I mean.

OLIVER. She's very, very talented.

PHILIP. Can't stop talking about it. Something about a garden.

OLIVER. Well, it's more of a jungle, really.

PHILIP. A jungle.

OLIVER. Let's call it a jungle in the heart of England. Or at least a very overgrown and rather tropical garden.

PHILIP. What is it with children's writers and gardens? There seems to be a proliferation of them. Most of them secret, I dare say.

OLIVER. You're right.

PHILIP. Well, she's very busy with it in any case. Sketches of strange creatures all over the place. I came across a rather alarming picture of something that resembled a two-headed antelope in the bathroom the other day. Fascinating.

OLIVER. That'll be the Bellyfinch. I'm supposed to be having a first look at it on Friday morning, I believe.

PHILIP. Bellyfinch indeed. I'm afraid by comparison my life seems rather lacklustre.

OLIVER. I don't honestly believe there is such a thing as a lacklustre life.

PHILIP. You haven't sold property for a living.

OLIVER. Unexplored perhaps, but not lacklustre.

PHILIP *hands him his drink. They sit.*

PHILIP. I've never met anyone like you before. A writer, I mean.

OLIVER. Haven't you?

PHILIP. Apart from this ghastly friend of my mother's who's published a book on baking cakes.

OLIVER. Baking cakes?

PHILIP. I'm not sure that really counts.

OLIVER. That sounds a little unfair. Nothing wrong with books about cakes.

PHILIP. Have you only ever written for children?

OLIVER. For the most part. But I've written two travel books as well.

PHILIP. Sylvia mentioned it. One on Athens.

OLIVER. I lived there for a year.

PHILIP. And the other?

OLIVER. The other on the Lebanon.

PHILIP. The Lebanon?

OLIVER. But mostly I'm drawn to writing for children.

PHILIP. I wonder why.

OLIVER. I don't really know. I think it might have something to do with running completely wild.

PHILIP. Wild?

OLIVER. The possibilities are infinite. The parameters and conventions of adult fiction I find a great deal more restrictive.

PHILIP. I see.

OLIVER. I feel a lot happier in a world of talking tigers and magic mirrors. More in my element, really.

PHILIP. Fair enough.

OLIVER. Maybe one day adult fiction will embrace my more extravagant flights of fancy, but for the time being I'm quite happy writing for the under-twelves.

PHILIP. Well, it seems to keep a roof over your head.

OLIVER. A leaking one, but yes, just about.

PHILIP. Well, here's to the book anyway.

OLIVER. The book.

They toast.

PHILIP. It's strange.

OLIVER. What is?

PHILIP. When I opened the door.

OLIVER. Yes?

PHILIP. You look familiar, is what I think I'm saying.

OLIVER. Yes, I thought so too.

PHILIP. Did you?

OLIVER. Yes, I think I did.

PHILIP. Well, maybe we've bumped into each other. On the Underground or something.

OLIVER. Maybe.

PHILIP. Stranger things have happened.

Pause.

Or maybe it's just because she talks about you so often.

OLIVER. Talks about me?

PHILIP. So perhaps that's why I felt like I'd seen you before.

OLIVER. How d'you mean?

PHILIP. Oh, it's just that sometimes if you've heard a great deal about someone, if you've been expecting them in some way, you sort of imagine them before they actually arrive.

OLIVER. Yes.

PHILIP. If you know what I mean.

OLIVER. Yes, I think I do.

SYLVIA *enters. She is smartly dressed for an evening out.*

PHILIP. Here she is.

SYLVIA (*to* OLIVER). Has he been interrogating you?

PHILIP. Mercilessly.

OLIVER. Hello, Sylvia.

SYLVIA. He's a very jealous kind of man.

PHILIP. Rabid with it.

SYLVIA. Can easily become violent. Philip, be a darling and do me up.

She turns her back to him so that he can help her with the top hook of her dress.

Comes in handy though from time to time, I must say. I see he's offered you a drink.

OLIVER. He's been the perfect host.

SYLVIA. So all that training wasn't a complete waste of time after all.

PHILIP. I'm learning fast. Gin?

SYLVIA. I've booked the table for eight.

PHILIP. A quick one.

SYLVIA. Thank you, darling.

PHILIP *goes to the bar to pour her a drink.*

PHILIP. I've been telling Oliver how you keep talking about him.

SYLVIA. You haven't been embarrassing me in front of my employer, have you?

PHILIP. Probably.

SYLVIA. I've been rather nervous, you know. God knows why.

OLIVER. Nervous?

SYLVIA. About the two of you meeting.

PHILIP. She has been putting it off, hasn't she, Oliver?

OLIVER. Now that you mention it.

SYLVIA. It's a silly thing, really. I suppose it's just that I want you to get on.

PHILIP. We were doing just fine.

SYLVIA. To like each other, I mean.

OLIVER. I don't see why we shouldn't.

PHILIP. As long as I don't discover you've been having a torrid affair behind my back we should get on just fine.

SYLVIA. I did warn you about his sense of humour, Oliver.

PHILIP. Sense of humour?

SYLVIA. Or lack of it, I should say.

PHILIP. You're heartless.

SYLVIA. Just honest.

A slightly awkward pause. PHILIP *hands* SYLVIA *her drink.*

I hope you like Italian food, Oliver.

PHILIP. We've made a reservation at a little Italian place around the corner.

OLIVER. Lovely.

SYLVIA. Philip's always making fun of it but I find it charming.

PHILIP. It's extremely red. Everything in it is red.

OLIVER. I'm partial to a little red.

PHILIP. The walls, the tablecloths, the waiter's face. Everything's red.

SYLVIA. Philip's convinced they're not real Italians.

PHILIP. They're Yugoslavians. I'm convinced they're Yugoslavians pretending to be Italians.

OLIVER. It sounds interesting.

SYLVIA. But the food is good.

PHILIP. With a strong Serbian flavour to it.

OLIVER. Delicious, I'm sure.

A slight pause as they all sit down.

I'm very pleased to hear that a Bellyfinch has been spotted hanging around the house.

SYLVIA. Just a preliminary sketch, I'm afraid, but it's getting there.

OLIVER. I can't wait to see it.

SYLVIA. Hopefully by Friday it will be a little more confident. As we speak it's looking a trifle too purple for its own good.

PHILIP. All this talk of Bellyfinch and Hampshire jungles has made me very curious. I can't wait to read the damn thing.

SYLVIA. Well, you'll have to be patient, won't you?

OLIVER. Nearly there.

SYLVIA. Nearly. And in the meantime, you're not to snoop.

PHILIP. It's not my fault if you leave pictures of alarming things scattered across our home.

OLIVER. Is he a snooper?

SYLVIA. Of the very worst kind.

PHILIP. In the bathroom. On the sofa. Even in the fridge.

OLIVER. The fridge?

SYLVIA. Just once.

PHILIP. Something brown crawling up a tree. In the fridge. It was most disconcerting.

SYLVIA. The doorbell was ringing. I was preparing dinner. A moment of absent-mindedness, that's all.

PHILIP. Your story has invaded us. And then I'm accused of being a snooper.

OLIVER. Please accept my apologies.

PHILIP. Apologies accepted.

They laugh. There is a pause.

I am envious of you two, you know.

OLIVER. Envious?

SYLVIA. Whatever of?

PHILIP. Oh, you know, your work. Doing something creative I suppose is what I mean. Being able to invest a certain amount of passion in what you do for a living.

OLIVER. It doesn't feel passionate. Lonely more like.

SYLVIA. Philip is very frustrated in his work, aren't you, darling?

PHILIP. I sell houses, Oliver.

OLIVER. You were saying.

PHILIP. Houses and flats.

SYLVIA. The thing that you really ought to know is that Philip came into his line of work almost by accident.

OLIVER. Accident?

PHILIP. My father died.

SYLVIA. Philip's father died when he was just twenty-one.

PHILIP. I'd just left university.

SYLVIA. Philip's father had spent years running his own business buying and selling property. Philip's brother was all set up to take it over.

PHILIP. Well, he was being groomed for it, really. Father was grooming him for it. I was the useless one. Rather aimless, I'm afraid.

SYLVIA. But then two years later, Roger –

PHILIP. That's my brother.

SYLVIA. Roger was killed.

PHILIP. It was an accident.

SYLVIA. A car accident. A terrible thing.

PHILIP. I had to look after my mother.

SYLVIA. And your sister.

PHILIP. So I had no choice, really. The business just sort of fell into my hands, as it were.

SYLVIA. I sometimes wonder what you would have done. What you would have been. If things had turned out differently, I mean.

PHILIP. God knows, so do I. I'd have emigrated, probably.

OLIVER. Emigrated?

SYLVIA. Philip's always had this terribly mad idea of emigrating.

OLIVER. How exciting.

SYLVIA. Australia, Canada, that sort of thing.

PHILIP. Somewhere new.

SYLVIA. Do you remember you became obsessed with the whole idea of moving to Africa?

PHILIP. Africa, yes.

SYLVIA. He read every possible book that he could get his hands on. Books on Kenya, books on Rhodesia. They were strewn all over the house.

OLIVER. I'd love to visit Africa.

PHILIP. Never did make it further than Brighton, I'm afraid.

SYLVIA. One day.

OLIVER. One day.

PHILIP. Then next thing you know you wake up and you've spent the good part of your life showing people around empty flats.

SYLVIA. There are worse things one could do with one's life.

PHILIP. Are there?

OLIVER. I'm sure Sylvia's right.

PHILIP (*kindly*). She always is.

Pause.

Now you on the other hand, Oliver, have made it beyond Brighton.

OLIVER. I've been to a few places.

SYLVIA. Oh, stop being modest, you've been absolutely everywhere.

OLIVER. Not quite everywhere.

SYLVIA. Oliver lived in Greece.

PHILIP. Yes, he was saying…

SYLVIA. And Italy. And Beirut. And Syria.

OLIVER. I do have an affinity with that part of the world.

PHILIP. How exciting. To have lived there.

SYLVIA. Oliver was based in Athens.

PHILIP. How wonderful.

OLIVER. I lived in a tiny little house at the foot of the Acropolis. Infested with mice, but absolutely charming.

SYLVIA. How utterly romantic.

OLIVER. If you craned your neck outside the kitchen window you could just about catch a glimpse of the Parthenon.

PHILIP. The Parthenon.

SYLVIA. Philip and I are determined to drive down to Greece one day, aren't we, darling?

PHILIP. If you say so.

SYLVIA. Down through France and Italy and across the Adriatic.

PHILIP. One day.

SYLVIA. And then on to the islands.

OLIVER. The islands are beautiful.

SYLVIA. Philip, myself, a couple of copies of *The Odyssey* and a chessboard.

PHILIP. Not forgetting the gin, of course.

OLIVER. Not forgetting the gin.

SYLVIA. One day.

There is a pause. Suddenly, SYLVIA *remembers something. She turns to* OLIVER.

Tell him about Delphi.

PHILIP. Delphi?

SYLVIA. Yes, Delphi. The story about what happened to you in Delphi.

OLIVER. Oh, that…

SYLVIA. Your epiphany in Delphi.

PHILIP. What epiphany in Delphi?

SYLVIA. Oliver told me a wonderful story…

OLIVER. It's nothing really.

PHILIP. An epiphany in Delphi.

SYLVIA. It's wonderful.

PHILIP. Sounds like the title of a dreadful novel. *An Epiphany in Delphi.*

OLIVER. I don't know whether Philip…

SYLVIA. We took a break from work the other day and Oliver told me he'd been to Delphi.

OLIVER. It's not much of a story. Maybe some other time.

SYLVIA. And that something had happened to him there. Is it fair to call it a mystical experience?

PHILIP. Oh, you must say.

OLIVER. I really don't think…

PHILIP. Please.

OLIVER. It's not really that exciting or interesting. In a matter of fact it's not much of a story at all. It was just this funny thing that happened.

PHILIP. I'm all ears.

OLIVER. You'll be very disappointed, I'm afraid.

SYLVIA. Oh, go on, Oliver.

OLIVER. Well, I'd gone up to Delphi because it was one of the places in Greece, one of the sites I most wanted to visit.

SYLVIA. The oracle.

OLIVER. So I'd taken this rickety old bus from Athens and it took hours and hours and it twisted its way through the mountain roads and I remember we arrived just before the sun was going down and it dropped us off just outside this little hotel. The Hotel Zeus or something. And there were a few other foreigners – an old American couple and a German and a few other English people including this insufferable woman with a loud pompous voice and very confident opinions.

PHILIP. Not the most winning combination.

OLIVER. And we all had a bite for dinner and then went straight to sleep.

PHILIP. I'm riveted already.

OLIVER. And the next morning I woke up and opened the shutters and, well... the view was absolutely...

SYLVIA. Breathtaking.

OLIVER. The view was absolutely breathtaking. I mean, I can't do it justice. I can't attempt to describe it. You'd have to go and see it for yourself. To believe it.

PHILIP. One day.

OLIVER. The landscape, you see, the position of it. It is quite mesmerising. Very, very dramatic. Because you are high up in the mountains and on the peaks above us there was even snow, but then you look down, down through these silver slanting olive groves and you can see the sea.

SYLVIA. How beautiful.

OLIVER. You can see the waters of the Corinthian Gulf. So there is something very spectacular. I mean, truly, truly beautiful. And you begin to realise why it is that the Greeks chose that place for their oracle. That maybe in a place of such beauty and stillness you could have a sense of things to come. It takes you out of your time, out of time. You could see the bigger picture in a way.

PHILIP. Is that it? Your epiphany?

OLIVER. I've barely started.

SYLVIA. Oh, Philip, give the man a chance.

OLIVER. So after breakfast I set off towards the ancient theatre and the site of the oracle and I had the old Americans in tow. I think they thought I was a classics scholar or something. They kept asking me these questions and were very disappointed when my answers weren't quite as thorough as they were expecting.

SYLVIA. You do look the part. Especially when you're wearing your specs.

OLIVER. Well, eventually I succeeded in shrugging them off. I lost them somewhere and was able to continue on my own. Which was rather a relief, I must say.

PHILIP. I'm not surprised. One does not want to have a spiritual experience with American tourists in close proximity.

OLIVER. I just started wandering around the site. I was completely on my own and it was very, very quiet. All you could hear was the incessant humming of the cicadas. And a bit of a breeze playing through the trees. And I just walked through the place in a bit of a daze, really.

PHILIP. I feel an epiphany coming.

OLIVER. And then I heard it.

PHILIP. Told you.

OLIVER. I suppose I can only describe it as a voice. Not a voice in any conventional sense. Not the kind of voice one could immediately identify as in any way recognisable.

PHILIP. Are you sure it wasn't one of the Americans?

SYLVIA. Oh, Philip, do be quiet.

PHILIP. Pearls before swine.

OLIVER. I just stood there and I heard this voice. And it pretty much said that everything was going to be all right.

PHILIP. All right? What was going to be all right?

OLIVER. Well, that one day, maybe many, many years from now, there will be an understanding of certain things, a deeper understanding of certain aspects of our natures that would make all the difficulties we now feel, all the fears we now hold onto and the sleepless nights we now have seem almost worthwhile... And that the people who live in those times, be it fifty or five hundred years from now will be happy with that understanding and wiser for it. Better.

SYLVIA. How wonderfully Chekhovian.

OLIVER. And it sort of felt that this voice was coming to me in some way from that very future. Some future awareness of ourselves as it were. And that's it, really. That was my epiphany.

SYLVIA. There are certain places which have an effect on one. Certain places that touch one.

PHILIP. Yes, I know what you mean. I can't imagine experiencing a similar sort of self-revelation in Pimlico.

OLIVER. Knightsbridge maybe, but certainly not Pimlico.

PHILIP. In any case, my darling, I wish you'd informed me that we were having dinner tonight with a man who regularly hears voices. I'd have been more prepared.

SYLVIA. Oh, Philip, you're awful.

OLIVER. I feel positively embarrassed now.

SYLVIA. Oh, don't. He's just being silly.

They laugh and then there is a pause.

We ought to get a move on.

OLIVER. Yes.

PHILIP. We don't want to upset the Yugoslavians.

SYLVIA. God forbid. I have to fetch my cardigan. I'll only be a minute.

PHILIP. You can't possibly leave us alone. We'll have nothing to talk about.

SYLVIA. You could have fooled me.

PHILIP. Well, hurry along then.

SYLVIA. All right, all right, stop being a bully.

PHILIP. Hurry up.

SYLVIA *leaves the room and the two men are left alone. There is a pause and then they both begin to talk at the same time.*

I can't begin to tell you…

OLIVER. There's something that…

PHILIP. After you.

OLIVER. No, please…

PHILIP. I was just going to say I can't tell you what this job means to Sylvia. How much she enjoys working for you.

OLIVER. It means a great deal to me too.

PHILIP. I don't think she's ever thrown herself into a project with such zeal. And the timing was so fortunate.

OLIVER. The timing?

PHILIP. The commission. It's what she needed after everything that happened.

OLIVER. She did mention that she hadn't been very well.

PHILIP. Yes.

An awkward pause.

You know she used to be an actress, don't you?

OLIVER. She told me.

PHILIP. Before she took up illustrating.

OLIVER. Yes.

PHILIP. Only for a couple of years.

OLIVER. I wish I'd seen her on the stage.

PHILIP. Then she decided to give up. She said she was doing it for us.

OLIVER. Oh.

PHILIP. But I think it scared her in some way.

OLIVER. Scared her?

PHILIP. She was exceptionally good. It was rather terrifying how good she actually was. She would *become* these people. Enter these people's lives so fully, so completely. Her imagination, I suppose.

OLIVER. I can believe she was very good.

PHILIP. Of course, that whole world…

OLIVER. The theatre?

PHILIP. Not really her cup of tea, I don't think.

OLIVER. Wasn't it?

PHILIP. But she was very good. Instinct, I suppose, intuition. And empathy. Those sort of qualities.

OLIVER. Yes.

PHILIP. But I think it's wise.

OLIVER. Wise?

PHILIP. That she gave up, I mean.

OLIVER. Do you?

PHILIP. She's fragile.

There is a pause.

Have a lot of sleepless nights, do you?

OLIVER. I beg your pardon?

PHILIP. You said earlier. In your story. The oracle. You said something along the lines of one day there will be an understanding of certain things that will make all the sleepless nights we now have seem almost worthwhile.

OLIVER. Oh.

PHILIP. And I was just wondering if there's lots of them. Sleepless nights.

OLIVER. A few.

PHILIP. All those Bellyfinches floating around in your head no doubt.

OLIVER. Probably.

A long pause. Something has happened. Then SYLVIA *enters.*

SYLVIA. I'm ready.

PHILIP. It's about time.

OLIVER. You look lovely.

SYLVIA. Thank you, Oliver.

> PHILIP *starts turning off the lights.*

I was thinking.

PHILIP. What?

SYLVIA. How important this evening is.

PHILIP. Is it?

SYLVIA. For me. For all three of us, really.

PHILIP. Why?

SYLVIA. Oh, I don't know.

PHILIP. Have you got the keys?

SYLVIA. Yes.

PHILIP. Come on then.

> *They make a move towards the door. As they move towards it, a* MAN *enters the room. He is wearing a Nazi uniform. He is invisible to them but on his entrance he brushes up close to them.*

SYLVIA. What was that?

PHILIP. What was what, darling?

SYLVIA. I felt… I felt something.

PHILIP. You felt what?

> *The* MAN *moves to the centre of the room and stands there silently.*

SYLVIA. Nothing.

PHILIP. Don't forget your coat.

OLIVER. It's not warm.

> SYLVIA *picks up her coat. They open the door to leave.*

PHILIP. So why is tonight so important then?

SYLVIA. Don't mind me. Just thinking out loud.

OLIVER. Do that often, do you?

SYLVIA. That's all.

PHILIP. Mad as a hatter, Oliver.

OLIVER. Is she?

SYLVIA. Don't be a beast.

PHILIP. Mad as a hatter.

They close the door behind them. Slowly, a scene change happens imperceptibly, in semi-darkness. Perhaps some music could be played – something that could well have been played in the scene change of a 1950's production – something soft, elegant. A couple of changes to the room – maybe a giant modern photograph is revealed or a plasma screen appears – so that now this could be a modern flat decorated in a 1950's retro style. But the room is essentially the same, the changes are superficial and decorative. The 1950's music begins to meld into something new, something loud, maybe violent. All the while, the MAN *in the Nazi uniform remains in the centre of the room, still and silent.*

2008

Still in semi-darkness, OLIVER *enters, but he is now in his underwear. Behind him he drags a dressing gown. He sits on the floor somewhere in the room with the* MAN *standing over him, looking down at him. The lights return and the music comes to an abrupt end. For the first few lines, the* MAN *speaks in a German accent.*

MAN. Don't fucking look at me, you fucking piece of shit.

OLIVER. I'm sorry. I'm sorry.

MAN. You better be.

OLIVER. I'm sorry.

MAN. You never fucking look at me, you worthless piece of shit. What are you?

OLIVER. What am I?

MAN. What are you? Tell me what you are!

OLIVER. What am I.

MAN. You fucking tell me what you are, you fucking piece of human shit.

OLIVER. I'm a fucking piece of human fucking shit.

MAN. Yeah, das ist good. Now lick my fucking boots.

OLIVER *bends over to lick the* MAN*'s boots, but before he gets there he stops.*

OLIVER. Okay, I'm sorry, I'm going to stop you.

MAN. Shut your fucking mouth.

OLIVER. No, seriously, can you just stop. Please. Time out. Stop. Abracadabra.

MAN. Abracadabra?

OLIVER. Yes. Please. Stop. Abracadabra. Definitely abracadabra.

MAN (*in his own rather camp London voice now*). You'll have to pay me.

OLIVER. Yes.

MAN. I mean, I spent two fucking hours trying to get here. From Earls Court.

OLIVER. Yes. The Victoria line. It broke down. You told me.

MAN. And I got wet. Soaking.

OLIVER. I'm sorry.

MAN. Soaking wet.

OLIVER. Yes.

MAN. You'll have to pay me.

OLIVER. Of course. Of course I'll pay you.

MAN. I came a long way.

OLIVER. I know.

Pause.

I'm just not in the mood. I should never have called. I was bored.

MAN. Okay.

OLIVER. And a bit lonely.

MAN. A lot of them are.

OLIVER. I think I just drank a bit too much.

MAN. All right.

Pause.

OLIVER. Have a drink with me.

MAN. You're paying.

OLIVER. You might as well.

MAN. It's still pissing it down.

OLIVER. Have a Scotch.

MAN. Oh, go on then.

OLIVER *pours the* MAN *a Scotch and hands it to him. They sit in silence for a while and listen to the sound of the rain.*

OLIVER. You're very good at it. Convincing, I mean.

MAN. Oh.

OLIVER. The accent and everything.

MAN. Thank you.

OLIVER. You're welcome.

Pause.

The picture's good as well. On the website.

MAN. So they say.

OLIVER. Is the Alsatian yours?

MAN. My sister's.

OLIVER. Glad you didn't bring him along.

MAN. Yes.

OLIVER. Effective though.

Pause.

You an actor?

MAN. Was.

OLIVER. Thought so.

MAN. Couldn't really make ends meet.

OLIVER. Theatre?

MAN. Mostly. All over the place. Northampton. Bristol. Fucking
    Ipswich.

OLIVER. Rep.

MAN. Did an ad once though. Dog food. Made a mint.

OLIVER. I thought you looked familiar.

MAN. And the odd voice-over.

OLIVER. It's a hard life.

MAN. You're telling me.

Pause.

OLIVER. So what do you do now?

MAN. Oh, you know. Bits and pieces. This, for a start.

OLIVER. Of course.

MAN. Help out in a florist's twice a week.

OLIVER. Nice.

MAN. Teach drama.

OLIVER. Great.

MAN. That kind of thing.

OLIVER. Okay.

Pause.

My boyfriend's left me.

MAN. Oh right.

OLIVER. Third time this year.

MAN. Makes a habit of leaving you, does he?

OLIVER. But this time it's for real. Took his vinyls.

MAN. How long you been together?

OLIVER. Year and a half.

MAN. That's a lifetime.

OLIVER. It is, isn't it?

MAN. I've never managed anything longer than eight months.

OLIVER. Haven't you?

MAN. No.

Pause.

Had a thing with this guy from Ecuador last year. Asked me to marry him. Had a dick the size of my forearm.

OLIVER. That's nice.

MAN. Never seen anything like it.

OLIVER. I'm sure I have.

MAN. Weird though.

OLIVER. Weird?

MAN. Wanted to shit on me. Come out of nowhere. 'I want to shit on you,' he says. Some people.

OLIVER. Strange.

MAN. Fucking perverts.

Pause.

You sad about your boyfriend leaving you then?

OLIVER. Yes. Yes, I think I am.

MAN. Oh right.

Pause.

No.

Pause.

OLIVER. It's been three days.

MAN. Three days?

OLIVER. Since he left.

MAN. Oh.

OLIVER. I haven't really gone anywhere.

MAN. Right.

OLIVER. Just sat here. Thinking about stuff.

MAN. You'll get over it.

OLIVER. I don't know.

MAN. You get over things.

OLIVER. No food left. Have to make the trip to Tesco's.

MAN. You don't want to starve.

OLIVER. No.

MAN. You'll get over it.

OLIVER. Who knows?

Pause.

MAN. So what is it you do for a living?

OLIVER. I'm a journalist. I write.

MAN. Oh, nice.

OLIVER. Is it?

MAN. Proper job. Not like me.

OLIVER. If you say so.

MAN. Not like dressing up.

OLIVER. Freelance. Write for the *Mail* a lot.

MAN. Got to pay the bills.

OLIVER. Yes. About to start working on a new magazine though.

Pause. The sound of keys in the front door. It opens. PHILIP *enters. He sees* OLIVER *and the* MAN *and looks surprised.* OLIVER *jumps up.*

PHILIP. Fuck.

OLIVER. Shit.

PHILIP. Fuck it.

OLIVER. It isn't…

PHILIP. I thought…

OLIVER. Fuck.

Pause.

PHILIP. I thought you were going to Glasgow.

OLIVER. I cancelled.

PHILIP. You said you were going to Glasgow.

OLIVER. I didn't realise you still had keys.

PHILIP. You said you wouldn't be here.

OLIVER. I thought you left the keys.

PHILIP. I came to get the case. The last case.

OLIVER. Yes.

PHILIP. The books.

OLIVER. I know.

> OLIVER *notices* PHILIP *looking at the* MAN *and taking in the uniform.*

> This is…

PHILIP. It's fine. I'll be quick.

OLIVER. Take your time.

PHILIP. They're in the bedroom.

OLIVER. I know. By the bed.

PHILIP. I'll be quick.

OLIVER. Okay.

> PHILIP *hovers for a second, then darts out of the room and into the bedroom.*

> Fuck. Fuck, fuck, fuck, fuck, fuck, fuck. Please go.

MAN. Sorry?

OLIVER. Just go. Please. Go.

MAN. I've only just started my drink.

OLIVER. Just please go.

MAN. You haven't paid me.

OLIVER. Yes.

MAN. I'm not moving till you pay me.

OLIVER runs over to where his wallet is and takes out a few twenty-pound notes.

OLIVER. There. Keep the change. Just go.

MAN (*counting the money*). I need to get out of this.

OLIVER. No. You really must go. It's important to me.

MAN. I'm not travelling on the fucking Victoria line dressed up as a Nazi.

OLIVER. You know where it is. Just be quick. Please.

The MAN takes his bag and starts walking towards the bathroom, then turns around.

MAN. He's not coming back to you.

OLIVER. Fucking get dressed.

The MAN exits. PHILIP returns carrying a small suitcase.

PHILIP. Got it.

OLIVER. Great.

PHILIP. I'll be off.

OLIVER. No.

Pause.

Please. Just wait. Just for a minute. A drink. That's all. Promise.

PHILIP. Not a good idea.

OLIVER. Please.

PHILIP. You have company.

OLIVER. Oh, him.

PHILIP. Yes.

OLIVER. He's just… he's…

PHILIP. You needn't explain.

OLIVER. Friend of Nick's. Fancy dress. Fancy-dress party. On his way to Nick's. Had a drink. That's all. He's leaving.

PHILIP. Nick's in Brazil.

OLIVER. Of course he is. I know that.

PHILIP. For fuck's sake.

OLIVER. I know Nick's in Brazil.

PHILIP. For fuck's sake, Oliver.

OLIVER. Yes.

Pause.

Please. Please just stay for a minute. Fifteen minutes. That's all.

Pause.

PHILIP. That man.

OLIVER. Yes.

PHILIP. That man is wearing a Nazi uniform.

OLIVER. I know. Weird, isn't it?

PHILIP. You must wonder sometimes to yourself: what's next?

OLIVER. Yes. I do. I do.

Pause.

Please stay.

PHILIP. I don't want to.

OLIVER. Please.

Pause.

The cupboards look empty.

PHILIP. What?

OLIVER. What I'm saying is I hadn't quite realised how many clothes you had.

PHILIP. Oh.

OLIVER. All of a sudden they look empty.

Pause.

You look well.

PHILIP. I haven't changed.

OLIVER. No.

PHILIP. It's been three days, Oliver. People don't change in three days.

OLIVER. Feels like longer. You look different.

PHILIP. Yes.

OLIVER. Like I've lost you.

Pause.

The thing is, Philip, I'm not sure I can live without you.

The MAN *returns from the bathroom dressed in his own clothes and carrying his bag.*

MAN. It's still pissing it down.

OLIVER. Right.

The MAN *walks over to the table and drinks down what's left of his Scotch.* OLIVER *and* PHILIP *just watch him.*

MAN. I don't actually mind the job. For the most part. You meet some interesting people. And there's definitely variety. I'd never be any good at the whole office thing. Hours and hours behind a desk staring at a computer screen. And I don't even mind travelling around London on the Tube and walking around in the pissing rain. But you do expect to be treated with a modicum of respect.

He walks towards the door.

I'm not asking for much, am I? I suppose it's what everybody's after. The thing is this, you see. I'm not a piece of furniture or a wind-up doll. I'm a human being. And I deserve to be treated as one. You can't just discard me like a piece of rubbish. I may dress up for your entertainment but I do have feelings, is what I'm saying.

(*To* PHILIP.) Nice to meet you.

He exits. A pause. Just the sound of the rain.

OLIVER. Some people.

PHILIP. I better go.

OLIVER *rushes to the bottle of Scotch. Pours him one.*

OLIVER. Just the one.

PHILIP *takes it reluctantly.*

Sit. Five minutes. Then you go.

They sit. Pause.

Had Sylvia on the phone this morning. Trying to console me. Bless.

PHILIP. How is she?

OLIVER. Sylvia? Oh, Sylvia's fine. 'I'll come by on Saturday,' she says. 'Come by with Mario. We'll go to Pride. Have a laugh.'

PHILIP. Pride?

OLIVER. On Saturday. I said... I said, 'I don't know if I'll be in the mood. Philip's gone. I don't... I don't know if he's coming back.'

PHILIP. I'm not, Oliver.

OLIVER. That's what I said to her. I said, 'Sylvia, I don't think he's coming back.' 'Well, you can't just sit there,' she said. 'Sit there being sad. We have to get you out. Out of the house. Cheer you up.'

PHILIP. What did you say?

OLIVER. I said, 'It's going to take a bit more than a park full of fairies to cheer me up.'

Pause.

I didn't love him, Philip. The American guy. I didn't love him.

PHILIP. I don't want to talk about it.

OLIVER. It's not love. I *love* you.

PHILIP. I'm going.

OLIVER. No.

Pause.

Okay. Here goes. There are things about myself that I don't understand. Things I want to but can't. It's as if it's something in me. Something in my DNA.

PHILIP. For fuck's sake.

OLIVER. With you it's different. With you it's love.

PHILIP. You lied to me.

OLIVER. It didn't mean anything. The other thing. You know that.

PHILIP. So why did you do it?

OLIVER. Because I need it.

PHILIP. You lied to me.

OLIVER. I know.

PHILIP. Over and over again.

OLIVER. Yes.

PHILIP. Fucking lying all the time. A year and a half of lies.

OLIVER. D'you remember when we met?

PHILIP. It's as if I don't know you.

OLIVER. At that party.

PHILIP. As if I don't know who the fuck you are.

OLIVER. At Sylvia's party.

PHILIP. Of course I fucking remember.

OLIVER. She knew we'd get on. She knew we'd fancy each other. There's this photographer, she said. Always travelling. You'll like him, she said.

PHILIP. I've got to go.

OLIVER. You'd just got back from Israel.

PHILIP. The West Bank.

OLIVER. Yes…

PHILIP. So?

OLIVER. So we talked. About your trip. About the photographs you'd taken.

PHILIP. Why the fuck are you saying this now?

OLIVER. I wonder what happened to that woman.

PHILIP. What woman?

OLIVER. The one you talked about. The one whose photograph you'd taken. The Palestinian woman.

PHILIP. Oliver.

OLIVER. You spent an hour describing her. You said her eyes were the blackest you'd ever seen and the most demanding.

PHILIP. Fucking hell.

OLIVER. Her son had died.

PHILIP. Why the fuck are you saying all this?

OLIVER. And I asked you what they were demanding.

PHILIP. So?

OLIVER. And you said they were demanding the dignity that comes with being heard. Not responded to. Just heard. The dignity that comes with being heard. The privilege of having a voice.

PHILIP. For fuck's sake.

OLIVER. That's when I recognised something in you.

Pause.

PHILIP. I'm leaving.

OLIVER. I felt a connection with you. There. At the party. And then here, when we came back. And now, I feel it now. I feel it now, Philip.

Pause.

And I think it's rare.

PHILIP. You're a cunt, Oliver. You're a stupid, stupid cunt.

OLIVER. Thank you.

PHILIP. You're welcome.

Pause.

A month and a half after we met, you fucking shagged someone.

OLIVER. I know.

PHILIP. I was in Brussels. The night before I went we were together. In that fucking bed. You saying I've never loved anyone like this. Then you drove me to Waterloo.

OLIVER. I know.

PHILIP. Eight – what? – ten hours after that, you're sucking someone else's dick.

OLIVER. I know.

PHILIP. What's that about, Oliver? What's that about?

OLIVER. I don't know.

PHILIP. To be fair, you told me. You said, 'I've done this thing. I don't know why but I've done this thing.'

OLIVER. I did tell you.

PHILIP. 'I've sucked a man's dick,' you said. 'In the park.'

OLIVER. I told you.

PHILIP. 'I could hardly see him,' you said. As if that made a difference. 'I could hardly see his face.'

OLIVER. It was dark.

PHILIP. 'I could hardly see his face.' You said that like it would make me feel better.

Pause.

The fact is, it depresses me. There. I've said it. The reason I can't stay with you. It depresses me.

OLIVER. Depresses you?

PHILIP. I did think about it. I thought maybe there's something wrong with me. Maybe I'm a fucking prude. A puritan. God knows. Maybe I should be a fucking priest. He never saw his face, I kept thinking. Sucked his dick, maybe…

OLIVER. Philip –

PHILIP. Sucked his dick, maybe, but never saw his face. Perhaps I'm the one who has the problem. They're not out on a date, they're not spooning, they're not planning their fucking holidays together, all they're doing is sucking each other off in a park. But it bothered me.

OLIVER. It's not your problem.

PHILIP. It's because we're men, I thought. That's what they say, isn't it? It's because we're men. It's not a gay thing. It's a man thing. Men need it.

OLIVER. That's what they say.

PHILIP. But all I know is what I felt. And that night, when I got back from Brussels, after you'd told me, I just lay in bed and looked at the ceiling. And I felt the loneliest I'd ever felt in my life.

OLIVER. I'm sorry.

Pause.

Sylvia's got that job.

PHILIP. What job?

OLIVER. That job she went up for. The Shakespeare. She said it's a break. The lead. Viola. *Twelfth Night*. Stratford.

PHILIP. She deserves it.

OLIVER. And Mario. The Italian boyfriend. It seems to be good. They're in love. He's a good man, she says. And very, very straight.

PHILIP. Good.

Pause.

OLIVER. I don't know what it is about me, Philip. Something about my name. It feels as if someone's calling me by my name.

PHILIP. What are you talking about?

OLIVER. The name I respond to. Like the other night. I'm walking by the gay place on the corner.

PHILIP. Right.

OLIVER. And I'm walking by it and I'm thinking, you need to go home, you need to work. Had to write a piece for the *Mail* on God knows what. The end of the world is nigh, that kind of thing. And I'm walking by the pub and it's as if this voice is calling my name.

PHILIP. Your name?

OLIVER. As if this voice knows my name. So I walk in. Coz this voice is calling me by my name. Have a couple of drinks. And there's a guy there... and he's not even good-looking. Actually, come to think of it, he's actively quite ugly. And you can smell the beer. You're six feet away from him and you can smell it. Wafting off his breath. And he's got a look in his eyes and he's looking at me as if he knows my name too. He's a bit pissed and he's leering... I mean *leering*, and I'm thinking, God, you're really kind of gross and next thing you know I'm actually standing next to him and he's telling me he's married and his wife's at her mother's for the week and he's kind of talking to me and rubbing his groin at the same time...

PHILIP. I'm not sure I want to hear the rest of this.

OLIVER. And the next thing I know we're in a cubicle. And I'm on my knees.

Pause.

PHILIP. Thanks for that.

OLIVER. It's an addiction is what I'm trying to say.

PHILIP. An addiction.

Pause.

OLIVER. There's something I never told you.

PHILIP. I'm beginning to miss your economy with the truth.

OLIVER. This thing that happened when I was young. Once, I must have been seventeen or something and I was staying at my aunt's. My mother's sister. The one you met.

PHILIP. Right.

OLIVER. And this woman came by. A friend of hers. And I was on my way out. So my aunt introduced me to this woman and I said hi, how are you and all that and then ran out. But a minute later I realised I'd left something. My sweater or something. So I ran back in the house to get it and then I realised that the two women – my aunt and her friend – were talking about me. But they hadn't heard me come back in the house. And I stood there, rooted to the spot. And listened. I couldn't hear everything but then – then this thing happened. I heard my aunt saying something along the lines of, 'He's a good boy but a bit of a lost soul.' Actually, it wasn't along the lines of. It was her exact words. I heard them. 'He's a good boy but a bit of a lost soul.' And the weird thing is – the weirdest – was that even before she said it, I kind of knew what she was going to say, like I'd heard her speak the words before, like her saying it and me knowing what she was going to say was all kind of tied up. Happening at the same time. 'He's a good boy but a bit of a lost soul.'

Pause.

PHILIP. I must leave.

OLIVER. Yes.

PHILIP. I can't stay.

OLIVER. No. You can't.

PHILIP. There is a part of you I'll always care about.

OLIVER. Thank you.

PHILIP. But this other thing… this thing you call your addiction. I can't deal with it.

OLIVER. No.

Pause.

PHILIP. Okay.

OLIVER. Yes. Yes. Okay.

Pause. PHILIP *stands. Picks up the suitcase.*

PHILIP. I'm sorry. I really am.

OLIVER. Don't go.

PHILIP. I have to.

PHILIP *walks towards the door. He stops and turns to* OLIVER.

I still don't know why I hung around as much as I did. I was thinking that on my way over. I mean, it's not as if I didn't know. And yet I kept… I kept at it. I believed in something. You. I don't know. I believed. I thought I knew you is what I think I'm saying.

He leaves. OLIVER *is left alone in the room. He stands and walks over to where the Scotch is to pour himself a drink. Then, suddenly he stops. There is a gesture – a move of the hand to the head, a bowing of the head, something – a gesture that suggests aloneness.*

He walks over to one of the light switches and turns off the lights. In semi-darkness, SYLVIA *emerges from the door that leads to the bedroom. She is wearing a dressing gown. The room reverts to its previous state.* OLIVER *slowly drifts off, walking into the room that* SYLVIA *has just entered from.*

1958

SYLVIA *comes to sit on the sofa. After a few seconds,* PHILIP *enters. He too is wearing pyjamas and a dressing gown.*

PHILIP. There you are.

SYLVIA. Darling.

PHILIP. I woke up. You weren't there.

SYLVIA. I had a dream.

PHILIP. One of your nasty dreams, darling?

SYLVIA. Yes.

PHILIP. All that Serbian food.

SYLVIA. Probably.

He joins her on the sofa. They sit in silence for a few seconds.

Did you enjoy yourself tonight?

PHILIP. I had a perfectly pleasant evening.

SYLVIA. Did you?

PHILIP. Drank a little too much of that awful wine perhaps.

SYLVIA. We all did.

PHILIP. But it was a nice enough evening.

Pause.

SYLVIA. You were quiet.

PHILIP. Was I?

SYLVIA. Not to start off with. Not at the beginning of the evening.

PHILIP. I thought –

SYLVIA. You were chatty before. In a good mood. But then during dinner you became quiet.

PHILIP. I'm sorry you thought I was quiet.

SYLVIA. I didn't mean it like that. It wasn't a criticism. Just an observation.

PHILIP. An observation?

SYLVIA. It didn't bother me… I just felt that you became slightly pensive. Melancholy.

PHILIP. That's a big word.

SYLVIA. Maybe as if something was bothering you.

PHILIP. I was listening, that's all. I felt I didn't have all that much to contribute, but I'm sorry you thought I was an awful bore.

SYLVIA. I didn't mean it like that.

PHILIP. No.

SYLVIA. I wish I hadn't said anything now.

Pause.

So you liked him then?

PHILIP. Liked whom?

SYLVIA. Oliver, of course.

PHILIP. He seems like a nice enough chap.

SYLVIA. Isn't he though?

PHILIP. I'm not sure that we have an awful lot in common, but he's a
perfectly decent fellow.

SYLVIA. Why do you say that?

PHILIP. Why do I say he's a perfectly decent fellow?

SYLVIA. No, why do you say that you don't have a lot in common?

PHILIP. Because we don't. That seems clear enough.

SYLVIA. I thought you'd get on.

PHILIP. Well, it's true, isn't it? I mean, the man's a writer and all
that. Very intelligent and outgoing, isn't he?

SYLVIA. Whereas you...

PHILIP. Well, I'm nothing like him, really. There isn't an artistic
bone in my body.

SYLVIA. I don't know.

PHILIP. Anyway, what does it matter what I think of him? The point
is the two of you get on famously and that's all that really matters.

SYLVIA. Well, I wanted you to like each other.

PHILIP. And the work, of course. That's important.

SYLVIA. Yes.

PHILIP. You seem to have discovered a way of understanding each
other when it comes to the work and that's the most essential
thing.

SYLVIA. I suppose so.

PHILIP. So what I think of him is irrelevant, really.

SYLVIA. Well, I wouldn't go that far.

PHILIP. The work is what matters.

Pause.

SYLVIA. You sound as if you loathed him.

PHILIP. I protest.

SYLVIA. As if you absolutely hated him.

PHILIP. I can't win with you, can I?

SYLVIA. Poor Oliver.

PHILIP. Why is it so important to you that I should like him?

SYLVIA. I think he'd be upset.

PHILIP. Why is it so important?

SYLVIA. If he even suspected how much you loathe him.

PHILIP. Now you're exaggerating.

SYLVIA. How you detest him.

PHILIP. Why is it so important?

Pause.

He has a manner to him, that's all.

SYLVIA. A 'manner'?

PHILIP. That's all.

SYLVIA. What sort of 'manner'? How do you mean, he has a 'manner'?

PHILIP. I can't put my finger on it.

SYLVIA. What sort of 'manner'?

PHILIP. I don't know. Just a manner.

SYLVIA. How do you mean?

PHILIP. We just don't have a lot in common.

Pause.

I don't know about you but I'm very, very tired.

Pause.

SYLVIA. I think of you, my darling, sometimes.

PHILIP. That's reassuring.

SYLVIA. No, I mean I think of you sometimes when you're at work. During the day, when I'm here. I'll be sitting in this very room, having my cup of tea or listening to the wireless, and I think of you at work. I see you in one of those large flats standing in the corner of the room in your brown suit as they look around. Then I see you locking those large doors behind you and walking down the road and back to the office.

PHILIP. What a strange thing to say.

SYLVIA. And I think you must be lonely. Philip must be lonely.

PHILIP. What a strange and funny thing to say, my darling.

SYLVIA. What you were saying tonight about not being happy in your work. About being envious of Oliver and me. I found it sad.

PHILIP. Oh, that.

SYLVIA. And I thought about you and the things that make you happy.

PHILIP. You needn't worry about me, darling.

SYLVIA. And I thought how terrible it will be if you never attain them. If you never hold close to you the things that really make you happy.

PHILIP. You needn't worry about me.

SYLVIA. Is there anything sadder?

PHILIP. You're exaggerating.

SYLVIA. Than a life lived like that?

PHILIP. You make me happy.

SYLVIA. And even if Dr Marsden is right –

PHILIP. Darling.

SYLVIA. Even if there isn't a reason –

PHILIP. We said we wouldn't –

SYLVIA. Even if we can, and will –

PHILIP. Sylvia.

SYLVIA. I'm wondering if that will –

PHILIP. We said we wouldn't.

SYLVIA. If it will make a difference.

Pause.

If having children will make a difference. To that.

Another pause. PHILIP *stands.*

PHILIP. Maybe you did have too much wine.

SYLVIA. We've never talked about it.

PHILIP. I think I'm going back to bed.

SYLVIA. Please don't.

PHILIP. I'm tired. And tomorrow's a long day.

SYLVIA. Please wait. Just for a moment.

PHILIP. I have to be up at seven.

SYLVIA. Stay.

Pause.

Please stay.

Pause.

I should have felt relief when Dr Marsden said that he couldn't identify a reason we couldn't have children. He seemed to imply that if we just kept trying...

PHILIP. For God's sake, Sylvia...

SYLVIA. But then I started to question why I wanted it so much. A child. Why it meant everything to me. The desperation. Sometimes, I prayed with my whole body. I would lie next to you in bed and pray with my whole body to feel it... the beginnings of it. The stirrings. A new life inside me. I was sure I'd know the very night it happened.

PHILIP. For God's sake.

SYLVIA. And I thought it's natural, it's because I'm a woman. To be a mother. That's all. So I prayed and prayed and prayed.

PHILIP. What are you saying?

SYLVIA. But then I realised that there was something else. I wanted a child because I was frightened of us being left alone, Philip. The two of us. Just us. Alone.

Pause.

There was something I didn't tell you. Something that happened.

PHILIP. I don't understand you.

SYLVIA. Do you remember that actor I worked with?

PHILIP. Not now. Not the way you're speaking to me.

SYLVIA. Richard his name was. Richard Coveley.

PHILIP. Sometimes I simply don't understand you.

SYLVIA. He was in *The Cherry Orchard* with me. You came to see it.

PHILIP. What about him?

SYLVIA. He was tall and fair. He played Yepihodov.

PHILIP. I remember the play.

SYLVIA. You met him. After the performance one night we all went
to have a drink together. We went to that little pub just off
Shaftesbury Avenue. Do you remember?

PHILIP. Why are you telling me about this now?

SYLVIA. I liked him. He was a kind man. Unusual and quite private.
But kind.

She pauses.

You didn't like him very much. I remember you said you didn't
like him.

PHILIP. That was years ago. I met the man for a quick drink. There
were many other actors there. I can hardly remember. Why is it
important all of a sudden what I thought of this one man?

SYLVIA. You took exception to him. You said, I think you said, 'I
find him offensive.'

PHILIP. I honestly can't remember.

SYLVIA. 'He offends me,' you said.

PHILIP. What has this to do with anything?

SYLVIA. You may have even called him mannered. Like you did
Oliver tonight. You may have said he had a 'manner'.

PHILIP. I'm not quite sure of the significance of this conversation.
But I'm very tired. Maybe you can explain to me in the morning
what this is all about.

SYLVIA. Three days ago I read in *The Times* that he had killed himself. I didn't tell you at the time. I don't know why. But I didn't.

PHILIP. Well, I'm sorry to hear it.

SYLVIA. Maybe it's because I remembered that you hadn't liked him. That he'd offended you in some way.

PHILIP. You've obviously been very affected by it.

SYLVIA. He hung himself. There'd been a scandal. A court case. Gross indecency, that sort of thing.

PHILIP. I see.

SYLVIA. I think he was homosexual. I think Richard Coveley must have been a homosexual.

Pause.

When I read it I just thought of that night. Of why it was that you seemed to take such a dislike to him.

PHILIP. I can hardly remember the man. He seems to have made a lasting impression on you, but I can hardly remember the man. I'm very sorry that he's taken his own life and I'm sorry you seem to have been so upset by the whole affair but I hardly met the man.

SYLVIA. Why was it that you found him so repugnant?

PHILIP. I don't remember finding him repugnant. That's an exaggeration on your behalf. I found him mildly offensive, that's all. In a way that those men can often be offensive. Effeminate. I do recall him looking at me in a way I found overt.

SYLVIA. But even if he did look at you, even if he did, why would you find that so objectionable?

PHILIP. This discussion is absurd. You seem intent on upsetting me.

SYLVIA. I just couldn't fathom why it was that Richard Coveley disgusted you so. And that's why I didn't tell you.

PHILIP. This is wonderful. You're accusing me in some perverse way of being responsible for the death of a man I met on one occasion for approximately twenty minutes.

SYLVIA. I'm not accusing you of anything, Philip. I'm just asking you a question.

PHILIP. Well, I can't deny to you that I'm concerned. That you seem to have regressed.

SYLVIA. I'm sorry you feel that way.

PHILIP. You're sounding alarmingly similar to what you sounded like before Devon.

SYLVIA. Before my illness. That's what we decided to call it, wasn't it? My illness.

PHILIP. Are you finished?

SYLVIA. As if it were a bad case of the flu.

PHILIP. Is there anything else you wish to discuss? Or am I free to go now?

SYLVIA. I didn't mean to keep you here by force.

PHILIP. You asked me not to leave. You obviously felt a burning need to communicate these disparate and disturbing thoughts to me and I'm simply asking you if you've now finished.

SYLVIA. Did Oliver offend you in the same way that Richard Coveley did?

PHILIP. If you're asking me if I think Oliver Henshaw is a homosexual, I really wouldn't know. I haven't given it a moment's thought. His private life after all is none of my business and neither do I think it should be any of yours. I will try and explain to myself your somewhat strange behaviour tonight by the fact that you have clearly been upset by this man Coveley's death. This, combined with the possibility that you had a few too many glasses of wine, can go some way to justifying what can only be described as an outburst of irrationality. Now if you'll excuse me I really do need to return to bed.

SYLVIA. Goodnight, Philip.

PHILIP. Come to bed with me. You're tired.

SYLVIA. In a little while.

> PHILIP *exits and* SYLVIA *stays in the room alone. A few seconds pass and she slowly stands. She is about to follow him into the bedroom but then, suddenly, there is a gesture – an echo of* OLIVER*'s gesture from the end of the previous scene. An anguish. She leaves the room.*

2008

OLIVER *enters and sprawls out on the sofa, still in his dressing gown. By his side is a near-empty bottle of Scotch and a glass. The lights are dim. The television is on and the room is full of the sound of* Big Brother *or something similar, contemporary. Then there is a knock at the door. He doesn't stir. The knocking becomes louder, more determined. Eventually he crawls to the door to open it.* SYLVIA *enters. She's carrying a bag of groceries.*

SYLVIA. Fuck.

OLIVER. Lovely to see you too.

SYLVIA. I thought you'd slashed your fucking wrists.

OLIVER. I have told you on numerous occasions that if I ever choose to follow the path to self-obliteration it will be noxious fumes.

She sweeps by him and disappears into the kitchen. She speaks the next few lines from offstage.

SYLVIA. You have fifteen minutes.

OLIVER. How very generous you are with your time. It's a good thing we're such good friends.

SYLVIA. Mario's just flown in. He's taking me out. And then I'm staying at his. Call me old-fashioned but I've missed him.

OLIVER. Sweet.

SYLVIA. I bought you food. Avocado mousse. Organic feta. Madagascan vanilla yogurt. Basics.

OLIVER. Thanks, Mum.

SYLVIA. I'm having a beer.

OLIVER. Help yourself.

She reappears at the kitchen door, beer in hand.

SYLVIA. You look like shite.

OLIVER. Funny, I thought there was a portrait in the attic doing that for me.

SYLVIA. What happened?

Pause.

OLIVER. He said I depress him.

SYLVIA. You depress him.

OLIVER. The anonymous sex thing. He said it depressed him.

SYLVIA. Okay.

OLIVER. So I told him it's not the same thing. I mean, when we're together... when I'm with Philip, that's different. But you know the other stuff, the park, the sauna, the internet, whatever, that stuff...

SYLVIA. The slut stuff.

OLIVER. The slut stuff, thank you, that's not the same. It's kind of... what's it like, it's kind of like going to the loo. Only with someone else.

SYLVIA. Like going to the loo with someone else.

OLIVER. Exactly.

SYLVIA pauses. Her phone is vibrating.

SYLVIA. Excuse me, I'm feeling a vibration in my nether regions.

OLIVER. Lucky you.

She takes out the phone and checks to see who it is.

Is that Pesto-breath?

SYLVIA. Racist.

She answers it.

(*On the phone.*) Hi. Welcome back. How was the trip?...

OLIVER. Say hi from me.

SYLVIA. Good... no, I'm fine. I missed you. I'm at Oliver's.

OLIVER. Say hi.

SYLVIA. Ollie says hi. Hello back. Yup. Okay. I won't be long.

OLIVER. He's eating into my time.

SYLVIA makes a face at OLIVER, telling him to shut up.

SYLVIA. I haven't got the car, I'll take the Tube. (*She looks at her watch.*) I can be there by nine. Or nine-thirty at the latest.

OLIVER. Tell him he's eating into my fifteen minutes.

SYLVIA (*to* OLIVER, *with her hand covering her mobile*). Please shut up.

(*On the phone again*.) That sounds nice. Yummy. I'll see you then – call you from Hammersmith. *Ciao*. Welcome back. *Ti amo*.

She turns it off.

OLIVER. '*Ti amo*'?

SYLVIA. Shut up.

OLIVER. Vintage Cartland.

Pause.

SYLVIA. Okay, so let me try and get into Philip's mind here. Figure out what it is… what it might be that depresses him.

OLIVER. Be my guest.

SYLVIA. Okay, here goes.

OLIVER. I'm all ears.

SYLVIA. Okay, so you're walking through a park, it is night-time and then suddenly you see this guy.

OLIVER. I'm with you.

SYLVIA. And he is gorgeous. I mean *gorgeous*. And he takes his dick out.

OLIVER. I like it.

SYLVIA. And it is big. I mean *big*. And he is waving it, nay, brandishing it in your face. And your urge –

OLIVER. My urge is to get down on my knees and give him satisfaction.

SYLVIA. Your urge, as you so succinctly put it, is to kneel down and give him satisfaction. But stop. Newsflash. You find out, after you've seen his man-tool but before you do the actual kneeling-down bit, you find out through some psychic newsflash something about him. A few facts. I don't know. Someone tells you this man is a racist. Or he sells crack to fourteen-year-olds. Do you still suck his dick? Do you still give him satisfaction?

A pause as OLIVER *thinks about it.*

OLIVER. When you say big, how big?

SYLVIA. Be serious. Do you suck his dick?

OLIVER. Probably.

A short pause.

SYLVIA. I'm siding with Philip on this one.

OLIVER. It's not like we're having a conversation. I'm not endorsing his world view. It's not like I'm saying of course I agree with you that the Holocaust never happened. I'm just sucking his dick, for God's sake, I'm not voting for him.

SYLVIA. Definitely with Philip on this one.

OLIVER. Anyway, the point is you pick the worst possible scenario. You say this man is a freak and kills babies. Whatever. That's the exception. I mean, most of these men, most of the men in the saunas or whatever, are like you and me. I mean, why did you have to choose a fascist freak? Why couldn't it be a concert pianist who gives all his money to the Save the Children fund?

SYLVIA. It could be. But the point is – and I've got a feeling that this is the detail that depresses Philip – the point is *you don't know*. You don't know whose dick you're sucking.

OLIVER. Whatever.

Pause.

Are we playing the honesty game?

SYLVIA. I hope so.

OLIVER. The honest truth?

SYLVIA. And nothing but.

OLIVER. However unattractive?

SYLVIA. That's what friends are for.

OLIVER. In that case the honest truth is that not only I'd do it, I mean the cock-sucking thing, but I kind of really like it. The example, I mean. What you chose. Kind of turns me on.

SYLVIA. I knew you'd say that.

OLIVER. The fact is – oh, fuck, fuck, fuck, I wasn't going to tell you this, but when Philip came round, there was a man here and he was, fuck, I don't know how to say this…

SYLVIA. Just try.

OLIVER. Well, he was a Nazi.

SYLVIA. A Nazi? You had a Nazi over?

OLIVER. Not a real Nazi.

SYLVIA. How d'you mean, 'not a real Nazi'?

OLIVER. A make-believe one.

SYLVIA. A make-believe Nazi.

OLIVER. I mean, you know, from the internet. So they have these various costumes and you choose one and then they come over and... well, it's roleplay, really.

SYLVIA. Roleplay.

OLIVER. I mean, you can have *anything*. A fireman. An air pilot. A plumber.

SYLVIA. But you chose a Nazi.

OLIVER. And you roleplay. You know, kinky stuff. It's not serious. It's fantasy land.

SYLVIA. Okay, so. What's your part? I mean, he's a Nazi, but what are you? A Viking?

OLIVER. No, I'm just me.

SYLVIA. You?

OLIVER. Yeah, he's a Nazi but I'm just me.

SYLVIA. So you're in the middle of this roleplaying thing and Philip walks in on you.

OLIVER. Kind of.

SYLVIA. 'Kind of'?

OLIVER. Well, we'd stopped. I'd stopped it. We were just having a drink.

SYLVIA. You were having a drink with the Nazi?

OLIVER. Yes. And Philip came in.

SYLVIA. That's not good.

OLIVER. Thanks for that. I know.

Pause.

I was once looking through the personals in *Gay Times*. Long ago. Before Philip. And this one personal caught my eye. It went something like this: 'Gay man, thirty-three, non-smoker, into bondage, rape simulation, leather, rubber, chains, rimming, felching. Looking for romance.'

That's my life.

SYLVIA. And then you find someone.

OLIVER. Why do I have to choose?

SYLVIA. Maybe you don't. Maybe you just have to understand it.

SYLVIA*'s phone makes a vibrating noise again.*

Excuse me. More vibrations.

It's a text. She reads it; smiles.

OLIVER. Is that the Italian again?

SYLVIA. Might be. Shit, I've got to go.

He doesn't answer. She stands up and starts putting on her coat.

OLIVER. Sebastian called earlier. They've been given the green light for the magazine – the money's come through. Said it was going to do to gay literature what Marie Antoinette did for the guillotine. Widen its appeal.

SYLVIA. 'Literature'?

OLIVER. Apparently they have the biggest names on board. BA, BMW, Gucci, Gap. You name it. The big boys. Everyone wants a piece of it.

SYLVIA. Well, you guys are cool. And have disposable income.

OLIVER. They're already floating ideas by me: a Tom Ford interview. A gay rich list.

SYLVIA. Have they got a name?

OLIVER. A name?

SYLVIA. For the magazine.

OLIVER. *Blissful.*

SYLVIA. Okay.

OLIVER. And something else too. Sebastian's recommended me for a one-off. Some lad-magazine editor wants to meet me tomorrow. I'm intrigued.

SYLVIA. I'll call you in the morning.

OLIVER. Anyway, it's all good. Salvation. Wash the man right out of my hair. I need to keep busy. Otherwise…

SYLVIA. Otherwise what?

OLIVER. Otherwise I'm going under.

SYLVIA. 'Under'?

Pause.

OLIVER. I've never been this bad. Not ever. I mean it.

SYLVIA. Well, that should do the job. *Blissful.* And then there's your book, of course.

OLIVER. Book?

SYLVIA. Your fucking book, Oliver, remember?

OLIVER. Oh, that.

SYLVIA. I could have sworn you were writing a novel.

OLIVER. So like you to bring it up.

SYLVIA. Love. Life. Some sort of meaning. Or at least an effort to find it.

She moves towards the door. She opens it.

SYLVIA. We'll talk.

OLIVER. I don't know what I want any more. But it's not good.

SYLVIA. What isn't?

OLIVER. I'm scared.

A pause, and then:

I mean, I'm sitting here and I'm joking with you, but I don't really see the point any more. And I have to figure it out. Otherwise…

SYLVIA. Otherwise what?

OLIVER. Who knows?

Pause.

I'm going to ask you the biggest favour. And it's not easy for me. But I have to do it. Just this once. Never again. You know I wouldn't. If I didn't have to.

Pause.

SYLVIA. Fuck.

OLIVER. Stay with me. Just tonight. Please, Sylvia.

SYLVIA. I can't.

OLIVER. Just this once. Please. Please. Please.

SYLVIA. No, Oliver.

OLIVER. I'd never ask. You know that. Not if I didn't feel I had to. Not if I didn't feel –

SYLVIA. Please don't do this.

OLIVER. Not if I wasn't scared of me.

SYLVIA. Scared of you?

OLIVER. Of being left alone tonight. Of being me alone tonight.

A pause as she lets these words sink in.

PHILIP *enters in his 1958 clothes; a ghost.* SYLVIA *can't see him and neither can* OLIVER, *but his presence, somehow, is felt. He emerges from the shadows.*

Somewhere inside me a feeling that… a kind of betrayal.

SYLVIA. Betrayal?

OLIVER. Yes.

SYLVIA. You're the betrayer or the betrayed?

OLIVER. Both. I don't know. Both.

SYLVIA. Okay. Take a deep breath. Start again. Try and make sense. I mean, articulate, for God's sake, and then maybe, *maybe*, I can start to help you.

OLIVER. I'm trying, you shit.

SYLVIA. Try harder.

OLIVER. I keep returning to this one same place. So I have to figure it out.

SYLVIA. What same place?

OLIVER. And I'm not threatening to wake up a born-again Christian or a Muslim or God knows what. Or shave off my hair and walk around Soho singing 'Hare Krishna'. But something needs to happen, some sort of realisation. Because otherwise, well, fuck me, it's untenable.

SYLVIA. What is?

PHILIP. Oliver.

OLIVER. The voice.

SYLVIA. What voice?

OLIVER. The voice that says –

PHILIP. Oliver –

OLIVER. You're no good –

PHILIP. Oliver –

OLIVER. You're unlovable –

PHILIP. Oliver –

OLIVER. This is what you deserve.

Pause. PHILIP *stands back into the shadows.*

SYLVIA. I'll call Mario.

OLIVER. I'm so sorry.

SYLVIA. So am I.

OLIVER. Thank you. Thank you. Thank you.

SYLVIA. I don't know why. I don't know *how* –

OLIVER. Thank you so much.

SYLVIA. *– how* you do it.

OLIVER. And then tomorrow you can spend the whole day with him. Morning, afternoon, evening.

SYLVIA. Thank you. For your permission, I mean. How generous.

OLIVER. Don't be mean.

Pause.

SYLVIA. I'm having another beer.

OLIVER. I'll get you one. Make yourself comfortable. *Mia casa, tua casa.*

He goes to the kitchen. SYLVIA *sits.*

SYLVIA. I can't keep doing this, you know. Ollie. Being here for you. Not like this. It's not fair. On either of us. I need to say that.

OLIVER. I'll never forget this.

Pause. The sound of him opening a drawer and then a bottle.

SYLVIA. The irony is that Mario can't wait to meet you. I talk about you all the time. He said he wants to come to Pride on Saturday. He's only ever been to the one in Rome. He swears he saw a priest throwing an egg but I think that's just his own brand of anti-Catholic propaganda. Did I tell you he wants to have a baby? I said, 'Not until I meet your mother.' Her name's Filomena. Can you believe it? Filomena. Sounds like a bloody volcano. Apparently, her gnocchi is to die for.

Pause. She stands and walks over to the door that leads to the kitchen just as PHILIP *emerges again from the shadows and comes to sit in the chair she has just left.*

The thing is you need to sort it out yourself is what I'm saying.

PHILIP *stares ahead as if lost in his own thoughts. There is a knocking at the door. He ignores it for some time – it persists. Then, slowly, he stands up and walks towards the door just as* SYLVIA *disappears into the kitchen.* PHILIP *opens the door and* OLIVER *is standing there in his 1958 clothes. He is in a raincoat and soaking wet.*

1958

PHILIP. Hello.

OLIVER. I'm sorry.

PHILIP. You're drenched.

OLIVER. Yes.

Pause.

I wasn't planning to come. We said…

PHILIP. We said we wouldn't meet.

OLIVER. I know.

PHILIP. We said we'd try not to talk to each other.

OLIVER. Yes.

PHILIP. I think we both agreed it wasn't a good idea.

OLIVER. I know.

Pause.

PHILIP. You're drenched.

OLIVER. I was absent-minded.

PHILIP. Soaking.

OLIVER. I left my umbrella in the library.

PHILIP. Well, you'd better come in.

OLIVER *enters. He hovers.*

OLIVER. I'm sorry.

PHILIP. Sylvia's in Wimbledon staying with a friend. She'll be back tomorrow.

OLIVER. I know. We spoke on the telephone. That's why I came.

PHILIP. I don't think it's a good idea.

OLIVER. I needed to talk to you, Philip.

PHILIP. I didn't realise there was anything else to say.

OLIVER. Just one last time. And then I won't bother you.

Pause.

PHILIP. Well, you'd better have a seat.

OLIVER. Thank you.

They sit facing each other. There is a long pause before OLIVER *starts talking.*

I wanted…

PHILIP. What?

OLIVER. Nothing. I thought… I hoped…

PHILIP. You hoped what?

Pause.

OLIVER. I walked across the park. It was pouring with rain. I was forgetful. I'd been in the library. Trying to write. But I couldn't. I couldn't write. So I left. To come here. But I forgot my umbrella.

PHILIP. Yes.

OLIVER. I couldn't... I know we said... but I couldn't...

PHILIP. You couldn't do what?

OLIVER. All my life I've been waiting for some sort of confirmation that I'm not alone.

PHILIP. Yes.

OLIVER. When it comes, when that confirmation comes, you can't... I can't – I had to come here. And see you. I'm sorry.

PHILIP. For God's sake.

Pause.

OLIVER. It's funny. I thought I knew.

PHILIP. Knew what?

OLIVER. Knew what it meant to be lonely. To be alone. I thought I knew.

PHILIP. What do you mean?

OLIVER. But now. Now I know.

A long pause.

PHILIP. What is it you want to say to me?

OLIVER. That I love you.

PHILIP. Please don't say that again. I find it absurd.

OLIVER. I have no choice. It isn't a choice.

PHILIP. We agreed. You said... I asked you not to talk like that.

OLIVER. I love you so much.

PHILIP. Stop saying those words.

OLIVER. At night, I can't sleep. I see your face. I hear your voice.

PHILIP. Stop it.

OLIVER. When we were together, the last time, when we were together it did feel, didn't it, as if… as if. Did it not feel to you as if all of a sudden, everything, everything you *were* and are…

PHILIP. No.

OLIVER. I miss you.

PHILIP. I'd rather you left.

OLIVER. No. Please. One moment. Please let me stay for a moment.

Pause.

These four months… I understood something.

PHILIP. You understood what?

OLIVER. I used to think it was just a sexual lust. A physical need. A deviation.

PHILIP. It *is* a deviation.

OLIVER. That if I met the right girl, that if I married, if I had children, the physical need, the *sexual* need would stop.

PHILIP. It is a deviation.

OLIVER. That it would go away. That I could fight it.

PHILIP. That's right.

OLIVER. But then, when I met you…

PHILIP. You *can* fight it.

OLIVER. I knew it was more than that.

Pause.

That it was everything I am. Not something I can put away. Not just one part of me.

Pause.

When we were together. The times we met. All those times. When we talked.

PHILIP. We've been over this.

OLIVER. I realised that it was more. And that what I slowly learnt…

PHILIP. For God's sake…

OLIVER. Was that what happens between two people can be sacred. And important. And that it doesn't matter who those two people are.

Pause.

I remember being a boy. I remember having this dark, secret knowledge of what I pined for. Of who I was. It kept me up at nights. I was terrified. Everything, everyone, told me it was wrong.

PHILIP. It *is* wrong.

OLIVER. I thought so too. I believed that if the whole world told me so, the whole world must be right. Who was I to question that?

PHILIP. I don't see what it is you're trying to say.

OLIVER. I'm saying that when I met you, when I fell in love with you... I knew that it was true. That the world *was* wrong. That what I felt was honest and pure and good.

Pause.

There was a place. In the park. Where certain men went.

Pause.

PHILIP. I don't want to hear this.

OLIVER. I went... there was this one man and he... I didn't know him. He didn't know me. We barely talked. Just a word. We didn't even really look at each other. And then... then it was as if I wasn't quite there. It was over in a couple of minutes.

PHILIP. I think you should leave, Oliver.

OLIVER. But then when I... when we... it wasn't, it *isn't* the same. Because, you see, there was something *else*, Philip. We had spoken and I felt that I knew something of who you were. Your fears. Your loneliness. Your wants. I saw in your eyes, that you too, like me, are a good man.

PHILIP. A good man?

OLIVER. Yes, Philip, a good man. A *good* man. A good man. And it was the first time, when we were together, when we were embracing that I felt that I had a pride. A pride for the person I was.

PHILIP. Is this what you needed to tell me?

OLIVER. Yes, I suppose it is. I suppose I needed to tell you that what happened between us is not the same thing. Not the same as that place I went to.

PHILIP. It is the same. You're deceiving yourself. It's wrong.

OLIVER. And I thought that some of those men, if only you had seen them you would know what I mean, that some of those men, hovering, waiting in that dim flickering light, some of those men would also choose this, that maybe that's what many of them want, but because they don't know where... *how* to find it, and because they have been told that this is who they are, that they are these men who stand waiting to touch someone, to touch another man's skin, that they've believed that's *all* they are, but that what they want, what they really want is more than that, what they want is what we can have... an intimacy with someone they can hold onto for a while.

PHILIP. Have you finished?

OLIVER. Because from the minute I met you it felt as if you were the only person who had ever known my real name.

PHILIP. How do you mean?

OLIVER. As if we spoke the same language.

Pause.

PHILIP. But I don't feel the same way, Oliver.

OLIVER. Don't you?

PHILIP. No, Oliver, I don't. I don't. I don't.

Pause.

You see, Oliver, I love Sylvia. And Sylvia loves me. We're a couple and we love each other. What happened... I mean, what happened between us, between you and me, Oliver, between the two of us, that was simply a mistake. Call it what you will. A moment of weakness. A weakness. That's all.

OLIVER. But you said –

PHILIP. I may have said many things, Oliver, but unfortunately I probably didn't mean them. You see, I wasn't being myself. I was like a man possessed. I want you to understand though that I hold nothing against you. No rancour, no spite. I have some affection for you. I believe you are a decent man. I don't believe you influenced me or tempted me in any way or that your motives were malicious. I was as responsible as you were. We both made a mistake. That's all. I wish you well, Oliver. There are no hard feelings. But the memory of what happened... now that I seem to have regained my senses, the memory of what happened between us, of the things that happened between us, that memory fills me with shame. And disgust.

OLIVER. Disgust?

PHILIP. You came here today to persuade me that what we felt for each other, what you felt for me was noble and pure.

OLIVER. I did.

PHILIP. Well, you can feel that for me as a friend. And I can do likewise. I can like you and respect you, *try* to respect you, as a friend. But the other thing... that thing that you talk about... that place, those people.

OLIVER. What about them?

PHILIP. That place... the one you so eloquently described, Oliver. They are not like me and I am not like them. If you want me to be honest, Oliver, if you want to know the honest truth, I despise them. That isn't too strong a word. I have to be honest with you. I pity and despise them. I've seen them... I *see* them, I notice them in a crowd, on a bus, on the street and they disgust me. The way they walk, the way they look at you, all in the same way. I'm not like that, Oliver. And I don't think you are either. So we must put this behind us. It's for the best. I promise you it's for the best.

OLIVER. Is it?

PHILIP. One day you'll thank me. You'll understand that I did this to protect you in some way. From yourself. You'll understand that in my own, strange way it was my gift to you. My parting gift.

A long pause.

OLIVER. I suppose I should leave.

PHILIP. Yes.

Pause.

OLIVER. She knows, Philip.

PHILIP. Knows what?

OLIVER. She knows everything. About you. She knows everything about you, Philip.

PHILIP. How do you mean?

OLIVER. About what keeps you up at night. About the stirrings of your heart. The many things you're frightened of. The lonely thoughts you have. And you have to now – because you will not be offered another opportunity – you have to now ask yourself why it is you repay her with the worst possible deception. And I'm not talking about us. About what happened between us. I'm talking about the opposite – I'm talking about your refusal to acknowledge it for what it really is.

PHILIP. Please don't talk about Sylvia to me.

OLIVER. Why not?

PHILIP. I don't want her talked about in this way. Between us, like this. I don't want us to discuss the subject of my wife.

OLIVER. Do you honestly think it's easy for me? I care about her. Deeply.

PHILIP. I don't want to talk about it.

OLIVER. But then I understood that this is what she wanted. Not *this*. Not how things are now. But us. The meeting. That is what she wanted.

PHILIP. You're insane.

OLIVER. She brought us together, Philip. I know that she brought us together.

PHILIP. You're mad.

OLIVER. Maybe not consciously, maybe not in full awareness of what she was doing. But I can put my hand on my heart and swear that Sylvia brought us together.

Pause.

I wonder when you first started thinking of emigrating.

PHILIP. Emigrating?

OLIVER. Yes. Emigrating. You mentioned it. The night I met you. Sylvia said the flat was strewn with books on Africa.

PHILIP. What has that to do with anything?

OLIVER. So I was wondering when it was that you started having that dream. Seventeen, eighteen, when? Maybe when you were becoming a man. Discovering yourself. Who you really were and what it was you wanted from your life. The open plains, you thought. The open plains of Africa. Not a bad place. I can see you there. This country is small. You need somewhere bigger. Somewhere to breathe. So you set off. I can see you. You said you never got further than Brighton, but I can see you miles, miles away. Across the cold waters of the Channel, down across the Mediterranean, down in Africa where you long to be. What are you doing there? Farming? Hunting game? Teaching? I suppose it doesn't really matter. In that sort of place, under that kind of sky you'll eventually discover what it is you're there for. In your own time.

PHILIP. Oliver.

OLIVER. I won't see you again then.

PHILIP. No.

OLIVER. That's what you want.

PHILIP. That's what we both need. To continue. To return to things as they were.

OLIVER. So what is the point?

PHILIP. The point?

OLIVER. What is the point of this stupid, painful life if not to be honest? If not to stand up for what one is in the core of one's being?

PHILIP. I don't know. I don't know.

OLIVER. Something's happened to me, Philip. I can't go back. Not to how things were before.

PHILIP. What do you mean?

OLIVER. Don't worry, I'm not expecting you to come with me. I'm not expecting anything any more. Not from you.

PHILIP. I'm sorry.

OLIVER. You're weak, Philip.

PHILIP. I wasn't…

OLIVER. What?

PHILIP. It isn't that…

OLIVER. Tell me.

PHILIP. No. Nothing.

OLIVER. Please tell me.

PHILIP. It isn't easy. It isn't easy.

Pause.

I wish I'd never met you. I wish she'd never brought you here.

OLIVER. Who are you?

PHILIP. I don't know. Not any more.

OLIVER. You've never known. This was your chance to find out. But you're not strong enough. You'll die, Philip, not knowing who you are.

PHILIP. Be quiet

OLIVER. What a foolish, sad way to live a life.

Suddenly, PHILIP strikes him across the face. It is a reflex; the reaction of a cornered animal. PHILIP is as shocked as OLIVER, who reels. There is some blood in the mouth.

PHILIP. I'm sorry. Oh, God, I'm so sorry, Oliver. I'm so sorry.

He moves towards him; OLIVER flinches.

Let me see.

OLIVER *lets him.*

I'm so sorry, I'm so sorry, I'm so sorry.

OLIVER. It's all right. I'm fine.

PHILIP. I'm so sorry. I didn't… I'm so sorry…

OLIVER. I'm fine. Really, I'm fine.

And then, PHILIP begins to cry. He collapses into OLIVER's arms and begins to sob like a child.

PHILIP. I'm sorry, I'm sorry, I'm sorry.

OLIVER. It's all right, Philip, it's all right.

OLIVER comforts him. Then, a kiss. But OLIVER tries to remain tender. PHILIP has been taken over by something else – there is something urgent, aggressive stirring in him.

OLIVER. Wait, Philip, wait.

PHILIP. No.

> *A struggle of sorts as* PHILIP *pulls* OLIVER *over towards the sofa – his movement becoming more violent. He begins to pull at their clothes.*

OLIVER. No, Philip. Not like this. Not now. Not here. Wait.

PHILIP. Why not now? Why not here? It's what you want, isn't it? It's what you want me to be, isn't it?

> PHILIP *has become violent. He throws* OLIVER *down.* OLIVER *is resisting.* PHILIP *unzips his own trousers and has managed to pull* OLIVER*'s halfway down. He mounts him with* OLIVER *resisting at first, then succumbing. In just a few, frenzied seconds he has ejaculated and the noise he makes at the moment of orgasm is a terrible, anguished cry of release. They lie on the floor for some time –* PHILIP *hiding his face in shame,* OLIVER *hiding his.*

> *Eventually,* PHILIP *stands. Quietly, methodically, he dresses and leaves the room.* OLIVER *does not move. He is lying on the floor, his face down against it.* PHILIP *returns a minute or so later. He pours himself a drink and sits. He lights a cigarette. A moment passes.*

> *Slowly, painfully,* OLIVER *gets up and begins to rearrange his clothing. A minute or two pass in complete silence.*

I knew you should never have come here.

> *Pause.*

I think you should leave, Oliver. This thing… this thing is…

I want you to leave and never come back.

> OLIVER *moves slowly across the room to the door. He does not look at* PHILIP*. He looks down at the floor. He opens the door, then pauses.*

OLIVER. I'm sorry… I…

> *He pauses, confused. As if trying to gather his thoughts.*

What I… the thing… I… was…

> *Pause.*

I'm sorry. I thought I knew you.

He leaves the room, closing the door behind him.

PHILIP *does not move. He remains seated, drinking his whisky and smoking his cigarette.*

The lights gradually fade.

End of Act One.

ACT TWO

2008

An office. Behind the desk sits PETER. *A bit of a wide boy.* OLIVER *is sitting on the other side of the desk.*

PETER. So I'm talking to Seb Nichols and he says, 'If you're looking for a good queer writer, I know the best one in town.' Is that all right? I mean, using that word, the word 'queer', is that all right? No offence, I hope.

OLIVER. No offence taken.

PETER. Coz you never fucking know, do you? I mean, if you're using the right word. I mean, I know the whole political correctness thing's over – what the hell was that about? – but I'm not the kind of guy who enjoys offending people. Thing is, you never know what the right word is. I thought the word queer might be to you guys what the N-word is to blacks. All right amongst yourselves, but...

OLIVER. Queer's fine, queer's fine.

PETER. Pushing out the boundaries, that's what I'm talking about. I don't know if you happened to see the piece we did on Iraq.

OLIVER. No, I missed that.

PETER. This young kid gets back from the war and he's lost both his fucking arms. And we follow him for a week, I mean, it's like his diary or something, you know, stuff like how his life has changed and all the shit he has to deal with, stuff like his girlfriend walking out on him, and little shit too, everyday things like using a cashpoint and how the fuck he gets from A to B and this piece is very moving, I mean, it pushes people's buttons, makes them think. Powerful.

OLIVER. I'm sure.

PETER. Coz there's more to life than tits and arse, tits and arse, tits and arse with a little football thrown in for good measure. And I'm not saying we're gonna turn into the *New Statesman* overnight, but we've got a wide readership out there, and most of them are impressionable young lads and, you know what they say, with power comes responsibility and all that.

OLIVER. So they say.

PETER. Coz the thing is, Oliver, most of these lads just love sex. Fuck, most of them would fuck a pig. And you know what I'm saying about 'times are changing', I mean, they are, believe me. The other night I'm out with all these mates and this one guy, his name's Dave and he's a bit of an arsehole but not a bad guy, and he's had a few and he's telling us about his trip to Thailand and he's left his girlfriend back at the Shangri-La or wherever the fuck they're staying at and he's walking the streets and feeling horny, as you do, and next thing you know he's having his dick sucked by a lady-boy. A fucking lady-boy. So he's telling us this and we're all fucking, 'You did what?' and he's saying, 'Best fucking blowjob I ever had,' and we're all taking the piss and everything and having a laugh, and two minutes after that we're all playing snooker again and the thing's forgotten. That wouldn't have happened ten years ago, times are changing, Dave would have kept that to himself. I mean, who gives a fuck these days? I mean, at the end of the day, Oliver, and forgive me if I sound crude, but if you've got a problem with it don't look down.

OLIVER. Fair enough.

PETER. So I'm thinking, come on, let's push the boat out here, nothing to be afraid of, lads, we're all fucking human after all, and you don't have to fucking get married or anything. Time to say to these lads it's okay if you get turned on by it, and it's cool to be gay or whatever and fucking face your homophobia or get over it. So what I really want is a piece on gay sex, I don't mean all the details but kind of the whole thing of sex in public and that kind of thing, making them a bit jealous, you know, kind of saying, well, if you could just walk into a park or a fucking public loo any time of the day and there's these gorgeous girls just waiting to be shagged, wouldn't you be up for it? Kind of like gay sex for the straight man.

OLIVER. Gay sex for the straight man.

PETER. So really what I want to do is a piece which will make them identify in some way and at the same time say, 'It's okay to be gay.' Change the way you think. Gay is cool. That kind of thing. These gay guys know what they want and they know how to get it. Innovators in various fields – music, fashion, fucking dogging.

And just by putting that into the magazine – just by having it there – you are making people change their minds. Coz it's not every lad's magazine that does a piece on gay sex. It's what I was saying at the beginning – breaking down barriers.

OLIVER. Yes.

PETER. And basically what I'm saying is, if I can do my job and do the right thing at the same time then that's a good thing. And breaking down barriers is a fucking important part of that. Coz you guys fucking deserve it.

Pause.

I mean, you guys fucking fought for your rights. You had a lot of shit to fight against. A lot of fucking ignorance.

OLIVER. Sure.

PETER. I'm not gonna deny to you, Oliver, that I've got a personal connection. I mean, to the whole gay thing. The gay cause, if you like. Had an uncle.

OLIVER. Don't they all.

PETER. No, but I fucking did. Great bloke. Fucking ace. My mother's brother. Uncle Harry. Fucking lovely man. Heart of gold. Couldn't hurt a fly. Worked for the council. Fucking AIDS got him.

OLIVER. I'm sorry.

PETER. Seared on my memory. Fucking engraved. This one day. Last time I saw him. And he's dying. And I'm, what? Twelve, thirteen. And my mum takes me and my little bro to the Royal Free coz that's where he is. Some special ward and they don't really know what it is, I mean, they know it's AIDS but this was the early days, I mean, you didn't really know if you could catch it, *how* you could catch it, so my mum's like throwing the glasses away, you know the ones he's drunk out of after he's been to ours, not in front of him, of course, but after he's gone, and it sounds fucking ignorant but you didn't really know what was going on back then. So we get to the Royal Free, this special ward, like, and Uncle Harry's under this fucking sheet thing, like a special sheet with wires coming out of him and drips and stuff. Fucking mad. And he's on a ventilator coz he can't fucking breathe and it's making this noise, I mean, enough to drive you mad, this kind of wheezing noise, like the sound of death. Never seen anything like it. And it's all a bit weird and I lean forward and I'm a bit freaked out by the whole thing and my mum's saying, 'Say hello to your Uncle Harry,' but what she really means is, 'Say goodbye to your Uncle Harry,' coz we all kind of know he's on his way out so I lean in and this fucking sheet thing is between us, but I look down and I see and. Fuck. Fucking hell. His eyes. Like every other part of him is dying but his eyes. Windows of the fucking soul. That kind of thing. Eyes full of fucking love. Breaks my fucking heart.

Pause.

So we're turning around to go and there's this guy sitting there, a few feet away from us and he sees me and smiles and I'm a bit like, 'Who the fuck are you?' coz I'm twelve or whatever and don't know any better and my mum kind of drags us out of the place and I'm asking her who that guy was and she's like, 'That's your Uncle Harry's friend.' And later I found out that they've lived together for twenty-five years. Fucking twenty-five years. I mean, that's a long fucking time. I mean, that's fucking serious. So I'm asking my mum why we've never met him, how come we've never met Uncle Harry's friend before and she doesn't really have an answer. 'We just haven't,' she says. People are weird.

Pause.

So that's my own personal connection. I mean, to the gay thing. Uncle Harry. I want to honour that.

OLIVER. Thank you. I mean, thank you for sharing that.

PETER. So what I'm thinking, Oliver, it's been great to have this initial chat and I'll email you some more ideas. About the kind of thing I'm after. But the main thing is to keep it light. And kind of exciting.

OLIVER. Exciting.

PETER. And you're all right about the money.

OLIVER. Four grand.

PETER. Two up-front.

OLIVER. Yes.

PETER. And two on completion.

OLIVER. Great.

Blackout.

1958

The park. There is a bench. When the lights go up we find OLIVER *and* SYLVIA. *They are standing. It is an autumn afternoon.*

SYLVIA. Thank you for coming.

OLIVER. It's a pleasure. It's been a long time.

SYLVIA. I thought you might find it odd that I asked you to meet me here. In the park. But the weather is being so kind and it all looks...

OLIVER. It looks beautiful.

SYLVIA. And I needed to get out, really. I've been spending ever so much time at home these days. Sometimes you forget that there's a whole world out there. Other people.

OLIVER. It's a lovely place to meet.

SYLVIA. And what with Philip being away so much. He's very busy. All of a sudden, work seems to take up all of his time. So it's nice to get out.

OLIVER. You look well.

SYLVIA. Do I?

Pause.

I walked by Hatchards the other day. Our book was in the window display. I felt so proud for a minute. So very, very proud.

OLIVER. You should.

SYLVIA. I do hope we get to work together again, Oliver. I hope that's not forward of me.

OLIVER. Not at all.

SYLVIA. Asking you, I mean. But I've plucked up the courage because it was important to me.

OLIVER. Of course we'll work together again.

SYLVIA. I thought maybe you were disappointed.

OLIVER. Disappointed?

SYLVIA. Oh, you know. That when it was actually over, that when the book was done and dusted maybe it didn't quite live up to your expectations. That it was a disappointment. My work, I mean, my contribution.

OLIVER. Not at all.

SYLVIA. That maybe it didn't quite live up to its initial promise.

OLIVER. You musn't think that, not for a minute. I couldn't have been happier.

SYLVIA. I suppose I was trying to come up with a reason why we hadn't seen each other for such a long time.

OLIVER. I've just been very busy.

SYLVIA. Of course.

OLIVER. But I'm so sorry if I gave you the wrong impression. Nothing could be further from the truth.

SYLVIA. Thank you for putting my mind at rest. That little part of me that remains sensible kept trying to tell me that it wasn't the case.

Pause.

I'm sure Philip thinks I'm completely mad most of the time.

Pause.

Your friendship is very important to me.

OLIVER. Are you all right, Sylvia?

SYLVIA. When I worked in the theatre there were a few people with whom I felt a similar kind of bond. There were people I could talk to openly about things which seemed vital and interesting and maybe even personal. Things I couldn't really talk to most people about. Even Philip. Especially Philip.

OLIVER. That's the theatre for you.

SYLVIA. And then when I met you I felt the same thing. That we didn't belong within that absurd little world in which talking about anything remotely significant seems an affront to one's dignity. A kindred spirit. Somebody you know you can be frank with and whom you hope can be frank with you.

She sits. A pause.

I'm lonely.

Pause.

Is that a terrible thing to say?

OLIVER. Not at all.

SYLVIA. I mean, I'm a married woman. I live with my husband. But sometimes I wake in the middle of the night and I lie in bed thinking how lonely I am. And the loneliness I feel is like a blanket. But not a blanket that comforts you. Something darker. More oppressive. It feels almost as if it stops me from breathing. I'm so sorry.

OLIVER. What are you sorry about?

SYLVIA. Calling you here. You were at home, writing probably, minding your own business and then you are summoned to the park to hear the ramblings of a mad woman.

OLIVER. You're not mad, Sylvia.

SYLVIA. There are things you suspect. And then, you brush them aside. Things maybe a part of you knows but to acknowledge them renders your life a lie. And then…

OLIVER. Then what?

SYLVIA. Then the foundations of everything you've ever depended on, the ground you've moved on, the home you've built for yourself, everything, the walls, the furniture, the air you breathe, everything seems unreal. And you cease to be able to distinguish truth from lies. Or at least from something you know is *not* the truth. An appearance of sorts. Life becomes a little like some horrible fancy-dress party. And it becomes unbearable.

Pause. Slowly, SYLVIA *starts to look through her bag for something.*

I found something of yours.

OLIVER. Of mine?

SYLVIA. At home. It must have fallen out of your pocket. I was wondering when it was. Three times you've been to our flat. Once, that first time when we asked you over so that you could meet Philip. The night we went to the Italian restaurant. And then twice after that. That morning you came to look at that last batch of illustrations when I couldn't come to yours because I had that awful cold. And then finally, the night of the party for the book's launch and that was only for five minutes when you dropped me off and we had a quick brandy. So only three times when I was there. And then, of course, on all those occasions you were only in the living room, unless of course you visited the bathroom, which to be honest I can't remember.

She pulls out a pen from her handbag.

Your gold pen. The one you love so much. The one your sister gave you. It was behind the cushion on the armchair. The green armchair in our bedroom. It must have fallen out of your jacket. You always kept it in the inside pocket, didn't you?

OLIVER. Yes. Yes, I did.

SYLVIA. So it must have slipped out.

OLIVER. Yes.

SYLVIA. I assume it was the time I'd gone to visit my mother. I was away for at least a week, wasn't I?

Pause.

Take it, Oliver. It's yours. It's your pen.

He takes it. There is a long pause.

I want you to know I don't blame you. I really don't. I did think it hurtful and disturbing that you should choose... I found it disturbing that you would... knowing that you have a flat, that you have your own flat, that you would choose... Isn't it funny that it should be that which upset me more than anything else? I suppose because it was the only aspect of the whole affair that surprised me. Your choice of location. How absurd.

Pause.

But then, you see, I thought about it and even that I don't blame you for. Because when one lives within that world of lying, of deception, then the details begin to blur. One's discernment is undermined I suppose is what I'm saying. One's sense of judgement. So under normal circumstances perhaps you wouldn't have chosen to insult me in that particular way. I like to think that.

She suddenly begins to cry.

OLIVER. I'm so sorry.

SYLVIA. All that wasted time. And I look at myself now, in the mirror and my face is the face of a woman who's forgotten herself and has been forgotten.

Pause.

Are you still in touch with Philip?

OLIVER. No. No, we're not.

SYLVIA. Was that his choice or yours?

OLIVER. His. I would have chosen the same as you.

SYLVIA. The same as me?

OLIVER. To live an honest life.

SYLVIA. An honest life.

OLIVER. Yes.

Pause.

SYLVIA. Was he happy?

OLIVER. Happy?

SYLVIA. Tell me. Was he happy? For an afternoon, at least. A morning. Was he ever happy?

OLIVER. I can't... I find it...

SYLVIA. Difficult. You find it difficult.

OLIVER. Yes, I...

Pause.

Maybe once. For a very short while. When for a very short time he glimpsed the possibility of being... of being...

He pauses.

SYLVIA. Of being brave.

OLIVER. Yes. I suppose that's the right word.

SYLVIA. That thought filled me with a rage. Your happiness. For a day or two I hated you so much. Because I suspected then that even in your few, illicit meetings, in that very short time you describe, he would have been able to be his real self, something he has never been with me. In that glimpse you talk of.

Pause.

OLIVER. I'm so sorry. I'm ashamed.

SYLVIA. I know you are.

I hope...

OLIVER. Yes…

SYLVIA. I hope with all my heart you find what you're looking for. It isn't easy, I'm sure. You must be lonely too.

OLIVER. Yes, I am.

She moves to go, then stops.

SYLVIA. That first night when you came over, something happened, didn't it? I felt it. I wonder what that is. It was thick in the air. I want to feel that too. And someone to feel that for me. Goodbye, Oliver.

SYLVIA walks away, leaving OLIVER sitting on the bench. The lights fade to black.

2008

SYLVIA*'s flat. She's just opened the door.* OLIVER *is there. There's some blood in his mouth.*

SYLVIA. Fuck.

OLIVER. You really need to stop greeting me like that. I'm starting to take it personally.

SYLVIA. Jesus.

OLIVER. That's more like it.

SYLVIA. You're bleeding.

OLIVER. As ever, your powers of observation astound me.

SYLVIA. What are you doing here?

OLIVER. I was in the area.

SYLVIA. What happened?

OLIVER. An accident.

SYLVIA. An accident?

OLIVER. Could we discuss the details after I've stopped dripping blood onto your floor?

SYLVIA. What have you done?

OLIVER. It's a cut, that's all. A piece of kitchen roll will suffice, Miss Nightingale.

SYLVIA. Sit.

He sits. SYLVIA *runs into the kitchen to get the paper.*

OLIVER. It was my farewell tour. Let's call it a souvenir. One of my many fans. But this one had a predilection for the darker side. It seems you have the gift of prophecy, Miss Burton. Don't quite know what his voting profile was but I wouldn't have him down as a woolly liberal. A primitive man, I think it's fair to say. In a pinstriped suit though and he had shaved, I'll give him that. Shiniest brogues you've ever seen. You never can tell these days. I mean, he didn't look like he'd crawled out of a cave. Though the sweat was just about detectable under a velvety surface of Acqua di Giò.

SYLVIA *runs back with some kitchen roll. She gives him some to wipe his nose with.*

SYLVIA. I thought you said that whole aspect of your life was becoming untenable.

OLIVER. I was just checking.

SYLVIA. That was a conversation we had yesterday.

OLIVER. As recently as that?

SYLVIA. I thought you'd give it at least a week.

OLIVER. Obviously your powers of persuasion are not quite as effective as the lure of city cock.

SYLVIA. What the fuck happened?

OLIVER. I love a man in a suit.

SYLVIA. Clearly.

OLIVER. The signs were all there. During the actual act the whole verbal thing was slightly more convincing than usual.

SYLVIA. What verbal thing?

OLIVER. His use of adjective was alarming. And his imaginative use of the common noun left me speechless. It wasn't, of course, the only thing that made it difficult for me to put a word in edgeways.

SYLVIA. Spare me the details.

OLIVER. And then upon completion there was a push. Along the lines of – out of the way, I have important things to get on with: my friends are waiting, I'm taking my wife out to dinner, the markets are closing. That sort of thing. It was definitely just a push.

SYLVIA. You're bleeding.

OLIVER. It was the Rolex. One of the chunky ones. Caught my upper lip at an unfortunate angle. But it was a push. Not a punch.

SYLVIA. Well, that's all right then.

OLIVER. Hence my use of the word 'accident'. He was back in the office before I'd even realised what had happened.

SYLVIA. I'm sure if he'd noticed he would have driven you home in his Jaguar.

OLIVER. Without doubt.

Pause.

SYLVIA. Fuck, Oliver.

OLIVER. I was doing research.

SYLVIA. 'Research'?

OLIVER. The piece on anonymous sex. God knows why they chose me.

Pause.

Speaking of being surrounded by a sea of my gay brethren, I need to talk to you about tomorrow.

SYLVIA. Pride?

OLIVER. Yes. I'm not coming. Send my apologies to the Italian.

SYLVIA. You *are* coming.

OLIVER. Really, I'm not. I intend to spend the day in bed, nursing my wound.

SYLVIA. I spoke to Philip.

OLIVER. Liar.

SYLVIA. He said he might drop by. For me, he said. I told him you'd be there. He said that's okay, we're adults, we can cope. Something like that.

OLIVER. Are you being serious?

SYLVIA. Why would I lie?

OLIVER. Coz you're ruthless in the pursuit of your objectives.

SYLVIA. He's coming. Join us if you like. Or you could stay in bed having thoughts of loneliness and death.

OLIVER. Thanks for that.

SYLVIA. Let me know. I have to know how much food to make.

OLIVER. But the whole thing is so passé. All those tight T-shirts, all those preening queens. Anyway, what's the point? Remind me. Is it a demonstration, a celebration or a fashion show?

SYLVIA. Cynic.

OLIVER. Ten thousand mincers admiring each other's biceps. How could I be so dismissive.

Pause.

You look nice, by the way.

SYLVIA. Thank you.

OLIVER. Expecting visitors?

SYLVIA. A visitor. Singular. Yes, I am.

OLIVER. Okay.

SYLVIA. He's coming for dinner.

OLIVER. You cooking?

SYLVIA. Yes.

OLIVER. Smells good.

SYLVIA. Thank you.

OLIVER. Nothing Italian, I hope. He'll compare it to his mother's. That's what they do.

SYLVIA. Do they?

OLIVER. Hope you've stuck to something English. Frozen peas, that kind of thing.

SYLVIA. He'll be here any minute now.

OLIVER. That's exciting.

Pause.

So what else did he say?

SYLVIA. Philip?

OLIVER. No, Cliff Richard. Yes, Philip.

SYLVIA. We talked about books.

OLIVER. Books?

SYLVIA. He told me about this book he'd been reading. Something Hungarian.

OLIVER. But he didn't say anything about me.

SYLVIA. No. Apart from what I just said. It'll be okay to see you, he said.

Pause.

OLIVER. Fuck you. You know how to push my buttons.

SYLVIA. Of course I do.

OLIVER. You know I'm coming.

SYLVIA. Of course I do.

OLIVER. I want to see him again. Be with him.

SYLVIA. He's a special person. Profound, honest, loyal.

OLIVER. Deeply compassionate.

SYLVIA. And handsome to boot.

Pause.

OLIVER. Sometimes…

SYLVIA. What?

OLIVER. Do you ever get that thing?

SYLVIA. What thing?

OLIVER. When you've just fallen asleep, just before the dreams begin. Or maybe just after you've woken up and your eyes are open even though your mind might still be dreaming.

SYLVIA. What about it?

OLIVER. The brevity of life strikes you. The brevity. The randomness. A flash in the pan.

SYLVIA. I've had that.

OLIVER. And I kind of feel then that the only thing that matters is finding some meaning, some reason, something you can slap the face of brevity with. And say I was here. I existed. I was. And then I think that the only two ways to do that are through work and relationships. How you changed people. How people changed you. And how you held on. To each other. Or at least gave it a damn good try. That's what defines your flash in the pan.

SYLVIA. Amen.

Pause.

So what do you do?

OLIVER. What do I do?

SYLVIA. There's only one thing you can do.

OLIVER. Which is?

SYLVIA. You have to stop sucking his dick.

OLIVER. Whose dick?

SYLVIA. You have to stop sucking the dick of your oppressor.

OLIVER. That's deep.

SYLVIA. Of your Nazi-Rolex man.

OLIVER. Sounds like a City Lit course. 'Marxist Theory for the Promiscuous Homosexual.'

SYLVIA. But one day soon you'll look up at the fascist whose dick you're sucking and you'll say something like –

OLIVER. 'Now look here' –

SYLVIA. 'Now look here, Klaus or whatever the hell your name is, surprisingly enough your dick is marvellously big but I have decided, a little like those pioneering fish that crawled out of the deep, dark ocean so many zillions of years ago, that from now on I will only suck the dicks –

OLIVER. Of social workers and yoga teachers.

SYLVIA. – of people who I know for a fact or at least *suspect*, for God's sake, aspire to things like justice, equality, mutual respect. And I really need to make this evolutionary leap, otherwise God knows where I'll end up.'

OLIVER. In the gutter. Or a cage. In an existential gimp mask.

Pause.

SYLVIA. I'm glad we've sorted that out. And now I have to…

OLIVER. You have to what?

SYLVIA. Mario will be here any minute and I need to, you know, get ready. That sort of thing.

OLIVER. Are you asking me to leave?

SYLVIA. Well, I mean, you can stay for a quick drink and meet him, but –

OLIVER. But what?

Pause.

SYLVIA. The thing is this. It's not that I don't enjoy being there for you. Sometimes. Because I do.

OLIVER. Sometimes?

SYLVIA. I need a little space, Oliver. And I don't mean just tonight.

OLIVER. Space? How d'you mean, you need a little space?

The question hangs.

I'll fuck off then, shall I?

SYLVIA. You know how when you stay, when you're around you take over in some way.

OLIVER. 'Take over'?

SYLVIA. With your charm, if you like, your charisma, your presence.

OLIVER. Is that the spoonful of sugar?

SYLVIA. And tonight I don't want you here like that. I've met this man that I am very, very fond of –

OLIVER. She's kicking me out.

SYLVIA. And I have an overwhelming feeling that from now on I'm going to be focusing quite a bit more on him than I am on you.

OLIVER. Fucking kicking me out.

SYLVIA. And I don't think that's a bad thing.

OLIVER. It's over between us.

SYLVIA. For either of us.

Pause.

There. I've said it.

The buzzer rings.

Fuck.

OLIVER. That'll be the future.

SYLVIA. He's early.

OLIVER. I'll be off then.

SYLVIA. Stay. For a quick drink. And then go.

OLIVER. You've made me feel as welcome as a bacon sandwich at a bar mitzvah.

She runs towards the door. Then stops.

SYLVIA. But come tomorrow. To the park. I think…

OLIVER. You think what?

SYLVIA. I think it *is* important. And yes, it's all of those things. A demonstration. A celebration. And a fashion show. But definitely in that order.

OLIVER. The jury's out. Now answer the bloody door.

She runs out of the room. OLIVER *stays there, alone. He becomes pensive, as if trying to remember something. He closes his eyes, and then, almost in a whisper:*

Philip.

1958

A doctor's surgery. Simple. A desk, two chairs, maybe an examination couch. The DOCTOR *and* PHILIP *sit facing each other.*

DOCTOR. When was it that you first experienced sexual attraction to a member of your own sex?

PHILIP. I don't really… I suppose…

DOCTOR. Was it during or after adolescence?

PHILIP. I suppose it was during. Maybe when… maybe when I was thirteen or thereabouts. At school. But of course… well, you understand at that age. I didn't really know. I was frightened, I imagine. So I didn't really. I tried not to think about it. I made myself not think about it.

DOCTOR. Were you interfered with?

PHILIP. I beg your pardon?

DOCTOR. Were you ever interfered with? During your childhood or adolescence. By an adult of your own sex. Were you seduced into any sort of sexual activity by an older male? Either a member of your own family or a teacher or perhaps even a stranger.

PHILIP. No, I wasn't. I didn't…

DOCTOR. You do understand it is absolutely necessary to be truthful in your answering of these questions.

PHILIP. Yes. Of course.

DOCTOR. That unless you answer every one of these questions with absolute honesty and courage you are not only wasting my own time but your own as well. You must attempt to put all inhibitions aside.

PHILIP. I was never seduced. Or interfered with. By anybody.

DOCTOR. So you remember being about thirteen years of age when you first felt sexually attracted to a member of your own sex.

PHILIP. Thereabouts.

DOCTOR. And you indulged in sexual fantasies involving yourself and this boy?

PHILIP. When I was with him I felt… when I was close to him. A strong, overwhelming attraction.

DOCTOR. And your penis would become erect? I mean, there was arousal?

PHILIP. I suppose. I can't really. It was all, sort of connected. Everything was connected.

DOCTOR. 'Connected.' How do you mean, it was 'connected'?

PHILIP. Well, I definitely felt something physical, but it was…

DOCTOR. Did you ever participate in any sort of sexual activity with this boy?

PHILIP. Good God, no. I wasn't... I didn't really know that anyone else... that anyone else had that kind of feeling. Looking back, I suspect that maybe it was mutual, but at the time.

DOCTOR. Describe to me the fantasies that you had which involved yourself and this boy whom you say you were infatuated with.

PHILIP. I can't really. I suppose we were together. Physically.

DOCTOR. Did you fantasise about anal penetration?

PHILIP. I can't really... Perhaps. Maybe.

DOCTOR. Do you remember if in those fantasies you adopted the sexually passive or the sexually active role?

PHILIP. I honestly can't remember. I do remember wanting to be with him. In a physical sort of way. But I can't remember the details. Maybe I've forced myself to forget them. I'm not sure.

A pause as the DOCTOR *looks over some of the papers he has before him.*

DOCTOR. It says here that you were recently involved in a sexual relationship with a man which persisted over a number of months.

PHILIP. I was, yes.

DOCTOR. I'm assuming that anal intercourse was included in these relations.

PHILIP. Yes. Yes, it was.

DOCTOR. On how many occasions did you have sex with this man?

PHILIP. Well, we were... well, it was over a period of four months.

DOCTOR. And over those four months how many times were you sexually intimate with each other?

PHILIP. Well, it's difficult to say really. Maybe on average two, three times a week.

DOCTOR. And what brought this... this relationship to an end?

PHILIP. I did. I put an end to it.

DOCTOR. In a concerted effort to struggle against this tendency you both shared.

PHILIP. Yes.

DOCTOR. And have you kept in touch with this man? I mean, have you been successful in keeping him out of your life?

PHILIP. Yes.

DOCTOR. And have you banished him from your thoughts?

PHILIP. Sorry?

DOCTOR. Have you been successful in banishing him from your
thoughts? Your sexual fantasies.

PHILIP. Yes. I have tried.

DOCTOR. Have you, since the end of this relationship, been
involved in any other sexual activity with any other men?

PHILIP. No. No, I haven't.

Pause.

DOCTOR. This is an extreme form of therapy, there is no question
about that. Firstly, let me congratulate you on taking the steps you
have taken which have brought you here today. I'm sure it has not
been easy. From speaking to you briefly this afternoon and from
the conversations I have had with Dr Davies, I gather it has been a
struggle for you. But fighting this pernicious enemy, this
perversion, is an essential part in the development of your
personality. I'm sure you agree.

PHILIP *says nothing.*

You've brought your belongings.

PHILIP. Yes, I have. A change of clothes. A toothbrush.

DOCTOR. Good. In a few minutes the nurse will take you to your
room. The objective is to stay in the room for the length of the
treatment. I would suggest till at least tomorrow morning.

PHILIP. All right.

DOCTOR. The room is simple. Spartan. Nothing extraneous. A bed.
That is all. There is no window. You may want to brush your teeth
beforehand. And get into your pyjamas. Though, of course, we can
provide you with something appropriate. Something to wear, I mean.

PHILIP. I've brought my pyjamas.

DOCTOR. Excellent.

Pause.

There are pictures in the room. Publications. We will encourage
you to look at them. They are of a pornographic nature and of

homosexual content. You will be left alone in the room for approximately an hour. I suggest you spend most of that time looking at these pictures. You will probably be aroused.

Pause.

An hour later, at approximately nine p.m., the nurse will enter the room and inject you with a generous dose of apomorphine. This is a drug that induces vomiting. Around ten to fifteen minutes after the injection you will begin to feel nauseous. You will then be violently sick and may suffer dizziness. Most of the patients undergoing this therapy in the past have asked for a basin, something to vomit into, some sort of receptacle. I have discovered, however, that in order for the treatment to be at its most effective, it is best not to provide you with any such objects. You will vomit in the room and you will have to remain surrounded by your own vomit till the therapy is over in the morning. After the first injection and the first bout of vomiting, it is vital that you try to return to perusing the pornography. A couple of hours later, the nurse will enter again and inject you a second time. This will be repeated three times during the course of the night. And between each injection I would strongly suggest you return to the pornographic images we have provided you with. This will help facilitate the therapy and increase its chances of success.

Pause.

Do you have any questions?

PHILIP. Yes… I… Dr Davies said that in certain cases. Where there is an individual involved.

DOCTOR. Ah, yes. He mentioned it. A few of our patients have asked for the same procedure. I mean, when a particular individual…

PHILIP. Yes.

DOCTOR. You have brought a photograph then. Of this individual.

PHILIP. Yes. Yes, I have.

DOCTOR. Good. Well, it's quite simple, really. You take the photograph with you. Into the room, I mean. Of the individual. You include it. You incorporate it into the treatment. You look at it with the other photographs. This is a common sort of request.

PHILIP. Yes.

Pause.

The thing is, Doctor…

DOCTOR. Yes?

PHILIP. What I need to know is… the other things. The other feelings. I mean, the ones that aren't *exclusively* sexual.

DOCTOR. Yes.

PHILIP. Do they… will they…

There is an awkward pause.

DOCTOR. The nurse will be ready for you now. And I will be seeing you again in the morning.

PHILIP. Yes.

DOCTOR. So there's nothing else then?

PHILIP. No. No, there isn't.

PHILIP *stands up.*

DOCTOR. By the way…

PHILIP. Yes, Doctor?

DOCTOR. Do you mind me asking you what brought you here? What tipped the scales as it were and made you decide to come here? It's an important part of my research.

Pause.

PHILIP. Forgetting.

DOCTOR. Forgetting?

PHILIP. I want an easier life.

DOCTOR. Don't we all?

PHILIP. We do.

Blackout.

2008

The park bench – it is the same one as before. SYLVIA *is sitting on it with* OLIVER. *They have opened a bottle of champagne and are drinking out of flute glasses. In the background there are lots of noises from the Pride party – whistles, shouts, music. The sound of celebration.*

SYLVIA. So we're on the 31 as it's crawling up Kilburn High Road and there's this blonde girl, she's about fifteen and scary and surrounded by her adoring fan club and she's very loud and every second word is 'gay'. Gay this, gay that, gay everything. That song's gay, and *EastEnders* is gay and even the chicken sandwich she had for lunch was gay. So I muster up a little bit of courage and I turn around to her and in my most authoritative voice say, 'Excuse me...'

OLIVER. Excuse me, miss.

SYLVIA. Excuse me, miss, but can I ask you a favour and do you mind not using the word 'gay' in that particular context...

OLIVER. Gay is shit. Sub-standard.

SYLVIA. Or at least think twice before you do so because in some way that perhaps you can't quite fathom yet it is damaging to many people and that upsets me.

OLIVER. And she didn't stab you?

SYLVIA. And then an hour later I'm at Jennifer's for dinner.

OLIVER. Why you insist on being her friend is beyond me...

SYLVIA. And she's invited another five or six people including Millie Wallis, who by the way has had a massive nose job and looks completely transformed but nobody's allowed to talk about it so we're all pretending that even though her face is *entirely* different we haven't noticed a thing and there's this one guy called Harry or something who's saying something along the lines of 'well, it kind of makes sense for the inheritance stuff but they don't really care about the other stuff,' whatever that means, 'I mean, most of them just want to have fun' and then Sonya's joining in and saying, and I quote, that 'some of her best friends are gay'...

OLIVER. And most of her exes.

SYLVIA. 'But why do they need to get married, I mean, why aren't civil partnerships enough?' and then Harry's back joining in with 'who wants to get married anyway?' and 'they're much better off shagging in the parks, I know I'd be' and everyone's having a good laugh and at that point I stood up, I actually pushed my chair back and stood up on both legs...

OLIVER. One leg would have been awkward.

SYLVIA. And I said, 'Harry, the reason a lot of them were in the parks to begin with is because they couldn't be at home in the first place. They were in exile.'

OLIVER. 'In exile.' I like that.

SYLVIA. But I looked at these people, Ollie, and they're not stupid, I mean, a little unimaginative maybe but not necessarily stupid, and I looked at them all and I thought...

OLIVER. You thought what...?

SYLVIA. Oh, I don't know, I thought, Ollie, of all the battles that had been fought. And what they had been fought against. Not only hatred but something else too, quieter but just as persistent. A world telling you what you are. I listened to these people and in some way they reduce you. And somewhere, you, Ollie, have believed them.

OLIVER. I'm gullible, it's true.

SYLVIA. And then I thought of what the things were that those battles had been fought for. What they'd been fought for.

OLIVER. That's a lot of thinking.

He pours her some champagne.

Have some more. And now will you kindly step off your fucking soapbox.

PHILIP *enters.*

PHILIP. I could hear you down the hill.

OLIVER. The voice of an actress.

SYLVIA. Was I loud?

PHILIP. Brilliantly so.

SYLVIA. Oh God. I'm a cliché.

Pause.

PHILIP. I brought sandwiches.

SYLVIA. Oliver made some too. Mario's on his way.

OLIVER. What's in them?

PHILIP. Chorizo. Duck. Tapenade.

SYLVIA. What's wrong with cheese and pickle?

PHILIP. And there's blueberries too.

OLIVER. Yum.

   Pause.

SYLVIA. So last night he's talking about kids again.

PHILIP. Kids?

SYLVIA. 'I've always wanted children,' he says.

OLIVER. He's keen.

SYLVIA. And I love this man.

PHILIP. Haven't you just met?

SYLVIA. He writes his own songs. He has a guitar.

OLIVER. That's all she needs to know.

SYLVIA. He never misses an anti-war march. He reads, and reads, and reads.

PHILIP. And?

OLIVER. The signs are all good is what she's saying.

SYLVIA. He's great in bed.

PHILIP. An important thing.

SYLVIA. He makes love to me and I'm thinking… if something should come of this love… If this love is fruitful in that particular way, well then I'm ready for it, and then that's great, I mean, we'll be lucky, it will be a gift. From God. Life. Whatever.

OLIVER. She's having babies.

SYLVIA. And if not, I mean, if it doesn't happen, if it's not meant to happen then that's fine as well. What we have is enough, I mean.

   Pause. She's suddenly aware she should leave them alone.

   I'm going to… get an ice cream.

OLIVER. An ice cream? But we haven't had lunch.

PHILIP. She wants an ice cream, Oliver.

OLIVER. I'll come with you.

SYLVIA. With me? How d'you mean, you'll come with me?

OLIVER. I want one too.

SYLVIA. Don't be stupid.

OLIVER. Oh, that's right. I'm to stop stalking her.

PHILIP. Stalking her?

OLIVER. Off you go then. You're a free woman.

SYLVIA. At last.

OLIVER. The operation was successful. My arms have been surgically removed from your waist.

SYLVIA. About time.

OLIVER. It's been lovely knowing you.

She starts to move.

SYLVIA. Have some champagne. Finish the champagne.

OLIVER. Okay.

PHILIP. Will do.

SYLVIA. And remember the battles, Ollie.

OLIVER. What battles?

She leaves.

Oh, *those* battles.

Pause.

Hey.

PHILIP. Hi.

OLIVER. How are you?

PHILIP. Fine. I'm fine.

OLIVER. Good.

A long pause. They look out over the park. They start talking at the same time.

I wasn't –

PHILIP. I hope you don't –

OLIVER. Sorry.

PHILIP. No. What?

OLIVER. After you.

PHILIP. It's fine. You go first.

A pause.

OLIVER. Do you believe in change?

PHILIP. Do I believe in change?

OLIVER. We're lucky really, aren't we?

PHILIP. Lucky?

OLIVER. I mean, think about it. The freedom. What we have.

PHILIP. What freedom?

OLIVER. All these people who were mute. Had been mute for hundreds, thousands of years.

PHILIP. Most of the world still is. Mute.

OLIVER. I know. Which makes it all the more…

PHILIP. All the more what?

OLIVER. Important, I think I mean. Not to throw the baby out with the bathwater. For us. If you follow me.

PHILIP. Not really.

OLIVER. I mean, you watch those nature documentaries…

PHILIP. Nature documentaries?

OLIVER. I mean, they're all fucking killing each other, for God's sake. That's all they ever do. Kill each other. And procreate. Inflict terrible pain and kill each other…

PHILIP. Apart from dolphins.

OLIVER. True. They spend all their time swimming with autistic children. But apart from dolphins, they just kill each other. And the only thing, I mean, the only thing that separates us, that makes us different, that makes us *human* is this ability we're discovering, this *thing* we have to instil, to do things with and to give love. And some kind of respect. That's all we have. To listen to each other.

Pause.

That's what I'm going on about. It's what I was trying to say to you the other day.

PHILIP. What?

OLIVER. The night we met. The way you spoke about that woman. The one whose photograph you'd taken. Your ability to put yourself in her shoes. It was genuine.

PHILIP. Oh, that.

OLIVER. And that made me feel hopeful.

Pause.

You still haven't answered my question.

PHILIP. What's that?

OLIVER. Do you believe people change?

PHILIP. That wasn't your question. Your question was do I believe in change. Not do I believe *people* change.

OLIVER. A slight amendment.

PHILIP. What for?

OLIVER. Oh, you know. Us.

PHILIP. What about us?

OLIVER. The thing is…

Pause.

I love you so much. Profoundly.

Pause.

PHILIP. God knows why I came here today.

OLIVER. I'm irresistible?

PHILIP. Impossible is the word I have in mind.

OLIVER. Charming.

PHILIP. You can be shallow.

OLIVER. Thank you.

PHILIP. Vain.

OLIVER. Lovely.

PHILIP. And you're addicted to sex with strangers.

OLIVER. I've been thinking about that.

PHILIP. But I keep giving you the benefit of the doubt.

OLIVER. Thank you. For the faith, I mean.

PHILIP. The sheer, pig-headed stupidity.

OLIVER. You're very wise in your persistence.

PHILIP. Or completely fucking mad.

OLIVER. Maybe.

A pause and then OLIVER *is suddenly overwhelmed by an emotion. He pulls back.*

PHILIP. What?

OLIVER. Nothing... I...

PHILIP. What is it?

OLIVER. Nothing. Can I...

PHILIP. Can you what?

OLIVER. Sleep on your sofa for a little while?

PHILIP. Sleep on my sofa?

OLIVER. Work. I may not be earning. Until things... I want to work on my book.

PHILIP. I thought you had all these jobs lined up...

OLIVER. They've kind of fallen through.

Not really me. So times may be hard. For a little while.

PHILIP. Okay. But definitely the sofa.

OLIVER. Agreed.

Pause.

PHILIP. After all...

OLIVER. What?

PHILIP. Well, it may not be a long time…

OLIVER. What isn't?

PHILIP. A year and a half, I mean.

OLIVER. Nineteen months. Next Thursday.

PHILIP. Since we've known each other.

OLIVER. That's years.

PHILIP. It may not be much but…

OLIVER. But what?

PHILIP. It's a history of sorts.

OLIVER. Yes.

PHILIP. You and I…

OLIVER. What about us?

PHILIP. We have a history of sorts.

Pause.

And I'm sorry.

OLIVER. What for?

PHILIP. I don't know. If… If I did anything. Ever. To hurt you. To upset you. Whatever. Anything I may have done.

OLIVER. Betrayed me.

PHILIP. Betrayed you?

OLIVER. Yes.

PHILIP. I don't really…

OLIVER. Never mind.

A pause. They look out over the park at the people who surround them. OLIVER *pours* PHILIP *a glass of champagne.*

Have some champagne.

PHILIP. Do you know, I think I will.

They continue to look out.

OLIVER. Have you seen those two? On the bicycle.

PHILIP. They're in love.

OLIVER. The blond one's had his tongue in the other one's ear since we got here.

PHILIP. Yummy.

OLIVER. They're sweet.

PHILIP. And he must be ninety-five.

OLIVER. Who?

PHILIP. The one over there. By the ice-cream van.

OLIVER. I can't see.

PHILIP. Two o'clock. The string vest.

OLIVER. Oh, him. Oh my God.

PHILIP. Ninety-five.

OLIVER. Good on him. A survivor.

PHILIP. Bless him.

OLIVER. If I look like that when I'm ninety-five I'm having a party.

PHILIP. If you look like that when you're ninety-five I'll have you arrested.

SYLVIA *returns but she comes back in her 1950's incarnation. She is wearing her nightie and holding a small suitcase.* OLIVER *and* PHILIP *do not see her and she comes to stand in a pool of light on the other side of the stage from them. It is as if she is sleepwalking.*

SYLVIA. When I next wake it will be to leave. You will still be sleeping. I will kiss you on your forehead and quietly go. I cannot blame you for what you have been. You have been the prisoner of fear. You have only known how to hold on to things and the things you have held on to have died in your hands.

The birth pangs will be the pains of you hanging on to the way things are. And all I can do is whisper from a distance: it will be all right, it will be all right, it will be all right.

Blackout.

The End.

APOLOGIA

This version of *Apologia* was first performed at the Bush Theatre, London, on 17 June 2009, with the following cast:

PETER	Tom Beard
KRISTIN	Paolo Dionisotti
TRUDI	Sarah Goldberg
SIMON	John Light
CLAIRE	Nina Sosanya
HUGH	Philip Voss

Director	Josie Rourke
Designer	Peter McKintosh
Lighting Designer	Hartley T A Kemp
Sound Designer	Emma Laxton

A revised version of *Apologia* was produced by Howard Panter for Trafalgar Entertainment Group, DB Productions and Dodger Theatrical, and first performed at the Trafalgar Studios, London, on 29 July 2017, with the following cast:

KRISTIN	Stockard Channing
CLAIRE	Freema Agyeman
HUGH	Desmond Barrit
TRUDI	Laura Carmichael
PETER/SIMON	Joseph Millson

Director	Jamie Lloyd
Set Designer	Soutra Gilmour
Lighting Designer	Jon Clark
Sound Designer	Ringham Bros
Associate Director	Rupert Hands

103

Characters

KRISTIN MILLER, *in her sixties*
PETER, *her son, fortyish*
TRUDI, *his American fiancée, in her late twenties/early thirties*
SIMON, *her other son, in his late thirties*
CLAIRE, *his girlfriend, in her thirties*
HUGH, *an old friend of hers, in his sixties or early seventies*

PETER *and* SIMON *may be played by the same actor.*

The play takes place entirely in the kitchen of Kristin's cottage somewhere in the English countryside, in the present.

ACT ONE

Scene One

The kitchen of KRISTIN*'s cottage. Impressive, chaotic, eclectic – like its owner. Full of interesting and beautiful objects. The space is dominated by a large dining table.*

KRISTIN *is standing on one side of the room,* PETER *and* TRUDI *are on the other side, by the door. They have just arrived. They have two bags with them – an overnight travel bag and a large plastic one.*

PETER. Mother.

KRISTIN. Darling.

PETER. We're early.

KRISTIN. You are.

PETER. No traffic.

KRISTIN. It's fine.

PETER. And Trudi wanted to see it before the sun went down.

KRISTIN. Did she?

TRUDI. The countryside is so beautiful.

KRISTIN. As long as you don't mind me in my dressing gown.

Pause. PETER *and* TRUDI *put the bags down.*

PETER. Mum, this is Trudi.

KRISTIN. Hello, Trudi.

TRUDI. Hi, Mrs Miller.

KRISTIN. Kristin.

TRUDI. Kristin.

KRISTIN. Welcome to my house.

TRUDI. I've heard so much about you.

KRISTIN. Have you?

TRUDI. And I've read your work.

KRISTIN. What a pretty name you have, Trudi.

TRUDI. Thank you.

KRISTIN. It's so American.

TRUDI. I know.

KRISTIN. Like Disneyland.

A slight pause.

We have a bit of a crisis on our hands.

PETER. What kind of crisis?

KRISTIN. I need you to look at the oven.

PETER. The oven?

KRISTIN. It just doesn't feel to me like it's getting hot enough.

PETER. Have you got something in there now?

KRISTIN. Chicken.

TRUDI. Okay.

PETER. I thought I told you Trudi was a vegetarian.

KRISTIN. There's potatoes. And vegetables, of course.

TRUDI. I love potatoes.

KRISTIN. But I can't remember you telling me she was a vegetarian.

TRUDI. Really, Kristin, it's fine.

PETER *opens the oven.*

PETER. It's not that hot.

KRISTIN. And I've put it on full.

PETER. What time is it?

TRUDI. Just turned six.

KRISTIN. I mean, we won't be eating for at least another hour so
    maybe –

PETER. It doesn't feel that hot in there.

KRISTIN. Can you look at it?

PETER. Look at it?

KRISTIN. I mean, check the electrics, that kind of thing. Might be a switch.

PETER. It's not a switch, and no, I can't look at it. I mean, I wouldn't know where to start. You need an electrician.

KRISTIN. The irony of it. I mean, tonight of all bloody nights. I wanted everything to be –

PETER. What's your contingency plan?

KRISTIN. Contingency plan?

PETER. I mean, if it doesn't get any hotter. Pasta, or something?

KRISTIN. The hobs seem to have gone as well. I tried them earlier. I was thinking I could poach it or something. As a last resort. Cut it up and fry it.

PETER. Fry the chicken?

KRISTIN. But the hobs seem to have gone as well. The whole damn thing.

PETER. So what do we do?

KRISTIN. I could drive it over to Phil and Lou's. Borrow their oven.

PETER. That's twenty miles away.

KRISTIN. I know.

PETER. You can't be driving up and down the motorway with a chicken in the back seat.

KRISTIN. Or we could just have a cold meal. I'm sure I could be inventive. Forage for food in the cupboards, you know. Look for things.

PETER. Look for things?

KRISTIN (*looking in the cupboard*). There's anchovies, nuts.

PETER. Nuts?

KRISTIN. I have a cos lettuce in the fridge.

PETER. We're not bloody squirrels.

KRISTIN. Make a salad, you know.

PETER. Anchovy nut salad?

KRISTIN. Be inventive is what I mean.

TRUDI. I love salads.

KRISTIN. It's still early. It'll probably warm up.

PETER. Unlikely.

KRISTIN. We won't be eating for another hour.

PETER. It's broken.

KRISTIN. So in the meantime let's just try and be positive, shall we?

PETER. We'll try.

KRISTIN. And I'm sure you didn't tell me Trudi was a vegetarian.

PETER. My version of events against yours.

A slightly awkward pause.

KRISTIN. I was just about to have some tea.

PETER. Okay.

KRISTIN. But I think, under the circumstances, a glass of wine
would be more appropriate.

TRUDI. That would be lovely.

KRISTIN. Good.

PETER. I'll do it.

PETER *gets three glasses out of a cupboard and a bottle of wine
out of the fridge. It is already uncorked – maybe* KRISTIN *has
had a glass before they arrived.*

TRUDI *(remembering)*. Oh, happy birthday.

PETER. Of course.

KRISTIN. Thank you.

TRUDI. Shall we…?

PETER. What?

TRUDI. You know…

PETER. Oh.

TRUDI. Should we…?

PETER. Oh, that.

TRUDI. We've brought you something.

PETER. Maybe we should wait.

TRUDI. Or you could open it now.

She opens the plastic bag she's brought with her and takes out quite a large, strangely shaped object which is wrapped in paper.

KRISTIN. My goodness.

TRUDI. Happy birthday.

KRISTIN. Well, it isn't a book.

TRUDI. It's from somewhere far away.

KRISTIN. How exciting.

TRUDI. I hope you like it.

KRISTIN. Shall I open it now?

PETER. Go on then.

KRISTIN. All right.

She starts to unwrap it. PETER *has poured the three glasses of wine.*

TRUDI. We kind of chose it together.

PETER. Trudi chose it.

TRUDI. I thought it was very, very beautiful.

PETER. She sort of fell in love with it.

TRUDI. And I said to Peter, 'Maybe your mother will love it too.' I knew it was kind of risky but –

PETER. But we took the chance.

TRUDI. And we really hope you like it.

KRISTIN has taken the paper off and the object is revealed – an African tribal mask. It is beautiful and disturbing the way these masks can often be – it has an exaggerated long face and a very broad forehead. PETER has handed TRUDI her glass of wine but holds onto KRISTIN's because she is holding the mask.

KRISTIN. A mask.

TRUDI. Yes.

KRISTIN. An African mask.

PETER. It's from Liberia.

TRUDI. When Peter was there and I went with him. He was working all day and I was stuck in the hotel watching CNN.

KRISTIN. A tribal mask.

TRUDI. I was kind of nervous of going out on my own.

KRISTIN. It's quite something.

TRUDI. We were in Monrovia.

PETER. The capital.

TRUDI. But there's only so much news you can watch. So Peter was out all day with the people from the bank, meeting with all these guys from the Government. And I got bored. So I ventured out.

PETER. Not on your own.

TRUDI. With this guy from my hotel who was like my bodyguard or something. Peter arranged it. It was crazy.

KRISTIN. A bodyguard?

TRUDI. And we just walked around this marketplace and then this woman suddenly came up to me. She was very, very beautiful and quite young but when she opened her mouth I noticed she had no teeth. I mean, not a single tooth. It was kind of freaky. Anyway, she grabbed me by the arm and asked me to stay there and she ran into her house and then came out with this mask and said that she would sell it to me. And I kind of fell in love with it.

PETER. And the next day she took me over and showed it to me and persuaded me to buy it.

TRUDI. For you. Because I knew you liked beautiful objects of art. And of course, it's the real thing, what I mean is, it's not like the ones they sell at the airport. It's the real thing.

Pause as KRISTIN *takes in the mask.*

I really hope you like it.

KRISTIN *continues to examine it.*

KRISTIN. It's a tribal mask.

TRUDI. Yes.

KRISTIN. It's definitely impressive.

TRUDI. Oh, I'm so glad you like it.

KRISTIN. But what's its significance?

TRUDI. Its…?

KRISTIN. Its significance, history, function, its life.

TRUDI. How do you mean?

KRISTIN. Which tribe does it belong to? Was it made to conjure rain out of the sky or to bring punishment to those who had transgressed?

TRUDI. I don't –

KRISTIN. Did the person who wore it dance a dance of delirium so as to be taken over by the spirit of an ancestor or to pray for the crops?

TRUDI. I don't know –

KRISTIN. Or perhaps to bring famine and death to his enemies?

TRUDI. I really don't know. She didn't say.

KRISTIN. I suppose what I'm saying is that these objects – these strange, mysterious objects – are steeped in their own histories and we know very little of them, so to expatriate them in exchange for a few hundred dollars seems a little –

PETER. Mother.

KRISTIN. It's not that I'm superstitious because I'm not. I just suppose I wish I knew something of the context in which it was created. Because its main purpose was definitely not decorative. So for it to be here, in this house, as a decorative object seems to be… how can I put this… disrespectful, I suppose. Both of it and of the artist who created it.

PETER *gives her a look.*

But thank you. It's very kind.

TRUDI. I just thought it was beautiful.

KRISTIN. It is. It is. It is.

TRUDI. And I thought that –

KRISTIN. Somewhere in my study I have a book on African tribal art. We'll have a look later. See if there's any point of reference. Not my area of expertise, I'm afraid. So we'll have a look at the book.

TRUDI. That would be good.

KRISTIN. But thank you.

TRUDI. Happy birthday.

Pause. KRISTIN *places the mask down on one of the kitchen counters somewhat awkwardly as if she is uncomfortable with it. It stares out at them for the rest of the evening.* PETER *hands her the glass of wine.*

I was wondering...

KRISTIN. Yes?

TRUDI. I need to powder my nose.

KRISTIN. How sweet. Through the door on your right.

TRUDI. Thank you.

TRUDI *leaves the room. A short pause.* KRISTIN *takes some napkins out of a drawer and starts to fold them.*

KRISTIN. She's pretty. In a North American kind of way. Wholesome.

PETER. Be nice to her.

KRISTIN. I'm not an ogress, my darling. I won't have her on toast.

PETER. I think this is it.

KRISTIN. She's definitely the right age.

PETER. What do you mean?

KRISTIN. You know. Children.

PETER. For fuck's sake.

KRISTIN. Well, you have to think about these things. If you want a family.

PETER. We're in love.

KRISTIN. She looks fertile.

PETER. I want you to be nice to her.

KRISTIN. Like a peach tree.

PETER. A peach tree?

KRISTIN. And she's got that look.

PETER. What look?

KRISTIN. Like she's going to be a good mother.

PETER. How d'you mean?

KRISTIN. Some women just have it. It's in the eyes.

PETER. The eyes?

KRISTIN. The eyes that say, 'I'm going to be a good mother.'

Pause.

I've missed you.

PETER. Yes.

KRISTIN. It's been –

PETER. I've been busy.

KRISTIN. How's that awful bank you work for?

PETER. The bank is fine.

KRISTIN. Still raping the Third World?

PETER. Brutally.

KRISTIN. I was thinking that in the present climate your job would have lost some of its allure. I keep hoping you're going to pack it all in and grow your own vegetables. Teach yoga. Anything. You've always looked awkward in a suit. Then I can be proud to call you my son again.

PETER. Please don't moralise. You know nothing about what I do.

KRISTIN. I know you're with the takers and not the givers.

PETER. Enough.

Pause.

And Simon?

KRISTIN. What about him?

PETER. Is he coming?

KRISTIN. Claire said she'd pick him up after filming. But you don't really know these days, do you?

PETER. Know what?

KRISTIN. She said he disappeared for three days last week. She called the police.

PETER. Fuck.

KRISTIN. I think she was implying he'd been living rough.

PETER. Living rough?

KRISTIN. On the streets, under the bridges, God knows.

PETER. Jesus.

KRISTIN. The point is, Peter, your brother is having a complete mental breakdown and the sooner we start recognising it for what it is, the better it is for all of us.

PETER. I suppose.

KRISTIN. He's left his job.

PETER. When did that happen?

KRISTIN. On Thursday.

PETER. The café?

KRISTIN. Three jobs in as many months.

PETER. Shit.

KRISTIN. He said he needs the time to work on his novel.

PETER. Okay.

KRISTIN. He's been working on it for seven years.

Pause.

PETER. And Claire?

KRISTIN. What about her?

PETER. What's she doing about it?

KRISTIN. Nothing.

PETER. Nothing?

KRISTIN. She's a soap actress, Peter.

PETER. What's that got to do with it?

KRISTIN. I'm convinced she's driven him to it in the first place. There's something *missing* in her.

PETER. Missing?

KRISTIN. You try living with a big gaping hole in close proximity. Must be unnerving, I would imagine.

PETER. Claire's not the problem.

KRISTIN. Isn't she?

PETER. No.

KRISTIN. I just want him to be happy.

Pause.

PETER. I read your book.

KRISTIN. Oh?

PETER. It made me…

KRISTIN. What? It made you what?

TRUDI *comes back.*

PETER. Hey.

TRUDI. I love your bathroom. All those books. And that beautiful picture of the old man over the toilet.

KRISTIN. That's Karl Marx.

TRUDI *picks up her glass of wine.*

TRUDI. You have such a wonderful house, Kristin. It's so artistic.

KRISTIN. Thank you.

TRUDI. Peter had said you had great taste.

KRISTIN. Is that what he said?

TRUDI. And of course I knew you were a famous art historian.

KRISTIN. I wouldn't go that far.

TRUDI. Well, your books are on sale in all the major US bookstores.

KRISTIN. Oh well, in that case.

TRUDI. When Peter and I were in New York there was like one of those island things in Barnes and Noble on Lexington Avenue dedicated to the memoir. And they had like a big picture of you mounted on cardboard.

KRISTIN. How impressive.

TRUDI. I have been quite nervous about meeting you. But you're a lot nicer in real life. Nicer than your cardboard version.

KRISTIN. A little more animated, I should hope in any case.

TRUDI. Definitely.

Pause.

KRISTIN. I need to turn the hot water on. I wasn't expecting you till at least seven.

PETER. You said.

KRISTIN. And I want you to change that bulb for me. The one I mentioned on the phone.

PETER. I'll do it now.

KRISTIN. I don't like standing on that stool. My balance –

PETER. I'll do it.

KRISTIN. Back in a second.

KRISTIN *leaves the room.* PETER *walks over to* TRUDI *and puts his arms around her.*

PETER. What do you think?

TRUDI. She's amazing.

PETER. And?

TRUDI. She hates the mask.

PETER. No.

TRUDI. I thought she'd like it.

PETER. I don't think she hates it.

TRUDI. I really thought she'd like it.

PETER. Maybe she just needs time.

TRUDI. Time?

PETER. You know, to get used to it. It's that kind of thing, isn't it?

TRUDI. What kind of thing?

PETER. Kind of thing you need time for it to grow on you. She'll end up loving it. You'll see.

Pause.

TRUDI. Why does she have a picture of Marx in the bathroom?

PETER. She's an old commie. Having said that, poor old Karl used to hang over the stairs but was recently demoted to the downstairs loo.

TRUDI. She's very glamorous. Bohemian.

PETER. She's a bloody nightmare.

TRUDI. Don't say that.

PETER. Opinionated, didactic, dictatorial.

TRUDI. I don't see that.

PETER. Okay.

He kisses her.

My brother's coming, hopefully.

TRUDI. I can't wait to meet him.

PETER. He's been having a rough time.

TRUDI. You said.

PETER. As usual.

TRUDI. How do you mean?

PETER. Things just never seem to stick.

TRUDI. Stick?

PETER. They never have.

TRUDI. Poor Simon.

PETER. He's been trying to write.

TRUDI. It must be difficult.

PETER. It is.

TRUDI. He sounds fragile.

PETER. And now…

TRUDI. What?

PETER. He feels broken, I suppose.

Pause.

I love you.

TRUDI. I love you too, Petey poo.

Pause.

Will we tell them before or after the meal?

PETER. Let's see.

TRUDI. See what?

PETER. See how it all goes.

TRUDI. I thought after would be nice. Maybe dessert. And then we'll have champagne. Her second birthday present.

PETER. Maybe.

TRUDI. Please, Petey.

PETER. Okay. We'll see.

KRISTIN *comes back, light bulb in hand.*

KRISTIN. Here it is.

PETER. I'll do it now.

KRISTIN. Thank you, darling.

PETER. And I'll put our bag in the room.

KRISTIN. You're in the yellow one. I've left towels on the bed.

PETER *takes the bulb from her, leaves the room and takes their overnight bag with him.* KRISTIN *goes to the oven, opens it.*

Do you know, it feels like it's getting ever so slightly warmer.

TRUDI. That's hopeful.

KRISTIN *goes and opens a cupboard and takes out some plates.*

Can I help you with anything, Kristin?

KRISTIN. I suppose you could help me set the table. We'll need to eat something, whatever the outcome. The cutlery is in the second drawer from the right.

TRUDI. Sure.

During the next few moments the two women set the table together – mats and plates with cutlery and then the glasses.

KRISTIN. How did you meet my son, Trudi?

TRUDI. Oh, I thought he told you.

KRISTIN. Not a word.

TRUDI. We met at a prayer meeting.

KRISTIN. A what?

TRUDI. A prayer meeting. It was Peter's first. A mutual friend of ours brought him along. A girl called Sarah who works at the bank with him.

KRISTIN. A prayer meeting?

TRUDI. Well, that's what they call it, but actually it's more of a get-together. It's really quite social. I mean, there is a little prayer but mostly people talk about their lives. And have coffee and biscuits.

KRISTIN. How do you mean, a prayer meeting?

TRUDI. A Christian prayer meeting.

KRISTIN. A Christian prayer meeting?

TRUDI. Yes.

KRISTIN. So you're a Christian?

TRUDI. Most of the people who go to the Christian prayer meetings usually are.

KRISTIN. And Peter?

TRUDI. I'm sorry, I'm being facetious. But yes, Kristin, Jesus is an important part of my life.

KRISTIN. I'm happy for you. But what was my son doing there?

TRUDI. I just think he came to see what it was like.

KRISTIN. Good God.

TRUDI. Does that surprise you?

KRISTIN. He's just never really been into all that.

TRUDI. Into?

KRISTIN. Please tell me he hasn't been talking in tongues.

TRUDI. He hasn't been talking in tongues.

KRISTIN. Into religion. That's one thing I thought I got right.

TRUDI. Have you never had faith, Kristin?

KRISTIN. By the bucket loads. And I believe in mystery and imagination. But not obsolete patriarchal propaganda.

TRUDI. That's interesting. Where are the glasses?

KRISTIN. That cupboard there. Just put some of the plain ones out, for water. Oh, and some flutes for the champagne. You can leave those on the counter.

TRUDI opens the cupboard and starts bringing the glasses to the table.

I'm slightly shocked. Money's been more Peter's thing.

TRUDI. Well, maybe this is a reaction against that.

KRISTIN. I don't know which is the worst of the two.

TRUDI. That makes me sad.

KRISTIN. All of a sudden the idea of him keeping the whole of sub-Saharan Africa in crippling debt doesn't seem quite as bad a proposition.

TRUDI. I don't think you mean that.

KRISTIN. Please don't tell me what I mean.

A slightly awkward pause. They continue laying the table.

TRUDI. He's really been looking forward to coming. To see you, I mean.

KRISTIN. Oh?

TRUDI. He talks about you a lot.

KRISTIN. I'm surprised.

TRUDI. You've obviously played a very big part in his life.

KRISTIN. I am his mother.

TRUDI. Of course.

KRISTIN. Parents, you'll find, generally have a way of doing that. Playing a big part in your life.

TRUDI. It's true.

KRISTIN. It's less of a talent and more of a God-given right. So please forgive me if I'm not overtly enthusiastic in responding to what I assume was intended to be a compliment.

TRUDI. I didn't mean...

KRISTIN. But I'm glad to hear he talks of me. Fondly or with hatred?

TRUDI. Something's happening to Peter.

KRISTIN. Happening?

TRUDI. I have to tell you, Kristin, that ever since I've known him I feel that Peter is a man on the brink of a quite important change in his life.

KRISTIN. I'm almost certain you're implying that has something to do with the grace of our Lord Jesus Christ.

TRUDI. Like he's asking all these questions he's never asked himself before. And maybe this new curiosity is just one symptom of that journey.

KRISTIN. That's such an American word. 'Journey.'

TRUDI. Is it?

KRISTIN. It really is time you allowed the immigrant experiences of your ancestors to stop shading your entire take on life.

TRUDI. Why should we? An immigrant's life is full of hope and optimism. They are good qualities to hold onto, I think.

KRISTIN. I couldn't agree more. But it all becomes a bit distasteful when the immigrant is raping and pillaging half the world.

TRUDI. He did warn me about your hatred of Americans.

KRISTIN. Oh, I like Americans. It's what you've been up to lately that I don't like. I'm sure you can relate. It's very much along the lines of hate the sin, love the sinner.

TRUDI. Times are changing, Kristin. We've just elected our first African-American president.

KRISTIN. Let's wait and see.

TRUDI. He told me you were a passionate woman.

KRISTIN. Did he?

TRUDI. But I like you. I like you a lot.

KRISTIN. Lucky for you. Otherwise this evening would be most unpleasant.

TRUDI. He did warn me.

KRISTIN. Good.

Pause. They have finished laying the table. They sip their wine.

TRUDI. It's such a shame his father died.

KRISTIN. Is it?

TRUDI. It would have been nice to have met him, is what I mean.

KRISTIN. If you say so.

TRUDI. What was he like?

KRISTIN. The boys' father?

TRUDI. Yes.

KRISTIN. Irascible, moody, manipulative.

TRUDI. Okay.

KRISTIN. And I'm trying to be objective.

TRUDI. That's funny.

KRISTIN. Emotionally stunted, mentally cruel, chauvinistic and very, very lucky.

TRUDI. Lucky?

KRISTIN. Even in death he was lucky. He had a massive stroke. It took him thirty-six seconds to die. The bastard.

TRUDI. That's quick.

KRISTIN. Much to my disappointment he escaped the joys of self-reflection on a deathbed.

TRUDI. You must be very angry with him.

KRISTIN. Oh no, I've let it go. I used to be but it was killing me.

TRUDI. Kristin, forgiveness is such a liberating emotion.

KRISTIN. I'll bear that in mind.

Pause. TRUDI *is trying to tread carefully.*

TRUDI. Peter told me about the divorce.

KRISTIN. Did he?

TRUDI. He said there was a lot of blood on the floor. I'm convinced he was speaking metaphorically.

KRISTIN. I can't remember.

TRUDI. It must have been difficult for you.

KRISTIN. What was?

TRUDI. I mean… what happened. You know.

KRISTIN. I haven't a clue what you're talking about, my dear.

TRUDI. Peter told me about…

KRISTIN. Yes?

TRUDI. Peter told me about the separation.

KRISTIN. Separation?

TRUDI. It must have been very painful losing your children. Not watching them grow up. How old were they when he took them away from you? Nine and seven?

There is a pause and TRUDI *realises that she has overstepped the mark.*

Things were so different then, weren't they?

Pause. KRISTIN *doesn't respond.* TRUDI *is working hard.*

I think we take things for granted nowadays is what I'm saying. Women, I mean.

KRISTIN. Do you?

PETER *returns.*

PETER. Done.

KRISTIN. Thank you, darling.

PETER. Anything else?

KRISTIN. Not that I can think of.

PETER. Good.

KRISTIN *opens the oven door again.*

KRISTIN. It feels a little warmer.

PETER. Let's see.

He sticks his hand in the oven.

KRISTIN. It definitely feels warmer.

PETER. A little.

KRISTIN. We'll just have to eat a little later than planned, that's all.

PETER. Midnight, you mean.

KRISTIN. But I'm sure it's getting warmer.

A slight pause. PETER *walks over to the fridge and opens it. He pours himself another glass of wine.*

Trudi and I have been talking.

PETER. That's good.

KRISTIN. Trudi was telling me about your prayer meetings.

PETER. Oh, that.

TRUDI. Your mother was a bit surprised that you came along, Peter.

PETER. She would be.

KRISTIN. Just a little surprised.

PETER. Mother calls herself a humanist.

KRISTIN. The word 'prayer' on its own is bad enough. When it's a prefix to the word 'meeting' it's absolutely terrifying.

PETER. You were very much one for meetings in your youth, Mother.

KRISTIN. They were not religious. They were political. We were not worshipping some big illusion in the sky.

PETER. Only yourselves.

KRISTIN. It was more of a case of putting your house in order because you care about it as opposed to putting it in order because that big bad landlord up above is watching your every move.

PETER. Is that what it was?

Pause.

TRUDI. I read your book, Kristin. It's wonderful.

PETER. Sweetie.

KRISTIN. I'm flattered.

TRUDI. I'd never really read your work so when Peter took me to Florence a few weeks ago I thought it was a good opportunity. It was very thrilling for me to be able to read about your life while being surrounded by the places and art that inspired you. Not only in Florence but Assisi too. It was fascinating. And your book was informative and inspiring.

KRISTIN. What a rich array of adjectives.

TRUDI. It must have been amazing spending seven years there. In Florence, I mean.

KRISTIN. It had its moments.

PETER. I told her about your flat overlooking the Arno.

TRUDI. And your passion for Giotto. Of course, all of that is in the book.

KRISTIN. I was working.

PETER. And wearing kaftans.

TRUDI. And I kept asking myself, I mean, when we were there, when I was looking at his work, I kept asking myself what it was about him, I mean, about that particular artist, that grabbed you so. Why him and not the others. I mean, I realise that he was the first one, I realise that he was the father of the Renaissance…

KRISTIN. And mother…

TRUDI. But I kept thinking, why him and not the others? What it was about him in particular that moved you so?

Pause.

KRISTIN. Let's have a top-up. And then I'll have my shower. Trudi? More wine?

TRUDI. Thank you.

KRISTIN. Good.

She walks to the fridge and gets out the bottle of wine and refreshes their glasses.

Did you read the book, Trudi?

TRUDI *throws a quick, confused glance over at* PETER.

PETER. Mother.

KRISTIN. Because surely, if you read it properly, if you applied yourself, the answer to your question would be somewhat obvious.

TRUDI. I didn't mean to…

KRISTIN. Surely, if my book is half as good as you say it is, you wouldn't really need to ask that question because the answer would be self-evident.

TRUDI. Maybe I didn't quite understand all of it.

KRISTIN. Maybe.

KRISTIN *pours wine into* TRUDI's *glass and then into her own.*

TRUDI. It's a whole new territory for me, Kristin. Art history, I mean. I've never really studied it before.

PETER. Trudi's a chiropractor.

KRISTIN. He was a revolutionary. He took religious iconography and completely transformed it.

TRUDI. Okay.

KRISTIN. Let me tell you a story, Trudi, and maybe this will answer your question more effectively than three hundred and seventy-five pages seems to have done.

PETER. Not now.

KRISTIN. Imagine you are living in the early years of the fourteenth century in some small village a few miles outside Padua. You're in your early thirties but you look sixty-five because you work in some field all hours of the day and at night you have to care for a family of nine...

TRUDI. That's a big family.

KRISTIN. Including a husband who regularly and happily beats you. Four of your children have died in childbirth. Your fingers are constantly blistered and you smell of your own sweat. Despite the brutal conditions of your life, however, you happen to be a sensitive and inquisitive soul.

TRUDI. Okay.

KRISTIN. You are constantly reminded by the wonderful Catholic Church that just in case you ever entertained the thought of patting yourself on the back for surviving this horrible adversity, you are in fact a bad, carnal creature, intemperate and steeped in original sin. As a matter of fact, you're also constantly reminded that in all likelihood you will end up in some crowded furnace being prodded by all sorts of objects including pitchforks and dog's genitalia whilst surrounded by flesh-eating goblins and assorted whores and perverts.

TRUDI. How disturbing.

KRISTIN. As a consolation, and some sort of carrot, you are also offered an alternative but this alternative is strange and foreign to you. These two-dimensional, alien faces stare down at you with absurd expressions, set against a gold backdrop. They don't look remotely human. They are supposed to promise some sort of an after-life but it all stretches your credulity because they reflect nothing familiar and gold is a colour reserved for the rich, those who have paid for a place in this hallowed heaven through patronage. That much you've sussed out. Brown is more your colour, the colour of the clumps of earth you dig out with your hands every day and the colour of your shit. Then suddenly one day this funny thing happens.

TRUDI. A funny thing?

KRISTIN. You are in a chapel and you kneel down to pray. This is an acquired habit, something you were taught to do from infancy and even though you do it with some feeling there is a question that accompanies that feeling and the question, which fills you with shame and fear, is whether the receptor of your prayer, in His might and power will be able, in all truth, to understand and commiserate with your petty needs, your small and humble pains. This thought brings you out of your meditation and your eyes drift upwards to just one part of a giant fresco that adorns the vaulted ceilings above you: an image of the Madonna cradling the body of her son in her arms. Your eyes move further up slowly, curiously, taking in the soft skin, the nape of the neck, the gentle contours of the face and then... then you actually stare at the face for the first time and a chill runs up your spine and your whole view of life changes for ever. The Madonna's expression is one of anguish and loss, her mouth tilted slightly upwards as if she is asking the same questions that you are, her left hand touching her son's neck as if trying to stroke him back to life. You realise now that this face is not only recognisable – the face is yours. *Your* weeping eyes, *your* pale cheeks, *your* mouth that slightly curls with doubt. It's a mirror. That's all. But all of a sudden your whole perspective changes and maybe things become a little more bearable. Someone else has connected with you and you discover the meaning of the word *empathy*. With that you begin to realise that you are part of a collective experience. You will perhaps continue to pray but in a completely new way. Your prayers will be directed more to something within yourself, a nascent capability. And the knowledge that you carry that within you gives you a little strength. And a little reassurance.

TRUDI. That's beautiful.

KRISTIN. That's why I love Giotto, Trudi. That's humanism emerging from the religious matrix. Evolving. He was the first who did that. The vision, the power and the responsibility of the artist. The rest is superstition.

Pause.

TRUDI. Thank you for welcoming me to your home. You're an interesting and extraordinary woman.

KRISTIN. This hyperbole has to stop.

Pause.

TRUDI. And the book's title.

KRISTIN. The title?

TRUDI. *Apologia.*

KRISTIN. What about it?

TRUDI. It's one of those words. Like you think you know what it means but then maybe you don't. Or at least what you think it means is not exact. Not precise. *Apologia.*

KRISTIN. It means a formal, written defence of one's opinions or conduct.

TRUDI. Okay.

KRISTIN. Not to be confused with an apology.

Pause.

I'm off to have my shower.

PETER. Okay.

KRISTIN. Why don't you take Trudi to the bottom of the garden. Show her the magnolia tree and the view over the hills. It's the right hour of the day for it.

TRUDI. That sounds wonderful.

KRISTIN. And then I suppose we'll have to solve the problem of what exactly it is we're going to eat tonight in the unfortunate event of that fucking oven not getting its act together.

She puts her wine glass down on one of the counters and makes a move towards the door. But just as she gets to it she turns around. She looks at PETER.

Your face has changed.

PETER. My face?

KRISTIN. I was looking at you just now when the sun caught it.

PETER. How has my face changed?

KRISTIN. And I thought, 'He's not a boy any more.'

PETER. Congratulations for noticing.

KRISTIN. He's not a boy.

Pause and for a minute she's lost in thought. And then she brings herself back.

Welcome.

She leaves the room.

Blackout.

Scene Two

An hour later. PETER *and* TRUDI *are standing in the kitchen with glasses of wine in hand. They have been joined by* CLAIRE *and* HUGH *who are also drinking.* CLAIRE *is wearing an expensive-looking, light-coloured dress.*

TRUDI. It really is so wonderful to meet you, Claire. I've heard so many things about you.

CLAIRE. You have?

HUGH. Your reputation precedes you, my dear.

TRUDI. About your career, I mean. Your acting.

CLAIRE. Oh, that.

TRUDI. It sounds so exciting.

CLAIRE. It has its moments.

TRUDI. Peter was saying you're quite famous.

CLAIRE. Comes with the territory, I'm afraid.

TRUDI. That's fun.

CLAIRE. I'm a very private person so it's kind of weird. I miss my anonymity.

HUGH. You do?

CLAIRE. Of course I enjoy being appreciated for my work.

TRUDI. Everybody does.

CLAIRE. But fame was never my objective.

HUGH. Of course not.

A slight pause.

TRUDI. So what's the soap opera about? Where's it set?

CLAIRE. Sorry?

TRUDI. Peter mentioned in the car that you were in a soap opera and I'm just wondering what it's about.

CLAIRE. Oh.

TRUDI. I mean, the kind of world it takes place in.

CLAIRE. Well, it's not really a soap opera.

HUGH. Isn't it?

CLAIRE. Not really. Not technically.

PETER. Oh, I'm sorry.

CLAIRE. It's more of a serialised drama that happens to follow the trajectories of various people's lives.

HUGH. A *what?*

CLAIRE. It's just a different genre is what I'm saying.

HUGH. A different genre?

CLAIRE. But it's about the lives of these people who work in an advertising agency.

HUGH. How thrilling.

CLAIRE. Their relationships, their works, their dilemmas. They're seriously good scripts.

TRUDI. I'm sure.

CLAIRE. Subtle and ambitious.

TRUDI. What a great job.

CLAIRE. They have depth.

Pause.

As a matter of fact, I had some good news yesterday.

TRUDI. You did?

CLAIRE. They've just renewed my contract for another year.

TRUDI. That's great.

PETER. Well done.

CLAIRE. Thanks, Peter.

HUGH. Who's a clever girl?

CLAIRE. I did have a moment. 'Do I really want to do this for the rest of my life?' I asked myself.

HUGH. And then you thought, 'Why ever not?'

CLAIRE. I've had to turn down quite a bit of theatre work.

HUGH. Have you?

CLAIRE. But I weighed everything up and decided that it's the right thing to do.

TRUDI. Congratulations.

CLAIRE. Because it really is quite classy.

Pause. Suddenly HUGH *spots the African mask.*

HUGH. Oh my God, what is that thing?

PETER. It's a mask –

TRUDI. That Peter and I bought Kristin –

HUGH. It's hideous.

TRUDI. As a gift.

HUGH. And beautiful at the same time. You know how some things have that ability to be hideous and beautiful at the same time? It's fascinating.

CLAIRE. Did you get it at that shop behind the British Museum?

TRUDI. No, it's the real thing.

CLAIRE. *Taboo* or something. Just off Russell Square.

PETER. It's from Africa.

TRUDI. Liberia. We bought it in Liberia.

CLAIRE. Coz it looks very much like the ones that they sell at that shop.

TRUDI. It's the real thing.

HUGH. Extraordinary.

Pause.

So how's our boy?

CLAIRE. Not good.

PETER. I heard.

TRUDI. Poor Simon.

CLAIRE *(slightly monitoring the volume of her voice)*. Your mother's book.

PETER. What about it?

HUGH. The memoir?

CLAIRE. I think that's what she calls it.

TRUDI. She writes so beautifully.

CLAIRE. He finished it this morning.

PETER. Oh?

CLAIRE. He said the strangest thing after he'd read it.

PETER. He did?

CLAIRE. 'Why did she have children?' That's all he said.

HUGH. That is strange.

CLAIRE. He just threw it across the room and said, 'Why the fuck did she have children?'

KRISTIN *enters the room. She is showered and dressed.*

KRISTIN. Why did who have children?

HUGH *(thinking on his feet)*. Anna Karenina.

KRISTIN. Anna Karenina?

CLAIRE. We were talking about books.

HUGH. Nineteenth-century Russian literature.

KRISTIN. I see.

CLAIRE. And I was just asking why Anna Karenina had bothered having children –

HUGH. If all she wanted was to shag Vronsky.

CLAIRE. That's all.

KRISTIN. That's an interesting take on it.

She kisses HUGH *on the cheek.*

I've made a bed for you. In case you want to have a few and stay the night. You and Simon are in the green room, Claire.

HUGH. Thank you, darling. And by the way, we've ordered the Chinese.

KRISTIN. I'm embarrassed.

HUGH. Don't be. We're all rather relieved at having avoided death by poultry.

KRISTIN. It's not my fault the bloody thing conked out on me.

Pause as she realises SIMON *isn't there.*

Where's Simon?

CLAIRE. He might be joining us later.

KRISTIN. How do you mean, he might be joining us later?

CLAIRE. I came straight from the studio –

KRISTIN. I thought the whole point was that you were going to pick him up.

CLAIRE. I was. But then we spoke on the phone and –

KRISTIN. And what did he say?

CLAIRE. He said he couldn't make his mind up.

KRISTIN. Couldn't make his mind up?

CLAIRE. He was being monosyllabic.

KRISTIN. He's depressed.

CLAIRE. I know. I live with him, Kristin.

KRISTIN. So he's not coming?

CLAIRE. He said he might drive over later.

KRISTIN. Maybe we should try calling him.

CLAIRE. I just did. He didn't answer.

KRISTIN. As long as he's not drinking.

CLAIRE. I'm his girlfriend, Kristin.

KRISTIN. I was just under the impression that you were going to bring him here safely.

CLAIRE. Not his baby-sitter.

CLAIRE *takes a gift-wrapped box out of her bag and hands it to* KRISTIN.

But happy birthday anyway.

KRISTIN. You shouldn't have.

CLAIRE. Don't be ridiculous, it's your birthday.

KRISTIN. You really shouldn't have.

CLAIRE. It's just a little something. Oh, and I've brought a cake. Mango meringue. It's in the fridge.

HUGH. Mango meringue?

KRISTIN. I wasn't expecting anything.

HUGH. How delicious.

CLAIRE. Open it.

KRISTIN *starts to unwrap the present.*

TRUDI. I love watching people opening presents.

HUGH. I know what you mean. Especially that priceless moment when they have to conceal their disappointment behind an inane grin.

KRISTIN *has unwrapped the gift and an expression very similar to the one just described by* HUGH *is etched on her face as she reads the writing on the box.*

KRISTIN. 'TRANSFORMATIVE REJUVENATION.'

HUGH. Just in the nick of time.

CLAIRE. It really is a miracle worker. They only sell it at Selfridges. There's a waiting list. Works on the toughest skin. My mother swears by it.

KRISTIN. How kind.

CLAIRE. I was torn between that and the new Virginia Woolf biography. But I read a stinking review in the *Observer* so I got you the face cream instead.

KRISTIN. How thoughtful.

CLAIRE. Enjoy. And keep it in the fridge.

KRISTIN. You really shouldn't have.

> HUGH *has gone to the fridge and he pops open a bottle of champagne.*

TRUDI. That's my favourite sound in the world.

HUGH. Good girl.

TRUDI. I always associate it with celebration. And I love celebrations.

> *She goes over to where* HUGH *is standing and helps him with the champagne – holding up the glasses one by one for him to pour it into and then handing them out to everyone. As she does this,* HUGH *is holding up his glass in a toast. He camps it up.*

HUGH. And this evening we are celebrating the birthday of the legend that is Kristin Miller. Pioneer of Arts and Letters, Champion of the Voiceless and Redemptive Saviour of the Western World.

TRUDI. That's funny.

HUGH. We have lovingly watched you evolve over the years through your many varied personas and graduate to a place of peace and self-knowledge.

PETER. Have we?

HUGH. We have observed you whisk your way gracefully through your many incarnations – from placard-carrying waif to hammer-and-sickle-wielding Communist, from alarmingly coiffed Courtauld graduate to even more alarmingly coiffed hippy bride. In your pursuit of the common good you have offered yourself to as many causes as I've had social diseases. From the backstreets of Palestine to the NUM frontlines, and from the Parisian barricades to the tents of Greenham Common –

CLAIRE. Without a moisturiser in sight.

HUGH. You have made your presence felt most emphatically –

PETER. In some quarters.

HUGH. And most importantly, with your passionate, often lambasted contribution to the traditionally male-dominated bastion of art history you have always done things – and this is where I get serious and maybe even a little teary-eyed – with a whole load of *heart*. Tonight, Kristin Miller, we salute you.

CLAIRE. We salute you.

They all raise their glasses, though PETER *is a little unenthusiastic.*

TRUDI. Happy birthday.

KRISTIN. Thank you, thank you, thank you. Very heartfelt if a little over-the-top.

HUGH *is suddenly holding a small wrapped gift which he presents to her.*

HUGH. And here is a little something to go with my well-rehearsed eulogy. Not quite as essential as Transformational Regeneration –

CLAIRE. Transformative Rejuvenation.

HUGH. But a gift nonetheless of rare and priceless significance. At least to me.

He hands over the gift and she begins to unwrap it.

I was clearing out some old shoeboxes in my study the other day. Found it in there in amongst a heap of WRP pamphlets and a whole lot of yellowed news clippings. It made me laugh.

She has unwrapped it and the object has revealed itself. It is a beautifully framed photograph.

KRISTIN. Good God.

HUGH. Isn't it extremely fabulous?

TRUDI. What is it?

KRISTIN. We look so young.

HUGH. We *were* young. And fucking gorgeous.

CLAIRE. Can I see?

They all start to crowd around KRISTIN *to look over her shoulder at the photograph.*

HUGH. With our lives stretched in front of us like scrolls waiting to be written upon in indelible ink.

TRUDI. That's so poetic.

CLAIRE. Is that a poncho you're wearing?

HUGH. And our eyes glittering with the possibilities of all our tomorrows.

PETER. Jesus.

CLAIRE (*looking at the photograph*). That is hilarious.

HUGH. And our hearts thumping in anticipation of forthcoming sexual encounters.

TRUDI. You look so beautiful.

HUGH. Thank you, darling. She's not bad either, is she?

KRISTIN. A lifetime ago.

Pause.

TRUDI. Where was it taken?

HUGH. Appropriately enough, at a demonstration.

KRISTIN. *The* demonstration.

HUGH. In Grosvenor Square. We threw some eggs at your embassy, Trudi, and then ate the rest back at mine with an awful bottle of plonk.

PETER. What fun.

HUGH. It was the two of us and a mutual friend.

KRISTIN. Melissa Jones.

HUGH. A feminist poet with a gift for subtlety. Her first anthology, I believe, was entitled *Devil Penis*.

KRISTIN. I remember that floral shirt. People whistled at you in the street.

HUGH. I was provocative in my youth. Madam was down from
Cambridge. A wee thing with a shockingly disproportionate
amount of self-confidence.

PETER. Of course.

HUGH. I suppose we just wanted to change the world. At least your
mother did. I was just looking for diversion or someone's cock to
suck.

TRUDI. Okay.

HUGH. But your mother really was serious about the whole thing.
She stood somewhere between reactive anger and the new
hedonism like a beacon.

KRISTIN. A beacon?

HUGH. Because all those men really ever wanted was to be top-dog.
It's biological, for God's sake, cloaked in the guise of political
causes. It's the reason the Communist experiment died such a
slow and ignominious death. Not evolved enough.

KRISTIN. Not quite ready.

HUGH. But your mother really did want to transform the world in a
more permanent way. And I kind of tagged along for the ride. I
was a follower, like a fucking disciple. The woman was
persuasive.

PETER. I'm sure.

CLAIRE. That's hilarious.

*KRISTIN puts the framed photograph down somewhere in the
room and it joins the tribal mask in staring out at them for the rest
of the evening.*

TRUDI. Photographs are such beautiful things. I mean, I know that
sounds obvious but all I mean is, maybe it's one of the many
things we take for granted. To hold the past in your hand like that,
just like you were, Kristin, to hold the past in your hand and look
at it and remember what it was like to be young – the clothes, the
friends, the many dreams you had. To hold the past in your hand
as if it were a ball or a little mirror or something, to hold it as if...

*She suddenly realises she's getting a little carried away and loses
her confidence.*

To hold the past in your hand.

HUGH. I really rather like you, you know.

TRUDI. Thank you.

Pause.

KRISTIN. So what was it exactly that you found hilarious, Claire?

CLAIRE. Sorry?

KRISTIN. Twice you used the word 'hilarious'. Once when you saw the photograph and then a second time a minute ago when Hugh said something kind about what drove me. And I'm just wondering what exactly it was that you thought was hilarious. Why the use of that specific word.

CLAIRE. Oh, you know, the sixties, the early seventies. Everything about it. The clothes, the hair, the raging idealism. It's sweet.

KRISTIN. Sweet?

CLAIRE. The thought of you all marching in your sandals. The bandannas, the CND logos, make love not war, the braided flowers, the whole damn thing. '*The answer, my friends, is blowing in the wind.*' I love it.

HUGH. It was rather glorious.

CLAIRE. I just have this image of you all sprawled out in Hyde Park with daisies in your hair, planning ways to overthrow the Government.

PETER. Or smoking Gauloises on the Left Bank as you dipped your toes in the ocean of student revolt.

KRISTIN. Is that what we were doing?

CLAIRE. Until you could afford a Bang and Olufsen stereo system and a house in Islington.

Pause.

That was a joke.

PETER. I know what you mean, though.

CLAIRE. But at least you're the real thing, Kristin. I mean, you've given *everything* you have and don't think we haven't noticed.

PETER. Everything.

CLAIRE. Because you have all these other people, these sixty-eighters or whatever you want to call them, who go around as if they'd personally fought on the side of the Vietcong or single-handedly brought civil rights to America and then you find out that what they really mean is that they used to shop at Biba.

Pause. HUGH *grabs the bottle of champagne and starts to top up the glasses.*

HUGH. Who's for more bubbly?

CLAIRE. Thanks, Hugh.

TRUDI. Lovely, thank you.

PETER. Thanks.

He empties the bottle and rests it on the counter.

KRISTIN. I really am worried about Simon, you know.

CLAIRE. We all are, Kristin.

KRISTIN. No, but I mean, tonight. I'm especially worried about him tonight. Knowing that he's quite happy to have a few drinks and jump behind the wheel of his car –

CLAIRE. He'll be fine.

KRISTIN. Knowing that, I'm really quite surprised that you didn't make sure he got here safely –

CLAIRE. I keep thinking he's like one of those buildings.

KRISTIN. Buildings?

CLAIRE. In Iran. God knows. Turkey.

KRISTIN. How is he like a building in Turkey?

CLAIRE. When there's an earthquake. And of course it's the earthquake that does it – I mean, that's what does the damage, that's the thing that brings the building down, that kills the people inside.

HUGH. What *are* you talking about?

CLAIRE. But then they find out corners were cut. In the construction of it. Shoddy work, that kind of thing. The edifice was weak.

PETER. The foundations.

KRISTIN. I'm not quite following this analogy.

CLAIRE. I think all I'm saying is that I'm worried too, Kristin.

PETER. Of course you are.

CLAIRE. But enough said.

The doorbell rings.

TRUDI. Maybe that's him.

HUGH. That'll be the chop suey.

PETER. That's quick.

KRISTIN *takes her purse out of her bag and starts to make her way out of the room.*

HUGH. Don't even think of paying, it's on me.

KRISTIN. Don't be ridiculous, you can't afford it.

HUGH. For fuck's sake, woman, it's your birthday.

KRISTIN. You're very, very poor.

HUGH. I've asked you not to bring that up in public.

KRISTIN. Anyway, you're a guest.

HUGH. I'll bloody fight you for it.

He follows her out of the room.

TRUDI. They're very lovely.

PETER. That's one way of putting it.

CLAIRE. Such a double act.

PETER. Symbiotic.

CLAIRE. Laurel and Hardy.

Pause. They know KRISTIN *and* HUGH *are in the next room so the next few lines are spoken quietly.*

It's weird timing, I'll give her that.

PETER. Timing?

CLAIRE. The book, I mean.

PETER. Oh.

CLAIRE. I just hope it's not the straw that breaks the camel's back.

PETER. I'm livid.

CLAIRE. I mean, it says it on the back, doesn't it? It actually says something like 'The Life and Times of'.

PETER. That's what it says.

CLAIRE. So to call it that and then not even mention you. To not even mention that she ever had children.

PETER. It's weird.

CLAIRE. As if you didn't exist. It's a little spooky.

PETER. Stalinist more like.

CLAIRE. I couldn't quite get my head round it. I mean, what was she thinking?

PETER. Fuck knows.

CLAIRE. I mean, it's hurtful.

TRUDI. Maybe she was –

CLAIRE. It's just a very strange choice. And I can understand you both feeling very...

PETER. What?

CLAIRE. Wounded, I suppose. Betrayed.

PETER. I need to talk to her.

TRUDI. But not tonight, please, Petey.

Pause.

I'm sure there's an explanation. I'm sure she didn't mean to upset you. Sometimes people behave in the strangest ways and there's usually a reason.

PETER. Maybe.

KRISTIN *and* HUGH *return with a bag of Chinese food.*

HUGH. The witch wrestled me to the ground.

KRISTIN. You didn't give me a choice.

HUGH. With her nasty protruding claws.

TRUDI. That smells delicious.

KRISTIN. We should just shove it in the oven and wait till Simon gets here.

PETER. The oven's kaput, remember?

KRISTIN. I don't want us to start without him.

PETER. Which is why we're not eating your chicken in the first place.

HUGH. Thank heaven for small mercies.

PETER. And if we wait the food will just get cold.

KRISTIN. I just think we should wait.

PETER. And we don't want to eat cold Chinese.

HUGH. We don't.

PETER. So we don't really have a choice.

CLAIRE. I'll just make sure we put some food aside for him, Kristin.

PETER. I think we should eat.

HUGH. I'm famished.

TRUDI. Me too.

KRISTIN. All right, I'll put these down here and then we can all help ourselves.

KRISTIN starts taking the cartons out of the bag, opening them and placing them on mats in the middle of the table. There is a general commotion for the next few minutes as they all hover round the table in preparation to sit down. They are all talking at the same time, almost overlapping.

TRUDI. Can I do anything to help?

KRISTIN. You could just get some serving spoons out of that drawer.

TRUDI. Sure.

TRUDI opens the drawer and gets serving spoons out which she then brings to the table and places by the cartons of food.

KRISTIN. Peter, why don't you get another bottle of wine out of the fridge? And there's red in the bottom cupboard if anyone wants any.

HUGH. White is good.

CLAIRE. I think I'll have white as well.

PETER. Honey?

TRUDI. Can I have red, sweetie?

PETER. Sure.

> PETER *gets a bottle of white wine from the fridge and a red one*
> *from the cupboard, which he uncorks. They all start taking their*
> *seats around the table. There is much movement and again, the*
> *conversation almost overlaps. Once they sit,* KRISTIN *ends up at*
> *the end of the table with an empty seat opposite her which is for*
> SIMON.

TRUDI. That is such a beautiful dress, Claire.

CLAIRE. Thank you. I splashed out on it.

TRUDI. It's beautiful.

KRISTIN. You splash out on yourself a lot, don't you?

CLAIRE. It's true, I confess.

PETER. Where shall we all sit?

TRUDI. I'm sure you deserve it.

KRISTIN. Anywhere you like.

TRUDI. Is it from a designer store?

HUGH. You sit at the end, birthday girl, like the queen that you are.

CLAIRE. It's Tomako Mihara.

TRUDI. Tomako who?

HUGH. Imperatrix Kristina.

PETER. Sweetie, why don't you sit opposite me?

TRUDI. Okay, honey.

HUGH. Regina Terribilis, reigning over her dominions.

CLAIRE. Tomako Mihara, she's a new Japanese designer.

TRUDI. I've never heard of her.

HUGH. Overseeing the lands of her subjects with a steely eye of
disapproval and despair.

TRUDI. I'm not really familiar with designers. I don't really read
Vogue or anything.

CLAIRE. No?

HUGH. And wondering where it all went horribly wrong.

TRUDI. I mean, I've heard of Gucci and stuff.

PETER. Are we using these spoons to serve with?

KRISTIN. We are.

TRUDI. But I don't generally know a lot about fashion.

PETER. That's one of the things I love about you.

TRUDI. Though I do know a beautiful dress when I see one.

CLAIRE. That's very kind, thank you, Trudi.

They are all serving themselves the food.

TRUDI. This smells so delicious.

PETER. These are veggie, sweetie.

TRUDI. Thanks, honey.

CLAIRE. This really is a treat.

HUGH. What's that one?

CLAIRE. Beef in oyster sauce or something.

HUGH. Something weird is floating in it.

CLAIRE. I can't see anything.

HUGH. Like a fingernail or something.

TRUDI. A fingernail?

HUGH. Or maybe I'm just imagining things.

CLAIRE. Oh no, I see it, I see it too.

PETER. This one doesn't have meat in it either.

TRUDI. Thanks, sweetie.

CLAIRE. I think I'll give that one a miss.

PETER. Sure, honey.

Pause.

KRISTIN. So how much does a dress like the one you're wearing now set you back then, Claire?

CLAIRE. I never divulge my secrets.

KRISTIN. Two hundred pounds? Three hundred?

PETER. Why do you want to know how much her dress costs?

CLAIRE. I had an especially bad week at work so I decided to spoil myself.

KRISTIN. Good for you.

CLAIRE. It was just very stressful.

HUGH. Down the mines.

CLAIRE. And I said to myself, 'You know what, Claire? You deserve this.'

TRUDI. I'm sure your work can be quite gruelling.

HUGH. All those lines to remember.

CLAIRE. So I splashed out.

TRUDI. Sometimes it's good to do that.

KRISTIN. How much?

CLAIRE. Two thousand.

TRUDI. Pounds?

HUGH. Fuck me sideways with a bargepole.

KRISTIN. Trudi's looking rather pale.

TRUDI. No, I'm not I –

HUGH. That's like the GDP of Angola.

KRISTIN. Maybe she's re-evaluating whether you deserve it or not.

CLAIRE. And you know what, I don't feel guilty.

KRISTIN. Obviously not.

CLAIRE. I just think to myself, 'I've worked hard for this, I've paid my dues, I survived drama school, I've had my time out of work and if I want to spend seven hundred pounds on a Tomako Mihari dress –

TRUDI. It really is very beautiful.

CLAIRE. – then I will. I fucking will.'

KRISTIN. Congratulations.

CLAIRE. Cheers.

The beeping of a mobile-phone text message. PETER *starts to check his pockets.*

PETER. Was that me?

TRUDI. It didn't sound like yours, honey. It was more birdy.

CLAIRE. I think that was mine. Excuse me.

She stands up and starts looking for her handbag.

HUGH. This is delicious.

KRISTIN. It sounded like mine.

TRUDI. Aren't you going to have some rice, sweetie?

KRISTIN. Two thousand for a piece of clothing.

PETER. I'm okay, sweetie.

CLAIRE *sees a phone on the kitchen counter and picks it up.*

CLAIRE. Whose is this?

KRISTIN. I think that one's mine.

HUGH. God knows why you have one. You don't even know how to fucking use it.

CLAIRE. That's weird. It's just like mine.

KRISTIN. Peter chose it for me.

CLAIRE *is rummaging through her handbag looking for her phone.*

CLAIRE. I'm sure it was mine. I just want to check in case it's Simon.

TRUDI. Hugh, can you pass me that one there, please?

HUGH. The one with the fingernail in it?

TRUDI. No, the one next to it. The pak choi.

He hands it over to her. CLAIRE *has found her phone and reads the text.*

CLAIRE. It is from Simon.

KRISTIN. Is he on his way?

CLAIRE. That's weird.

PETER. What does it say?

CLAIRE. 'Coming over. Need to talk to her.'

KRISTIN. Talk to who?

CLAIRE. That's all it says.

KRISTIN. I expect he means me.

HUGH. That sounds ominous.

>   CLAIRE *puts the phone down on the counter, right next to*
>   KRISTIN*'s and then sits down at the table again.*

TRUDI. Oh, you know what, we should have another toast.

PETER. What for, sweetie?

TRUDI. For Claire. For the renewal of her contract.

KRISTIN. What contract?

CLAIRE. Never mind.

TRUDI. Claire has been asked to do another year of the serialised
    drama she's in.

KRISTIN. The what?

CLAIRE. It's really not very –

TRUDI. And she's just accepted so I think it's fitting that we raise
    our glasses to her and congratulate her.

KRISTIN. The soap?

TRUDI. Well, Claire was saying that it's not really a soap.

KRISTIN. It isn't?

TRUDI. That it's more of a –

CLAIRE. It's fine, Trudi, really it's fine. But thank you.

PETER. Yes, congratulations.

CLAIRE. Thank you, Peter.

TRUDI. So I thought we should have a little toast.

>   *They all raise their glasses.*

HUGH. Cheers. May you continue to grace our television screens
    with your compelling trajectories.

KRISTIN. What trajectories?

PETER. Cheers, Claire.

CLAIRE. Thank you, Peter.

HUGH. Now if you'll excuse me, I'm going to fish out the offending fingernail.

He picks up the carton of food and peers into it with his fork poised.

TRUDI. Have you ever watched it, Kristin?

KRISTIN. The soap?

HUGH (*still looking for the fingernail*). It's disappeared.

TRUDI. Well, yes.

CLAIRE. Simon made her once. Strapped her to the chair kind of thing.

HUGH. It seems to have submerged itself into the oyster sauce.

CLAIRE. Not really your thing, was it, Kristin?

KRISTIN. The camera loves your face.

CLAIRE. Thank you.

KRISTIN. But I remember finding it nihilistic.

TRUDI. Nihilistic?

CLAIRE. Told you.

HUGH (*serving himself from the carton*). Fingernail or not, I'm going to be brave and eat some.

KRISTIN. It was a little vacuous. I kept asking myself, 'Why do people watch this? And why do they make it?'

PETER. Maybe because it's entertaining.

KRISTIN. I suppose it's a question of making money. It's about product.

CLAIRE. That's funny.

KRISTIN. 'Aspirational', isn't that the word? Everybody wears wonderful clothes in it. The women especially are so beautiful. Criminally superficial and always ready to hop into bed with the boss but definitely beautiful.

HUGH. Sounds a corker.

CLAIRE. At least not everybody agrees with her. It's won awards and the ratings have gone through the ceiling.

TRUDI. How exciting to be a part of that.

CLAIRE. It is.

KRISTIN. I'm not surprised. It's definitely alluring in a way. Accessible and hypnotic.

CLAIRE. And I think the writer is a real genius. He's kind of glamourising the whole world but subverting it at the same time.

KRISTIN. I must have missed that.

CLAIRE. It's full of irony.

PETER. It sounds great, Claire.

CLAIRE. But it's never obvious.

KRISTIN. No.

PETER. We'll look out for it next week.

Pause.

HUGH. I'd avoid this one if I were you. It tastes a little funny.

PETER. Sweetie, can you pass me the chicken?

TRUDI. Sure, honey.

She passes him the chicken dish.

CLAIRE. I wonder what Simon wants to talk to you about.

KRISTIN. I'm sure we'll find out.

A slight pause as they all eat.

TRUDI. And do you ever act in the theatre?

CLAIRE. I have acted on stage, yes.

PETER. We came to see you in *A Doll's House* once, didn't we?

CLAIRE. That's right.

KRISTIN. In Camden. Over that pub.

CLAIRE. You were very supportive.

HUGH. Over a pub?

CLAIRE. It was off-West End. A fringe venue. But one of the ones with a really good reputation.

TRUDI. I'm sure.

KRISTIN. There was an overwhelming smell of deep-fried scampi.

CLAIRE. I played Nora.

TRUDI. I don't really know the play.

KRISTIN. But you were very good in it, I remember.

CLAIRE. Thank you, Kristin.

KRISTIN. The direction was a little funny. The concept. It was set in an army barracks.

CLAIRE. It was a meat factory. The set was expressionistic.

HUGH. Good God.

PETER. And everyone was wearing leather aprons.

HUGH. How exciting.

KRISTIN. But whatever the production is like, just to hear that play is enough.

TRUDI. I really wish I'd seen it.

KRISTIN. Groundbreaking.

HUGH. Isn't it, though?

PETER. You were very good in it.

CLAIRE. Thank you, Peter.

Pause.

TRUDI. Claire, can I ask you a question?

CLAIRE. Of course.

TRUDI. I mean, it's probably the most stupid, unoriginal question you've ever been asked along with 'How do you learn your lines?' but I really want to know the answer so I'm not just asking in a flippant way or to pass the time. I really am interested.

CLAIRE. Go ahead.

TRUDI. But why did you become an actress? I mean, what was it that made you choose that particular path in life?

CLAIRE. Okay.

HUGH. She likes the frocks.

KRISTIN. That's not a stupid question, Trudi. It's the most important question anyone can ever ask her.

HUGH. Along with 'Where you do you get your hair done?'

TRUDI. What was it that made you say to yourself one day, 'This is what I want to do for the rest of my life'?

KRISTIN. And I want to hear the answer too. Because what motivates people fascinates me.

Pause. All eyes on CLAIRE.

CLAIRE. I suppose it's coz I always enjoyed telling stories.

TRUDI. Stories?

CLAIRE. When I was a little girl I used to enjoy dressing up –

HUGH. Told you.

CLAIRE. And telling stories. And I suppose I enjoyed it so much that I decided to do it for the rest of my life.

KRISTIN. But I think what Trudi's really asking you is what makes you want to tell stories in the first place.

TRUDI. Well, I wasn't really –

KRISTIN. Is it because you are trying to communicate something which will in some direct or indirect way improve the world in which you live, point it towards a better understanding of itself –

CLAIRE. Well, I suppose –

KRISTIN. Or is it simply that you enjoy the sensation of having all eyes on you a great deal of the time?

CLAIRE. It's a combination of both, Kristin.

TRUDI. That makes sense.

CLAIRE. I feel ever so slightly that I'm being interrogated.

PETER. You are.

KRISTIN. Which one it is that constitutes your *raison d'être*. Your existential propeller if you like. Is it the will to live in service of some larger whole –

HUGH. I'm assuming that's 'whole' with a W before the H.

KRISTIN. – or is it an exercise in narcissism?

HUGH. Though living in service of a hole without a W before the H also sounds like a rather attractive proposition.

KRISTIN. Because it really is an interesting question.

Pause.

CLAIRE. It's the first. I'm an artist.

KRISTIN. And I remember that night, that even if the production misfired in certain ways, that there was something about sitting in that room watching you compete with the sounds of thumping bass drum and the smell of cheap food –

TRUDI. That must have been really challenging.

KRISTIN. Speaking words that had been written a hundred years before which questioned everything about the established order of the day, everything of what it meant to be a woman at that particular point in time, that there was something beautiful about it and strangely moving.

HUGH. But why was it set in a sausage factory?

KRISTIN. Which brings us back to the subject of your current work. The soap.

CLAIRE. Here we go.

KRISTIN. And I have to now repeat, within the context of this particular conversation, that it is the biggest pile of putrid shite I have ever seen in my life.

HUGH. Don't hold back, darling.

CLAIRE. We know how you feel about it, Kristin, and I'm sorry that it's not your thing but I think as I explained earlier I don't happen to agree with you. I think it's a clever and profound piece of television.

KRISTIN. Surely you can't mean that.

PETER. Why can't she?

KRISTIN. Because that's an even more frightening thought than you doing it just for the money.

HUGH. Do you know, I'm feeling ever so slightly queasy.

CLAIRE. You really are unbelievable.

KRISTIN. That would be understandable, doing it for the money.

PETER. Why can't you just respect the fact that people don't always see things the way you do?

HUGH. I think it was the beef thing.

PETER. Why can't you just respect that?

HUGH. I think I may have swallowed that fucking fingernail.

CLAIRE. I just don't think you get it. Maybe it's a generational thing.

KRISTIN. *That* I could understand.

CLAIRE. I mean, it is aimed at younger people and maybe there's something about it –

KRISTIN. Most people have been whores at some point in their life.

CLAIRE. – that you simply don't get.

HUGH. I really do feel rather sick.

   Pause.

CLAIRE. I'm sorry, did you just call me a whore?

   Pause.

HUGH. And ever so slightly dizzy too.

TRUDI. Maybe you're just allergic to Chinese food.

HUGH. Or fingernails.

TRUDI. The monosodium glutamate.

   Pause.

CLAIRE. And yes, of course I need the money as well, Kristin. I need to make a living. To survive.

KRISTIN. And drive a BMW.

CLAIRE. But that doesn't negate the fact that I think it's a good piece of work.

KRISTIN. Our capacity for self-delusion is phenomenal, Claire.

PETER. That's rich.

CLAIRE. And I'm fucking proud of it, if you really want to know.

KRISTIN. I'm sorry but it's something I feel quite passionate about.

HUGH. Obviously.

KRISTIN. The misappropriation of words.

PETER. What misappropriation of words?

KRISTIN. It's just that she said she was an artist.

CLAIRE. That's right, I am an artist.

KRISTIN. And I just don't know what that means any more. To be an artist.

CLAIRE. Don't you?

KRISTIN. I mean, you may laugh at this, you may find it sweet and hilarious but artists were people whose voices could be the instigators of social change. And that it's those voices that we hang onto in some way to save us from the rampant stupidity of religion on the one hand and vacuous consumerism on the other.

HUGH. I really think I'm going to be sick.

KRISTIN. So to waste that or to sell it to the highest bidder really seems to me like the worst possible betrayal.

TRUDI. I'll get you a glass of water, Hugh.

TRUDI *stands but as she does she knocks over the bottle of red wine which spills all over the place but mostly onto* CLAIRE*'s dress.*

TRUDI. Oh my God. Oh my God. I am so sorry… I am so –

CLAIRE *is in shock.*

HUGH. Sweet Jesus. That's an expensive accident.

TRUDI. I am so sorry, Claire, I am so terribly sorry –

CLAIRE. It's fine, really it's fine.

PETER. It was an accident, sweetie.

TRUDI. I am so terribly, terribly sorry.

CLAIRE. I said it's fine.

TRUDI. Here let me…

She picks up a bottle of water, pours some onto a napkin and starts dabbing the dress with it.

Maybe if we soak it.

CLAIRE. I don't think that's doing any good.

HUGH. Try salt.

CLAIRE. I really don't think that's doing any good.

HUGH. You need to put some salt on it.

TRUDI (*who keeps dabbing* CLAIRE *with water*). I'm so sorry, I'm so sorry.

CLAIRE. Trudi, please.

PETER. Sweetie, leave it.

HUGH. Why don't you put some fucking salt on it?

PETER. It needs to go to the dry cleaner's.

TRUDI. Maybe Hugh's right.

TRUDI *grabs the salt dispenser which stands in the middle of the table and starts to sprinkle it very liberally and rather hysterically onto* CLAIRE*'s dress.*

Maybe this will do it.

CLAIRE. I really don't think –

TRUDI. I just stood up too quickly –

PETER. It was an accident –

TRUDI. And the bottle was right next to the edge –

CLAIRE. I really don't think you covering me in salt is going to make that much of a difference –

TRUDI. And it all just happened so quickly –

CLAIRE. The point is the dress is fucked.

TRUDI. But I'm so terribly sorry.

CLAIRE (*forcefully*). So please stop doing that. Stop covering me in salt.

TRUDI. I feel really awful.

CLAIRE. BECAUSE I'M NOT A FUCKING PIECE OF MEAT.

Pause. TRUDI *is slightly taken aback, as is everybody else.*

PETER. It was an accident.

CLAIRE. I'm sorry. I didn't mean –

TRUDI. No, I'm sorry.

PETER. She's just trying to help.

CLAIRE. I didn't mean to snap at you, I'm sorry.

TRUDI. No, I'm sorry.

CLAIRE. It really isn't your fault.

Pause.

KRISTIN. I bet you now wish you'd invested that two thousand pounds in a slightly wiser way.

CLAIRE *takes a deep breath and turns to face* KRISTIN.

CLAIRE. How dare you criticise my choices? How dare you sit there in judgement on me?

KRISTIN. I only do it because I expect more from you.

HUGH. That's punchable, darling.

KRISTIN. Because you are my son's partner and I like to trust his judgement.

CLAIRE. You're a fucking dinosaur, Kristin.

KRISTIN. However challenging that may be.

CLAIRE. I'll tell you something, though. When you do eventually talk to Simon, or rather when he talks to you, tells you what it is, why it is, what the fuck it is that has driven him to this strange, dark place he now finds himself in –

KRISTIN. It's some of the choices you've made that I have problems with –

CLAIRE. If you choose to listen for once in your life, I mean really listen –

KRISTIN. Not the person you are.

CLAIRE. Well, maybe then you'll be in for a surprise. An unpleasant surprise or two.

KRISTIN. I'm simply saying that as an artist and as a partner you are taking the route of least inconvenience to yourself but the route of most peril to others.

CLAIRE. You are fucking unbelievable.

KRISTIN. The one thing one could say in your favour is that at least you're consistent in your lack of commitment to the things which are the most imperative.

PETER. I think you're barking up the wrong tree.

KRISTEN. Concepts, stories, human beings – my son!

PETER. I said I think you're barking up the wrong fucking tree.

KRISTIN. Consistent in your profound inability to give a fuck about anyone other than yourself.

PETER. I said YOU'RE BARKING UP THE WRONG FUCKING TREE.

TRUDI. Sweetie, please.

There is a pause as they're all taken aback by this sudden explosion.

KRISTIN. Why am I barking up the wrong tree, darling?

PETER. Let's talk about your book, Kristin.

KRISTIN. It always makes me nervous when you start calling me Kristin.

PETER. Let's talk about your fucking book.

TRUDI. Sweetie.

CLAIRE. Your memoir.

Pause. KRISTIN *stands up and starts to clear up the plates.*

KRISTIN. I'll start clearing these up and then maybe we can have some of that cake you brought, Claire.

HUGH. I can't say I'm in the mood for mango meringue.

KRISTIN *starts to take the plates over to the counter.*

PETER. The way you write about art is thrilling.

TRUDI. It really is a wonderful book, Kristin.

PETER. The supporting characters, however, seem a little sketchy.

KRISTIN. The supporting characters?

PETER. I myself happen to be a little more thick-skinned, shall we say, but if I were Simon – if I were my brother Simon, whose skin perhaps has never been quite as thick as mine – whose *soul* has never been quite as resilient –

CLAIRE. It hasn't.

PETER. I might ask myself how, in a book that calls itself a memoir, that purports to be your fucking life story, I don't get a single fucking mention.

CLAIRE. Not one.

PETER. I am your son, I would say to myself, and though we didn't see much of each other as we were growing up, it's true, I would have liked to have played a slightly more pivotal part in what I'm sure it describes on the back flap as 'The Life and Times of'. Would that be churlish of me?

CLAIRE. He was devastated.

KRISTIN. It's a work memoir. I wasn't interested in airing my dirty laundry.

PETER. Fuck me, now she's calling us dirty laundry.

TRUDI. I don't think that's what she means, honey.

PETER. That awful Italian you shacked up with for a couple of years got a whole fucking chapter.

KRISTIN. Only because he was the foremost Renaissance-painting-restorer of his generation. But I'm sorry if you felt the book *neglected* you in some way.

PETER. 'Neglected.' Interesting choice of word. And I have to now ask you the question I have been leading up to, the question I have been secretly asking myself for many, many years, the question that has been gnawing in my fucking chest since I was a small boy, the same question I've just been informed your other son is also keen to hear the answer to.

TRUDI. Sweetie, please.

KRISTIN. Go on then.

PETER. And the question is why did this woman have children if she wasn't prepared to do the job properly?

Pause.

And I honestly don't think that Claire being in a soap opera is the problem here.

TRUDI. It's not a soap opera, sweetie.

Another pause and KRISTIN *quietly tops up her glass with wine.*

KRISTIN. Have you finished?

HUGH. Hopefully.

PETER *doesn't answer.*

KRISTIN. You know nothing.

PETER. Tell me then.

KRISTIN. Not now. Not like this. Not like a witch hunt.

She continues to put things away, clearing up, piling plates up on the counter. Nobody speaks and the others remain seated.

I'm going to bed. If Simon does show up, tell him I'll see him in the morning.

Nobody speaks. She moves towards the door, then stops and turns to look at PETER *and* CLAIRE. *She directs her words to both of them.*

You know nothing about what it means to live for something slightly larger than yourselves so anything I say in my defence will sound like a foreign language to you. I don't know how, I don't know *why* this happened but somewhere along the line earning money – for the most part at the cost of other people's suffering – seems to have become your only objective. And I honestly think, Peter, that this new religious path you've decided to follow is just a way of assuaging what can only be a troubled conscience. Of course, taking responsibility for your actions would release just as many endorphins as swaying in the pews does. The only difference is that they'd be a slightly better class of endorphins. You'd have earned them.

PETER. What the fuck has that to do with anything?

KRISTIN. I could sit here for twenty-four hours and try and describe to you what it means to be *political*, what it means to fight for something other than your own material and domestic well-being, and you wouldn't understand. We could debate on what defines a good parent through the night and still we wouldn't agree. But yes, I'm sure that in *your* version of what constitutes a good mother you are right that I have failed you in every possible way.

PETER. You have.

KRISTIN. But more than anything what appals and depresses me is that you have never once asked yourself – not really, not *honestly*, Peter – what it might have been like for me. Then, I mean. In Florence. When he took you away from me. In that way, you have persistently shown a quite catastrophic failure of imagination. Your father would be proud of you.

Suddenly, CLAIRE*'s mobile rings.*

That'll be Simon.

Thinking it's her phone, KRISTIN *answers it.*

Hello?

CLAIRE. I think that's my phone, Kristin.

There is a pause as KRISTIN *listens to someone on the phone.*

I said I think it's mine.

KRISTIN (*on the mobile*). I believe it's Claire you want to talk to.

CLAIRE. Who is it?

KRISTIN (*still on the mobile*). Please don't apologise, it's been informative and entertaining.

CLAIRE. Can I have my phone, please?

KRISTIN. Well, it isn't Simon.

She walks towards CLAIRE, *mobile in hand.*

But whoever it is said he's booked the room for Thursday night and he can't wait to fuck you up the arse.

She hands the mobile to CLAIRE.

Goodnight, everyone.

She leaves the room. CLAIRE *is left holding the mobile.*

CLAIRE. It isn't… it's a friend… it's not… it really isn't what it… the thing is…

Pause as she realises she's losing a battle.

Fucking bitch.

She storms out of the room, mobile in hand.

HUGH. Lucky girl.

TRUDI. I wish I'd never asked her why she wanted to be an actress.

PETER. It's not that, sweetie.

Pause.

HUGH. What did she mean when she called her a dinosaur?

Pause.

Excuse me, but I think I'm going to be sick.

HUGH *rushes out of the room.*

PETER *and* TRUDI *are left alone. There is a pause and then* TRUDI *starts to quietly cry.*

PETER. Trudi?

TRUDI. I'm sorry, I –

PETER. Sweetie?

TRUDI. I'm sorry. I'm just a little emotional, that's all. It's just that –

PETER. Of course you are –

TRUDI. It's just that I wasn't expecting this.

PETER. Neither was I.

TRUDI (*through her tears*). And everything you said made me so sad, so very, very sad and I started thinking about poor Simon and then earlier when your mother was talking to me about Giotto, about what he did as an artist, I mean about how he changed the world, how he transformed the way we looked at each other and that made me quite emotional too, I don't know why but it did, it kind of all made sense and then I started thinking, later, when she was talking about art and about everything like that, and what she just said now about responsibility, I started thinking about Jesus, about what it is about him that I love so much, about why it is I'm a Christian, and I had a terrible thought that what if the only reason I like Jesus, I love Jesus is just because... because... is just because...

PETER. Because what?

TRUDI. Is just because he makes life simpler.

PETER. Oh, sweetie.

TRUDI. And I ruined her Japanese dress.

PETER. Honey.

TRUDI runs out of the room in tears.

Jesus.

He runs after her.

The room is empty. Then SIMON *enters. He is wearing his coat and looking slightly dishevelled. His right hand is bleeding and he has wrapped a handkerchief around it. He looks around the room as if wondering where everyone has disappeared to. He sits at the table.*

Blackout.

End of Act One.

ACT TWO

Scene One

The middle of the night, a few hours later. The food has all been cleared away. SIMON *is sitting at the table with* KRISTIN. SIMON *is fully dressed but* KRISTIN *is in her dressing gown. He has taken the handkerchief off his hand and* KRISTIN *is inspecting his palm.*

KRISTIN. There's definitely some in there.

SIMON. Okay.

KRISTIN. Little pieces of glass. Tiny splinters.

Pause.

We'll have to get them out.

SIMON. Fine.

KRISTIN. How did you do it?

SIMON. I got off the train. I was walking down the road looking for a cab. It was raining.

KRISTIN. Claire should have brought you here.

SIMON. I was trying to do up my shoelaces. There was broken glass in the undergrowth by the road. I lost my balance and fell on it.

KRISTIN. There's definitely some in there.

SIMON. It could have been worse.

KRISTIN. So let's get it out.

She stands and walks over to a cupboard. She opens it and takes out a first-aid kit.

I've been looking forward to the day this thing would come in handy.

She brings it over to where he's sitting. She sits down and opens it. She starts to take out all the contents of the box, laying them out carefully on the table.

Are you sure you don't want something to eat?

SIMON. I'm not hungry.

KRISTIN. We can't warm it up, I'm afraid, but you could eat it cold.

SIMON. I said I'm not hungry.

KRISTIN. Let me know if you change your mind.

She opens up a bottle of disinfectant and dabs a little of it onto a piece of cotton wool.

The evening didn't go quite as we expected.

SIMON. I heard.

KRISTIN. We had a heated discussion.

SIMON. Claire said.

KRISTIN. On various subjects.

SIMON. Okay.

KRISTIN. But if there was one overriding theme, I suppose it would be priorities.

SIMON. Priorities?

KRISTIN. What's important. The things that count.

SIMON. I see.

KRISTIN. The choices that define us.

SIMON. That's interesting.

She begins to dab the disinfectant onto his palm.

KRISTIN. We'll put this disinfectant on it and then I'll use the tweezers to get the glass out.

SIMON. Thank you.

KRISTIN. But it doesn't need stitches.

Pause.

The thing about Claire and me is that we're very different kinds of people.

SIMON. Are you?

KRISTIN. We don't always see eye to eye.

SIMON. No.

KRISTIN. So it's inevitable that there'll be a little friction between us, isn't it?

Pause as she continues to apply the disinfectant to his open palm.

How are the two of you?

SIMON. How are we?

KRISTIN. I imagine it will be harder now that you're not working.

SIMON. Will it?

KRISTIN. Money, for a start.

SIMON. I see.

KRISTIN. Until you feel better. Until you feel ready again.

SIMON. Money?

KRISTIN. Until you feel you're strong enough.

SIMON. Strong enough?

KRISTIN. To find another job, I mean.

SIMON. Oh.

KRISTIN. But that money, or rather lack of it, shouldn't be a reason –

SIMON. What?

KRISTIN. For you to feel trapped in any way.

SIMON. Trapped?

Pause.

KRISTIN. I suppose what I'm saying is that I can lend you money. As much of it as you need.

SIMON. Okay.

KRISTIN. *Give* you money. And then when – *if* – you ever feel you can afford to pay me back, well, then you can.

SIMON. I see.

KRISTIN. But that I wouldn't be expecting it is what I'm saying.

SIMON. Thank you.

KRISTIN *puts down the disinfectant and picks up a pair of tweezers.*

KRISTIN. Keep it still. Some of them are tiny. Tiny shards.

She starts to take out the splinters of glass one by one. She does this with great care, fastidiously.

And if you ever needed to get away. I mean, for a few days, or even longer, you know you can always come here. If you need some sort of break, a little distance. You know there's always a room for you here.

SIMON. Thank you.

Pause.

KRISTIN. I know you wanted to talk to me. And I want you to know that there is nothing you can't say.

SIMON. Good.

KRISTIN. However uncomfortable.

Pause.

I want us to be friends.

SIMON. Yes.

Pause.

KRISTIN. Your brother is very worried about you. But I think he's got the wrong end of the stick.

SIMON. Has he?

Pause. She is trying to tread carefully.

KRISTIN. How do you think Claire is coping?

SIMON. How do I think Claire is coping?

KRISTIN. It must be difficult for her.

SIMON. I'm sure.

KRISTIN. She must feel inadequate at times.

SIMON. Maybe.

KRISTIN. What I mean is that when someone close to you is suffering you must often carry the burden of it.

SIMON. Must you?

KRISTIN. And that can be an isolating place for you to find yourself in.

SIMON. I expect so.

KRISTIN. Lonely.

SIMON. Yes.

KRISTIN. And that can't be easy.

SIMON. I'm sure.

Pause.

KRISTIN. But you're coping all right. The two of you, I mean. As a couple.

SIMON. A couple?

KRISTIN. Because if there's anything you want to talk to me about, I want you to know that you can.

SIMON. You've said that already.

KRISTIN. However personal.

She waits for something but nothing comes. She continues to take the splinters out of his palm.

Try and keep it still, darling.

Pause.

She said you went missing last week.

SIMON. Yes.

KRISTIN. For three days. She said you went missing for three days and that when you returned you never told her where you'd been.

SIMON. No.

Again she waits, again he gives her nothing.

KRISTIN. What did you make of your brother's new girlfriend?

SIMON. Her name is Trudi.

KRISTIN. What did you make of Trudi?

SIMON. She seems nice enough.

KRISTIN. I can't say I'm not surprised.

SIMON. Surprised?

KRISTIN. You know she's a Christian.

SIMON. Is she?

KRISTIN. Born again, that sort of thing, I imagine.

SIMON. So?

KRISTIN. They met at a prayer meeting. They shared coffee and biscuits.

SIMON. That's nice.

KRISTIN. I'm just a little bewildered, that's all.

SIMON. Are you?

KRISTIN. Just a little.

SIMON. I'm not.

Pause.

I woke up one morning and realised that pretty much everything we are and everything we do is a response against you. So, no, I'm not bewildered in the least.

KRISTIN *continues as if she didn't hear this.*

KRISTIN. But she seems nice enough. And he seems to like her which is the most important thing.

SIMON. It is.

Pause. She looks closely at his palm.

KRISTIN. We have to make sure they're all out otherwise it could get infected. And then we can go to sleep. You look tired.

SIMON. I'm not.

KRISTIN. I am.

SIMON. I came to talk to you.

She continues taking out the splinters.

KRISTIN. Your brother had a go at me for not mentioning you in the book. He didn't understand that the book was about the work, more about my professional life and less about the personal things. He seemed offended in some way and implied that you were as well. I suppose I ought to apologise if it wasn't clear enough. I certainly didn't set out to upset you.

SIMON. No.

KRISTIN. So that's that.

SIMON. Yes. That's that.

KRISTIN. I was thinking, in the morning we should go for a walk. At least to the foot of the hills and maybe even halfway up them. The weather will be good, it said.

SIMON. All right.

KRISTIN. And we could all do with the exercise.

SIMON. We could.

KRISTIN. Fresh air.

SIMON. Yes.

KRISTIN. The oxygen.

Pause.

SIMON. Lately I've been doing some retracing.

KRISTIN. Retracing?

SIMON. Locating the moments, finding the locations, remembering, and then suddenly going, 'Ah! So this is where it was. This is the place, that was the time when I first said to myself: this is who I am, how it is, what I'm worth.'

KRISTIN. What you're worth?

SIMON. This is where I was shaped. This is where the music started.

KRISTIN. What music?

SIMON. This is the moment that set the soundtrack for the rest of my life. Finding those moments. That's what I mean by retracing.

Pause. She puts down his hand and the tweezers.

KRISTIN. I need to talk to you about something.

SIMON. Because the thing is I've always felt this way.

KRISTIN. What way?

SIMON. Disjointed.

KRISTIN. Disjointed?

SIMON. And dislocated. Disillusioned. Dis – this, dis – that. Disturbed, distracted, discombobulated.

KRISTIN. I don't understand what you mean.

SIMON. But you keep going. You shrug it off. You say to yourself, 'This is the way it is for everyone.' And then one day you realise that it isn't. That your complete incapacity to feel any sort of self-worth is your own personal brand of misery.

KRISTIN. I don't understand you.

SIMON. So you keep going until that day. And then suddenly you run out of fuel. You can't lie to yourself any more. You've always felt that way. And so it catches up with you, that's all.

Pause.

KRISTIN. There's something you need to know.

SIMON. So that's why I came. To tell you about my retracing. And to ask you a question or two.

KRISTIN. It isn't easy but I've decided that it's the right thing.

SIMON. What is?

KRISTIN. I need to talk to you about Claire.

SIMON. What about her?

KRISTIN. I wasn't going to. I didn't want to.

SIMON. What about Claire?

KRISTIN. But I think I have to. Talk to you.

SIMON. About what?

KRISTIN. About something that happened this evening.

SIMON. I see.

KRISTIN. Because maybe knowing things for what they are is important now.

SIMON. That isn't why I came.

KRISTIN. So maybe it's for the best.

SIMON. Not to talk about Claire.

Pause.

KRISTIN. Her phone rang earlier. I thought it was mine. I answered it. Something embarrassing happened.

SIMON. I don't want to talk about Claire.

KRISTIN. I answered it by mistake. Thinking it was mine.

SIMON. That's not why I came here.

KRISTIN. So I answered it.

SIMON. SO PLEASE LET'S NOT TALK ABOUT CLAIRE.

Pause. She returns her attention to his hand.

KRISTIN. We're nearly finished. And then we'll put a plaster on it. There's only a couple more.

SIMON. Lately I can't stop thinking of that year.

KRISTIN. What year?

SIMON. The year you took us to Florence.

KRISTIN. What about it?

SIMON. After the divorce. You were working on your book.

KRISTIN. The first one.

SIMON. And you took us with you.

KRISTIN. I did.

Pause.

SIMON. Do you remember the house?

KRISTIN. Of course I do.

SIMON. Overlooking the city.

KRISTIN. That view.

SIMON. There was an orange tree in the garden.

KRISTIN. I remember.

SIMON. It was vast.

KRISTIN. We used to sit in its shade. In the afternoons. The three of us. I'd be traipsing around churches in the mornings doing my research. Then I'd pick you up from that funny school and then we'd spend the afternoons in the shade of that vast orange tree. I'd be ploughing through those heavy tomes and making notes for the book and you and your brother would be doing your homework.

SIMON. Do you remember?

KRISTIN. How could I forget?

SIMON. I've been thinking about it a lot.

KRISTIN. It was the happiest year of my life.

SIMON. Sometimes on Sundays you'd take us with you. To the basilicas, the galleries. Or we'd get in the car and drive to some other town. You were always working. I remember spending hours in the back of some church somewhere, watching you scribbling notes with your head tilted back staring up at some fucking fresco.

KRISTIN. I was obsessed, it's true.

SIMON. I always felt I was competing for your attention.

KRISTIN. I suppose it was a vocation. A calling.

SIMON. Yes.

KRISTIN. But I took you with me. I took you to Florence with me.

SIMON. I know.

KRISTIN. And then he took you away.

Pause.

SIMON. We always thought you'd follow us.

KRISTIN. I'm sure.

SIMON. We thought you'd come for us.

KRISTIN. I know you did.

SIMON. Fight for us.

KRISTIN. Yes.

SIMON. Because that's what we thought parents did.

KRISTIN. Of course.

SIMON. Mothers.

KRISTIN. Of course you did.

SIMON. So we waited, and waited.

KRISTIN. Yes.

SIMON. And waited.

KRISTIN. I know.

SIMON. But you never came.

Pause.

I was seven years old.

KRISTIN. I know how old you were.

Pause. She takes out a plaster and starts to apply it to his hand.

They're all out. We'll just put a plaster on it and then we're done.

SIMON. I mean, if your parent dies when you're that age, then obviously you feel something, I don't know, irreparable, long-lasting, something you never quite get over.

KRISTIN. Of course you do.

SIMON. A loss, an injury, something that never quite mends.

KRISTIN. Yes.

SIMON. But when a parent, when your mother –

KRISTIN. I know what you're going to say.

SIMON. Doesn't come for you, it's just as damaging.

KRISTIN. Of course it is.

SIMON. Abandons you, it's just as harmful.

KRISTIN. I didn't abandon you.

SIMON. And maybe even worse.

KRISTIN. He took you away.

SIMON. But you never came. And then you became this person we'd spend holidays with.

Pause. She starts to pack away the first-aid kit.

Do you remember once I came to Italy on my own? It was the summer. I must have been – what – eleven? Peter had gone to stay with a friend in Cornwall. Dad put me on the train in London. You were supposed to pick me up in Genoa.

KRISTIN. I can't remember.

SIMON. But something happened and you never made it. I mean, you did eventually but it was like a day later.

KRISTIN. I really can't remember.

SIMON. But I'd been on my own through the night. I had a phone number for you in Italy but I rang it and there wasn't an answer. I remember all the trains had come in and all the people had been greeted by their families or friends and I sat watching them and waiting to spot your face in the crowd.

KRISTIN. Why are you telling me this now?

SIMON. But it got dark and you never came. The station emptied and these two women came out and started mopping the platforms. I remember that.

KRISTIN. Why are you telling me this?

SIMON. It must have been one in the morning and I was lying on this bench when this man approached me.

KRISTIN. A man?

SIMON. There was a café on the side of the platform and I think he'd been sitting there for quite a long time and had noticed this boy in a suit looking rather lost. So he came to talk to me.

KRISTIN. I think I do remember now.

SIMON. Remember?

KRISTIN. There'd been a misunderstanding. Crossed wires. Your father had said –

SIMON. It doesn't really matter.

KRISTIN. He'd left a message with the cleaning lady who came in once a week. Which was a stupid thing to do as she didn't speak a word of English and his Italian was non-existent. Anyway, she got it wrong. Or wrote it down on a piece of paper which I didn't find until it was too late. But that's what caused it all. It was a stupid thing to do. And I'd been working. I remember there was a lecture that I –

SIMON. He must have been – I don't know, about forty, or something. Probably had bad acne when he was younger because his skin was slightly pock-marked.

KRISTIN. But that's what happened. Your father had been careless.

SIMON. He spoke quite good English but I think he was German or
    Dutch or something. Doesn't really matter, though, does it, what
    nationality he was. Anyway he asked me if I was all right –

KRISTIN. Why are you telling me this now?

SIMON. And I said that I was and that I was waiting for my mother
    but that she would be there soon and that I would wait for her
    until she got there.

KRISTIN. Why are you telling me this?

SIMON. He then said that he was worried about a boy of my age
    spending the whole night on my own and asked me if I wanted to
    have a Coke with him in the cafeteria. I said why not so we went to
    the cafeteria but it had just closed and there was nowhere else to go.

KRISTIN. So did he leave you alone?

SIMON. I remember then we sat down on a bench outside the
    cafeteria and we talked and at one point he said something like,
    'If I was your parent I would never leave you waiting for me on a
    station platform all night long.' This made an impression on me
    because half of me was angry at him for saying it and I wanted to
    defend you and explain to him that it was all a misunderstanding,
    that you would show up and everything would be all right, and
    half of me agreed with him and was happy that he'd expressed it
    in that particular way.

KRISTIN. What a strange thing to say.

SIMON. And then he said, 'Why don't you come back to my house
    and have something to eat and you can rest and then I'll bring you
    back in the morning.'

KRISTIN. What happened?

SIMON. And even though I felt, no, I *knew* that it was dangerous,
    that it was wrong for me to follow this man back to his house, I
    stood up and picked up my bag and followed him.

KRISTIN. You went to his house?

SIMON. And part of me was thinking – 'This will show her, this will
    show her, this will fucking show her.'

KRISTIN. You went to this man's house?

SIMON. So we walked through the streets of Genoa and it was in the
    middle of the night and there was nobody about. I remember

thinking that we must be very near the sea because there were many seagulls in the sky.

KRISTIN. Why have you never told me this before?

SIMON. Then eventually we got to this old building and he opened the door and we walked up these stairs that stank of urine or something. His flat was at the top and he opened the door and let me in. He asked me to sit down and then he gave me a glass of wine and made some joke about not telling my parents.

KRISTIN. What happened?

SIMON. And then he cooked a meal. I watched him taking things out of a cupboard and out of the fridge and he started preparing a meal. He made pasta with a tomato sauce and as he cooked he talked to me about what had brought him to Italy and about other things too and I noticed that he was nervous and that his hands were shaking a little and I could feel the wine whooshing around in my head.

KRISTIN. Did he hurt you?

SIMON. At one point I asked him if I could use the bathroom so he took me down the hall and showed me where it was and I went in and closed the door behind me. I remember the light in the bathroom was very weak as if the bulb was broken or something, it was quite dark. So that when I looked into the mirror I could only just see my face. I stood there for some time just staring at myself and wondering why you hadn't shown up at the station.

KRISTIN. Why have you never told me all this before?

SIMON. And it was when I was trying to see my face in the mirror that I heard him breathing outside the door. So he'd been standing there all along, on the other side of the door. And then I tried to open it, to open the door but it was jammed.

KRISTIN. Jammed?

SIMON. As if it was blocked. As if he was blocking it from the other side.

KRISTIN. What did he do to you? What did this man do to you?

SIMON. Then after a little it opened and he wasn't there. He was back in the kitchen. So I went back. I wanted to run away but I was too scared.

KRISTIN. Did he hurt you?

SIMON. The food was ready so we ate in silence. After we'd eaten we sat on the sofa for some time and he kept talking nervously and then he asked me if I wanted to sleep in his bed with him and I said that I didn't. Then he took some sheets out of a cupboard and turned the sofa into a bed for me and then he said he'd wake me at six in the morning and walk me back to the station. And that's what he did. He walked me back to the bench that he'd found me on.

KRISTIN. So he never hurt you?

SIMON. Lately I can't seem to get that night out of my head. I keep thinking of myself trying to find my face in the mirror in the dim-lit bathroom of that dark building in that strange and foreign city.

Pause.

Where were you?

KRISTIN. I told you. Your father had made a mistake and had –

SIMON. No. I mean, where were you? Where were you? Where were you?

Pause.

You were never there. I have to tell you now that the thing I remember most about you is your absence. I have to be honest and tell you that. That's what I wanted to tell you when I read your book. That's my response to it.

Pause.

So you look for those moments. And you say to yourself, 'That's when it was.'

Pause. KRISTIN stands and picks up the first-aid kit. She walks over to the counter and puts it back into the cupboard.

KRISTIN. I'm very tired. We can continue talking tomorrow. I've left a towel at the end of the bed if you want to have a shower in the morning.

SIMON. I saw it.

KRISTIN *walks over to him and kisses him on the forehead.*

KRISTIN. Goodnight.

SIMON. I know about Claire. What it was you wanted to tell me. Do you blame her? I haven't been around for some time now. In any way.

Pause.

KRISTIN *leaves the room.* SIMON *leans over and picks up the framed photograph that* HUGH *gave* KRISTIN *as a gift. He looks at it closely, as if trying to understand something about it.*

Lights fade to darkness.

Scene Two

The next morning. HUGH, TRUDI *and* CLAIRE *are in the kitchen. They are having breakfast –* TRUDI *is eating a bowl of cereal and* CLAIRE *is playing with a piece of toast.* HUGH *is drinking coffee and casually leafing through the newspaper.*

CLAIRE. All I'm really saying is that I think you're very lucky.

TRUDI. I am?

CLAIRE. To have your faith, I mean.

TRUDI. Okay.

CLAIRE. Especially nowadays.

TRUDI. How do you mean?

CLAIRE. Although I wouldn't be surprised if religion is about to make a big comeback.

HUGH. Is it?

CLAIRE. People looking for some sort of certainty.

HUGH. I see.

CLAIRE. In times of turmoil.

HUGH. All of a sudden, dictators – biblical or otherwise – seem rather alluring.

CLAIRE. It's inevitable.

HUGH. Anyone who promises they can sort things out for you in one way or another.

TRUDI. Maybe.

HUGH. And maybe punish the suspected perpetrators.

TRUDI. Okay.

HUGH. Another example of human nature in all its shimmering
intelligence.

Pause.

CLAIRE. I do like Jesus, though.

TRUDI. Like him?

HUGH. How do you mean, you like him?

CLAIRE. Well, what I mean is –

HUGH. He's not a brand of toothpaste, for fuck's sake –

CLAIRE. That everything he stands for kind of makes sense –

HUGH. Or a pasta sauce.

TRUDI. Does it?

CLAIRE. I mean, like everything he says in the sermon on the
mountain –

HUGH. What mountain?

CLAIRE. Kind of resonates with me.

TRUDI. Okay.

CLAIRE. Love thy neighbour and all that.

HUGH. Yes, that's a good one.

CLAIRE. To err is human, to forgive divine.

TRUDI. I don't know if –

HUGH. I think that was Oscar Wilde.

CLAIRE. So I completely understand why you would want to make
it such an integral part of your life.

TRUDI. It's not really –

CLAIRE. I did get drawn to Buddhism for a time.

HUGH. Oh?

CLAIRE. The chanting really stills you.

TRUDI. Does it?

CLAIRE. And I suppose if Christianity still held onto its more
    mystical side –

HUGH. I know what you mean.

CLAIRE. I might be more drawn to it.

HUGH. Might you?

CLAIRE. The Orthodox Church still has some of that.

HUGH. It's very dramatic.

CLAIRE. Incense, candles, chandeliers.

HUGH. Those funny hats.

CLAIRE. It kind of draws you in.

HUGH. English vicars don't quite have the same allure.

CLAIRE. But religion generally gives me the creeps. Especially the
    more fundamental Muslims. The *anger*.

    Pause.

TRUDI. The thing is…

CLAIRE. Yes?

TRUDI. I don't want to be rude but –

CLAIRE. Rude?

TRUDI. I mean, the way you talk about it, I mean, about religion, I
    don't really understand you. I mean, I think Hugh is right to point
    out that it's not a product. It's much more than that.

CLAIRE. I wasn't –

TRUDI. It's like, I'm sorry but the way you were talking about it just
    now, about Christianity and Buddhism and the Orthodox Church,
    you make them all sound like items on a shopping list but for
    most people –

CLAIRE. I'm sorry, I didn't mean to offend you.

TRUDI. For most people it's probably not like that. The thing is for
    many people it might be less of a luxury item and more like the
    only thing they have – a lifeline, a reason to continue, their only
    hope. I think what I'm saying is that it's about the way we look at

life, about the way we live, so to trivialise it or demean it is not necessarily helpful and I know a lot of the times when you see those men –

HUGH. What men?

TRUDI. Those men, in Pakistan or wherever, screaming and shouting, they seem, I don't know, crazy, or mad or completely *medieval* or something – well, I know that when you see these things, it's easy I suppose to laugh at it or be appalled by it or condemn it as some sort of ancient superstition but the point is – the thing to understand is – that maybe some of us had an opportunity – *have* an opportunity, I don't know if it's too late – to offer some sort of viable alternative but because we were greedy or selfish or just plain stupid, we've wasted it. And that is really quite sad.

CLAIRE. I didn't really mean –

PETER *has entered the room. He stands by the door, slightly surprised by* TRUDI*'s tone of voice.*

TRUDI. I mean, we have been so privileged, I'm sure people will look back at us five hundred years from now and be amazed at just how rich we were and they'll ask what we did, I mean, what the legacy of all that phenomenal wealth was, but when they, I don't know, excavate or whatever, all they'll find is a few infinity pools and a whole lot of expensive clothes.

CLAIRE. The thing I was trying –

TRUDI. And if you really don't have clean drinking water and a little education I'm sure waving a banner and frothing at the mouth seems like the only option.

HUGH. Hear, hear.

TRUDI. I'm sorry but I really felt like I needed to say that.

PETER *catches her eye and there is a look between them. He looks a little worried – as if there is something of* KRISTIN *growing in her.*

PETER. Are you feeling okay?

TRUDI. I'm fine.

PETER. I can't find my toothbrush.

TRUDI. I put it in the bag.

PETER. It isn't in there, I checked.

TRUDI. I'm sure I put it in the bag.

PETER. I couldn't see it.

TRUDI. I'll find it for you.

They leave the room just as KRISTIN *is entering.*

KRISTIN. Good morning.

HUGH. Hello, darling.

TRUDI. Hi, Kristin.

CLAIRE. Hello.

PETER. Hi.

HUGH. The coffee's hot.

PETER *and* TRUDI *exit.*

KRISTIN. Is Simon still in bed?

CLAIRE. No, he's gone.

KRISTIN. Gone?

CLAIRE. He left at seven.

HUGH. None of us got to say goodbye.

KRISTIN. How do you mean, he's gone?

CLAIRE. He'll be home by now.

KRISTIN. I thought he'd stay for breakfast.

CLAIRE. He didn't sleep much.

KRISTIN. I thought I'd see him.

CLAIRE. And then I woke up and he was gone.

KRISTIN. I see.

Pause. HUGH *senses that he should leave the two women alone. He checks his pockets.*

HUGH. I've left that bloody car key on the bedside table.

He leaves the room. There is a pause as KRISTIN *goes to the cafetière and pours herself a cup of coffee.*

KRISTIN. I'm surprised you're still here.

CLAIRE. Are you?

KRISTIN. Just a little.

CLAIRE. I'm not in make-up till eleven.

Pause.

Besides, I wanted to talk to you.

KRISTIN. Oh?

CLAIRE. I don't think I'll be seeing you again.

KRISTIN. Won't you?

CLAIRE. So I thought it only right to say goodbye. Consider it a mark of respect.

Pause.

I don't know what you and Simon talked about last night. But when he came back to the room he woke me up and we chatted till dawn. You'll be happy to hear we've decided to part ways.

KRISTIN. Have you indeed?

CLAIRE. Don't flatter yourself into believing that it was your doing. It was inevitable. We've just been putting it off, that's all. I'm surprised we lasted for a year and a half.

KRISTIN. So am I.

CLAIRE. He said he realised the only reason he was attracted to me was because I was the polar opposite of you.

KRISTIN. I'm sure he meant it as a compliment.

CLAIRE. I'm sure he did.

Pause. KRISTIN *puts down her coffee and starts to busy herself around the kitchen – she gets a dishcloth from the sink and starts to wipe down the kitchen table.*

It's funny. When you said last night that you thought I was good in *A Doll's House*, my heart missed a beat. I nearly leapt for joy. How do you do that?

KRISTIN. I really wouldn't know.

CLAIRE. Did I ever tell you about my father?

KRISTIN. Your father?

CLAIRE. I watched him slowly drown in a mountain of unpaid bills.
When I was thirteen he was declared bankrupt. I used to come
home every day after school and the bathroom door was always
closed and the sound was always the same – the sound of my
mother's stifled sobs. Then she'd come out with a smile on her
face and cook dinner. One day, he left and never came back. My
mother and I moved to a small rented flat and lived on benefits.
The first day I moved my bed and there was a whole lot of blood
on the wall. I spent all my time in that flat wondering what had
happened before we arrived. I came up with quite a few upsetting
scenarios. I had a vivid imagination.

Pause.

Since then most of my life I've been running away from unpaid
bills, stifled sobs and those dark-red stains. That may have
affected some of my artistic choices.

Pause.

That's my individual story. But something tells me that
somewhere along the line you've stopped listening to people's
individual stories. I wonder when that happened.

Pause. She waits for something from KRISTIN *but nothing
comes.*

There's a part of me that admires you. The way you've held onto
the things you've believed in. But your idealism has turned into
hardness, Kristin. It has a thick, thick shell. *You* do. A carapace.
Isn't that the word?

KRISTIN. Is it?

CLAIRE. 'Why does she demonise me like that?' I kept asking
myself. 'Why does she vilify me? Why does she scrutinise
everything I do and then condemn it without a second thought?'

KRISTIN. Is that what I do?

CLAIRE. And then I decided it's got nothing to do with me really.
It's not about me.

KRISTIN. Isn't it?

CLAIRE. It's about you, Kristin.

KRISTIN. Oh?

CLAIRE. When I was in my room last night I had a little bit of a revelation.

KRISTIN. That must have been a novel experience.

CLAIRE. They say, don't they, that when people get older they just become worse versions of themselves.

KRISTIN. Is that what they say?

CLAIRE. Maybe in some people that's a little more pronounced.

KRISTIN. Maybe.

CLAIRE. And I expect it's really a case of having to hold onto everything you are. Everything you *were*. The choices you made, the paths you followed. Because if you start to question them, if you start to doubt them… well, then you're fucked really, aren't you?

KRISTIN. I wouldn't know.

CLAIRE. So you hang on with every fibre of your being.

Pause.

It must be exhausting being you.

KRISTIN. Thank you for that searing insight. But I'd stick to the acting if I were you.

TRUDI *and* PETER *return, followed by* HUGH.

TRUDI. It was in the bag, of course.

KRISTIN. Have you all had breakfast?

TRUDI. I've had some cereal.

HUGH. I called the electrician. He'll be here by noon.

KRISTIN. Thank you.

PETER. Sweetie, do you want some more coffee?

TRUDI. Thanks, honey.

PETER *fills up theirs cups.*

CLAIRE. I really ought to be making a move.

KRISTIN. Drive carefully.

PETER. We ought to get going soon too.

TRUDI. Your flight is at two.

KRISTIN. Where are you off to this time?

PETER. Botswana.

HUGH. You really do go to the most extraordinary places.

PETER. Yes.

HUGH. You global adventurer, you.

TRUDI. And you haven't even packed yet.

CLAIRE. Bye, Peter.

She kisses PETER *on the cheek.*

PETER. Bye. I'm sorry that –

CLAIRE. It's fine.

PETER. But I hope we see you again.

CLAIRE. Maybe.

TRUDI. We'll look out for the…

CLAIRE. Weeknights at seven. On Sky.

TRUDI. I look forward to it.

CLAIRE. Trudi.

TRUDI. It was great to meet you. And I'm sorry if I sounded a little defensive just now –

CLAIRE. It's fine.

TRUDI. But I felt at that particular moment that I needed to say what was on my mind.

CLAIRE. As I said, you're very lucky to have something to believe in.

TRUDI. And I'm sorry about your Japanese dress.

CLAIRE *walks up to* KRISTIN.

CLAIRE. Kristin.

KRISTIN. Claire.

CLAIRE. Don't forget to eat the mango meringue.

CLAIRE *gives* KRISTIN *an unexpected kiss on the cheek.*
KRISTIN *is slightly taken aback by it.*

KRISTIN. Take care.

CLAIRE. It's been challenging.

TRUDI. Bye, Claire.

HUGH. Cheerio.

CLAIRE. Bye.

She leaves.

HUGH. Enjoy Thursday.

Pause.

Right. I have some urgent gardening to attend to.

KRISTIN. Don't want to neglect your turnips.

HUGH. Certainly not.

A slight pause.

TRUDI. Before you go, Hugh, I… sweetie?

She looks at PETER *but he doesn't pick up.*

The thing is that when we came here last night we were expecting… well, we had something that we wanted to share with you –

PETER. Oh.

TRUDI. Something that we wished, something that we *hoped* would make you very happy.

HUGH. I'm riveted.

TRUDI. But then the evening took an unexpected turn.

HUGH. Did it?

TRUDI. And it just didn't seem appropriate at the time to…

PETER. To tell you.

HUGH. The suspense is killing me.

TRUDI. But now, this morning, I don't see why we shouldn't, so the thing we wanted to tell you is –

PETER. Sweetie.

TRUDI. Is that we're engaged. To be married. To each other.

Pause.

HUGH. How glorious.

TRUDI. Of course, I didn't really envision telling you like this.

PETER. No.

TRUDI. I had imagined that after dinner, maybe after you'd blown out the candles on your cake –

HUGH. That fucking mango thing.

TRUDI. And we were all sitting around the table, all together, that Peter and I, well, one of us at least would stand up and sort of announce it and then we'd have some more champagne. That's how I imagined it.

KRISTIN. Things rarely turn out the way we expected.

TRUDI. I'm beginning to see that.

PETER. Anyway, it's true, we're getting married.

KRISTIN (*checking the fridge*). I'm afraid we're all out of champagne.

HUGH. Must have been all that marvellous celebrating we did last night.

KRISTIN. But congratulations.

TRUDI. Thank you.

KRISTIN. Really, congratulations.

HUGH. Have you got a date?

PETER. A date?

HUGH. For the big day.

TRUDI. May next year.

HUGH. A spring wedding.

TRUDI. And then a honeymoon in the Middle East.

KRISTIN. The Middle East?

HUGH. Interesting choice.

TRUDI. Syria, Egypt, the Holy Land.

KRISTIN. Will you be looking for the Holy Grail?

TRUDI. It's just that I've always wanted to see that part of the world.

PETER. Me too.

KRISTIN. You've never told me that.

PETER. I don't tell you everything.

HUGH. Israel?

TRUDI. Sure. Jerusalem. Bethlehem. Just to see, really, what it's like.

KRISTIN. A pilgrimage of sorts.

TRUDI. If you want to call it that. It's just I'm not really a beach person.

KRISTIN. No.

TRUDI. So I prefer trips that have a cultural relevance. Historical, that kind of thing.

KRISTIN. Religious.

TRUDI. I promise I won't have Peter baptised in the River Jordan.

KRISTIN. That's a relief.

TRUDI. Just to see where it all started.

KRISTIN. Why don't you do Greece? Athens, Delphi.

HUGH. Even their choice of honeymoon is a threat to her.

KRISTIN. The Greek islands are beautiful in May.

She walks over to PETER *and kisses him on the cheek.*

But congratulations.

Pause. With some hesitation and awkwardness she also kisses TRUDI *on the cheek.*

TRUDI. Kristin, can I ask you a favour?

KRISTIN. Go on then.

TRUDI. One more thing before we go.

KRISTIN. What is it?

TRUDI. You know how much I love your house. I mean, the way you've decorated it. And Peter was saying the other day that the most beautiful room in the house is your study. The room you work in.

KRISTIN. I'm listening.

TRUDI. And I was just wondering if before we leave I could just look at it. Stick my head in the door kind of thing. But I realise that you may not want me to. That it's private, sacred to you. So if you don't want me to, that's fine. I'll understand.

KRISTIN. Why wouldn't I want you to?

TRUDI. I'll completely understand.

KRISTIN. It's not private, at least not when I'm not in there working and it's certainly not sacred. I'm not a priest.

TRUDI. Thank you. I'll just stick my head in the door.

KRISTIN. I'll show it to you.

TRUDI. Thank you.

KRISTIN. Oh, and we might as well pick up that book I was telling you about. The one on African tribal art. It's to the right of my desk somewhere, in a pile. We'll have a look at it and see if I can find anything.

TRUDI. Sure.

KRISTIN. We'll be back in a minute.

HUGH. And then I really must move my skinny arse.

KRISTIN *and* TRUDI *leave the room.* HUGH *has returned to perusing the newspaper.*

PETER. Anything interesting?

HUGH. Just the usual. Famine, war and celebrity facelifts.

PETER. Nice.

HUGH. What an enlightened species we are.

Pause.

Call me a witness for the defence.

PETER. Sorry?

HUGH. I think it's time for my testimony.

PETER. What testimony?

HUGH. I was there. I saw. I heard. I know.

PETER. Know what?

HUGH. I'm not saying you don't have an argument, I'm not saying that you – and Simon, God bless him – haven't paid a price, haven't a right to recriminate, to attack, to feel all those tangled, seething feelings that you do. But I was there.

PETER. What are you talking about?

HUGH. And last night, when you went for her jugular, I wanted to go for yours. Even though I was trying to hold down a very disagreeable serving of beef in oyster sauce.

PETER. So?

HUGH. So, I'm the peacemaker. I'm also rather English. I'd rather have a limb amputated than make a scene. But last night I wanted to go for you, boy.

PETER. I was provoked.

HUGH. Oh, I know, she is to moderation and diplomacy what I am to heterosexuality – she just doesn't do it.

PETER. She doesn't.

HUGH. But I still wanted to grab you by the neck and say, 'I was there. I'm a witness.'

Pause.

You may joke about Gauloises cigarettes but you didn't know her back then. Before it all went so terribly wrong. I don't know about the others. Those men and women who were also there, doing what we were doing. Marching in our sandals, as Claire put it. And maybe she's right, maybe all they really wanted was to move to big houses in Islington. But there was something in your mother's eyes that was genuine.

PETER. Genuine?

HUGH. She was extraordinary. '*Visionary*' is the word.

PETER. Okay.

HUGH. The thing you really need to know is that I can put my hand on my heart and say to you that in those eyes I saw that she thought – naively, maybe, who knows – that she was doing it all for you.

PETER. Is that what you saw?

HUGH. But then you'd need to believe that people like that actually exist. People who care in that particular way. And maybe you don't any more.

PETER. I don't understand what you –

HUGH. Chew on that a little while, you ingrate.

KRISTIN *and* TRUDI *return.* KRISTIN *is holding a large book on African art.*

TRUDI. That is such a beautiful room, Kristin.

KRISTIN. I'm glad you like it.

TRUDI. It's atmospheric and so cosy.

KRISTIN. Thank you.

KRISTIN *sits at the table, opens the book and starts to scour the index.*

Right, what country did you say it was from?

PETER. Liberia.

TRUDI. And all those books. Books, books, books. Books everywhere.

KRISTIN. Yes.

TRUDI. I've never seen so many books in my life.

KRISTIN. Haven't you?

TRUDI. And the view. The way you've positioned the desk. To sit there, looking out over the fields and the hills, thinking of what you're going to write next.

KRISTIN. I won't be writing anything for some time. Here we go – Liberia. Masks.

HUGH. I'm off.

TRUDI. It's been really wonderful to meet you, Hugh.

HUGH. Likewise. You really are a rather adorable creature.

TRUDI. Thank you.

HUGH. And I'm very happy that you're planning to teach this man a little sense. Religious or not is not really the point. You're a sensible girl, I can tell.

KRISTIN. I'll call you this evening.

HUGH. Do. And I'll see you on Saturday.

KRISTIN. You will.

HUGH. I'll pick you up and then we'll take the train. We need to be in London by eleven at the latest so I'll be here eight-thirtyish.

KRISTIN. Good.

TRUDI. What's happening on Saturday?

HUGH. A pro-Kurdish march.

PETER. Naturally.

HUGH. So I'll see you then.

KRISTIN. I'll be ready.

He kisses her.

HUGH. We never ate that fucking cake.

KRISTIN. No.

HUGH. Have it for lunch.

KRISTIN. Or we could have some now.

TRUDI. I'm okay, thanks, Kristin.

PETER. Me too.

HUGH *kisses* TRUDI.

HUGH. Look after the brute.

TRUDI. I'll try.

HUGH. Have fun in Burundi.

PETER. Botswana.

HUGH. Try not to exploit the locals too horribly.

KRISTIN. It's his job.

PETER. Goodbye, Hugh.

HUGH. Goodbye.

He moves towards the door then stops and turns to look at PETER.

Remember what I said about the eyes.

KRISTIN. What eyes?

HUGH *leaves*.

PETER. We really should make a move too.

TRUDI. Okay, sweetie.

PETER. I just need to use the bathroom. And I'll get the bag.

TRUDI. Sure.

PETER *leaves the room. There is a pause.* KRISTIN *continues to look through the book.*

It's funny.

KRISTIN. What is?

TRUDI. When we were in your study I happened to glance up at your bookshelves and I let my eyes scan all the titles, you know, the spines of the books and… Can I ask you something?

KRISTIN. You may.

TRUDI. Is it just my imagination or have you… what I'm asking is have your books been ordered chronologically? Have you ordered them chronologically?

KRISTIN. I have.

TRUDI. Why have you done that?

KRISTIN. At heart I'm an optimist.

TRUDI. An optimist?

KRISTIN. I like to believe that we're evolving in some way.

TRUDI. Anyway, I noticed. I started at one side and there were lots of names and many of them were women. And then slowly there were fewer and fewer of them. Women, I mean. And I think it was only like the 1950s. And by the end of the second shelf it was all men. And poor George Eliot, all on her own.

KRISTIN. Yes.

TRUDI. I mean, you forget how recent it is.

KRISTIN. Do you?

TRUDI. I suppose what I'm saying is that something happened in the sixties, the seventies. All these women's voices.

KRISTIN. Yes.

TRUDI. I mean, we all know that we've been living in a patriarchal world, in a masculine… What's the word?

KRISTIN. Ordering?

TRUDI. Ordering of the world, that's right. They've made a bit of a… what's that expression that Peter's always using… a dog's dinner?

KRISTIN. Yes, that's a good expression.

TRUDI. They've made a bit of a dog's dinner of it on their own, haven't they?

KRISTIN. You could say that.

TRUDI. But that something happened that had never quite happened before. And if there was one thing worth fighting for, one thing worth holding onto, it was that. So thank you, I suppose is what I'm saying.

Pause. KRISTIN *has found what she was looking for.*

KRISTIN. Eureka. Well, it's close enough anyway.

TRUDI. What is?

KRISTIN. Wouldn't you say? I mean, look – the forehead, the broadness of it, the shape.

KRISTIN *shows* TRUDI *the photograph she has found in the book.* TRUDI *picks up the mask to compare it.*

TRUDI. Oh my God, that's incredible.

KRISTIN. The similarity.

TRUDI. They're almost exactly the same.

KRISTIN. Aren't they just?

TRUDI. What does it say?

KRISTIN. Wait. Let's see.

TRUDI. How weird. They're almost identical.

KRISTIN (*reading from the book*). 'Mask from the Sande society, a woman's association found in Liberia, Sierra Leone and Guinea that champions women's social and political interests and promotes their solidarity vis-à-vis the Poro, a complementary institution for men. The broad forehead and long face, commonly used in masks from this region, are associated with the sense of responsibility and duty that accompanies the privileged position of power and influence. The wearers of this mask would connect to the spirit of the community in which they lived and experience the insight that the survival and well-being of the individual is inexorably interdependent with the survival and well-being of that very community.'

TRUDI. I was thinking. The pioneers. The first ones in uncharted territory. The map-makers. They're the ones who pay the price so that the rest of us don't have to.

Pause.

And I know why you didn't write about them in your book. Why you didn't even mention them.

KRISTIN. Oh?

TRUDI. Because you couldn't.

Pause.

Some things are so big, aren't they? Too big. If you had even put pen to paper and written their names, the earth would have opened up beneath your feet. You would never have been able to write the book. The *loss*.

She waits for KRISTIN *to respond but she doesn't.*

I know. I understand. It's only human.

PETER *returns. He is holding their overnight bag.*

PETER. Done.

KRISTIN. Are you sure you don't want another coffee for the road?

PETER. We really must be going.

TRUDI *realises that she needs to leave* PETER *alone with* KRISTIN *for a moment.*

TRUDI. I've left my coat next door.

PETER. Okay.

TRUDI. I'll only be a minute.

She leaves the room. There is a pause as PETER *and* KRISTIN *are left alone.* KRISTIN *picks up the mask which* TRUDI *has left on the table.*

PETER. The things I said last night.

KRISTIN. What about them?

PETER. Maybe I got carried away.

KRISTIN. No, you didn't. You said what you've always wanted to say, and so did your brother. It's fine. I can take it. I'm a big girl.

PETER. Can you?

Pause.

KRISTIN. That day. I went to the school to pick you up and he had taken you. I ran around the streets like some mad woman. I opened your cupboards. Your clothes were gone. Your books, your toys. In one day the house seemed to change for ever. Its rooms echoed. I was alone.

Pause.

Something about me finding my voice threatened him. Oh, he was progressive. He called himself a liberal. An enlightened man in every sense of the word. Theoretically. But when the moment came he couldn't quite live up to it. So he twisted my arm, twisted *my soul* into making a choice. And I had to take a stand.

TRUDI *comes back in her coat.*

TRUDI. Okay.

PETER. Let's go.

KRISTIN. I know. Botswana.

TRUDI. I'm ready.

KRISTIN. Off you go.

TRUDI. It's been such a privilege to meet you, Kristin.

KRISTIN. I've enjoyed meeting you too.

TRUDI. I'd love to see you again soon.

KRISTIN. I'm sure we'll be seeing a lot of each other.

PETER. Not if I can help it.

TRUDI. Thank you so much for everything.

KRISTIN. You're very welcome.

PETER. I'll call you when I'm back.

KRISTIN. Do that.

TRUDI. Bye, Kristin.

They open the door and are about to leave.

KRISTIN. Don't let the thugs win, Peter.

PETER. I'll do my best.

TRUDI. Bye-bye.

KRISTIN. Remember, work is about offering.

PETER. Is it?

KRISTIN. Not usury.

PETER. I'll make a note of that.

PETER *leaves and* TRUDI *is about to follow him but she stays back.*

TRUDI. Kristin.

KRISTIN. Trudi?

TRUDI. One last thing.

KRISTIN. Go on.

TRUDI. That thing I said last night. About forgiveness.

KRISTIN. Oh, that.

TRUDI. I think you misunderstood me.

KRISTIN. I did?

TRUDI. I didn't mean their father. I wasn't talking about you forgiving their father.

There is a beat as TRUDI *waits to see if* KRISTIN *has understood what she means. Then, when she knows that she has, she walks forward and embraces her.* KRISTIN *does not respond – it is as if she is frozen.*

TRUDI *leaves the room and* KRISTIN *does not move. She is like a pillar of stone. A few seconds pass. She looks down and notices that she is still holding the mask. She studies it. And then, slowly, her mouth slowly opens and a sound starts to emerge – something like a wail, something like the sound of an animal in distress. She begins to tremble, her body is taken over by a sweeping surge of emotion, something that has been restrained and repressed for many years.*

Slowly, with difficulty, she recovers. She comes to stand in the middle of the room, clutching the mask against her chest and staring ahead.

The End.

THE FAITH MACHINE

'Life is lived forwards but understood backwards'

Søren Kierkegaard

The Faith Machine was first performed at the Jerwood Theatre Downstairs at the Royal Court Theatre, London, on 25 August 2011, with the following cast:

TOM	Kyle Soller
SOPHIE	Hayley Atwell
EDWARD	Ian McDiarmid
PATRICK/LAWRENCE	Jude Akuwudike
TATYANA	Bronagh Gallagher
SEBASTIAN	Alan Westaway
ANNIE	Maya Wasowicz
AGATHA	Kezrena James

Director	Jamie Lloyd
Designer	Mark Thompson
Lighting Designer	Neil Austin
Music & Sound Designer	Alex Baranowski

Characters

in order of speaking

TOM, *ages from twenty-four to thirty-seven during the play,*
    American
SOPHIE, *ages from twenty-two to thirty-four during the play, English*
EDWARD, *in his seventies, English*
PATRICK, *in his forties, Black Kenyan*
TATYANA, *in her thirties or forties, Russian*
SEBASTIAN, *in his forties, Chilean*
LAWRENCE, *ages from thirties to forties, Black British*
ANNIE, *in her thirties, American*
AGATHA, *seventeen*

PATRICK *and* LAWRENCE *are to be played by the same actor.*

Bold letters in the Russian pronunciation indicate stress.

ACT ONE

Scene One

2001

New York radio: something about the weather, it being a sunny September morning, maybe a traffic update.

Lights up:

The bedroom of TOM*'s apartment in downtown Manhattan. A slick, expensive place, sparsely but tastefully furnished – the home of a young, successful man.*

Early morning. TOM *is still in his dressing gown but gets dressed during the scene.* SOPHIE *is half-dressed. She is putting things into a suitcase. She packs throughout the scene.*

TOM. So what are you asking me to do?

> *She doesn't answer.*

> Because I have a feeling that if you finish packing that bag – will you please stop, just put that down, stop packing that bag, will you, GIVE ME THAT AT LEAST, put the fucking – whatever that is – put it down.

> *She stops packing.*

> Thank you. That if you finish packing that bag, that if you leave New York this afternoon, if you go back to London, then fuck me I don't know where that leaves us, but I don't know –

SOPHIE. I need to think.

TOM. – if we can ever pick things up is what I'm saying, *resume* things, because if you really want me to be honest here –

SOPHIE. You know I do.

TOM. – well, to be honest I feel judged, *vilified* in some way, frowned upon, Jesus, yes, just continuously judged –

SOPHIE. By me?

> *She resumes packing her bag.*

TOM. – and I'm sorry I'm not Jesus or Mahatma Gandhi or fuck knows who you want me to be –

SOPHIE. I want you to be you.

TOM. – but the fact is, Sophie, this is who I am, and you just have to *accept* that: a good man who happens to work in a field that you – fuck me, I don't know, *disapprove* of – a good man who just happens to work in advertising.

SOPHIE. I know you work in advertising, Tom, I know how things evolved –

TOM. It's what I do.

SOPHIE. – to what they are, and I know that the world needs to keep turning.

TOM. Oh, you do?

SOPHIE. Buying, selling, supply, demand.

TOM. And it's advertising that helped us move into this apartment –

SOPHIE. I liked Brooklyn.

TOM. – and that happily funded your postgraduate degree at Columbia.

SOPHIE. My inheritance could have paid for that.

TOM. It's all you fucking have.

SOPHIE. But there's a line, Tom. That's all. A line.

TOM. A line?

SOPHIE. Let's call it the Fletcher line.

TOM. Jesus.

Pause.

SOPHIE. Why did you take the Fletcher contract, Tom?

TOM. Because it's a means to an end.

SOPHIE. Why did you chase it?

TOM. Because it opens doors. Because another two contracts like it and I can stop working. And then fuck knows, maybe we *can* save the world –

SOPHIE. You're believing your own sound bites.

TOM. Build a fucking orphanage in Kenya, Vietnam.

SOPHIE. 'It's a means to an end.'

TOM. Fucking Mozambique.

SOPHIE. Jesus, Tom.

TOM. I mean, I have been working so fucking hard –

SOPHIE. *What for?*

TOM. Joe Ikeman called me yesterday and said, 'It's unheard of.'

SOPHIE. I'm sure it is.

TOM. He said, 'For someone who's been writing copy for less than three years to head the Fletcher account is amazing. It's history, advertising history.'

SOPHIE. '*The Power to Heal*'. It's pithy, I'll give you that. No wonder they liked your pitch, you should be proud.

TOM. Well, fuck you, Sophie, I am proud and you know I too wish we lived in some idyllic, some, no, what's the word, *utopian* world, yes, if we lived in a fucking utopia then I would be earning a hell of a lot of money –

SOPHIE. We don't need a lot.

TOM. – for writing confessional novels about dysfunctional childhoods, but I'm afraid we don't, we live in the real world –

SOPHIE. Is that what it's called?

TOM. – and the real word is harsh, and cruel and full of compromise.

SOPHIE. Leave the ad-speak at work, I beg you. Let's keep something untouched.

Pause. EDWARD *walks into the room: they cannot see him.*

TOM. And this is all about your father, by the way.

SOPHIE. No, it isn't.

TOM. And I keep saying to myself it's part of the mourning process, one of the phases, you know, what do they say, the seven stages of mourning –

SOPHIE. Five.

TOM. So this is maybe stage five because ever since he died he's like, I don't know like, he's in this bedroom with us –

SOPHIE. The bedroom?

TOM. And I can understand it, I mean, the man was exceptional in every possible way, visionary and courageous and profound –

SOPHIE. He was.

EDWARD. Thank you, darling.

TOM. But having him in our bedroom twenty-four-seven isn't exactly conducive to a healthy relationship.

SOPHIE. Are you saying I can't think for myself?

EDWARD. His socks are inside out.

TOM. I'm saying that you need to let go of certain dogmatic ways of seeing things which are filled to the brim with the love of humanity, whatever you want to call it – but which are also incompatible with the world we happen to be living in right now and – dare, I say it, ever so slightly obsolete and archaic.

EDWARD. Ethics?

SOPHIE. Ethics are obsolete and archaic?

TOM. So it really is time to let him go.

EDWARD. Oh, he provokes.

SOPHIE. Your socks are inside out.

TOM. Jesus, the time!

Pause. He takes them off, puts them on again the right way round.

EDWARD. Show him the file.

SOPHIE. The file.

TOM. What file?

EDWARD. You've done your homework, you have the evidence. Show him the file.

SOPHIE. I've put together a file.

TOM. What file?

EDWARD. Show it to him, Sophie.

She walks over to the bedside table and opens the drawer. She takes out a thin cardboard file.

SOPHIE. The Fletcher file.

TOM. First we had the Fletcher line, now we have the Fletcher file. I'm intrigued.

EDWARD. That's a start.

TOM. And pray tell, what is this Fletcher file?

EDWARD. Read it to him.

SOPHIE. Cases, case histories, that kind of thing. Clippings, articles, the odd opinion piece. Gleaned from the internet mostly, and the library.

TOM. You've been busy.

EDWARD. Very.

SOPHIE. I know you're late for work so I'll keep it brief.

TOM. How considerate.

She opens the file and starts going through the clippings.

SOPHIE. Most of it I won't bore you with, endless examples of corruption, bribery, fiddling, what not, unethical this, unethical that, pretty much what you'd expect from one of the world's leading pharmaceuticals.

TOM. Okay.

SOPHIE. I won't even go into the spurious marketing of four drugs including –

TOM. Detoxtrin.

SOPHIE. – thank you, and Flaxorin which led to seven deaths including that of a six-year-old epileptic girl in Minnesota last year, which followed the wilful suppression of unfavourable studies –

TOM. There was a settlement –

SOPHIE. Yes, I'm sure her parents are living in splendour somewhere –

TOM. Remind me again why we're doing this.

EDWARD. Because you need to hear it.

SOPHIE. Or the continuous promotion of various drugs for non-approved uses, including, of course, the misbranding of Fenerak, the destroying of documents pertinent to the investigation being a detail I'll just skim over in this instance –

TOM. What is your point?

SOPHIE. And instead I'll just focus if you don't mind on the one case –

TOM. Uganda.

SOPHIE. – using it perhaps – as the most telling example of your new client's – *character* and – as a launch pad, if you like, for me to discover –

TOM. Interrogate.

SOPHIE. – who it is I'm living with these days.

TOM. Fuck you, Sophie.

EDWARD. Read it to him.

Pause. She takes a deep breath before launching into it. She reads from a clipping, interjecting from time to time with her own remarks.

SOPHIE. 'Two years ago, in 1999, an outbreak of measles, cholera and bacterial meningitis occurred in a region of Eastern Uganda –

TOM. I know all this.

EDWARD. Louder, with feeling.

SOPHIE (*increasing in volume and intensity*). About one hundred and twenty miles north of the capital, Kampala. Representatives of Fletcher's were there within a fortnight to assist' –

EDWARD. Assist!

SOPHIE. That's the word it uses – *assist* – 'the affected population. An experimental antibiotic, Maloflaxacin, was administered to approximately three hundred children. Local officials reported that more than one hundred of those children died from infection within two days of ingesting the drug, whilst the great majority of the rest developed mental and physical deformities.

TOM. I said I know all this.

SOPHIE. According to consistent reports of various witnesses, Fletcher administered the Maloflaxacin *without* parental consent.'

TOM. It's going to court.

SOPHIE. I know, here it is, there's more: 'In the lawsuits, Fletcher is accused of using the outbreak to perform unapproved human testing as well as allegedly under-dosing a control group –

EDWARD. *Unapproved human testing*.

SOPHIE. – being treated with traditional antibiotics in order to skew the results of the trial in favor of Maloflaxacin.'

TOM. Would you please tell me where the fuck this is leading?

SOPHIE. It's leading, I suppose, to the fundamental question, Tom, which is not 'What are you doing working with these people?' or 'How do you feel in your heart helping this company promote an image of themselves which is at the very least dishonest?' or not even 'In abetting a criminal – '

TOM. Abetting?

EDWARD. That's the word.

SOPHIE. ' – do you in fact become an accomplice to the crimes of murder, perjury, corruption…'

TOM. For fuck's sake.

SOPHIE. But the question it's leading to, the essential question to which I need to know the answer, Tom, if we are to continue living together, trying to form a *home* together, is quite simple really and the question is –

TOM. You're unbelievable.

EDWARD. 'Who are you?'

SOPHIE. Is 'Who are you, Tom?' Who are you? Who are you?

TOM. Who am I?

Pause.

SOPHIE. Are you, for instance – and this is just one possible strand, one of many directions we can choose to go in – are you, for instance, a *racist*, Tom?

TOM. How can you even ask that?

SOPHIE. And as a racist I don't necessarily mean someone who walks around in a hooded white top with – I don't know – a pitchfork or a blazing torch in his hand – no, that would be crude, too obvious –

TOM. How can you fucking ask that?

SOPHIE. But more someone who believes that the life of a child born in another part of the world, who just happens to be of a different colour and belongs to a whole other socio-economic group from his dear self, is not quite worth the same as that of a child living in, let's say, I don't know, Hartford, Connecticut or Paris, France?

TOM. The fact that you even –

SOPHIE. Because it feels to me, Tom, that your new friends at Fletcher do make that distinction, they make it most emphatically by choosing to send their teams to Uganda in order to 'assist' in this particular way, knowing full well that they're using those children as laboratory animals all in the pursuit of nothing more than the bottom dollar.

TOM. You're simplifying things.

SOPHIE. Because their lives are expendable, worthless, replaceable.

EDWARD. Simplifying things?

TOM. Things don't change overnight.

EDWARD. *The best lack all conviction.*

SOPHIE. Things don't change at all, Tom, unless you force them.

Pause.

TOM. So what are you asking me to do? I don't have the time to sit here in this room having abstract conversations about –

EDWARD. Abstract?

SOPHIE. They're *abstract*?

TOM. – about the choices we make, about moral decisions, about what it means to survive in a particular society –

EDWARD. To *thrive* in a particular society.

SOPHIE. Nothing abstract about what we're talking about.

TOM. Of which we are all a part, like it or not, in which we all try to do the best we can –

EDWARD. Do we?

TOM. – realistically, I mean, within the confines, the constrictions of the real world –

SOPHIE. There it is again, that real world you insist on referring to –

EDWARD. You create that world, Tom, you're creating it now.

SOPHIE. – as if you're implying you're trapped in it, some hapless prisoner –

TOM. Realistically, practically, what are you asking me to do?

SOPHIE. – instead of an active, conscious member of it who has the power not only to question it but to challenge, oppose, radicalise and reconstruct it.

TOM. Realistically.

SOPHIE. Because that is the person I thought you were.

EDWARD. *The Power to Heal.*

TOM. Jesus.

Pause.

EDWARD. Test him.

SOPHIE. I want you to go in today and turn it down. Turn down the Fletcher contract.

EDWARD. Test his mettle.

TOM. You what?

SOPHIE. I want you to go into work today and tell Roger Hartmann that you are turning down the Fletcher contract. That you don't want anything to do with it.

TOM. An ultimatum.

SOPHIE. Other jobs, fine, other contracts. But not this one.

TOM. So you're blackmailing me.

SOPHIE. Am I?

TOM. I think that's what it's called. I think you're saying 'Turn down the Fletcher contract or I'm going to England and there's a good chance I may not return.'

EDWARD. That is what she's saying.

TOM. Well, I can't do it, even if I wanted to.

SOPHIE. Why not?

TOM. Not that I do because I will not be blackmailed, Sophie, held to fucking ransom.

SOPHIE. Why can't you do it?

TOM. I can't turn around after eight months of prepping for the fucking thing and say, 'You know what, Roger, I have ethical concerns.'

SOPHIE. I don't want to go, Tom. But the simple fact is that if you go ahead with the Fletcher contract, I don't know if I'll be able to live with you any more.

TOM. Be careful what you're saying, Sophie.

SOPHIE. I know what I'm saying, Tom.

TOM. Be careful what you're saying.

EDWARD. She knows what she's saying.

TOM. You fucking wait till now –

SOPHIE. You knew how I felt about it.

TOM. And you fucking threaten me –

SOPHIE. We talked about it in the summer, when it first came up –

TOM. Blackmail me –

SOPHIE. You knew what I thought –

TOM. Not like this, you never said –

SOPHIE. You always knew.

TOM. Not that you were going to put me in this position.

EDWARD. Because you wanted him to do it himself.

SOPHIE. And if nothing else, I mean, even if you can't dig deep enough to find some kind of regret, I don't know, something in you like a conscience, something stirring deep inside your soul that reminds you that there are inescapable –

EDWARD. Ancient.

SOPHIE. Inescapable ancient truths nagging at you, tearing at you, saying over and over again –

EDWARD. You are your brother's keeper, Tom.

SOPHIE. – that you are your brother's keeper, Tom, but if nothing else, then realise at least that this constant injustice, *racism*, these laws that favour only the fortunate –

TOM. Jesus Christ.

SOPHIE. – will come back to you –

EDWARD. A hundredfold.

SOPHIE. – a thousandfold, Tom, like some fucking karmic boomerang, because everything, every choice you make has its consequences. Whether or not you're consciously aware of it.

Pause.

That's all.

A long pause.

TOM. You're mad, Sophie. I love you so much but you're completely mad. If you feel that you have to go –

SOPHIE. I don't want to.

TOM. – then you must go. But I can't drop the job. Not now. I *won't* drop the job. I'd like it if you stayed and supported me but if you…

SOPHIE. *Please, Tom.*

TOM. I can't. I won't. End of.

Pause.

EDWARD. *The blood-dimmed tide is loosed.*

And then, suddenly, the sound of a jet engine can be heard approaching. It increases in volume and then for a second, as it passes overhead, it is deafening.

Just as suddenly, silence.

Blackout…

Scene Two

1998

…or maybe a single light remains on EDWARD*: he stays in the middle of the space and the scene changes around him. The apartment fades away and we are transported to* EDWARD*'s house on the island of Patmos in Greece. In sharp contrast to the slick minimalism of the first scene, this space is warm, colourful, soulful. It is a terrace but at the back of the space we see some of the*

interior: a room full of books, pictures, strange and beautiful objects – many of them with religious or tribal significance – collected from various trips and experiences around the world. The living museum of EDWARD*'s soul.*

As if it can't contain itself, some of the house's objects seem to have overspilt onto the terrace and have invaded some of the outside space as well: a pile or two of books, a picture leaning against an outside wall, an armchair, a stack of old newspapers tied with strings. At the centre of the terrace stands a large oak table, the kind of table around which the whole day is spent. This is the home of a brilliant, eccentric, slightly chaotic polymath.

It is an early evening in September. EDWARD *stands on one side of the terrace, and directly opposite him stands* PATRICK. *He holds a briefcase and is slightly out of breath; he has just arrived.*

EDWARD. You found me.

PATRICK. Persistence.

EDWARD. I'm warning you, I'm not a happy man.

PATRICK. We're not going to let go of you as easily as that.

EDWARD. You've come in vain.

PATRICK. Hello, Edward.

EDWARD. Patrick.

PATRICK. That was a dramatic exit you made.

EDWARD. I was feeling dramatic.

PATRICK. Well, you certainly made an impression. 1998 will be remembered as a vintage year.

EDWARD. Plenty of blood and gore but this time it was the gays who were being thrown to the lions and the Christians who were doing the cheering.

PATRICK. I wouldn't describe it like that.

EDWARD. I use the word Christians, of course, with just a tinge of irony.

PATRICK. Difficult days.

EDWARD. And then there were the ones sitting firmly on the fence. They're the worst of the lot, Patrick.

EDWARD *pours* PATRICK *a glass of ouzo from a bottle on the table. Hands it to him.*

I wish I could say this was unexpected.

PATRICK. Athens is halfway between London and Nairobi. And then there was the ferry from Piraeus.

EDWARD. I thought you might turn up.

PATRICK. But it's a fleeting visit.

EDWARD. What a shame.

PATRICK. The fact is that my flight leaves Athens for Nairobi tomorrow evening. And in order to catch it I have to be back on the ferry – the same one that brought me here – first thing tomorrow morning.

EDWARD. Is that all you've given yourself?

PATRICK. You know what I'm like.

EDWARD. An optimist, yes.

PATRICK. A man of faith. We both are.

EDWARD. Are we?

PATRICK. Stubborn and full of hope.

EDWARD. Full of something.

PATRICK. Are you turning cynical on me, Edward?

EDWARD. Trouble is we don't believe in the same God any more.

Pause.

PATRICK. The Archbishop sent me. Not that it was hard to convince me.

EDWARD. He's cleverer than I thought.

PATRICK. Why's that?

EDWARD. Because he knows there's only one man who could ever come close.

PATRICK. A compliment.

EDWARD. But not nearly close enough.

Pause.

PATRICK. Patmos. Your hideaway.

EDWARD. And now my retirement home. You've never been to the island before?

PATRICK. It's my first time in Greece.

EDWARD. Welcome.

PATRICK. Thank you.

EDWARD. To the land where Hebrew prophecy and Greek rationalism first entered their inevitable and complicated marriage.

PATRICK. Yes.

EDWARD. You don't even have time to visit the cave where John is alleged to have had his revelations.

PATRICK. Sadly not.

EDWARD. Half a kilometre down the road. Past the man selling pistachios and beach towels.

PATRICK. I'll get to the point. You can't leave, Edward. The Church needs you. Now more than ever.

EDWARD. Does it indeed.

TATYANA *walks on carrying a tray laden with plates and cutlery. When she speaks, she jumps between English and Russian.*

TATYANA. Did you eat the smokey salmon, Edward?

EDWARD. Not that I recall.

TATYANA. This morning it was big. Now it is small. And I do not have enough food. I have only beetroot salad, potato salad, and the meatballs.

EDWARD. Is that all?

TATYANA (*noticing* PATRICK). Who is this?

EDWARD. This, Tatyana, is the Reverend Patrick Mwangi, Bishop of Keriko.

TATYANA. I am Tatyana.

PATRICK. Hello, Tatyana.

EDWARD. Patrick and I met when I was living in Kenya many years ago.

PATRICK. We have remained friends over the years.

EDWARD. Against the odds.

TATYANA. You are eating the dinner with us?

PATRICK. Well, I –

EDWARD. We can squeeze him in.

TATYANA. Не хватит еды. [*Pronounced: 'Nyeh khvah-teet yay-dee.' Meaning: 'There is not enough food.'*]

PATRICK. If that's all right with you.

EDWARD. We'll manage.

TATYANA. I make more salad.

EDWARD. Do that.

PATRICK. But really don't go to any trouble.

EDWARD. We have to send him on his way well fed and with a smile on his face.

PATRICK. Now you're talking.

EDWARD. Even if all that's making him smile is a belly full of beetroot.

TATYANA. What are you talking about?

EDWARD. So yes please, one more place at our table. And the man will need a bed too. He can sleep in the downstairs room.

TATYANA. Как будто у меня без этого работы мало. [*Prounounced 'Kak butto u menia bez etava rabotu malo.' Meaning: 'As if I don't have enough work already.'*]

She leaves.

EDWARD. She's Russian. But from the Ukraine.

PATRICK. Formidable is the word that comes to mind.

EDWARD. I can think of a few more.

PATRICK. Forty-five years, Edward.

EDWARD. Forty-seven.

PATRICK. Of dedication.

EDWARD. You haven't even done your homework.

PATRICK. A lifetime.

EDWARD. Your point?

PATRICK. And now. Just like that.

EDWARD. I've had enough.

PATRICK. So because of this one point, this issue –

EDWARD. Yes.

PATRICK. The homosexuals.

EDWARD. Not only.

PATRICK. Because of the gays, Edward.

EDWARD. Though it's reason enough.

PATRICK. Because of this one disagreement.

EDWARD. It's *emblematic*.

PATRICK. You're going to leave.

 Pause.

EDWARD. I've never seen that sort of hatred. It beggars belief. I've tried hard to understand it but I can't. It has nothing to do with what I know of Christianity. It's irreconcilable.

PATRICK. We are fighting for the soul of Africa, Edward, you know it well. Christianity needs to prevail in its purest form. It is not the time for any sort of relativism. Moral certainties are necessary.

EDWARD. Nothing moral about them.

PATRICK. And so the Archbishop received your letter of resignation. He was upset, if not surprised.

EDWARD. Upset, was he?

PATRICK. Devastated.

EDWARD. That's more like it.

PATRICK. We want you to reconsider.

EDWARD. Do you now?

PATRICK. After all, you're a great asset.

EDWARD. An asset?

PATRICK. A crude word, I know, but I'm being blunt.

EDWARD. In what way am I an asset?

PATRICK. You have continuously challenged us with your many unorthodox opinions over the years, ranging in subject matter from the ordination of women bishops to ways of combating inner-city crime and the efforts to eradicate AIDS from sub-Saharan Africa.

EDWARD. Thank you for reminding me.

PATRICK. I think in that last example I mentioned you proposed the Italian Air Force bombarding Africa with condoms decorated with the face of the Pope.

EDWARD. Did I?

PATRICK. We all remember you chained to the railings of the Chinese Embassy.

EDWARD. Oh, that.

PATRICK. As well as the controversial piece you wrote in the *New Statesman* naming the three great Jewish prophets as Moses, Jesus Christ and Karl Marx.

EDWARD. That was good, wasn't it.

PATRICK. I suppose what I'm saying, Edward, is that everyone in the Church welcomes and actively appreciates your often uncomfortable, always exciting contribution to the larger theological debate.

EDWARD. I'm not sure all of your colleagues would agree.

PATRICK. Without voices like yours, the Church would slumber and stagnate.

EDWARD. Instead, it's right out there on the cutting edge.

PATRICK. We *need* you is what I'm saying.

EDWARD. Is that the best you can do?

PATRICK. The night is young.

Slight pause.

EDWARD. I hate to be the bearer of bad news but you're at a disadvantage.

PATRICK. I am?

EDWARD. Your timing is unfortunate, my daughter is here.

PATRICK. Sophie?

EDWARD. With an American. A *New Yorker*, he keeps correcting me. An aspiring novelist. They were working on a production of *Hamlet* together in Cornwall. I think it's love.

PATRICK. I look forward to seeing her, it's been years.

EDWARD. But there's a problem.

PATRICK. And the problem is?

EDWARD. I haven't told her yet.

PATRICK. Told her...?

EDWARD. That I'm resigning. That as of tomorrow morning I am no longer bishop of anywhere. That I'm a layman, a recluse, a defeated old man.

PATRICK. You've been deceitful, Edward?

EDWARD. I'm picking my moment, that's all.

PATRICK. And the moment is?

EDWARD. Tomorrow morning. At the port. As she's boarding the ferry.

PATRICK. And the reason...?

EDWARD. She's obdurate and determined like you.

PATRICK. And she'll try to dissuade you.

EDWARD. So tonight is our last night together. Please don't spoil it.

PATRICK. You're putting me in a very difficult situation.

EDWARD. I don't recall sending you an invitation to dinner.

PATRICK. You're asking me to lie.

EDWARD. I'm asking you to respect my wishes in my house.

PATRICK. And lie.

EDWARD. And wait until tomorrow morning.

PATRICK. At the port. When we're boarding the ferry.

EDWARD. That is correct.

PATRICK. I… Edward… I…

EDWARD. So let's be civil and respect each other's needs.

SOPHIE and TOM *enter from the house.*

SOPHIE. Oh. My. God.

EDWARD. Sophie, you remember Patrick?

SOPHIE. Remember him!

She runs up to him and they embrace.

PATRICK. Hello, Sophie.

SOPHIE. This is the man I was telling you about.

PATRICK. You were talking about me?

SOPHIE. The other day. I was telling Tom about this young priest who taught me children's songs in Swahili.

PATRICK. Young, yes.

EDWARD. And now he's old and a bishop.

SOPHIE. Patrick, this is Tom.

TOM. I'm from New York.

SOPHIE. What are you… (*To* EDWARD.) You didn't say… I mean, that you were coming.

PATRICK. No.

SOPHIE. I mean, this is –

TOM. It's great to meet you, sir.

SOPHIE. Fantastic, yes, but why didn't you say?

EDWARD. Because I didn't know.

SOPHIE. But what brought you here?

Pause.

PATRICK. Well, I…

EDWARD. He's passing through.

PATRICK. Edward.

SOPHIE. It's a seven-hour ferry trip from Athens.

EDWARD. He's come to ask me something. It's work-related.

SOPHIE. Work-related?

EDWARD. Things, you know.

TOM. Church things.

EDWARD. Yes, thank you, Tom, Church things.

SOPHIE. All this way? Why didn't you call.

TOM. Things to do with Jesus and things.

PATRICK. I have come to make an urgent request of your father.

SOPHIE. Concerning?

EDWARD. It's private.

SOPHIE. Nothing serious?

EDWARD. No, nothing serious.

PATRICK. Quite serious, yes.

EDWARD. Serious to us, but not to you.

PATRICK. That's not quite true.

SOPHIE. This is all a bit strange.

EDWARD. Nothing strange about it at all. And now, if you don't
mind. I will escort Patrick to his room so that he can leave his bag
and freshen up or whatever he has to do and then we will all
convene here on this terrace with this view of the Aegean to enjoy
dinner and discuss various topics, preferably all trivial.

TOM. That sounds cool.

EDWARD. Patrick, follow me.

He walks off with PATRICK *in tow.*

TOM. Jesus, that is so weird.

SOPHIE. What is?

TOM. I've never met a bishop in my life and then I meet two in three
days.

SOPHIE. They often hang out with each other.

He walks up to her, puts his arms around her.

TOM. Okay, so you ready?

SOPHIE. No.

TOM. Sophie, you need to do it.

SOPHIE. I don't want to.

TOM. Jesus, you must think he really hates me.

SOPHIE. It's not that.

TOM. Is it the 'living in sin' thing?

SOPHIE. I told you, he's cool.

TOM. A cool bishop.

SOPHIE. If he knows we love each other.

TOM. Then what?

SOPHIE. I'll tell him tomorrow.

TOM. *Tomorrow?*

SOPHIE. Before we get on the boat.

TOM *pulls away.*

TOM. Okay, you know what, this is not good, I mean, are you ashamed of me?

SOPHIE. You know I'm not.

TOM. Because I'm beginning to take this personally.

SOPHIE. He doesn't know you.

TOM. That's why we came here. So that he could meet me.

SOPHIE. It's three days.

TOM. Enough time for him to establish that I don't kill babies.

SOPHIE. I'm his only… the only person he has.

TOM. He's a bishop, he has his flock or whatever it's called, his… his herd.

SOPHIE. I'll take him aside tomorrow morning.

TOM. All you're doing is putting it off.

SOPHIE. Or maybe, I don't know –

TOM. If he needs references he can write to my parents. Well, maybe not my dad but my mother definitely. I love you. You love me. You are moving to New York and we are going to try the cohabitation thing. I will do this advertising gig –

SOPHIE. While you're working on your next draft.

TOM. So that we can have some money coming in and you can apply for the journalism course and I will help you and support you and be a good hunter-gatherer and we will be happy and perhaps one day bring forth new life onto this planet.

SOPHIE. You're scaring me.

TOM. So I am going to tell him tonight.

SOPHIE. No. I mean, I will. Please. Let me. I promise.

> TATYANA *walks on with another tray laden with more plates and glasses for the table, muttering in Russian as she does so.*

TATYANA. Я даже слушать его не должна; надо делать так, как я считаю нужным. [*Pronounced: 'Ja dazhe slushat evo ne dolzhna; nado delat' tak, kak ja cshitau nuzhnum.' Meaning: 'I shouldn't even listen to him, I should do what I know is right.'*]

SOPHIE. Do you need some help, Tatyana?

TATYANA. There is not enough food for everyone but it is not my fault, I said to him we need more.

SOPHIE. We'll manage.

TATYANA. And now he bring the black man.

SOPHIE. His name is Patrick, he's from Kenya.

TATYANA. Where are they?

SOPHIE. He's just showing him to his room. They'll be down in a minute.

> TATYANA *checks to make sure they can't be heard.*

TATYANA. Sophia.

SOPHIE. Tatyana.

TATYANA. Your father has the screw loose.

SOPHIE. And it's taken you this long to find out?

TATYANA. He forget everything. This morning I think he eat the smokey salmon. This is fine, I have no problem, he can eat it all, I don't care.

SOPHIE. So?

TATYANA. So now I say, 'Edward, did you eat the smokey salmon?' and he says, 'No, I did not eat the smokey salmon.'

TOM. But you don't believe him.

TATYANA. I don't think he is lying, why should he be lying, I think he forgets.

SOPHIE. Well, that happens.

TATYANA. But every day, twenty things like this.

SOPHIE. Maybe you're exaggerating.

TATYANA. And then he is so angry. And now, since we come from England, even more angry, very angry.

SOPHIE. He has his reasons.

TOM. It's to do with the gays.

TATYANA. He is angry with the gays?

SOPHIE. No, it's the opposite, but yes, he's angry.

TATYANA. Every day losing the temper, shouting, из всего устраивает сцену. [*Pronounced: 'iz vsevo us-tra-i-va-jet stzsenu.' Meaning: 'making a scene about everything.'*]

TOM. Maybe we should tell him tomorrow after all.

TATYANA. I say to him, 'Why are you angry, Edward, why always shouting?' He says to me something like, 'I am shouting against the closing of the light.'

SOPHIE. Raging, yes.

TATYANA. Maybe it is better now that we are not going back to England. That we are staying. Maybe he relaxes.

SOPHIE. What do you mean not going back?

TATYANA. And he is right to be angry with the gays. They are funny sometimes but dangerous too.

She leaves.

TOM. Okay. That's interesting. She's articulated what I've always felt. They *are* dangerous. I have this theory that they want to take over the world and force us all in tight vests.

SOPHIE. What did she mean, they're not going back to England?

EDWARD *and* PATRICK *return*.

EDWARD. So, yes, good, that's all sorted.

PATRICK. Now I see why you keep coming back to this place.

EDWARD. Sophie's mother bought it in the late seventies for a few thousand drachma.

SOPHIE. It was one of the last things she did.

PATRICK. A refuge.

TOM. No wonder it means so much to you.

SOPHIE. Dad, Tatyana just said something about you not going back to England.

EDWARD. Confused, as ever.

During the next few lines, EDWARD *pours* TOM *and* SOPHIE *a couple of ouzos and tops up his own.*

PATRICK. So, young man, Edward tells me you have just been involved in a production of *Hamlet*.

SOPHIE. In Cornwall, yes.

TOM. We both were. Sophie was playing Ophelia and I was assisting her.

EDWARD. I'm sure you were.

SOPHIE. He was the assistant director is what he means.

PATRICK. How interesting.

TOM. It's not what I had in mind when I decided to come to Europe for the summer.

PATRICK. An extended holiday?

TOM. Following my postgrad course, yes.

PATRICK. And prior to?

TOM. Moving back to the city. And a temporary job.

EDWARD. You never said what the job was.

TOM. Oh, it's just temporary.

SOPHIE. Tom is a writer.

TOM. Something to keep me going. A good cash job.

EDWARD. Doing what?

SOPHIE. What he really wants to do is write.

PATRICK. Well, good luck to you.

They've all settled in various points around the space, some sitting, some standing.

EDWARD. So what's *Hamlet* about, Tom?

TOM. What's *Hamlet* about?

EDWARD. In a word.

SOPHIE. He does this.

TOM. Well, let's see, I suppose –

EDWARD. Instinctively.

TOM. A call to arms?

EDWARD. Against?

TOM. Something spurious, I suppose, unreal.

EDWARD. I agree.

TOM. As well as the usurpation of power by the undeserving.

SOPHIE. The morally corrupt.

PATRICK. Something rotten.

TOM. Exactly.

EDWARD. And do you relate at all, *connect*, Tom? To Hamlet, I mean?

TOM. Doesn't everyone?

EDWARD. I'm not interested in everyone, I'm interested in you.

SOPHIE. Why the inquisition all of a sudden?

EDWARD. Oh, I'm sorry, I didn't mean to –

TOM. It's fine, really, I'm enjoying this.

EDWARD. It's just I don't really know you. I mean, you've been here for three days but all I really know is that you eat very quickly and have a penchant for psychedelic swimming trunks... But the *measure* of the man.

TOM. Of course I relate to Hamlet. I can't see how it would be possible not to.

EDWARD. In what way do you relate to him?

TOM. His procrastinations, anxieties, weaknesses.

EDWARD. And what about his calling?

TOM. His calling?

EDWARD. 'A call to arms,' you said. I'm assuming you meant it was Hamlet who was being called?

TOM. Oh, that.

EDWARD. And do you have a calling?

SOPHIE. He's a writer.

TOM. Well, maybe not as pronounced as yours.

EDWARD. What do you know of my calling?

TOM. No, I mean, what I mean is I haven't been called in that way, I mean, I'm not a bishop –

SOPHIE. Now you tell me.

TOM. I haven't a *religious* calling is what I mean, I haven't been blessed in that way.

EDWARD. Oh, it's a blessing, is it?

TOM. But yes, I suppose I have a calling –

EDWARD. Against the spurious, the unreal.

TOM. Doesn't everyone?

EDWARD. No, I don't think everyone does, but I assume that if I am to believe my daughter when she says that you are a writer of some importance –

SOPHIE. He is.

EDWARD. Well then, yes, I imagine that it is likely that you do have a calling. And it doesn't have to be religious.

PATRICK. Doesn't it?

EDWARD. You can choose your own word for it. For the time being let's hope it is a calling towards a state more truthful than the one we currently find ourselves in.

TOM. Okay.

EDWARD. And you are a procrastinator?

TOM. Well, I –

EDWARD. Because you said that's one of the characteristics that you share with Hamlet. It was the first word you used.

TOM. I, sometimes, yes, perhaps, I think –

EDWARD. You lack conviction?

TOM. It is harder for some of us to know what we believe. I envy the certainties of the religious-minded, that's for sure.

EDWARD. Yes, I envy Patrick too, but for the less literal-minded of us, certainty is a luxury we can't afford.

PATRICK. Edward, Edward, Edward.

EDWARD. Certainty is a state of mind, faith is a state of heart. There's a marked difference, I believe.

SOPHIE. What's got into you?

PATRICK. Edward, you're inviting a response.

EDWARD. I'm just trying to get to know the man.

SOPHIE. In a very weird manner.

EDWARD. But I'm sorry if it's coming across the wrong way.

TOM. It's cool.

EDWARD. Just getting to know you.

SOPHIE. Is that what it's called?

TATYANA comes in with the last of the dishes and some serving spoons.

EDWARD. At last, I thought you were trying to starve us.

TATYANA. It isn't very much but is ready anyway.

SOPHIE. There's loads.

TATYANA. Меня вы, конечно, никогда не слушаете.
[*Pronounced: 'Menia vu kone-shno ni-kag-da ne-slu-sha-e-te.'*
Meaning: 'But you never listen to me, of course.']

EDWARD. Well, help yourselves.

For the next few minutes they all help themselves to some of the
food and then sit in various places around the table. It's all very
casual.

PATRICK. This is a veritable feast.

TATYANA. I tell you there is not enough.

SOPHIE. This looks beautiful, Tatyana.

TATYANA. You are welcome.

They continue to serve themselves from the dishes. EDWARD
bows his head to say grace, the rest follow suit with TOM *doing a*
bit of an awkward imitation.

EDWARD. Bless oh Lord this food for our use and make us ever
mindful of the needs of others. Amen.

PATRICK. Amen.

TOM. Absolutely.

They all tuck in.

But you know it's interesting, continuing in this vein of 'getting to
know each other' –

EDWARD. Yes, let's.

TOM. Well, you know, I've never really met a bishop before, let
alone two, and it's an amazing thing –

EDWARD. What is?

TOM. Because you know I suppose I don't come from any sort of
religious background at all, I mean, my parents were very relaxed
about that kind of thing, I mean, the most religious thing they ever
did was baptise our Labrador but that was a kind of joke.

PATRICK. A joke?

SOPHIE. His parents were hippies, there were drugs involved.

TOM. But anyway, when I see you guys, I mean, even like now and
you're not even wearing your purple robes, isn't that what you

wear, purple things, what are they called, the bishop's habit, is it like a nun, do you say bishop's habit?

SOPHIE. Cassock.

TOM. The bishop's cassock, thank you, Sophie, and I mean when I see that and think of what you do for a living, and I mean I respect it, I really respect it, so this is not being said in a mocking or derogatory way at all –

SOPHIE. Tom-Tom.

TOM. But when I see that, what you guys do, what you are, I'm thinking this is so like *Mary Poppins*. Or *Bedknobs and Broomsticks*. That kind of thing.

No response.

What I'm saying is I'm sure it's an important, admirable thing, I mean, the Church and everything you guys are doing, is very important, I mean, really, but I suppose what I'm asking is, because maybe what I'm doing is asking a question here, that's part of what I'm doing, but what I'm really doing is asking really how it's possible in this day and age, for instance, you know after we've landed on the Moon and after Darwin and DNA and God knows what else, how it is possible to believe, for instance, that somebody a few thousand years ago turned water into wine and stuff like that and then actually was, not resuscitated, what's the word –

SOPHIE. Resurrected.

TOM. Resurrected, thank you, how it is possible to actually believe that, after, as I was saying, Galileo and Darwin and –

EDWARD. DNA, *yes*.

TOM. How that is possible.

Pause.

Unless you live in South Carolina.

Pause.

But I'm asking with respect.

Pause.

PATRICK. *Bedknobs and Broomsticks*, eh?

EDWARD. It's a valid question, Thomas. Let me think about it.

TOM. Cool.

They have all sat down by this point and are eating their dinner.

PATRICK. This is delicious, Tatyana.

TOM. It really is, it really is delicious. This thing you've done with the beets.

TATYANA. It is Russian.

TOM. I thought so, it has a kind of Slavic thing going on.

TATYANA. I am Russian.

PATRICK. Yes.

TATYANA. But from the Ukraine. Украина. [*Pronounced: 'Uk-ra-i-na.' Meaning: 'Ukraine.'*] A small town near Kiev called Horenka.

TOM. Well, they certainly know what to do with beets in Horenka.

Pause.

PATRICK. And how did the two of you meet, Edward?

TATYANA. Seven years ago. In Thessaloniki.

EDWARD. On my way to Mount Athos.

PATRICK. How interesting. And what brought you to Greece, Tatyana?

TATYANA. Prostitution.

PATRICK. I see.

Pause. They keep eating.

The potatoes are delicious too.

TOM. Yes, they're pleasantly moist.

Pause.

TATYANA. I am not ashamed to say. I did not choose that. I come with men who обещали [*Pronounced: 'o-be-csha-li' Meaning: 'promised'*] promise me work. I need to send money to my family. I thought maybe cleaning houses, looking after small children. But the men lie. Then one night, Edward pick me up in his car.

TOM. Kerb-crawling, Edward?

TATYANA. He take me back to his hotel. But no sex.

EDWARD. Alas, no.

TATYANA. No, talk, talk, talk, as always. He ask me if I enjoy the work.

EDWARD. Not quite the way I phrased it.

TOM. And you said…

TATYANA. You think I enjoy all the ugly men putting their things in me?

PATRICK. That can't be nice.

TATYANA. So, he says, 'I live in England, I will help you out with papers so you can come to the UK,' and he says, 'I also have a house on Patmos, in Greece and you look after me, I am an old man, maybe cooking and things' –

PATRICK. And that's what happened.

TATYANA. I ask him, 'Will you put your thing in me too, Edward?'

EDWARD. She did.

TOM. It's good to be direct.

TATYANA. And he says, I have not forgotten because I look up in the lexicon, the dictionary, he says, 'No, I will refrain from putting my thing in you.'

SOPHIE. That's a relief.

TATYANA. And is true, he refrain. But he is difficult man.

TOM. Very. I mean, yes, well, aren't we all in different ways.

Pause.

EDWARD. When I met Tatyana, she had an air of bewilderment about her.

TATYANA. What is this?

SOPHIE. It means like you were surprised, caught off-guard.

PATRICK. By what?

EDWARD. A bewilderment at finding herself in a country she hardly knew, trying to communicate in a language she didn't speak, doing a job she hadn't chosen, living a life she wasn't expecting –

TATYANA. It's true.

EDWARD. All decided for her by these men whose sole purpose was to accumulate more and more money at her expense.

TATYANA. I remember, Edward.

EDWARD. And so she was bewildered. And so am I.

Pause. They continue to pick at their food.

You two are going to miss each other, aren't you?

SOPHIE. We are.

EDWARD. Not that you can't go over from time to time. Holidays, that sort of thing.

TOM. We were going to talk to you about that.

SOPHIE. *In the morning.*

EDWARD. Talk to me about what?

TOM. About the fact that Sophie's moving to New York. To be. With me. In a couple of weeks. Sir.

Pause.

EDWARD. Well.

SOPHIE. It's true. For a little time. I mean, just for a while, Dad. And then we'll see.

TOM. There's this course at Columbia.

EDWARD. So it's more than just a summer romance.

TOM. Well, we certainly hope so.

SOPHIE. Just for a little time.

TOM. And then maybe for ever.

SOPHIE. But really I'm just going over to stay for a year or so. And then we'll see.

Pause.

EDWARD. What can I say? Big changes.

SOPHIE. Yes.

EDWARD. Congratulations.

TOM. Thank you.

EDWARD. So.

SOPHIE. Yes.

EDWARD. Congratulations. A toast. To change. New things. New days.

PATRICK. New days.

TOM. Yes. New days.

They toast.

SOPHIE. I wanted… I was going… to talk to you about it.

EDWARD. Were you?

SOPHIE. I didn't mean to tell you like this.

EDWARD. Of course not.

TOM. We just thought it best –

SOPHIE. So suddenly, I mean.

TOM. I think Sophie was a little nervous of telling you.

EDWARD. Whatever for? You love each other. You're moving to New York.

SOPHIE. For a few months anyway.

TOM. But you must come and visit.

EDWARD. I hate New York.

TOM. I'm sorry.

EDWARD. But congratulations.

A long, awkward pause. TOM *attempts a new subject with forced enthusiasm.*

TOM. So, the gay question.

EDWARD. What about it?

TOM. I was wondering if we could talk about it.

SOPHIE. Do we have to?

TATYANA. What is the gay question?

TOM. I just thought it would be interesting, seeing as it's such a hot topic, I mean, isn't that what you were all arguing about in… what's that place –

SOPHIE. Lambeth.

TOM. At the Lambeth conference of bishops and priests and I'm just wondering what the whole deal was about.

Pause.

In that 'getting to know each other' kind of way.

Pause.

EDWARD. All right then, Patrick, why don't you tell Tom what happened in Lambeth.

PATRICK. Why don't you?

EDWARD. Because history is written by the winners.

PATRICK. Oh, Edward.

TOM. But I really am very interested.

Pause. PATRICK *takes a moment before beginning.*

PATRICK. Let's see. Well, Tom, resolutions were passed that enforce the Church's commitment to helping support people of homosexual orientation –

EDWARD. As long as they're not homosexual.

PATRICK. Through pastoral care and God's transformative power –

EDWARD. Converting gays into straights with the power of prayer is what he means.

PATRICK. But ultimately affirming that homosexual practice is incompatible with Scripture –

EDWARD. Along with eating shellfish.

PATRICK. As is sexual promiscuity in all its forms –

EDWARD. Whilst paradoxically refusing to legitimise or give blessing to same-sex unions.

TOM. Jeez, it must have been a pretty busy conference. All those decisions made.

PATRICK. It wasn't easy.

EDWARD. The thing you need to understand, Tom, is that Patrick and many men like him just wish homosexuality didn't exist. Somewhere along the line he's confused what he doesn't like the idea of aesthetically with what is morally right or wrong.

PATRICK. Please don't speak for me, Edward.

EDWARD. Either that or he's just concerned about the dwindling global population.

SOPHIE. And a surplus of natural resources.

EDWARD. Along with this distaste of anything to do with matters anal, he also finds himself intimidated by any sort of ambiguity.

PATRICK. I do?

EDWARD. It is a known fact that the covert fascist in everyone appreciates clearly defined categories, not those murky shades in between.

PATRICK. You're calling me a fascist, Edward?

EDWARD. You will find, Patrick, that that particular characteristic is shared with the more militant European racist to whom the idea of a mixed-race child is an appalling aberration. Black and white with nothing in between.

PATRICK. That's a profoundly offensive comparison.

EDWARD. Straight men and straight women with nothing in between.

SOPHIE. Why are you being so aggressive?

EDWARD. Of course, here in Greece a few thousand years before Freud and Kinsey, Plato was already referring to the third sex which existed somewhere between the other two.

TATYANA. Like the transvestites.

EDWARD. So it is interesting to consider that if we'd inherited our morals from the Greek instead of the Hebrew tradition, Patrick could well be citing him to explain his passionate support for gay and lesbian rights.

PATRICK. As you can see, Edward feels strongly on the subject.

EDWARD. But then using scapegoats is the oldest trick in the book. The gays come in handy from time to time, don't they, Patrick?

PATRICK. Please, Edward.

EDWARD. So instead of worrying about the fact the world is riddled with corruption, horrific inequalities, random brutality and a criminal lack of education, let us decide to spend most of our energies condemning people who are only seeking a blessing for their loving relationships. This is what is left of Christianity.

He stands, his tone increasing in intensity over the next few minutes.

Go on then, Patrick. Tell them why you're here and then I'll answer Tom's question on what made me choose this particular path in life.

SOPHIE. What's he talking about, Patrick?

TATYANA. Why you stand up, Edward? Sit down and finish eating.

EDWARD. Tell Sophie why you're here.

PATRICK. Shouldn't you do that?

EDWARD. Patrick made this diversion on his way home in the futile hope of dissuading me from leaving the Church.

SOPHIE. Leaving the Church?

EDWARD. That's right.

SOPHIE. What are you talking about?

EDWARD. I told him, of course, that it's too late. That I'm already in exile.

SOPHIE. In exile?

EDWARD. In exile from a Church that is too busy reading the small print to hear anything of the meaning being imparted. A Church led by spiritual bureaucrats and their literalist lackeys.

SOPHIE. What d'you mean, you're in exile?

EDWARD. A Church intent only in maintaining its own warped version of social control.

TATYANA. Why you getting angry, Edward?

EDWARD. Whilst sacrificing the true tenets of the Christian message.

SOPHIE. Dad.

EDWARD. So let's talk about bedknobs and broomsticks, Tom.

TOM. That didn't come out right.

EDWARD. It came out just fine.

SOPHIE. Why aren't you answering my question?

EDWARD. Let me tell you why I gave my life – FORTY-SEVEN YEARS of my life to stories of virgin births, prodigal sons and healed lepers. First, I love a good fucking metaphor. Nothing quite like it to elucidate and inspire. Secondly, I fell madly, passionately – yes, Tom, *irrationally* – in love with another man.

TATYANA. You are a gay, Edward?

EDWARD. Don't worry, Patrick, bodily fluids were not exchanged and the anal passage was left untouched.

SOPHIE. What are you talking about?

EDWARD. A man who seemed at least to me to speak of love as the most subversive power in the world. The only power able to combat the innate greed and selfishness which now seems to be destroying everything around us.

TATYANA. Oh, he means Jesus, thank God.

EDWARD. The only power that can remind us that the markets are there to serve us and not the other fucking way around. That there is more to life than the lowest common denominator.

Pause.

That is why I gave my life to bedknobs and broomsticks, Tom. Not to perpetuate primitive prejudice. I hope that answers your question.

TOM. Emphatically.

Pause. They have all been taken aback by EDWARD's *outburst.*

TATYANA. My nephew in the Ukraine, I think he is gay. On his wall, two thousand pictures of Britney Spears.

EDWARD. Nietzsche was only part right. Your God is dead, Patrick. But not God. God changes with us, that's all.

PATRICK *stands, moves towards the house, then stops and turns to* EDWARD.

PATRICK. I've outstayed my welcome. Tatyana, thank you for the delicious food.

TATYANA. There was not enough.

PATRICK. There are some rooms on the harbour, they seemed nice enough. I'll stay there for the night.

EDWARD. Don't be a fool.

SOPHIE. Patrick.

PATRICK. The one thing we now agree on, Edward, is that my coming here was in vain. A few minutes ago I was praising your maverick spirit. But I fear that your arguments have now become more personal and just a little uglier.

EDWARD. I've been provoked.

PATRICK. You seem to think that you can impose your views on the rest of the world with scant consideration of the needs of different societies and a complete disrespect of their cultures. Some would call this attitude colonial and just a little arrogant. Old habits die hard, I see.

EDWARD. I'm running out of time.

PATRICK. Let us not forget, by the way, that fifty years ago you Brits were busy importing your own particular brand of homophobia to my country along with scones and strawberry jam.

EDWARD. That wasn't me.

PATRICK. Now, all of a sudden you've changed your minds.

EDWARD. It's called progress.

PATRICK. Oh, is that what it is?

Pause.

Forgive me, but to me, it appears different. From where I stand it seems like yet another manifestation of a society that has lost its moral compass at the altar of personal entitlement. I love the sinner as much as you do, Edward, you know that. But I will not be seduced into loving the sin.

EDWARD. The only sin is the absence of love.

PATRICK. The combination of your naivety and idealism is a dangerous one. You fail to understand what we need for the Church to survive is for moderation and gradualism. If we followed your ways in Africa, within a few years the Anglican Church would be dead and Islam would reign supreme. And where would that leave the gays, I wonder.

Pause.

Perhaps I was wrong. Perhaps it is right that you are leaving the Church, Edward. Perhaps it is time.

A pause and then PATRICK *enters the house.*

EDWARD. Don't let him go. Tell him to stay.

SOPHIE. I'll try.

She runs after him into the house. TATYANA *starts to clear the dishes.*

TATYANA. Why you always angry, Edward, why you shouting. You need to rest. No more screaming against the switching off of the light. Ты уже пожилой человек, тебе надо отдыхать. [*Pronounced: 'Tee oo-**zheh** pah-zhee-**loy** tcheh-lah-**vyek**, tee-**byeh nah**-da aht-dee-**khat**.' Meaning: 'You are an old man now, you need to rest.'*]

She walks off to the kitchen carrying a tray of dishes.

EDWARD *and* TOM *are left alone. There is a pause.* EDWARD *is looking out, towards the sea.*

EDWARD. This is the time of day. The sky.

TOM. It's beautiful.

Pause.

EDWARD. What's your novel called?

TOM. Working title: *The Missing Man.*

EDWARD. Sophie said it's important and urgent. Those were the words she chose.

TOM. She talks me up a little.

EDWARD. What's it about?

TOM. Okay, let's see. There's a hero. But he's this guy who kind of –

EDWARD. Procrastinates.

TOM. How did you know? And has this sort of –

EDWARD. Calling.

TOM. Towards a state more truthful than the one he finds himself in.

Pause.

It's mostly comic. And then tragic. Or the other way round.

Pause.

Are you really leaving the Church?

EDWARD *doesn't answer.*

EDWARD. Why do you want to be a writer, Tom?

TOM. You ask the easiest questions.

EDWARD. What compels you to write?

TOM. Things that I want to communicate.

EDWARD. Such as?

TOM. I am here. I feel this. I feel that. I hope this. I hope that.

EDWARD. Go on.

TOM. Do you feel this? Do you feel that? Do you hope this? Do you hope that?

EDWARD. Most probably.

TOM. And then…

EDWARD. I'm listening.

TOM. This is also possible.

EDWARD. Yes.

TOM. The way things are is not the only way. There's more. Something else.

EDWARD. I agree.

TOM. Which I can't quite rationally…

EDWARD. Grasp?

TOM. Not yet.

EDWARD. That's what I mean about loving a good metaphor. It's reaching for it.

TOM. Reaching.

EDWARD. That's who you are. Don't ever forget that.

Pause.

Stories.

TOM. What about them?

EDWARD. They're all we have.

TOM. Sure.

EDWARD. And the one I've given my life to is a good one. Even though many have done their best to warp it.

TOM. Yes.

EDWARD. But the battle is lost.

Pause.

Look after her.

Suddenly, he is overcome by an emotion but he restrains it.

Nihilism is the victory of the status quo, Tom.

TOM. Okay.

EDWARD. And so it's time for the storytellers again.

TOM. The storytellers?

EDWARD. The shamans. The real priests. The storytellers.

Their eyes meet. They stare at each other.

The storytellers, Tom.

Somewhere in the background, the sound of wings fluttering, a bird taking flight.

Blackout.

End of Act One.

ACT TWO

Scene One

2006

An afternoon in late summer in a large room in a country-house-type hotel, somewhere in England. The furniture has all been cleared and from the large doors towards the back of the room we can hear the sounds of a party in the next room – music, laughter, chatting, the clinking of glasses.

SOPHIE *hobbles in on one shoe, holding the other one in her hand, with* SEBASTIAN *following closely behind. Both are smartly dressed, both are holding glasses of something.*

SOPHIE. Shit, shit, shit.

SEBASTIAN. I'm not surprised.

SOPHIE. I need some glue.

SEBASTIAN. The way you were dancing.

SOPHIE. What about it?

SEBASTIAN. It was crazy.

SOPHIE. Is that a bad thing?

SEBASTIAN. It's just…

SOPHIE. Go on.

SEBASTIAN. Honestly? I have never known you drink this much, Sophie.

SOPHIE. Haven't you?

SEBASTIAN. Two mojitos, two champagnes before lunch –

SOPHIE. Oh my God, you're counting.

SEBASTIAN. And at least half a bottle of that Sauvignon Blanc.

SOPHIE. Where are you going with this?

SEBASTIAN. I'm just wondering if there's a reason.

SOPHIE. Sebastian, I got back just under a week ago.

SEBASTIAN. I know you did.

SOPHIE. I was there for three months.

SEBASTIAN. I know you were.

SOPHIE. During those three months I spent time with a thirteen-year-old girl who'd watched her father's head being sawn off for trying to make a living as an interpreter. I walked around a marketplace after a bomb had been detonated leaving a sea of severed limbs in its wake, I'm now at a gay wedding in Surrey. I'm letting my hair down. Is that a good enough reason?

SEBASTIAN. The American.

SOPHIE. What American?

SEBASTIAN. It is strange that you haven't talked to him.

SOPHIE. Is it?

SEBASTIAN. I thought maybe he was the reason.

SOPHIE. That must be his girlfriend. The very thin woman.

SEBASTIAN. Won't you speak to each other?

SOPHIE. I'm sure we will at some point. And if we do, we do, and if we don't, we don't.

SEBASTIAN. I love you, Sophie.

Pause. She smiles.

Okay, here goes. Fuck. I am a little nervous, it's understandable.

SOPHIE. Nervous?

SEBASTIAN. I've never done this thing before.

SOPHIE. What thing?

SEBASTIAN. Maybe I should blame my mother. On the phone every day from Chile, driving me crazy.

SOPHIE. I'm not sure I understand.

SEBASTIAN. Or maybe it's just because we're here. I've been inspired.

SOPHIE. Sebastian, what are you talking about?

SEBASTIAN. Funny to think I've always condemned marriage as a bourgeois convention.

SOPHIE. Have you?

SEBASTIAN. And I know we haven't been together for such a long time but sometimes you have to be bold and –

SOPHIE. Sebastian.

SEBASTIAN. Sophie.

SOPHIE. Glue.

SEBASTIAN. Glue?

SOPHIE. I need some glue. I feel at a disadvantage. Temporarily disabled, that sort of thing.

Pause.

Please find me some glue, something. And then we can… you can… but in the meantime I'm in desperate need of some glue.

SEBASTIAN. Yes. Glue.

He makes a move to go. LAWRENCE *bursts in, rummaging through his pockets as he does so. He is dressed to the nines. He is in a state of panic.*

LAWRENCE. Calamity, calamity, calamity. Appalling, horrendous calamity.

SOPHIE. What's wrong?

LAWRENCE. I've lost the speech, I've lost the speech, I've lost the speech.

SOPHIE. You've lost the speech?

LAWRENCE. I'd put it into my inside pocket this morning. But then I took the jacket off in that awful café where we had the fried eggs and it must have slipped out.

SOPHIE. Surely you remember it? I mean, it is the most important speech of your life.

LAWRENCE. I'd written it down, why would I memorise it? I was going to read it.

SEBASTIAN. Did you call the café?

LAWRENCE. Luke is doing that now. What's wrong with you? You're lopsided.

SOPHIE. My heel broke. Don't panic. We'll write it again.

LAWRENCE. It's a catastrophe.

SOPHIE. Sebastian was just going to get some glue. From reception. Can you ask them for a piece of paper and a pen as well?

LAWRENCE. I have a pen.

SEBASTIAN. Okay, I go.

SOPHIE. Thank you.

SEBASTIAN *rushes off*.

Breathe deeply. Maybe you should do some stretches or something.

LAWRENCE. Stretches?

SOPHIE. To relax, I mean.

LAWRENCE. Not the time for a fucking Pilates class, darling. This is a monumental crisis, up there with the Bay of Pigs.

SOPHIE. We'll write it again.

LAWRENCE. I feel sick.

Pause.

SOPHIE. I'm surprised Tom's here.

LAWRENCE. So am I.

SOPHIE. Why didn't you tell me, Lawrence?

LAWRENCE. I never thought he was going to come.

SOPHIE. But he's here.

LAWRENCE. All the way from New York, I mean. Why does it matter?

SOPHIE. Well, it doesn't. I mean, not a lot.

LAWRENCE. It's been five years. You're adults, you've moved on.

SOPHIE. Of course we have, I know that.

LAWRENCE. Unless, of course, you haven't.

SOPHIE. It's just I wish I was prepared.

LAWRENCE. In what way prepared? Armed with a chainsaw? Accompanied by a bullmastiff?

SOPHIE. These things are always awkward.

LAWRENCE. Anyway, darling, I hate to drag the spotlight off you but there are two hundred people waiting for me to make a brilliantly witty, unbearably moving speech and I have nothing to offer them other than an expression of absolute horror etched on my face.

SOPHIE. We'll write it together.

TOM and ANNIE walk in. TOM is holding a bottle of champagne in one hand and a glass in another. ANNIE is also holding a glass.

TOM. Jesus, Sophie.

SOPHIE. Hello, Tom.

LAWRENCE. Here he is.

SOPHIE. We were just talking about you.

LAWRENCE. In the kindest possible way.

SOPHIE. Yes, very kindly.

TOM. Sophie sweetie, this is Annie.

They both look at him.

I meant, Annie sweetie, this is Sophie.

LAWRENCE. A case of confused confectioneries.

ANNIE. I feel like I know you already.

SOPHIE. You do?

ANNIE. Tom has always said how wonderful you were as Ophelia. He said you were very convincing in the mad scenes.

TOM. Horatio was pretty damn hot as well.

LAWRENCE. The same, my lord, and your poor servant ever. That virginal Cornish summer.

TOM. Nothing virginal about it.

LAWRENCE. Speak for yourself. I was an un-plucked flower.

TOM. As far as I recall you were being plucked regularly.

SOPHIE. By Rosencrantz and Guildenstern, yes.

LAWRENCE. Don't bring up my sordid past, on this of all days.

SOPHIE. Good idea, let's not delve. What's done is done.

LAWRENCE. And here we are, just a little fatter, a little wiser.

SOPHIE. That's hopeful.

LAWRENCE. Cheers.

They toast.

And it was Rosencrantz and the Second Gravedigger.

SOPHIE *notices* ANNIE *staring at her.*

SOPHIE. It's my shoe. It's. The heel. It's broken.

She takes the other shoe off.

SEBASTIAN *runs in with glue in one hand and a piece of paper in the other.*

SEBASTIAN (*handing the glue to* SOPHIE *and the paper to* LAWRENCE). Glue for you, paper for you.

LAWRENCE. Thank you, thank you.

LAWRENCE *whips out his pen and gets to work.*

SOPHIE (*grabbing* SEBASTIAN *by the arm, digging her nails into him*). Darling, this is Tom and Annie.

SEBASTIAN. Hello, Tom, hello, Annie, I'm Sebastian.

TOM. Hi.

SEBASTIAN (*feeling her nails digging into him*). Ow.

SOPHIE. Sorry.

ANNIE. Hello, Sebastian.

LAWRENCE (*writing it down as he goes along*). *Ladies and gentlemen.*

SOPHIE. He's lost his speech. He has to write it again.

ANNIE. Oh, that's terrible.

LAWRENCE. *Ladies and gentlemen.* Then what?

SOPHIE. I didn't think you'd make it over.

TOM. It was the perfect excuse.

SEBASTIAN. Excuse?

TOM. To get on a plane. I miss it, is what I mean.

SEBASTIAN. You mean London?

TOM. And are you two, you know, married, or anything.

SOPHIE. No, not married, no.

TOM. Cool. I mean as in, who needs it, what I mean is, as long as you love each other, which obviously you do because otherwise you wouldn't be together, but marriage itself is overrated, I mean, it's just a piece of paper, it isn't really important…

LAWRENCE *throws him a look over his shoulder.*

… unless, of course, you're gay, in which case it is vital and significant because it is an essential validation of the love between. Two men. Or women. Because of the persecution, I mean. History of. Persecution.

ANNIE. We're engaged.

TOM. Yes, only just.

SOPHIE. Congratulations.

SEBASTIAN. Yes, congratulations.

SOPHIE (*beginning to work a little manically on the heel which she does over the next few lines*). If you'll excuse me, I need to apply myself.

TOM. I've been following your career by, the way.

SOPHIE. Is that what it's called?

TOM. That thing you wrote in *The Times* on the Indonesian sweatshops.

ANNIE. That was intense. Tom showed it to me.

LAWRENCE (*talking about his speech as he tries to remember it*). The resounding theme was undying love.

TOM. The letter you wrote to Donald Rumsfeld in *The New Republic*, that piece on Exxon Mobil.

SEBASTIAN. She has been busy making friends.

LAWRENCE. *Ladies and gentlemen.*

TOM. Lawrence said you just got back from Iraq.

SOPHIE. I did.

ANNIE. Oh my God, doing what?

SEBASTIAN. Examining the debris.

SOPHIE. Something for *Harper's*: 'After the Auction'. Is this the only glue they had?

SEBASTIAN. Investigating the consequences of imported freedom and democracy in the Middle East.

SOPHIE (*still struggling with the shoe and glue*). And doing interviews with the people on the ground as well.

SEBASTIAN. To use an American expression, Tom, the 'collateral damage' people.

TOM. I didn't actually coin that phrase myself, Sebastian.

SOPHIE. Not just the players, but the played.

ANNIE. The played?

LAWRENCE. It's coming back, it's coming back, it's coming back.

TOM. Well, I can't say I'm surprised. I always knew you were going to be more *Harper's* than *Harper's Bazaar.*

LAWRENCE (*writing away*). Oh my God, it's coming back.

SEBASTIAN. Sophie says you are a funny man.

TOM. How comforting to know that.

SEBASTIAN. You have a sense of humour?

TOM. I couldn't possibly say.

SEBASTIAN. Well, make the most of it. Laughing at everything is one of the luxuries of being privileged.

TOM. You never laugh, Sebastian?

LAWRENCE (*writing as he remembers*). *Jardin du Luxembourg…*

SEBASTIAN. I laugh at things that are funny, yes. But not as a means of distraction.

TOM. Sebastian, take it easy, we've only just met.

SOPHIE (*still struggling with the heel*). Sebastian's been angry lately. Oh, and he's a Marxist.

ANNIE. I *love* Europe.

SEBASTIAN. I'm from Chile.

ANNIE. Oh, I'm sorry.

TOM. Does that pay well these days?

SEBASTIAN. I teach.

TOM. Twentieth-century history?

SEBASTIAN. Political theory at UCL.

TOM. Is it difficult trying to be objective?

SOPHIE. This glue really isn't working.

SEBASTIAN. I just try and remind my students that the successful politician, like the successful economist, is the one that convinces the world that his way is the only option.

ANNIE. That makes sense.

SEBASTIAN. And that my students' job is to prove them wrong.

TOM. Good luck to you.

SEBASTIAN. I suppose I am inviting them to exercise their wills and minds in unexpected ways. To surprise themselves and never give up.

ANNIE. That's admirable.

SEBASTIAN. And you are in advertising, Tom?

SOPHIE. Only temporarily. This isn't going to work. We need some of that industrial-strength stuff.

SEBASTIAN. It's the only one they had.

SOPHIE (*sits on the floor to continue working on the broken heel*). Excuse me, don't mind me, I really need to focus on this.

SEBASTIAN. And what do you do, Annie?

ANNIE. I'm an interior decorator.

TOM. One of the best in New York.

SEBASTIAN. That's great.

SOPHIE (*focused on the shoe*). I love a good sofa.

ANNIE. I design houses for rich people.

SOPHIE. Lucky you. This really isn't working.

SEBASTIAN. Movie stars and things?

ANNIE. A few.

TOM. She's very successful.

SOPHIE. Ship owners, bankers?

ANNIE. That kind of thing.

SOPHIE. Arms dealers?

ANNIE. You two haven't seen each other since…?

TOM. Not in five years.

SOPHIE. It's the 11th on Tuesday.

LAWRENCE. You were right, it's all coming back to me. Okay, here goes, listen and then chip in if you remember any other bits.

SOPHIE. We're all ears.

LAWRENCE (*reading*). 'Ladies and gentlemen.

TOM. It's good to start with something familiar.

LAWRENCE. I wish I could say I met Luke in the Jardin du Luxembourg on an autumnal evening –

ANNIE. I love the Jardin du Luxembourg.

LAWRENCE. – or even in the Cotswolds at Christmas. Fact is I met him at a bar called Fist in Croydon. It was love at first sight even though we couldn't actually see each other. But when he took off his mask, I was smitten. Relax, Mother, I'm joking. It was at Costa Coffee and we were wearing Zara.' That's all I remember.

SOPHIE. There was something about opposites. The attraction of opposites.

LAWRENCE. Genius, you're a genius.

He resumes with the paper and pen.

ANNIE. Do you remember we spent that afternoon in the Jardin du Luxembourg when we were in Paris, sweetie? Just sitting on that bench with our books.

SOPHIE. I'll always associate you with that day, Tom.

TOM. Which part of it exactly?

ANNIE. Which day?

SOPHIE. Maybe just because it was the last time we saw each other.

TOM. The falling buildings, the jumping people or the sky on fire?

SOPHIE. – and then came back here.

TOM. Or just the general catastrophe?

SEBASTIAN. Oh, that day.

SOPHIE. Isn't it funny how there are days that come along every so often, these events, these things that happen that are like these big signposts saying –

ANNIE. Signposts?

TOM. Saying what?

SOPHIE. Okay, this isn't going to work. Fuck it, I'm going barefoot.

She tosses her shoes away. Stands up. She takes the bottle of champagne from TOM.

May I?

She pours herself a glass.

Anyone else?

ANNIE. Saying what?

SOPHIE. Saying: 'Stop! Stop where you are! Stop right there! Cease being what you are for just one minute and reflect a little, pause for just one millisecond before you simply *react in haste* and instead ask yourself in all honesty the imperative questions: "How did I get here? Where am I headed? Why has this happened?" ' Don't you think, Annie?

Pause.

Anyone else for a drink?

SEBASTIAN. No, thank you.

TOM. I'll have a little.

She pours him some.

ANNIE. Truthfully? I think people are jealous of us, that's all. In the West, I mean.

SOPHIE. Is that what it is?

SEBASTIAN. I think that's a little reductive.

LAWRENCE. I don't like where this conversation is headed.

ANNIE. And, you know, to be honest, I have to take issue with where you're going with this because you know I'm a liberal, and open-minded and yes, let's be aware of the bigger picture and all that, but there are certain things which are never justified –

SOPHIE. I don't think that's what I'm doing.

LAWRENCE. Can you go back to talking about sofas, please?

ANNIE. Acts of the most appalling barbarity and evil and when we start justifying –

SEBASTIAN. Who is justifying anything?

ANNIE. When we start *justifying* certain things then we're in trouble and maybe it's because I'm closer to the whole thing, I mean, apart from being a New Yorker –

LAWRENCE. Or fabrics, or swatches?

ANNIE. Apart from that, maybe it has something to do with the fact that I lost someone. A friend. Because I had a friend who died in the North Tower. Sandy. So maybe that's why I feel quite strongly on the subject.

SOPHIE. I'm sorry for your friend. I am *profoundly* sorry for everybody who suffered and died on that terrible day. But justifying isn't what I was doing. Trying to understand, perhaps. I think there's a marked difference.

ANNIE. So there are things I'm just not interested in listening to.

SOPHIE. So that history doesn't keep repeating itself –

ANNIE. Because I have that personal connection.

SOPHIE. – over and over again.

Awkward pause.

LAWRENCE. Wonderful. Thank you for taking a giant leak on the most important day of my life.

TOM. She wasn't really your friend, honey.

ANNIE. What?

TOM. I mean, you said you knew her coz you'd met her at Sarah Phillips's party in the Hamptons.

ANNIE. I saw her two weeks before she died.

TOM. I know you did, but you said you didn't like her very much. I mean, I think that's what you said.

ANNIE. I don't remember saying that.

TOM. But you only met her on that one occasion. For about fifteen minutes.

ANNIE. It was longer.

SEBASTIAN. It's funny how there are these buildings, edifices, constructions.

SOPHIE. What constructions?

SEBASTIAN. That come to signify empires, ideologies, whole economic and political systems.

TOM. What about them?

SEBASTIAN. And maybe, Tom, you are right about twentieth-century history, when the Berlin Wall came down that marked the end of Marxism, at least in the way that it had been exercised until then.

TOM. Not all that successfully, yes.

SEBASTIAN. But maybe the Twin Towers were the Berlin Wall of neo-liberalism, only it might take a little bit longer to acknowledge this.

SOPHIE. Because there's a lot more to be lost.

TOM. Well, in that case, I just hope your students are doing their homework.

LAWRENCE. Okay, you know what, stop, you are at my wedding. Show a little respect, for God's sake. I am about to make a very important speech.

TOM. Apologies.

LAWRENCE. So, the second bit. This is what I can remember.

SOPHIE. Go for it.

LAWRENCE (*reading from the paper*). 'Since then we have become completely domesticated and are excelling at impersonating our straightest friends. Next thing you know we'll be shopping at Morrisons and watching *Top Gear*. Which brings us to today. Here we are, bouquets, cakes, drunken relatives and all. We have arrived. It's official.

Opposites attract, they say. Looking at us you may think we're peas in a pod but believe me, appearances are deceptive. I'm Prada to Luke's Primark. I like oysters, he likes Nando's; I admire Buñuel, he's more *Naked Gun Three*. Somewhere between those two extremes there's that thing called common territory. Meet me there, Luke.'

ANNIE. That's beautiful.

SOPHIE. I told you that you hadn't forgotten it.

LAWRENCE. It's an abbreviated version but it will have to do. Follow me. I need an audience to laugh at all appropriate moments. And then weep copiously towards the end.

SEBASTIAN. We will do our best.

TOM. We shall, we shall.

LAWRENCE. And generally support with loving vibes.

ANNIE (*aside to* TOM). I can't believe you did that.

SEBASTIAN. We need to fill our glasses so we have some for the toast.

LAWRENCE. Annie, come with me, darling, let's talk interiors.

They start to make their way towards the door. They all head out, but SOPHIE *and* TOM *are towards the back.*

TOM. Sophie.

SOPHIE. Tom.

TOM. Just wait. Please. Just one second.

SOPHIE. What?

TOM. I just need to tell you something. One thing. In private.

SOPHIE. I'm listening.

Pause. They are alone.

TOM. Hello, Sophie.

SOPHIE. Hello, Tom.

TOM. You look well.

SOPHIE. I do?

TOM. Beautiful, I mean beautiful.

SOPHIE. Thank you, Tom.

Pause.

Is that what you needed to tell me?

SEBASTIAN *returns, sticks his head round the door.*

SEBASTIAN. Sophie, come, we'll miss the speeches.

SOPHIE. Yes.

SEBASTIAN. Come on, hurry.

TOM. Yes, we were coming. I just wanted –

SOPHIE. Just one minute, Sebastian. I'll be there in a minute.

SEBASTIAN *looks uncertain.*

SEBASTIAN. I'll keep your seat.

SOPHIE. Thank you.

Reluctantly, he goes.

TOM. I don't think he likes me.

SOPHIE. He has his reasons.

TOM. Can you tell him I'm a Democrat?

SOPHIE. It wouldn't make a difference.

TOM. Wouldn't it?

SOPHIE. His father was one of Allende's ministers. Two years after the coup, he committed suicide. He has issues.

TOM. I wasn't born in 1973.

SOPHIE. I'll pass it on.

Pause.

TOM. We were young.

SOPHIE. Yes.

TOM. And foolish.

SOPHIE. Yes, you were.

Pause.

TOM. How long have you and Sebastian…?

SOPHIE. A year and a half.

TOM. Not that long.

SOPHIE. He loves me. We love each other.

Pause.

We should get back.

TOM. I only flew over because I was hoping you might be here.

SOPHIE. I don't –

TOM. I was curious, is what I'm saying.

SOPHIE. Oh.

TOM. Curious to see you again. I can't lie.

Pause.

A year and a half isn't a long time, whatever you say.

SOPHIE. What are you talking about?

TOM. And then just now you said, 'He loves me,' and then a second later you added, 'We love each other.' Like an afterthought.

SOPHIE. Are you drunk?

TOM. I think so, yes. Are you?

She doesn't answer.

And if you want me to be honest –

SOPHIE. Why start now?

TOM. I don't think it's the same.

SOPHIE. What do you know about my life? About Sebastian? About me?

TOM. It's what I feel.

SOPHIE. And so to hell with everything else.

TOM. Yes.

SOPHIE. With everyone else.

TOM. It's how I feel.

Pause.

And maybe it's because we're here –

SOPHIE. What is?

TOM. But you must admit from the minute when we were both in this room and maybe if I hadn't drunk, I wasn't drunk I wouldn't be saying these things and maybe it is disloyal to Annie and low and I don't know, unfair or something –

SOPHIE. It is.

TOM. Reptilian, but from the moment we were in this room and we were making jokes and talking about what we all do and how we all were and blah blah blah but from the moment we were in the same room it was as if no time had passed and then maybe we could be back in New York and we wouldn't make the same choices –

SOPHIE. Which one of us?

TOM. But from the minute we were in the same room it was as if it was just us again, and these people we're with –

SOPHIE. Don't talk about them like that.

TOM. – were accidental in some way, or incidental, or not the real thing, and I wish them well, I wish them well, I wish them well but every so often you have to say 'this is how I feel right now' and that is all that really matters.

Pause.

What was Iraq like?

SOPHIE. Why do you care about Iraq, Tom?

TOM. Because you were there.

Pause. She thinks about it.

SOPHIE. I don't think Annie meant any harm by saying that that poor woman was her friend.

TOM. No.

SOPHIE. I think what she meant was 'We were alike. We shopped at the same places, and dressed in similar ways and knew the same people.' I think that's what she meant.

TOM. I think you're right.

SOPHIE. Well, in Iraq they don't shop at the same places or dress in similar ways or maybe know the same people. That's all.

Pause.

That's what Iraq was like.

TOM. Yes.

SOPHIE. And a little dustier.

TOM. Sophie.

SOPHIE. I did think about you when I was there. One night. I don't
know why. I'd been with this girl for about a week. Her name was
Janan. She… her parents had. Her father was. So she was
orphaned. Living with this aunt on the outskirts of Baghdad. I
became quite close to her. Inevitably. The things she'd lived
through. So this one night after I'd been with Janan I returned to
my hotel and I lay in my dark bedroom and I stared at the fan on
the ceiling whirring around my head and I thought of you. I felt
like I was going to be stuck in that room for the whole of eternity
and I thought: come and find me and take me away, Tom. Buy me
nice things, take me everywhere. I thought, fuck her. Fuck Janan.
Fuck the children, who cares if they're disabled or damaged or
dying or dead? Fucking fuck 'em. I didn't give a flying fuck. I
wanted to be with you. That's all. It's all I wanted. With you and
wearing something nice.

Pause.

I envy Annie.

Pause.

TOM. I don't think a single day goes by when I don't think of you in
some way or another.

She throws her glass of wine in his face.

Okay.

SEBASTIAN *returns.*

SEBASTIAN. You are still here.

SOPHIE. Yes. We got stuck.

SEBASTIAN. You all right?

SOPHIE. We're fine, we're fine.

TOM. I'll see you later.

SOPHIE. Yes, yes, later.

TOM *leaves. There is a pause.*

The answer is yes.

SEBASTIAN. Yes, what?

SOPHIE. To what you were about to ask me. To what your mother
wants. To bourgeois convention.

SEBASTIAN. Yes?

SOPHIE. Yes, yes, yes.

SEBASTIAN. Fuck.

SOPHIE. The answer is yes.

He walks up to her; they kiss.

SEBASTIAN. I love you.

SOPHIE. I just need another minute.

SEBASTIAN. Cool. And then come and dance with me. Barefoot.

*He starts to walk out of the room, stops. Punches the air
triumphantly.*

I'm going to go call Chile!

He leaves the room. She stands silently.

EDWARD *walks into the room.* SOPHIE *cannot see him. He is
looking much older than when we last saw him and more
dishevelled. He is holding a tattered old copy of the Bible and
reciting from it in a loud, meandering voice. Slowly, brushing past
him on the way,* SOPHIE *leaves the room.*

EDWARD (*reading*). 'One Sabbath he was going through the grain
fields; and as they made their way his disciples began to pluck
heads of grain. The Pharisees said to him: "Look, why are they
doing what is not lawful on the Sabbath?" And he said to them:
"Have you never read what David did when he and his
companions were hungry and in need of food? He entered the
house of God, when Abiathar was high priest, and ate the bread of
the Presence, which is not lawful for any but the priest to eat, and
he gave some to his companions." Then he said to them, "The
Sabbath was made for humankind and not humankind for the
Sabbath." '

Scene Two

2001

EDWARD *comes to stand in the middle of the space. Around him, the scene changes. The room fades and we are back in Patmos, an early spring evening.*

He wanders off, book in hand. TATYANA *enters, followed by* SOPHIE *and* TOM, *who is carrying a small case.*

TATYANA. He no listen to me, Miss Sophie. Never listen. I say 'Eat, Mister Edward, eat, in life you must eat' –

TOM. It helps.

TATYANA. But he no eat. Then he is always shouting. He is scaring me.

SOPHIE. Of course.

TATYANA. In only two years since he leave the Church everything stops working. He becomes crazy and all so quickly.

SOPHIE. He's had two strokes, Tatyana, that's why.

TATYANA. And then you know, there is the new problem.

SOPHIE. New problem?

TATYANA. How you say in English? У него недержание. [*Pronounced: 'U nevo ne-der-zha-ni-e.' Meaning: 'He is incontinent.'*] The poo.

SOPHIE. The what?

TATYANA. The poo. He does the poo-poo. под себя. [*Pronounced: 'Pad-sebia.' Meaning: 'On himself.'*] On himself.

SOPHIE. Okay.

TOM. Shit.

TATYANA. Yes, Tom, the shit, I know.

TOM. That's a whole new territory.

TATYANA. In his trousers, Miss Sophie.

SOPHIE. But surely he's wearing a pad.

TATYANA. Yes, Miss Sophie, he is wearing the pad but then he no let me change. He shout at me. 'Go away, Tatyana, leave me, I no need you.' Но оно ведь пахнет. [*Pronounced: 'No ono ved' pakh-net.' Meaning: 'But it smells.'*] But it smells, Miss Sophie, because he not let me change them.

SOPHIE. The minute you called we got on the flight. And I've made a few phone calls.

TATYANA. Yes, Miss Sophie.

SOPHIE. There's a home. In Athens. It's clean, pleasant –

TOM. It's perfect.

TATYANA. A home?

SOPHIE. For my father, I mean.

TOM. We're going to take him there. On Tuesday.

SOPHIE. But you need to know that you can stay here and we'll keep your salary going –

TOM. We'll definitely do that.

SOPHIE. So that you can look after the place and then when, if, you find somewhere else –

TOM. Only if you want to.

SOPHIE. Well, then you can go. But not unless you want to.

TATYANA (*fighting the tears*). Thank you, Miss Sophie, Mister Tom. You are golden, like your father.

SOPHIE. Now we need to sort out quite a few practical things.

EDWARD *drifts on, looking lost.*

EDWARD. Sophia.

SOPHIE. Hello, Dad.

EDWARD. Sophia.

TOM. Hello, Edward.

SOPHIE. You remember Tom, Dad?

EDWARD *looks at him blankly.*

TOM. Well, I remember you.

TATYANA. You see how crazy he looks?

SOPHIE. Why don't you go and have a rest, Tatyana.

TATYANA. I go make courgette pie. You call if you need me.

TOM. I love your pies.

SOPHIE. Thank you, Tatyana.

TATYANA *moves to go. Then she turns to* EDWARD.

TATYANA. Now you do what Miss Sophie says. And you no shout at her like you shout at me, Edward. Все время кричишь. [*Pronounced: 'Vse vremia kri-chish.' Meaning: 'Always shouting.'*]

EDWARD. I AM LIFE!

TATYANA *leaves*.

'Edward this, Edward that, Edward, Edward, Edward, Edward, you smell, Edward, Edward, Edward,' and I say to her, I say to her –

SOPHIE. What do you say to her, Dad?

EDWARD. I say to her, 'I am not Edward, so don't call me that, stop calling me it' –

SOPHIE. So who are you, Dad?

EDWARD. I AM LIFE!

TOM. Okay, Edward, no one's arguing with you.

SOPHIE. So, Life, do I get a kiss?

SOPHIE *walks up to him and puts her arms around him, kisses him*.

We came all the way from New York, Dad.

TOM. Just to see you. And so far, you haven't disappointed.

EDWARD. How's your book?

TOM. My book? You remember my book?

SOPHIE. He remembers your book.

TOM. Edward, I'm impressed.

EDWARD. How is it?

TOM. Oh, you know, simmering away.

TOM *imitates* SOPHIE, *gives him a slightly awkward hug*.

SOPHIE. I've missed you, Dad.

TOM (*aside to* SOPHIE). Okay, we need to talk.

SOPHIE. I know.

TOM. It's bad.

SOPHIE. I know it is.

TOM. And we are *outdoors*.

EDWARD. Sophia.

SOPHIE. What is it, Dad?

EDWARD. My daughter Sophia.

> SOPHIE *surveys the situation.*

SOPHIE. Okay, Dad. You're not going to like this but we need to give you a wash.

TOM. *We?*

EDWARD. I AM LIFE!

SOPHIE. I know, Dad, I know you're Life but you need to do what I tell you for a few minutes. Come with me, Dad.

> *She tries to lead him indoors but he resists.*

EDWARD. Don't you bloody start.

SOPHIE. Please, Dad.

EDWARD. I'm not going anywhere.

SOPHIE. Just for a while.

EDWARD. Unhand me.

SOPHIE. Please, Dad.

EDWARD. I want the sun.

TOM. He wants the sun.

SOPHIE. Okay, so we'll do it here.

TOM. *Here?*

SOPHIE. I'm not fighting a battle to get him inside and maybe it's better outdoors. Ask Tatyana to give you whatever you need.

TOM (*pulls* SOPHIE *to one side*). Sophie, I need to talk to you a minute.

SOPHIE. Go on.

TOM. The fact is, I don't know how to say this but –

SOPHIE. But what?

TOM. I'm not a fan of shit.

SOPHIE. You'll find that it's a very select minority of people who actually are.

TOM. You know I have a terrible gag-reflex thing.

SOPHIE. Just get the stuff.

TOM. That's all you need. Shit *and* vomit.

SOPHIE. Okay, Tom, *listen*. I am not expecting you to be an active member of this adventure. I know you well enough. I'm just asking you to get me a bucket of water, the disinfectant soap, the wash rag and whatever else Tatyana gives you. That is all, I promise.

TOM. I'm sorry.

SOPHIE. Just go.

TOM. Faster than an arrow from a Tartar's bow.

He goes.

EDWARD. I need to talk to you.

SOPHIE. What about, Dad?

EDWARD. Cornelius.

SOPHIE. Cornelius?

EDWARD. Acts of the Apostles.

SOPHIE. Oh, *that* Cornelius.

EDWARD. Everything evolves.

SOPHIE. I know, Dad, I agree, everything does evolve.

EDWARD. *Changes*, it has to, in order to survive.

SOPHIE. I know, Dad.

EDWARD. I am Life.

SOPHIE. I know you are.

EDWARD. Moving *towards*.

Pause.

SOPHIE. Look. The gulls. Can you see them? Diving into the sea.

EDWARD. For fish.

SOPHIE. Yes, fish.

Pause.

Okay, I need you to listen to me, it's important. Tom has gone to get some water and a clean pad. We need to change you, Dad, because... we need to change you. Please, just let me do that and then we can sit down, talk, whatever, walk in the garden, whatever you like. But please don't make a fuss. I need to change the pad and I'm asking you to cooperate.

EDWARD. It's come to that.

SOPHIE. Yes, I'm afraid it has. It's come to that.

TOM *comes back, bucket, pad and soap in hand.*

TOM. Operation De-shitification of Life is ready, Thunderbirds are go.

SOPHIE. Put them down there.

TOM. I can stand here and make sure people don't walk by. Or if they do, I can throw things at them.

SOPHIE. Tom.

She leads EDWARD *towards a bench.*

Sit here, Dad.

EDWARD. Only connect.

TOM. We're definitely about to connect, Edward.

EDWARD *sits.*

SOPHIE. Actually, Dad, wait, I need you to stand.

EDWARD. You said sit.

TOM. She's changed her mind, it happens.

SOPHIE. Sorry, Dad, I need to take your trousers off and I can't do it if you're sitting down.

EDWARD *stands and she starts unbuttoning his trousers.*

TOM. This is the bit where I go check if people are walking by.

SOPHIE. Open the soap thing.

TOM. Because that reflex is definitely starting to act up.

SOPHIE. Tom, I need you to do that.

TOM. Okay, sweetie.

SOPHIE. And moisten the rag, I mean wet it.

TOM. Wet the rag, Thomas, wet the rag. Focus on the rag.

He unscrews the bottled soap and dunks the rag in the bowl of water, while she starts to help EDWARD *step out of his trousers.*

SOPHIE. Okay, Dad, easy.

EDWARD. 'And there came a voice to him saying, "Rise, Peter, kill and eat," but Peter said, "Not so, Lord, for I have never eaten anything that is common or unclean," and the voice spake again the second time and said, "What God hath cleansed, that call not thou common."'

TOM. Okay, so a little scripture to distract us.

SOPHIE. Now sit down, Dad.

He sits.

EDWARD. Everything evolves.

TOM. I'm evolving as we speak.

EDWARD. The body, the mind, the soul, the grass, the earth.

TOM. I am definitely evolving here.

EDWARD. Nothing is stationary, nothing still.

SOPHIE. Give me the rag.

TOM hands her the rag.

Stand up, Dad.

EDWARD. You said sit.

SOPHIE. I need you to stand.

EDWARD *stands.*

TOM. He's the human yo-yo.

SOPHIE. Okay, you may want to look away, crunch time.

TOM. Oh, Jesus, yes, thank you, and deep breath in.

EDWARD. Love suffereth long and is kind.

SOPHIE. And pad is coming off.

TOM. Oh. Jesus. Fuck. No.

We see her taking off the pad.

SOPHIE. Where's the empty bowl?

TOM. What empty bowl?

SOPHIE. I need somewhere for the used pad.

TOM. You didn't say anything about an empty bowl.

SOPHIE. Shit.

TOM. Lots of it.

EDWARD. I AM LIFE.

TOM. You are definitely Life, Edward, you are definitely Life.

SOPHIE. I can't just put them on the floor.

TOM. In all its glory.

SOPHIE. I need a bowl, a bucket, something.

EDWARD. Love vaunteth not itself, is not puffed up.

TOM. Neither am I.

SOPHIE. Tom.

TOM. We're outdoors, put it on the floor and we'll sort it out later.

She places the used pad on the floor.

EDWARD. Beareth all things, believeth all things, hopeth all things, endureth all things.

TOM. It certainly does.

SOPHIE. Okay, step two.

The sound of a mobile phone ringing.

TOM. Jesus, the timing.

He takes his phone out, looks at it.

It's Roger, I need to answer it.

SOPHIE. Roger?

TOM. Hartmann, from the office. The Maybelline job. It's the deadline.

SOPHIE. Maybelline?

TOM. I need to answer it.

SOPHIE. Tom, I am holding my father's… in my hand, I can't hold him, I need you to be with me right now.

TOM. I told you before, Sophie, that if Roger called I needed to answer it, I promised him I was only going to Greece on the condition that I answered his calls. He's fine, you're fine, Edward, he's fine.

SOPHIE. Tom, I need you to hold him…

TOM. Thirty seconds.

He answers the phone, moves away from SOPHIE *and* EDWARD.
SOPHIE *puts the dirty pad on the floor and starts cleaning*
EDWARD *with the rag.*

(*Into the phone.*) Roger, yes, hi. We are, we are. Oh, you know, stuff. Doing stuff.

No, that's cool, I was just… it's fine, I can talk.

SOPHIE. No, you can't.

TOM. No, I left the proposals with Michelle. Did you see them? Oh, you did? Great. I'm happy you like them.

EDWARD. Though I have the gift of prophecy, and understand all mysteries –

TOM. What's that? Yes, I think so too. Dynamic, definitely.

EDWARD. And all knowledge –

TOM. And provocative too in a kind of young kind of way, I know… Hold on, Roger, can you just wait one second, thank you.

EDWARD. And though I have all faith so that I can remove all mountains –

TOM. Can you just, ask him to be quiet? Just like for thirty seconds, *please*, Edward –

SOPHIE. Go inside, why don't you go inside.

EDWARD. For we know in part and we prophecy in part –

TOM. You know that this is like the only spot on the whole goddamned island where I get a signal –

SOPHIE. Tough.

TOM (*into phone*). No, I'm still here, Roger, there's a problem with… em, with the signal, the signal is shit, I mean, the signal is bad, just hold on.

EDWARD. But when that which is perfect is come, then that which is in part shall be done away.

TOM. Can you not take him, I mean, finish inside? *I beg you.*

SOPHIE. TOM, I AM WIPING MY FATHER'S ARSE CLEAN, I CANNOT MOVE INSIDE.

TOM (*into phone*). No, that's fine, just interference, I can hear you fine.

EDWARD. When I was a child I spake as a child –

TOM (*into phone*). Sexier? How d'you mean sexier? Okay, cool.

SOPHIE. Why can't you ask him to call you back in five minutes?

EDWARD. I understood as a child, I thought as a child –

TOM (*into phone*). No, definitely, I know where you're coming from, young, innocent but also kind of you know, womanly, or at least more sophisticated.

EDWARD. But when I became a man I put away childish things.

TOM (*into phone*). No, not in a whorey way, good God no, but I mean, sexy yes, sort of beautiful and shall we say… nymphic, I don't know, is that a word, nymphic –

SOPHIE. Nymphic.

TOM (*into phone*). No, not lymphic as in lymph nodes, I said nymphic as in nymphs, you know, mythological spirits of nature –

EDWARD. For now we see things through a glass darkly, but then face to face.

TOM (*into phone*). As in maiden-like creatures.

SOPHIE. Maiden-like creatures.

TOM (*into phone*). I completely agree with you, cool.

EDWARD. Now I know in part, but then shall I know even as also I am known.

TOM (*into phone*). We're back in Athens Tuesday, I'll be landing in New York Wednesday afternoon. Cool. I'll call you the minute I land, thanks, Roger.

SOPHIE. Thanks, Roger.

TOM turns off his phone.

EDWARD. And now abideth faith, hope, love, these three.

SOPHIE. But the greatest of these is love. Thanks, Dad.

She rinses out the rag.

(*To* TOM.) Could you pass me the clean pad, please?

TOM. Sure.

TOM goes back to where they are and hands her the clean pad. None of them speak as she starts putting the clean pad on, then thoroughly washes her hands and then her father's too.

I had to take that.

SOPHIE. Can you take all the stuff back in, please.

TOM. Sure I can.

He picks up the bowl, the soap, everything excluding the used pad.

SOPHIE. Including the used pad.

He hesitates, then picks it up with great difficulty. It looks as if he's gagging.

We're finished, Dad. That was easy enough.

TOM is walking off with everything in hand.

TOM. Oh, Jesus, I'm going to be sick.

SOPHIE. And bring a pair of underwear and some trousers from his room. The big cupboard in the corner. Underwear second drawer down.

TOM runs off, his hands full, gagging as he goes.

Let's sit down. Sunset time.

EDWARD. Sunset time.

They sit on the bench. He is just in his shirt and pad.

SOPHIE. That's better, isn't it.

EDWARD. Better, better.

They look out.

They take it all literally.

SOPHIE. Yes.

EDWARD. Fools, fools, fools. Myths, poetry, myths, poetry, myths, poetry.

SOPHIE. I know.

EDWARD. Understanding it.

SOPHIE. Understanding what, Dad?

EDWARD. The soul of the world. Not the way they try. Fools. Sisters.

SOPHIE. Sisters?

EDWARD. Religion and art. Sisters.

SOPHIE. Okay, Dad.

EDWARD. And on the other side, the others.

SOPHIE. What others?

EDWARD. The militant atheist saying, 'Don't think like that, don't dream like that, don't wish like that, don't breathe like that.'

SOPHIE. Yes.

EDWARD. Like the right hand asking the left hand not to move.

SOPHIE. Oh.

EDWARD. The right hand saying to the left hand, 'Stop moving, stop moving, stop moving.'

SOPHIE. I see.

EDWARD. As if it can. As if the left hand can ever stop moving.

SOPHIE. No, I know, it can't.

EDWARD. As if it has a choice.

SOPHIE. It doesn't.

EDWARD. Fools.

SOPHIE. Yes.

Pause.

EDWARD. I'm sorry you had to. You know. I'm sorry. Stink of shit.

SOPHIE. No you don't.

Pause. Then EDWARD *starts to weep. She lets him.* TOM *comes back. He's carrying some underwear and a pair of trousers.*

TOM. Here you go.

He hands her the underwear and trousers.

SOPHIE. Come on, Dad. Let's get you dressed.

EDWARD. No.

TOM. Stand up, Edward, so we can get these boxers on.

TOM *helps him up slowly.* EDWARD *leans against* TOM *while* SOPHIE *manoeuvres the underwear around his ankles and up to his waist.*

I'm sorry but I really needed to take that call.

SOPHIE. You said.

TOM. It was important.

SOPHIE. It sounded it.

TOM. So I needed to take it.

SOPHIE. Let's just change the subject, shall we?

Pause. They keep on dressing him. EDWARD *suddenly abandons emotion and becomes very matter-of-fact.*

EDWARD. I need to speak to you.

SOPHIE. I'm listening.

EDWARD. My book.

SOPHIE. Which book, Dad?

EDWARD. The one I'm writing. Someone needs to finish it.

SOPHIE. You're writing a book?

EDWARD. The publishers are waiting.

SOPHIE. Are they?

EDWARD. It's revolutionary.

TOM. We expect nothing less.

EDWARD. Important.

SOPHIE. I'm sure, Dad.

TOM. And now for the trousers, Edward.

> TOM *hands the trousers to* SOPHIE, *who starts putting them on for* EDWARD. *Again* TOM *is holding him, making sure he doesn't lose his balance.*

EDWARD. I've left notes. Pieces of paper.

SOPHIE. Okay.

TOM. Pieces of paper?

EDWARD. Everywhere. Under the bed. In the hole.

SOPHIE. What hole?

EDWARD. You must find them.

TOM. A theological treasure hunt. What fun.

EDWARD. Here it is. Read it.

> *He takes a crumpled piece of paper out of his shirt pocket, and hands it to* TOM, *who reads it.*

TOM. '*The patriarchal gods will die.*' Not until they've put up a damn good fight, I'm sure.

EDWARD. Will you do that, Sophia?

SOPHIE. Do what, Dad?

EDWARD. Find the pieces. Finish the book.

SOPHIE. I can't, Dad.

EDWARD. Why? Why? Why?

SOPHIE. I can't finish your book, Dad.

EDWARD. Fuck it.

SOPHIE. After all, it's your book, Dad, it isn't mine.

EDWARD. What about the American?

TOM. You don't have to talk about me in the third person, Edward, I'm here.

SOPHIE. No, he works in advertising.

TOM. Did you have to tell him that?

SOPHIE. I'm sorry, Dad, I wish we could, but we can't. We can't write your book.

Pause.

EDWARD. Then do something else for me.

SOPHIE. What?

EDWARD. Remember me.

She's taken aback.

SOPHIE. Of course. Of course I'll remember you.

Pause.

EDWARD. He works in *advertising*?

TATYANA comes back.

TATYANA. You have changed him. The pad.

SOPHIE. Yes.

TATYANA. Edward, why you not let me change you? Why you let Sophie do it? When I say to you, 'Let me change you, Edward' –

EDWARD. Shut up.

TATYANA. Why you say, 'No, no, no, get away, get away from me, Tatyana'? Why you do this, Edward?

EDWARD. See what I mean?

SOPHIE. Maybe you shouldn't, I don't know, talk to him like that.

TATYANA. Why do you do this, Edward?

SOPHIE. Like a child, I mean. Please don't. Talk to him like that.

TOM. She's just trying to help, Sophie.

SOPHIE. I'm sorry. I didn't want. It's just that he's not a child, Tatyana.

TATYANA. He's like a child.

SOPHIE. But he isn't. He isn't a child. So maybe you shouldn't talk to him as if he were one.

Pause.

I'm sorry. I just needed to say that.

TATYANA. It is difficult because I am here all the time. Попробуй(те) поживи(те) с ним. [*Pronounced: 'Pah-proh-boo-ee-tyeh pah-zhee-vee-tyeh sneem.' Meaning: 'You try living with him.'*] Edward and Tatyana. Just the two of us. So maybe I forget. This is why.

SOPHIE. Yes.

Pause. EDWARD *is staring at* TOM.

TOM (*to* SOPHIE). You know when we started dating I never imagined, you know… but this is good, this is definitely good. Getting to know you and your family. It's just I never imagined it like this.

SOPHIE. Didn't you?

EDWARD *keeps staring.*

TOM. Some say staring at people like the way you're staring at me now, Edward, is bordering on rude.

EDWARD *keeps staring.*

But maybe it's just a culture thing. In America, that is definitely rude. But here, in the isles of Greece, perhaps it's considered a mark of respect, who knows.

EDWARD. Thomas.

TOM. I'll be damned.

EDWARD. Doubting Thomas.

TOM. Are you getting personal?

EDWARD. Thomas, Thomas. Thomas.

TOM. Edward, Edward, Edward.

EDWARD. Matter will yield but only when we're ready.

TOM. If you say so.

EDWARD. The dormant powers of the human mind.

TOM. 'Dormant', interesting choice of word.

EDWARD. Help me.

TOM. Your wish is my command.

EDWARD. The book. I need to finish the book.

TOM. And how can I help you do that?

EDWARD. The papers, find the papers.

TATYANA. Everywhere in the house little pieces of paper.

SOPHIE. Which paper do you mean, Dad?

EDWARD. They're here, somewhere here.

SOPHIE. Dad?

TATYANA. He writes little pieces –

SOPHIE. Like the one he showed us.

TATYANA. And everywhere in the house. Маленькие бумажки сводят меня с ума. [*Pronounced: 'Ma-len'-ki-e bumazhki svo-diat menia syma.' Meaning: 'Little pieces of paper, driving me crazy.'*]

> EDWARD *stands up and starts to scurry about looking for his piece of paper – under the bench, under pots, on the floor – he becomes increasingly distressed.*

EDWARD. Help me find it, Thomas, help me find it.

TOM. I need to know what it is we're looking for, Edward.

EDWARD. Paper, paper.

TOM. I need you to be more specific.

SOPHIE. A little piece of paper like the one he gave you earlier.

TOM. And I mean we're actually looking now? Or are we just pretending to look?

EDWARD. Find the paper, find the paper.

TOM. I'm looking, Edward, I'm looking.

> TOM *starts looking, imitating* EDWARD, *who is becoming more and more distressed.*

EDWARD. Quickly, quickly, quickly, paper, paper, paper.

SOPHIE *goes up to him, tries to calm him.*

SOPHIE. It's okay, Dad, we'll find it, we'll find the paper, try not
to –

EDWARD. I need the paper, I need the paper, I need the paper –

TOM. I'm working on it, Edward.

EDWARD. I need the paper.

SOPHIE. Please, Dad.

EDWARD. THE PAPER, THE PAPER, THE PAPER, I NEED THE
PAPER!

He collapses into SOPHIE*'s arms and begins to sob.*

SOPHIE. It's okay, it's okay, it's okay. I have you now, I have you
now, I have you now. Shhh.

TATYANA. Every day like this. Каждый день. [*Pronounced: 'Kazh-
dui den.' Meaning: 'Every day.'*]

Pause. And then TOM, *who had been searching through a
flowerpot, raises his hand. He's holding a tiny piece of paper.*

TOM. Well, I'll be damned.

SOPHIE. Look, Dad, Tom's found the piece of paper.

TOM. I found it! I found it! I found it!

SOPHIE. Thank you, Tom.

TATYANA. Everywhere in the house pieces of paper. Повсюду.
[*Pronounced: 'Povsudu.' Meaning: 'Everywhere.'*]

EDWARD. Read it.

TOM. Yes, sir.

*He opens it. It is obviously blank. He turns it over. Blank, both
sides. He looks in panic at* SOPHIE.

(*Mouthing.*) It's blank. Nothing on it.

SOPHIE (*prompting him to make something up*). What does it say,
Tom?

TOM (*stalling*). You mean the paper? What does the paper say?

SOPHIE. Yes, what does it say?

EDWARD. What does it say? What does it say? WHAT DOES IT SAY?

EDWARD *is waiting for the response.* TOM *takes a deep breath, stalls, improvises, but not with great conviction.*

TOM. 'Seek, and ye shall find'?

Blackout.

End of Act Two.

ACT THREE

Scene One

2010

A hotel room. Slick, impersonal. A bed, a chair, a plasma television screen and not much else.

It is a winter evening in London and maybe there is a snow falling outside.

SOPHIE *and* TOM *are under the sheets, making love. A lot of noise comes from the pair but most of it suggests discomfort, not pleasure. Then, finally:*

SOPHIE. Ow.

TOM. What's wrong?

SOPHIE. Something's hurting me.

TOM. What is?

SOPHIE. I don't know, something's in my back.

Suddenly the television switches on. It's BBC World News. *A news report: the date is mentioned and so is the year and then something about the financial situation caused by the banking crisis and about the cuts being made in the UK by the Coalition Government.*

It's the remote.

TOM. You turned the TV on.

SOPHIE. Not on purpose.

TOM. Am I boring you?

SOPHIE. Just turn it off.

TOM. Where is it? Where is the remote?

SOPHIE. It's near my bra. I can feel it.

TOM. Okay, wait.

There is some fumbling about. Then, suddenly the television switches off.

Oh, shit.

SOPHIE. What?

TOM. My watch is caught on your bra thing.

SOPHIE. What bra thing?

TOM. Your bra clasp.

SOPHIE. Well, undo… *ow*… undo it, Tom.

TOM. Can you just lie still until I do this?

SOPHIE. I am lying still.

TOM. Just wait.

There is fumbling about.

I can't get it off.

SOPHIE. You can't get what off?

TOM. The watch. I don't know what happened. I think what happened is it opened up. And then snapped shut again but kind of did it when the bra clasp was in the way.

SOPHIE. Well, take it off.

TOM. That's what I'm doing, Sophie.

More fumbling.

You have to take your bra off, Sophie.

SOPHIE. How can I take my bra off when your whole arm is in it?

TOM. We have to get out of bed.

They crawl out of bed. TOM's hand is attached to her bra clasp. It's like a game of Twister.

Foreplay improves with age.

They struggle around a little but to no avail.

Maybe we should call someone. Like reception, or something.

SOPHIE. That's a great idea, Tom.

TOM. 'Hello, sir, my lady friend and I seem to have got ourselves into a little bind here. Would you mind unclasping us?'

SOPHIE. I need to see what I'm doing, then maybe I can undo the bra.

TOM. Okay, so let's do that.

SOPHIE. I need a mirror.

TOM. The bathroom.

SOPHIE. Okay.

They hobble off into the bathroom. The next lines are spoken offstage.

Can you just stop moving for a second?

TOM. I'm not moving.

SOPHIE. Just keep your hand still.

TOM. I am. At least I'm trying to.

SOPHIE. That's better. Now I can see what I'm doing.

A little more struggling.

There.

TOM. Jesus.

SOPHIE. I need.

TOM. What? You need what?

SOPHIE. Can you just close the door, please.

The door closes. Then it opens again.

No, I mean, with you on the outside.

TOM *steps back into the room.*

TOM. You don't want to resume our... that thing we were doing? Before the watch incident?

SOPHIE. Please, Tom. Just a minute.

She closes the door. He stands outside it.

TOM. Are you okay? Because I have a distinct feeling I've lost you.

No reply.

It's not adultery. I'm divorced and you. Well, you said Sebastian and you were. Temporarily separated. After the incident with the French student. (*Sotto voce to himself.*) Private tutorials in Marxist theory.

Still no response.

It would be good if you could give me some sort of clue. A pointer. Like, I don't know: 'This wasn't a good idea because of your breath, Tom. Or that thing you said.' Or: 'You're a constant disappointment.' I don't know. Whatever. Just something.

She comes out of the bathroom wearing a bathrobe. She aims straight for the chair her clothes are on and begins to get dressed. Her actions have a purpose to them, as if all of a sudden she is in a hurry.

SOPHIE. Your breath is fine and no, it wasn't anything you said.

TOM. What then?

She continues to get dressed.

SOPHIE. I have something that belongs to you.

TOM. How exciting.

SOPHIE. I was clearing out some old boxes. In my study.

TOM. Okay.

SOPHIE. And I found this.

She opens her bag, takes out a manuscript, hands it to him. She returns to getting dressed.

TOM. Fuck.

SOPHIE. I thought you'd appreciate it.

TOM. '*The Missing Man*'.

SOPHIE. With your own notes in the margins.

She keeps dressing. He flicks through the manuscript.

TOM. Tolstoyan in its ambition if a little clunky.

SOPHIE. It was your first completed novel, Tom. You were twenty-four. It's not going to be *War and Peace*.

TOM. Did you call me nine years after we broke up to discuss the promise in my writing?

SOPHIE. It's a first draft. Maybe one day you'll work on the second one.

TOM. Unlikely.

SOPHIE. I know it is. After all, you're not very good at sticking to things.

TOM. I was good a minute ago.

SOPHIE. Seeing things through.

TOM. When I was stuck to your bra, I mean.

SOPHIE. Yes, you were good at that. And you're consistently good in seeing the lighter side of everything.

She makes a move to go. He runs to the door and blocks it.

TOM. You can't go. Not now. Not like this.

SOPHIE. Tom, get out of the way.

TOM. You call me up, you say –

SOPHIE. I know I called you.

TOM. 'When you're next in town, Tom' –

SOPHIE. It was a mistake, I said so –

TOM. 'I need to see you, Tom.'

SOPHIE. I thought I did.

TOM. And then you say, 'Let's go to the room,' I didn't drag you here –

SOPHIE. I didn't say you did.

TOM. You suggested it.

SOPHIE. I know, I know I did.

TOM. And now you're like 'I'm leaving.'

SOPHIE. I need to.

TOM. Not before you talk to me.

SOPHIE. Please get out of my way, Tom.

TOM. Before you explain.

SOPHIE. You don't want to hear what I have to say.

TOM. Because you can't keep doing this, Sophie.

SOPHIE. You really don't want to hear it.

TOM. Walking out on me every ten fucking years.

SOPHIE. You really don't.

TOM. BECAUSE YOU CAN'T KEEP FUCKING DOING THIS!

Pause. They are both surprised by the intensity of his reaction.
SOPHIE *takes a deep breath.*

SOPHIE. All right then.

TOM. Go on.

SOPHIE. I was hoping that when I read it I'd realise that I was young, and in love with you and unable to be objective and that you'd been right to give it up –

TOM. What are you talking about?

SOPHIE. But that now I'd see its flaws and agree with you and say, 'Yes, he has very little to say, he had to let it go,' but then I read it and there was –

TOM. There was what?

SOPHIE. A *reason* you were writing.

TOM. So you called me to tell me that?

SOPHIE. And I was sitting there in the middle of the night, thinking of why things turned out the way they did, why you lost that *belief* you had in yourself and when it was that happened, when it started *eroding* –

TOM. I have a feeling you're going to tell me.

SOPHIE. – and it was when we returned to New York and you started the job at Hartmanns –

TOM. What about it?

SOPHIE. – and it had something to do with words losing their definitions, their intrinsic meanings –

TOM. What the fuck are you talking about?

SOPHIE. – words like *success* and *happiness* and *aspiration*, *believe in better*, and that once the words went, then everything else did too and that things lost their shape and you weren't able to distinguish what was true from what wasn't and that was the intention and you fell for it so easily.

TOM. What intention?

SOPHIE. And that everything became not about what you were but about the way you were perceived, not about what connected you to others but about what *separated* you –

TOM. Separated me?

SOPHIE. And that, before you realised it, life had become meaningless and that every choice you made was unimportant because in a life with no meaning everything is acceptable, or laughable or weightless and everything is condoned –

TOM. Fucking hell, Sophie.

SOPHIE. And that we found ourselves in this world we had created that survived and prospered on the very fact that we no longer believed in *anything*.

TOM. Jesus Christ.

SOPHIE. And then I read your book, Tom, and it was by a boy, a boy who had this thing we call a *soul*, untutored and young and still searching, but a soul, a soul, a *soul*.

TOM. Jesus fuck.

SOPHIE. Until you sold it to the highest bidder.

Pause.

TOM. You fucking come here in judgement on me with your fucking ideals, your superiority, you fucking come here –

SOPHIE. You asked me.

TOM. And tell me these things and say words have lost their definitions, words like *success* and *happiness*, you have the fucking nerve to do that, to sit in judgement on me –

SOPHIE. That's not what I'm doing –

TOM. – you come and judge *me* and speak of souls and highest bidders –

SOPHIE. Because I knew what you were –

TOM. Well, let me tell you something now, and you listen to me, for once in your fucking life listen to me –

SOPHIE. – the things you were capable of.

TOM. – because I am going to tell you something now about how things are, not about what you'd like them to be but about the way they are, the way it is –

SOPHIE. What way?

TOM. The way it is, Sophie, the way it is, the way IT FUCKING IS.

He silences her.

Fucking atoms, fucking things, animals, fucking animals in the fucking dark, eating each other, fucking eating, killing, destroying each other, it's what we fucking are, fucking appetite that's all, ruthless and indiscriminate, floating around in a fucking universe that doesn't give a flying fuck about us, and all we fucking have, the only chance at happiness, the only fucking chance we have is to find that one fucking person who makes you want to get out of bed in the morning and we had that and you... and you fucking come to me as if *I* made the world, as if *I* fucking decided it, as if *I* chose the fucking way life is.

SOPHIE. You did, Tom.

TOM. And you talk about these words as if you know what they mean, about *happiness* as if you know what it means –

SOPHIE. I never said that.

TOM. – because excuse me if I've got the wrong picture here, forgive me if I have an erroneous idea, but from what Lawrence has told me –

SOPHIE. I never said I knew.

TOM. – from what I've heard in passing, ever since you came back from Iraq you find it difficult to get out of bed in the fucking morning, have to scrape yourself off the fucking floor –

SOPHIE. Because of what I saw –

TOM. – so excuse me for not thinking you would be the right person to consult for the most precise definition of that particular word –

SOPHIE. The *things* I saw.

TOM. Excuse me for thinking that but the fact is –

SOPHIE. And knowing that way we live, the *choices* we've made –

TOM. – that what I see in front of me is a woman who's spent her whole fucking life doing the right thing, honouring her dead fucking father, living the right way, doing the right thing –

SOPHIE. – have made us complicit.

TOM. – AT THE COST OF HAVING LIVED HER LIFE AT ALL.

Pause.

SOPHIE *slowly picks up her things, moves toward the door as if she is about to leave, then stops and turns to him.*

SOPHIE. I thought you were the one who left me.

Pause.

Afterwards I waited. I hoped. Foolishly, I know. That maybe you would change your mind. Maybe, then. The two of us. Together. Something like happiness.

She walks up to him and kisses him gently. Then she goes. He does not move for a few seconds.

Then, slowly, he walks to the chair and begins to dress. As he does, the snow ceases to fall and the scene changes around him.

Scene Two

2011

TOM *is back on the terrace in Patmos but it has changed: it has been invaded by books. They are all over the place, they have left the edges and corners of the space and have taken it over completely. In piles, in boxes, on chairs, on the floors: books everywhere.*

TATYANA *is standing in the middle of the space, dusting some of them.* TOM *has just arrived. It is an evening in September.*

TATYANA (*in between tears*). И я говорю себе: будь сильной, Татьяна, будь сильной, бывало и хуже; но даже когда умерла моя сестра, мне не было так плохо, как будто мое сердце вырвали и бросили его на пол. [*Pronounced: 'I ja gavaru sebe: bud' sil'noi, buvala i khuzhe; no dazhe kagda umerla maja sestra, mne nebula tak plokha, kakbutta majo sertse vurvali i brosili evo napal.' Meaning: 'And I say to myself: be strong, Tatyana, be strong, you have been through worse, but even my sister died I did not feel this sad, like my heart has been ripped out and thrown on the floor.'*]

TOM. Tatyana, I still haven't learnt any Russian.

TATYANA. I said it is like my heart has been thrown on the floor.

TOM. That's a powerful image.

Pause.

TATYANA. You are late.

TOM. I know I am.

TATYANA. I said to them, 'Wait, we must wait, Tom is coming from America.'

TOM. I missed the ferry.

TATYANA. He will want to be here.

TOM. The demonstrations. It took three hours to get to the port.

TATYANA. It is important for him to be here.

TOM. Thank you, it is.

TATYANA. But they could not change the time of the boat. Everything had been planned.

TOM. I understand.

Pause. She weeps some more.

TATYANA. It is a shame.

TOM. What is?

TATYANA. That you did not stay together. You and Sophia.

TOM. Yes.

TATYANA. You were much good together.

TOM. Yes.

TATYANA. Like butter and jam.

TOM. Was I the butter or the jam?

TATYANA. Like tomato and feta.

TOM. You're making me hungry.

TATYANA. Come, I make you something.

TOM. No, it's fine, I didn't really, I was being... In a while maybe, in a little while.

TATYANA. There is soup.

Pause. She looks around to make sure they are alone.

I prefer you to Sebastian. He is Communist.

TOM. He's all right.

TATYANA. How can you be Communist when you have not lived in Communist country?

TOM. I don't know.

TATYANA. It is easy. I have lived as a child, I know. Nothing works, everything ugly, and people telling you all the time 'Do this, do that.' And if you don't do it, у тебя будут проблемы [*Pronounced: 'utebia budut problemu' Meaning: 'well, you're in trouble'*], you are in trouble.

TOM. Yes.

TATYANA. That is Communism. It is easy being Communist when you are living in the centre of London with beautiful things everywhere: IKEA, Harrods. I do not like him.

TOM. I think he means well.

Pause.

TATYANA. Like butter and jam.

SEBASTIAN *and* LAWRENCE *come on, they are wearing casually smart clothes, maybe jackets.*

TOM. I'm late, I know.

SEBASTIAN. We waited.

LAWRENCE. It was all rather sublime. Apart from that fucking Greek wind.

SEBASTIAN. The *meltemi.*

LAWRENCE. Most of her ended up on the lapels of my jacket but I'm sure that's an honour. She always left her mark.

SEBASTIAN. At least there were not too many waves.

LAWRENCE. Nobody threw up which was a blessing.

TATYANA. At the same place with her father. You remember, Tom?

TOM. Beyond the second bay, yes.

TATYANA. Father and daughter in the sea now. Like fish.

LAWRENCE *and* TOM *hug.*

LAWRENCE. Luke sends his love. He couldn't make it but I told him you were coming.

TOM. How's married life?

LAWRENCE. Married life is good.

Pause.

TATYANA. Where is the girl?

SEBASTIAN. Agatha?

TATYANA. You have forgotten her?

LAWRENCE. She stopped off at the cave. To have a look, she said.

TATYANA. We have to finish the books.

SEBASTIAN. She will come soon and we can start.

TATYANA. So many books.

LAWRENCE. But now we have an extra pair of hands.

TOM. Just tell me what to do.

Pause.

LAWRENCE. We need some more of those boxes.

TATYANA. Come, I take you.

LAWRENCE. Take me, Tatyana, take me.

TATYANA. They are in the room near the kitchen.

LAWRENCE. Lead the way.

TATYANA. And I drop your suitcase in the room, Tom.

She picks up his suitcase and enters the house with LAWRENCE *in tow.*

SEBASTIAN. They said to me… this doctor in Kabul, he spoke beautiful English and he said to me. He said to me it was very quick.

TOM. A bullet in the back of her head.

SEBASTIAN. There were five of them. An ambush.

TOM. I read about it in *The Times*. But some was speculation, the details were vague.

SEBASTIAN. She had only been there two weeks but was already unpopular with some people. The more fundamentalist type.

TOM. The fear. The rage.

SEBASTIAN. It was about education. But for the first time she had a film crew with her. Lately she had become obsessed about the education of girls. From family planning to algebra. So she was doing a piece about three different countries for the BBC. She had done Angola and Pakistan. But from the minute she landed in Afghanistan she was making people quite angry.

TOM. Inevitably.

SEBASTIAN. Rocking the boat, as you say.

TOM. Forever rocking it.

Pause. And then suddenly SEBASTIAN *cries.*

SEBASTIAN. You fucking bastard.

TOM. I'm sorry?

SEBASTIAN. Always living in your fucking shadow.

TOM. Oh.

SEBASTIAN. For some reason she couldn't quite get you out of her system, her mind, I don't know. Not that she spoke about you because she didn't. But I knew, I knew, I knew.

TOM. Okay.

SEBASTIAN. You bastard.

He pulls himself together as quickly and suddenly as he broke down.

I'm sorry. I'm upset.

TOM. We both are.

SEBASTIAN. Some people you never can.

TOM. Never can what?

SEBASTIAN. Shake off…

TOM. No, never.

SEBASTIAN. But I'm glad you came. For her sake. It's what she would have wanted.

TOM. I hope so.

Pause.

SEBASTIAN. It's the grief. It makes you honest.

TOM. It certainly does that.

Pause.

That thing you said. The day we met. You said something about the Towers. You said –

SEBASTIAN. I remember.

TOM. I think you were right.

Pause.

First goes the conviction. Then everything else.

LAWRENCE *and* TATYANA *return, carrying some boxes. They immediately set about packing books in boxes.*

TATYANA. What time are they coming to pick the boxes?

SEBASTIAN. Ten in the morning.

TATYANA. All the books for the girl. Sophie had written especially 'If something happens all my father's books for the girl.'

TOM. What girl?

LAWRENCE. And the house?

SEBASTIAN. It's being sold. At least it'll pay off the debts.

TOM. What will you do, Tatyana?

TATYANA. I will return to Ukraine. My mother says there is some work at her cousin's shop, selling shoes in Horenka.

TOM. If I can do anything.

TATYANA. I leave on Tuesday from Athens to Kiev. My nephew he has arranged me the ticket. He is steward for Air Ukrayina.

TOM. Does he still like Britney Spears?

TATYANA. No. Lady Gaga.

LAWRENCE. Are we just putting these in randomly?

SEBASTIAN. For the time. And maybe we separate when in England. Agatha can take hers to Brighton, the ones she doesn't want I can keep in London.

LAWRENCE. Does she live in a bloody mansion?

SEBASTIAN. I told her I would pay for storage until she leaves university and has somewhere to put them.

TATYANA *has stopped at a particular book, she opens it.*

TATYANA. Ah, look, Tolstoy. He is Russian.

TOM. Indeed.

TATYANA. And Dostoyevsky, and Gogol, and Gorky, and Chekhov and Turgenev. All Russian.

LAWRENCE. A rich tradition.

TATYANA. Always he writes in the book, Edward. Putting the lines under everything.

TOM. Highlighting.

TATYANA. And little pieces of paper. And photographs in the books.

SEBASTIAN. For bookmarks.

TATYANA. Why is he always putting the line under things. Even in *Anna Karenina*.

TOM. Pointers. Reminders.

AGATHA *walks on but nobody notices her.*

TATYANA. Like here. (*Reads.*) 'I have been seeking an answer to my question but reason could not give it to me. It was life itself that gave me the answer, through my knowledge of good and bad. To love your neighbour could not have been discovered by reason, because it is unreasonable.'

It sounds nicer in Russian.

LAWRENCE *spots* AGATHA.

LAWRENCE. Here she is.

AGATHA. Hello.

LAWRENCE. How was the cave, darling?

AGATHA. Mysterious and a little damp.

LAWRENCE. That's caves for you.

AGATHA. They have built a church around it.

SEBASTIAN. A chapel, yes.

AGATHA. In the beginning it was just a man having dreams in a cave. Then they built a church around it.

SEBASTIAN. We are doing the books and then we will eat something.

AGATHA. I will help you.

TATYANA. I have made the fish stew that Sophie liked.

AGATHA (*spotting* TOM). Hello.

TOM. Hi.

AGATHA. I'm Agatha.

TOM. I am Tom.

TATYANA. Some of these writers have very strange names.

LAWRENCE. You two don't know each other?

TOM. I don't think so.

SEBASTIAN. I think the best thing, Agatha, is just to put them all in the boxes and then separate them in England. Then the ones you don't want I can take.

AGATHA. Until I've read them, I won't know.

LAWRENCE. Ooh, she's a smart one.

AGATHA. You are a friend of Sophie's?

TOM. From a long time ago, yes.

TATYANA. Again he has put pen all over it.

LAWRENCE. I'm amazed you've never met.

TATYANA (*reading*). 'Cease being what you are, what biology and circumstance have made you. Become, at the fearful price of abnegation, what you could be.'

TOM. You are a student of Sebastian's?

LAWRENCE. But then, of course, I forget that you and Sophie hadn't seen each other for a long time.

TOM (*covering*). Not for ages.

AGATHA. I am a student, yes, but not of Sebastian's. I have just finished my first year at the University of Sussex, studying Literature and Economics.

TOM. That's an interesting combination.

LAWRENCE. And hopefully a useful one. (*Pulls a face of mock terror.*)

AGATHA. Where are you from, Tom?

TATYANA. What is this word, 'abnegation'?

TOM. I'm from New York.

AGATHA. I've never been to New York.

SEBASTIAN. One day.

AGATHA. But I am a friend of Sophie's too. For a long time, like you.

TATYANA. What does this word mean? Abnegation?

LAWRENCE. I think it means a sacrifice.

TOM. From where?

SEBASTIAN. Like you have to give something up.

TATYANA. Why does he have to write all over the books?

AGATHA. From somewhere far away.

TATYANA. In Russia, this is a crime.

TOM. Whereabouts?

AGATHA. From a town called Amuria. It is about one hundred and forty miles from Kampala in the eastern part of –

TOM. Uganda. I know.

He takes this on board.

AGATHA. You have heard of Amuria?

TOM. I have, yes.

AGATHA. Either Sophie had spoken to you about it or you have a good memory for bad news.

TOM. A little of both.

AGATHA. My town is known for the wrong reasons.

Pause. They carry on going through the books. Apart from TOM, *who can barely move.*

LAWRENCE (*pronouncing it like 'Keats'*). Yeats. Or Yeats. I always forget.

SEBASTIAN (*correctly*). Yeats.

LAWRENCE (*pronouncing it like 'Yeats'*). So then why not Keats? (*Mispronouncing it again.*) 'Ode to a Grecian Urn' by John Keats.

SEBASTIAN. When the boxes are packed we should put them by the kitchen door so that the man picks them straight up from there in the car.

AGATHA (*holding up a book*). This one I want to keep. *The Complete Works of William Shakespeare*.

LAWRENCE. Yes, that's a good one.

TATYANA. Very difficult names. Kierkegaard. Wole Soyinka.

AGATHA. He is from Nigeria.

TATYANA. *Either/Or*. Strange name for a book. *Either/Or*.

AGATHA (*flicking through* The Complete Works). *As You Like It*, *Twelfth Night or What You Will*.

SEBASTIAN. Come, we start moving the boxes to the back of the kitchen. Then we can clear the terrace for dinner.

TATYANA. And I bring the fish soup.

AGATHA. *Romeo and Juliet*, *Hamlet*, *Othello*.

LAWRENCE (*picking up a box*). I'll take this one. Oooh, my hernia.

AGATHA. *Cymbeline*, *The Winter's Tale*, *The Tempest*.

She puts it carefully in a box and returns to packing the remaining books.

LAWRENCE, SEBASTIAN and TATYANA all go off carrying some of the boxes of books. The space starts to clear.

AGATHA and TOM are left alone. They are silent for a while. Then TOM speaks.

TOM. And how did you. What I mean is. How did you. Meet Sophie. How did she meet you.

AGATHA. When I was eight years old Sophie came to write a piece about the organisation which was helping us raise funds for the Fletcher case… Ten years ago.

TOM. And you were. I mean. One of the. You were affected by the events of?

AGATHA. My sister died but I was lucky. I was paralysed down the right side of my body for three or four years and it is still what I call 'my lazy half', but yes, I was one of what they came to call the Fletcher children.

TOM. The Fletcher children.

AGATHA. Afterwards, everyone packed up and left. But from the beginning Sophie was more involved. 'Hands-on', isn't that what you say?

TOM. Hands-on.

AGATHA. When she first came she lived in our house for a few weeks and became close to my parents. She seemed to have a purpose to be there. But then she was one of those people.

TOM. One of those people?

AGATHA. Who lived with some sense of purpose, I mean.

TOM. Yes.

AGATHA. So she became close to us and then it was she who paid for me to go to the International School in Kampala and then has helped me to come here to follow my higher education. Not only financially.

TOM. It was kind of her.

AGATHA. But she would be very angry if you called it charity. She does not believe in charity, she always said. As long as you see it as charity, things will never change.

TOM. No.

AGATHA. It is more than that. Something else.

TOM. Something else?

AGATHA. Maybe a different way of seeing.

TOM (*almost to himself*). Nothing is abstract.

  AGATHA *stands up and picks up the box.*

AGATHA. I will take the box to put it with the others.

  She leaves, carrying the box. TOM *is left alone onstage. He is reeling. There is a gesture, something like a hand to the face, a lowering of the head which looks almost as if he might be in physical pain, as if he is finding it hard to breathe.*

Then LAWRENCE *returns with* TATYANA.

TATYANA. Another five minutes and the stew is ready.

LAWRENCE. The last few to go and then we're finished. Come on, Tats, give us a hand.

They return to putting the last few books into the remaining boxes. They both look at them one by one as they put them into the boxes.

Graham Greene: *The End of the Affair*. Oh, that was a good one, despite the whole Catholic thing. But I enjoyed it.

TATYANA. And then afterwards maybe we have watermelon.

LAWRENCE. Maya Angelou, oh, bless her, Goddess Maya. Dickens, Dickens, Dickens, three Dickens in a row, I'm sure that was planned. George Eliot, E.M. Forster, Gabriel García Márquez, *The Kama Sutra*? Oh, well, an eclectic collection.

TATYANA. And then I make coffee.

AGATHA *and* SEBASTIAN *return.*

SEBASTIAN. One more box each and then we finish.

AGATHA. I will do these ones over here.

They join LAWRENCE *and* TATYANA *in piling away the books. For a short while, as they work, nobody talks.*

TOM. And when was the last time you saw her, Agatha? Sophie, I mean.

AGATHA. I was lucky. Over the Easter break I went to stay with her in London for a week. It was just the two of us.

SEBASTIAN. I was in Chile, visiting my mother.

AGATHA. For that week she was not working. Just before she went to Afghanistan. We stayed up at night and talked a lot, maybe had what you might call philosophical conversations.

TOM. Philosophical conversations?

AGATHA. About life, really, and about religion too. Things I could never really talk to my own parents about.

TOM. Couldn't you?

AGATHA. My parents are not educated, you see. They can read and write but that is about all. The only book they know is the Bible.

LAWRENCE. Speaking of which, I found this one earlier.

He leans over and picks up an old book, hands it to AGATHA. *She holds on to it until the end of the scene.*

AGATHA. Thank you.

LAWRENCE. An old King James.

TATYANA. It is Edward's.

LAWRENCE. And there's a Koran in that one there. (*Points to another box.*)

AGATHA. So they revere it and you cannot say anything against it. It would upset them. I think it is natural.

TOM. Very.

AGATHA. But with Sophie we could talk about other things, and all these other books too, other stories. So yes, we talked a lot, sometimes well into the night.

LAWRENCE. She certainly liked talking.

SEBASTIAN (*looking at the book he is holding*). Cervantes.

They carry on sorting the books.

TATYANA. Look. Look at us. I am from the Ukraine. You are from Chile. Tom is American. You are African. And you are from Croydon. We are the globalisation.

SEBASTIAN (*putting the last few books in the box*). Nearly there.

AGATHA. One night we were talking about Christianity.

LAWRENCE. Nothing on the telly then?

AGATHA. Edward her father was a bishop, you know.

TOM. I did know that, yes.

AGATHA. But, by all accounts, an unconventional bishop.

TOM. Definitely unconventional.

LAWRENCE. He fought our cause within the Church.

AGATHA. Well, one night I said to her – asked her – how she must have been shaped by him. By his Christianity. I said, 'Do you consider yourself a Christian, Sophie?'

TOM. And what did she say?

AGATHA. She said, no, she wasn't a Christian. When she was a child, maybe, but not any more. And then she used the funniest expression to describe herself.

LAWRENCE. And what was that?

AGATHA. She said: 'I am a faith machine.'

TOM. What did she mean?

AGATHA. She said of course Darwin was right, we had crawled out of our caves on all fours, and then slowly, painfully, risen onto our back legs and stood up and yes, yes we were still 'red in tooth and claw' – Don't look surprised, Lawrence, I did Tennyson for my A-level.

LAWRENCE. Oh, hark at her.

AGATHA. Anyway, she said that yes we had evolved from that but that somewhere along the line some people – and she said she was one of them – had inherited in their machinery something that made them need to believe. And when I said, 'Yes, but what is it you believe in?', she just replied, 'Against all empirical evidence and rational enquiry I continue to believe in the human being.'

SEBASTIAN. Finished.

SEBASTIAN closes his box and picks it up. They have all finished packing their boxes. Except for AGATHA *who has a few books left.*

TATYANA. Come, we take them. And then we go and get the soup. It will be delicious… Lawrence, you bring the plates.

LAWRENCE. Yes, ma'am.

TATYANA. And, Sebastian, you open some wine. And we have the toast. To Sophie.

SEBASTIAN. Agatha?

AGATHA. I'm coming.

There are just a handful of books left and TOM *helps put them into* AGATHA's *box. She is still holding the Bible which she now starts to look at. The rest are making their way into the house.*

LAWRENCE (*to* TATYANA). Why do you keep looking at me like that?

TATYANA. Like what?

LAWRENCE. Like the way you are now.

TATYANA. You know it is funny. Many years ago, this man was here, a friend of Edward's from Kenya. You look very like him.

LAWRENCE. Wonderful, so you're a racist.

TATYANA. I am not racist. I like the Africans, the Japanese and even some of the gays.

LAWRENCE. How enlightened of you.

TATYANA. The only ones I don't like are the Communists.

LAWRENCE. So you don't think it's racist to say that I look exactly like the only other black man you've ever spoken to?

TATYANA. He was your spitting brother.

SEBASTIAN. Why don't you like the Communists?

TATYANA. My grandmother she is the only good Communist I know.

SEBASTIAN. Oh, so there is a good one, is there?

TATYANA. She says to me you can only be a Communist with the heart. And then she says we are not ready yet.

LAWRENCE. Not evolved.

AGATHA. Maybe one day.

LAWRENCE. That's hopeful.

SEBASTIAN. So in the meantime we keep looking.

LAWRENCE. And eating.

TATYANA. Come for the soup.

TATYANA, LAWRENCE and SEBASTIAN *leave, carrying the last boxes.*

Except for AGATHA*'s.* TOM *puts the last few books into it. She is still leafing through the Bible.*

AGATHA. I cannot take the Bible word for word like my parents. I know that when it says something about – I don't know – eating pork, or about slaves or the gay people – my goodness, there are so many gay people in Brighton! – I realise it is very much part of the time it was written in. The times are like shedding skins. But what lies behind them, that lasts for ever.

TOM. The heart of the story.

AGATHA. Do unto others as you would have them do unto you.

TOM. The Golden Rule.

AGATHA. Don't hide you light under a bushel, Tom!

TOM. Stick it on your head?

AGATHA. Or my favourite.

TOM. Which is?

AGATHA. For what good shall it profit a man shall he gain the whole world…

TOM *interrupts before she can finish it.*

TOM. Yes, that is a good one.

She looks out at the view from the terrace.

AGATHA. It is so beautiful here.

TOM. This is the time of day.

AGATHA. But there is a chill in the air.

TOM. September.

Pause.

AGATHA. I'm sorry, I didn't…

TOM. You didn't what?

AGATHA. I know you are from New York and that you were a friend of Sophie's but the thing is you didn't really say.

TOM. I didn't say what?

AGATHA. This will sound very rude.

TOM. I can take it.

AGATHA. Because you didn't really say how. And I don't think Sophie had mentioned you, so I think what I'm asking is…

She thinks how she can phrase it.

Who are you, Tom?

TOM. Oh. Me? Let's see. Em. Now that's an interesting question. Who am I?

Pause.

I was. She and I. We were. Now, let's see.

He thinks long and hard.

The missing man. Let's call me the missing man.

AGATHA *looks at him, puzzled. She smiles.*

She closes the Bible and places it carefully into the box with the other books.

Then, at a distance, SOPHIE *appears. Like* EDWARD *in the first scene, she is an apparition.*

She stands at a short distance from TOM *and* AGATHA *and looks at them. They cannot see her but her presence is felt.*

AGATHA *and* TOM *close the box of books.*

Blackout.

The End.

BRACKEN MOOR

We must go down into the dungeons of the heart,
To the dark places where modern mind imprisons
All that is not defined and thought apart.
We must let out the terrible creative visions.

Return to the most human, nothing less
Will teach the angry spirit, the bewildered heart,
The torn mind, to accept the whole of its duress,
And pierced with anguish, at last act for love.

May Sarton, 1912–1995

Bracken Moor was first performed at the Tricycle Theatre, London, in a co-production between Shared Experience and the Tricycle Theatre, on 6 June 2013, with the following cast:

JOHN BAILEY/DR GIBBONS	Antony Byrne
HAROLD	Daniel Flynn
EILEEN	Natalie Gavin
ELIZABETH	Helen Schlesinger
GEOFFREY	Simon Shepherd
TERENCE	Joseph Timms
VANESSA	Sarah Woodward
COMPANY	Bili Keogh & Jamie Flatters

Director	Polly Teale
Designer	Tom Piper
Lighting Designer	Oliver Fenwick
Composer & Sound Designer	Jon Nicholls
Movement Director	Liz Ranken

Characters

EDGAR PRITCHARD, *twelve*
JOHN BAILEY, *fifties*
HAROLD PRITCHARD, *late forties/early fifties*
EILEEN HANNAWAY, *early twenties*
TERENCE AVERY, *twenty-two*
VANESSA AVERY, *late forties*
GEOFFREY AVERY, *fifties*
ELIZABETH PRITCHARD, *late forties*
DR GIBBONS, *fifties*

JOHN BAILEY *and* DR GIBBONS *are to be be played by the same actor.*

The play takes place entirely in the drawing room of the Pritchards' home on the hills overlooking a mining village in Yorkshire in December 1937.

With the house lights still up, the actors playing HAROLD *and* JOHN *walk on stage. The actor playing* HAROLD *is carrying his shoes, not wearing them. He sits in a chair and puts them on, tying the laces. He then stands and buttons up his waistcoat.*

Meanwhile, the actor playing JOHN *stands in front of a mirror which happens to be positioned somewhere on stage as part of the set and combs his hair.*

We watch the ritual of two actors in the last moments of preparation before a performance. Then, when their checks are complete, they both take their starting positions and look at each other as if to confirm that they are now both ready for the play to begin.

Blackout.

We can hear EDGAR'*s voice but we can't see him. The voice of an anguished child in the dark.*

EDGAR. Mother? Father?

Pause.

Mother, where are you? Father. Father!

Pause.

Mother, Father, please. I'm scared.

Pause.

Please, Father, please!

Pause.

Mother. Father. Where are you?

ACT ONE

Scene One

Lights up.

The drawing room of the Pritchards' home in Yorkshire. This is the main room in a grand old house of an affluent, land-owning family. It is a large, imposing room that announces wealth but not great style. It is masculine and somewhat oppressive in its dark hues and in its scale. The furniture too is heavy and graceless though undoubtedly expensive. The overall impression is one of formality but little joy; as if, in some way, the house has become unloved over the years.

It is an evening in December 1937.

HAROLD PRITCHARD *stands in the middle of the room. He is a man of magnetic and intimidating presence – handsome in an austere way and confident with the knowledge of his position in the world. He is smartly dressed.*

Opposite him stands JOHN BAILEY, *a well-built man who speaks in a strong Yorkshire accent and is wearing a well-worn suit and overcoat that have been exposed to the elements.*

JOHN. I urge you to reconsider.

Pause.

If we let Ramshaw Drift go – if you decide to close it – the village will be decimated.

Pause.

There is no alternative work – nothing left for these men to do. And they have given their best – as have their fathers and their fathers' fathers before them – to help make this industry the proudest Britain has to offer. But of course you know this already, sir, it is not my business to educate you on the matter, merely to remind you of the necessity to reflect on their dedication over the years and on our duty to honour it.

HAROLD. And you do so to great effect, Mr Bailey.

JOHN. Only because I have lived with these people, Mr Pritchard, I am one of them.

HAROLD. Indeed you are.

JOHN. I have known their toil and I recognise them by the sweat of their brow, the strength of their hands and their knowledge of the land.

HAROLD. You are becoming poetical.

JOHN. It is not a pretence, sir. If I speak with some passion it is only because I feel what I say.

HAROLD. I do not doubt your sincerity, Mr Bailey, I only question the way you are using language in order to persuade. And in that effort at least, it may prove to be a waste of your creative endeavours. I'm afraid the situation demands less poetry and more pragmatism; those, unfortunately, are the times in which we live.

JOHN. I stopped by Ramshaw Drift on my way here, sir. There was a problem with one of the cutters – the one I mentioned to you last week, do you remember? – and so I needed to inspect it and ascertain that it was in working order once again, which indeed it was.

HAROLD. Well, that's reassuring.

JOHN. And as I was leaving I noticed Alfie Shaw walking homewards. His shift had just finished and I caught sight of him by the edge of the road and asked him if he wanted a lift in the motor.

HAROLD. Good man.

JOHN. Alfie Shaw, sir – he was the red-haired lad who impressed us all a couple of autumns ago when he helped pull out that poor boy who broke his leg on his very first day. Brought him out on his shoulders like an Achilles.

HAROLD. And now you are invoking mythology.

JOHN. So I drove him to his cottage and he asked me in for a quick brew. I wouldn't usually have taken the time, Mr Pritchard, only I was keen not to give offence and made myself promise that it would be a quick one and as I wasn't expected here till six and a half o'clock I scurried in for a cup of tea.

HAROLD. You did well, Mr Bailey.

JOHN. And it was then that I remembered that Alfie Shaw was recently widowed. His young wife – a pretty thing she was though always weak in constitution – succumbed to consumption a year or so ago, not a day older than twenty-five, I'm sure. And as I'm having my tea I notice something moving around in the corner of my eye and in the doorway I catch three little girls – seven, five and three years of age I'd guess and pretty things all of them with their father's strawberry hair and his freckles too but thin like their mother, nay, more than thin, skin and bones, Mr Pritchard, skin and bones.

HAROLD. You are painting an evocative picture, Mr Bailey, but to what purpose? I must compel you to reach your point, I have guests who have just arrived from London and so my time is pressured.

JOHN. Skin and bones even with their father working and his mother, old Mrs Shaw helping him out no doubt though that's another mouth to feed and the girls' eyes full of hope and worry but there I was sitting in that cold house wondering, Mr Pritchard, what will become of them if you should go ahead and take his job from Alfie Shaw and another one hundred and forty men like him, what should become of those poor, helpless creatures standing in the doorway.

Pause. HAROLD *moves over to the drinks cabinet and pours himself a Scotch.*

HAROLD. Do you read the papers, Mr Bailey?

JOHN. When I have the time, Mr Pritchard, when I have the time.

HAROLD. Of course. But you have, I assume, over the last few months caught enough of a glimpse of them to formulate an impression of what I would call, the bigger picture?

JOHN. And what would the bigger picture be, sir?

HAROLD. The one, Mr Bailey, which often contradicts our more sentimental natures.

JOHN. Does it indeed?

HAROLD. But which we have to heed in order to survive. Not only as individuals but as communities and nations. And which now dictates that sacrifices need to be made.

JOHN. On that we are both agreed, Mr Pritchard.

HAROLD. Good.

JOHN. What we may not be in agreement about is the nature of the sacrifices that are demanded and who they are demanded of.

HAROLD. You are aware, Mr Bailey, that our country – indeed most of the civilised world – is only now beginning to emerge from the worst economic crisis it has ever known.

JOHN. So they say.

HAROLD. But that our industry – the one we have both given our lives to for better or worse, continues to be one of the main casualties of this crisis.

JOHN. I am aware of the challenges we all face.

HAROLD. Demand is down by fifteen per cent this year, Mr Bailey, and that is not my doing.

Surely you have heard that the Fitzwilliams have recently let more than two thousand of their men go – not a mere one hundred and forty but *two thousand*, Mr Bailey – in a concerted effort to keep the business going.

JOHN. To keep their costs down, sir, yes.

HAROLD. These are hard times, Mr Bailey, and so perhaps you need the clarity of mind to comprehend that closing Ramshaw Drift for a few years until demand picks up again is not a strange fancy of mine. I am simply the unfortunate man on whose shoulders the unenviable task has fallen of making these difficult but necessary decisions and believe me when I say that I gain little enjoyment from it.

JOHN. But there is an alternative.

Pause.

You may call me presumptuous but I have been working hard at trying to find it and I think I may have finally stumbled upon it.

HAROLD. Working hard at what, my man?

JOHN *hurriedly takes out a few sheets of paper from his inside pocket.*

JOHN. I was up all night thrashing ideas about and putting some of them in writing. But the solution I think I have arrived at will mean that we can hold on to those men whilst only marginally affecting the profits.

HAROLD. My guests will be down at any moment, Mr Bailey.

JOHN. It is to do with the forthcoming purchase of the new
conveyors for the Hook Hill mine. I do believe that they haven't
been paid for yet. I spoke to Mr Milson, the accountant and he
informed me that this was the case. He implied that should it all
go to plan the transaction should proceed at some point next week
and that the whole thing had been delayed because of the late
arrival of some of the machinery from America.

HAROLD. You had no business talking to Mr Milson, sir.

JOHN. Of course I understand the positive contribution that this
advanced technology will have on the efficacy of the mines in
general, speeding up the whole process of extraction.

HAROLD. That is the intention, yes.

JOHN. But if perhaps we could postpone this investment for another
two years we could keep the men in full employment whilst not
severely compromising the quantity of our output.

HAROLD. And how would that be possible, Mr Bailey?

JOHN. Close Ramshaw Drift if you have to, Mr Pritchard, but re-
employ the men – all one hundred and forty of them at nine
shillings a shift – two less than what they are currently earning –
on only five shifts each at Hook Hill. Those extra shifts will help
speed up the output without resorting to the new conveyors and if
my calculations are precise the damage to the profit margin will
be minimal, perhaps a few hundred short per annum.

HAROLD. Is that all?

JOHN. I've spoken to the men and they all without exception agreed
to take the cut in wages and shifts as a means of holding on to
their employment. I also called a meeting with the miners who are
already employed at Hook Hill and they are willing to lose a shift
each a week in order to help their colleagues from Ramshaw Drift
hold on to their jobs.

HAROLD. I begin to see why you are not a man of business, Mr
Bailey.

JOHN. So really I suppose what I am suggesting is that you
deliberately delay the acquisition of the new conveyors until
perhaps a more appropriate time. Perhaps when things are looking
a little brighter and the demand picks up again.

HAROLD. You're asking me to delay progress.

JOHN. Only perhaps to broaden the definition of that word.

HAROLD. My dear man, I honestly applaud the noble nature of your enterprise and the zeal with which you have just communicated it. Alfie Shaw and the other men have a champion in you, there's no denying.

JOHN. I am doing my duty by them, that's all.

HAROLD. But perhaps they would be better served by someone with fewer ideals and just a little more common sense.

JOHN. I am simply asking you –

HAROLD. You would rather I kept my business securely fastened to archaic methods thus making it wholly uncompetitive and in the long run jeopardising the jobs of many more than a hundred and forty.

JOHN. I repeat, sir, that productivity will not be compromised. The men will work fewer shifts for less money that is all.

HAROLD. You are asking me to sabotage my business in order to quench a sentimental yearning and dare I say it aspirations towards some type of moral heroism.

JOHN. Those are not my motives, I assure you.

HAROLD. Thank you for sharing your scheme with me and I only wish I could say I will give it serious consideration.

JOHN. And so I return to your point about the sacrifices that need to be made in these challenging days, Mr Pritchard.

HAROLD. But the irrationality of its premise excludes the possibility of me taking it with any seriousness at all.

JOHN. And venture to suggest something quite radical: that the sacrifices are not demanded of those who have nothing left to sacrifice.

HAROLD. We are finished, Mr Bailey. I suggest you return to your duties.

There is a knock at the door and EILEEN *enters.*

EILEEN. Oh, I do beg your pardon, sir, I didn't realise Mr Bailey was here.

HAROLD. Mr Bailey is on his way out, Eileen, so your timing is convenient, no need to apologise.

EILEEN. I've shown Mr and Mrs Avery to their rooms, sir, and young Mr Avery too and asked them to join you for drinks when they're ready.

HAROLD. Thank you, Eileen. And you best notify Mrs Pritchard of their arrival.

EILEEN. I shall, sir.

HAROLD. Goodbye, Mr Bailey, Eileen will show you out.

EILEEN. Follow me, Mr Bailey.

JOHN. Don't worry yourself, Miss Hannaway, I know my own way out. Mr Pritchard.

He leaves the room, followed by EILEEN. HAROLD *is left alone in thought.* TERENCE *enters. He is a striking young man, handsome in an unusual way, and charismatic.*

HAROLD *has his back to him so doesn't immediately notice him, which allows* TERENCE *to study him for a few seconds. But then* HAROLD *senses him and turns.*

HAROLD. Good grief.

TERENCE. I'm sorry, I didn't mean to startle you.

HAROLD. Hovering there like a ghost.

TERENCE. I do apologise.

HAROLD. You're Terence I presume?

TERENCE. Mr Pritchard, how d'you do?

He comes forward and shakes his hand.

HAROLD. You've changed.

TERENCE. Have I ?

HAROLD. You're not a child any more.

TERENCE. I'm twenty-two years of age.

HAROLD. Last time I saw you you were…

TERENCE. Just a boy, yes. Twelve years old to be exact. It's been ten years.

HAROLD. And what are you up to, young man? I do believe my wife mentioned that you were at Merton.

TERENCE. That's not quite accurate, sir. I mean I was, but I left.

HAROLD. You've graduated?

TERENCE. Not quite, sir. I decided to leave at the end of my second year. I found Oxford stifling if truth be told.

HAROLD. How do you mean you left?

TERENCE. And embarked on travelling to the East. Constantinople initially and then onwards to Greece from whence I've just returned. I've just spent three months of perfect solitude in the monastic retreat of Mount Athos.

HAROLD. And what do you plan to do with your life now? Sit around in London smoking a hookah pipe and reminiscing?

TERENCE. I haven't decided yet, sir, but I'm not one for sitting around for too long. But writing is my forte or at least my passion.

HAROLD. Writing what exactly?

TERENCE. Well I was commissioned by *The Burlington* to do a piece on Byzantine icons which is one of the reasons I travelled to the places I did. So I'm writing about those.

HAROLD. A writer then. An aesthete too?

TERENCE. I don't know if I'm that. The word aesthete at least to me suggests a certain type of decadence. Beauty and art are all very well but I believe they have a role to play other than sating the pleasure of the one who either creates or dwells on them.

HAROLD. What kind of role?

TERENCE. I'm more interested in their transformative qualities.

HAROLD. And what would they be?

TERENCE. Qualities which move one towards one's higher purpose, I suppose.

HAROLD. So you're religious as well are you?

TERENCE. Call it what you will, sir. I simply believe that the way we're living our lives and the social structures we have adopted are not the only possible ones. In a matter of fact I suspect that they don't represent our real capabilities to any extent at all.

HAROLD. What are our real capabilities then, young man?

TERENCE. I'm sure we'll find out in due time. A little mystery is a good thing when it's married to a little patience.

HAROLD. You speak in riddles.

TERENCE. I'm just trying to answer your questions.

HAROLD. You're not a damned Bolshevik are you?

TERENCE. I hope you're not offended when I say you're awfully keen on labels, sir.

HAROLD. Why shouldn't I be? They let you know what or whom you're dealing with.

TERENCE. As long as they're accurate.

HAROLD. I'm usually right in my impressions of people.

TERENCE. Or if you're not I expect you're very convincing at persuading yourself that you are.

HAROLD. You're a forward young man aren't you?

TERENCE. I do beg your pardon if I seem rude, sir. I don't mean to be.

HAROLD. And so what does the future hold?

TERENCE. We'll have to wait and see.

HAROLD. Your plans I mean. Schemes. Ambitions.

TERENCE. I'm not a locomotive, sir. My feet are not attached to any sort of track.

HAROLD. Standing on the platform are you?

TERENCE. I believe it's a good thing to know what exactly one is hurrying towards before one actually commences the hurrying.

HAROLD. I'm a hard-working man and the one thing I have learnt is that introspection is merely an excuse for indolence.

TERENCE. Surely that depends on the quality of the introspection.

HAROLD. And then of course you'll have to get yourself a good wife to help you on your way.

TERENCE. I'm not sure I'm the marrying kind.

HAROLD. Rubbish. Every man's the marrying kind.

TERENCE. Are they?

Pause. He holds his stare for a beat.

HAROLD. Will you have a drink with me?

TERENCE. I'll have whatever you're having, sir.

HAROLD *goes to the drinks cabinet and pours him a Scotch.*

HAROLD. Do you remember the house at all?

TERENCE. I do, yes.

HAROLD. Ten years is a long time.

TERENCE. And I remember the grounds as well. I remember playing in them. There's a brook if I'm not mistaken at the back of the garden. And beyond it an entire hill covered in heather.

HAROLD. More than one.

TERENCE. We used to… I remember playing there.

HAROLD. With my son.

TERENCE. Yes, sir, with Edgar.

HAROLD. You got on the two of you, didn't you?

TERENCE. Famously, yes.

HAROLD. That's right.

TERENCE. We seemed to understand each other instinctively. I think it would be fair to say in hindsight that Edgar was the best friend I ever had.

HAROLD. That made my wife very happy.

TERENCE. He was a kind boy I remember with a very wicked sense of humour.

HAROLD. Yes, yes, little devil.

TERENCE. We understood each other sometimes without even having to speak.

Pause. HAROLD *hands* TERENCE *his drink.*

Can I ask you something?

HAROLD. Ask away.

TERENCE. The bedroom I'm in. It looks familiar. It's his, isn't it? Edgar's I mean.

HAROLD. We've closed down the east wing for repairs so apart from the one your parents are in it was the only one we had left. You don't mind?

TERENCE. Not at all. If anything, I quite like it. It makes me feel rather close to him.

HAROLD. What a peculiar thing to say.

TERENCE. But I wasn't sure my memory served me well. The room looked familiar but all his… the objects have all been cleared.

HAROLD. One must keep looking forward.

   VANESSA AVERY *enters, followed by her husband* GEOFFREY.

VANESSA. Oh my dear Harold, we've arrived at last.

HAROLD. Hello, Vanessa. Geoffrey.

GEOFFREY. You haven't aged a day, you rascal.

HAROLD. All the fresh air I imagine.

VANESSA. Where is she, where is she, where is she.

HAROLD. The girl's gone to tell her you arrived, I assume she'll be down in a couple of minutes. Hello, Vanessa.

   They kiss.

VANESSA. Oh, we had the most ghastly time getting here, my dear.

HAROLD. I'm sorry to hear it.

GEOFFREY. Bloody awful actually.

VANESSA. Well, eventful at the very least.

HAROLD. What will you have?

VANESSA. Any old spirit to calm the nerves. Gin?

HAROLD. One gin for Vanessa and for Geoffrey?

GEOFFREY. I'll have a Scotch, old man. And quickly.

   HAROLD *pours them their drinks.*

VANESSA. First we were forced to share a compartment up to Stevenage with this awful woman who kept going on about how Herr Hitler was the best thing that's happened to Europe in a hundred years. Geoffrey didn't even contradict her.

GEOFFREY. She wouldn't let me get a word in edgeways.

VANESSA. Kept going on and on about how we were going to see the light and join forces with him and what she meant by that I'm really not quite sure. Invade the world I imagine.

GEOFFREY. She had a moustache very like his, perhaps that was what inspired the affinity.

VANESSA. Terence kept giving her the strangest looks didn't you, darling?

TERENCE. Did I?

VANESSA. As though she belonged to a whole different species.

TERENCE. I think she did.

GEOFFREY. She had a point about the show he put on for the Olympics though. Rather impressive it was, all those straight lines and things, very inspiring.

VANESSA. And then afterwards on the second leg of the journey we absolutely froze, the train felt positively Siberian.

GEOFFREY. And it just juddered to a grinding halt for half an hour somewhere outside Wakefield.

VANESSA. Then when we got off at Leeds the damned wind grabbed hold of my hat and threw it straight into the path of the Edinburgh train.

GEOFFREY. I told you to hold on to it. But thank you for sending your man to pick us up anyway.

HAROLD. I'm sorry you had such a time of it.

VANESSA. Oh, but it's worth it, Harold, every single mile of the way.

GEOFFREY. It's definitely worth it.

VANESSA. To be here again. To be here.

She suddenly begins to weep.

Oh, I'm so sorry, I'm so dreadfully, dreadfully, sorry. I'm being a complete fool.

GEOFFREY. What's got into you?

VANESSA. I'm ever so sorry, I really don't know. Probably just tiredness. That and the excitement of seeing my dearest friend after a whole ten years.

TERENCE. It's understandable, Mother.

VANESSA. You've been keeping her locked up, Harold, you brute.

HAROLD. I've done no such thing.

VANESSA. Not a single trip to London in ten years. And for four of them she didn't even answer my letters, I've been sick with worry.

GEOFFREY. I would imagine it's natural after all that happened.

HAROLD. But now she's ready to emerge again.

VANESSA. Like a butterfly from its chrysalis.

HAROLD. I wouldn't go that far. Tentatively, and with small steps.

VANESSA. I almost jumped with joy when I received her letter. I've missed her dreadfully. And she was so keen to see Terence too.

HAROLD. It was my idea, I won't lie to you. Not that I had to apply too much pressure once I suggested it. But I think it's time we tried to resuscitate her a little if you know what I mean.

VANESSA. Well, rest assured, you've called the right people for the job.

HAROLD. But a word of caution if I may.

Pause.

She's not the woman you knew, Vanessa.

VANESSA. I'm not expecting her to be.

HAROLD. And so you might need to acclimatise yourself as it were. She hasn't really left the house in years. And her moods tend towards the morbid.

GEOFFREY. Morbid?

VANESSA. Well, we'll do our best to cheer her up won't we, boys?

GEOFFREY. Our very best.

ELIZABETH *enters but nobody sees her, and for a while she stands framed in the doorway. She is a beautiful woman but sombre in her appearance – both her clothes and her expression are of a dark shade.*

VANESSA. I remember before you married her, Harold, and dragged her off up here she was the life of the party, wasn't she, Geoffrey? Most of London was absolutely seduced by her and she had a

number of impressive suitors, not least that French count with the
high-pitched voice and a penchant for miniature dogs.

GEOFFREY. Something tells me that union wouldn't have led to
much conjugal bliss.

VANESSA. And then when your father died and you inherited this
place you both decamped here and apart from the odd holiday we
lost you for ever. God knows what drove you to it. Trying to avoid
people like us most probably.

HAROLD. There was work to be done, Vanessa. I wasn't going to
stay in the bank for ever. Someone had to run the land, and the
pits.

VANESSA. And all of a sudden she was gone. But she was a beauty
and much admired.

ELIZABETH. Hello, Vanessa. Hello, Geoffrey.

They all turn and see her.

VANESSA. Oh my dear, darling girl.

ELIZABETH. Yes, those were the days weren't they, Vanessa?
Carefree and idle and gay.

VANESSA. My dear, dear girl.

VANESSA *runs up to her and embraces her.* ELIZABETH
returns the embrace but is much more held back.

ELIZABETH. Parties and parties and more parties even though the
war had just ended and the stench of it still hovered over
everything. Hello, Geoffrey.

GEOFFREY. Hello, my darling.

ELIZABETH. So we'd leave our boys with their nannies and party
through the night. As if all those poor souls who had perished
under the ground, in the darkness and the fear were just an
inconvenience to be forgotten.

VANESSA. We were doing our best to live our young lives.

ELIZABETH. Is that what we were doing?

Pause.

HAROLD. Come and sit down, darling, there's a good girl.

ELIZABETH. I think I'll stand.

She turns to VANESSA *and* GEOFFREY.

Thank you for coming. It's a long way I know.

VANESSA. I'd have travelled to China and back to see you again, my dear.

ELIZABETH. It means a lot to me that you made the effort. It gets lonely up here, especially when the days get short doesn't it, Harold?

She suddenly sees TERENCE.

Terence.

TERENCE. Hello, Mrs Pritchard.

ELIZABETH. Terence.

She goes up to him.

What a beautiful boy you are.

HAROLD. He's a man, Elizabeth, not a boy any more.

ELIZABETH. You haven't changed have you? I'd have recognised you anywhere.

HAROLD. I said the opposite.

TERENCE. It's lovely to see you again, Mrs Pritchard.

ELIZABETH. My Edgar loved you so.

HAROLD. Darling.

ELIZABETH. 'Mummy, he's the best friend I ever had' he used to say 'and he understands me better than I do myself.' Isn't that an extraordinary thing for a boy of twelve to say?

VANESSA. Very.

ELIZABETH. But then he was an extraordinary boy wasn't he, Vanessa?

VANESSA. He was, my darling.

ELIZABETH. Well, you both were, Terence.

Pause.

Welcome back.

TERENCE. Thank you, Mrs Pritchard. I'm happy to be here.

HAROLD. Right, enough of all this, where's that stupid girl, she needs to tell Cook we'll be eating in an hour.

He rings a bell.

And I'll pour you a drink. Gin?

ELIZABETH. Thank you, Harold, I'll do it myself.

She moves over to the drinks cabinet and pours herself a gin on the rocks.

I'm sorry I've changed so much since you last saw me, Terence. I've become rather an old lady before my time haven't I? So forgive me if my appearance comes as something of a shock.

TERENCE. You look beautiful, Mrs Pritchard, and I'm the forgiving type anyway.

VANESSA. Oh, he is, aren't you, darling, and open-minded and tolerant and all those things.

HAROLD. And so are you by the sound of it, Geoffrey.

GEOFFREY. Am I?

HAROLD. Hardly raising an eyebrow when he pulls out of his studies to go gallivanting round the world.

GEOFFREY. He's his own man, no use trying to stop him.

TERENCE. Mr Pritchard wasn't very keen on me exploring the East.

HAROLD. Or the Arctic Ocean or the Amazon. Travelling is all very well in times of leisure but leisure is the one thing we can't afford at the moment. This country needs to whip itself back into shape.

GEOFFREY. Hear, hear.

HAROLD. Only this week I'm having to let a hundred and forty men go. So to be passing one's times traipsing around the Balkans hardly seems to me like the right priority at this particular moment. Our young men should be here at home making the most of themselves and offering the best they have.

ELIZABETH. Harold enjoys lecturing people and he hasn't had much of a chance lately so to have a young man in the house is an opportunity he can't pass by.

TERENCE. Surely in times of crisis it's a good thing to look at things from further away, sir, as well as reflect a little on where we've come from as a means of perhaps forging the path ahead with some due thought.

HAROLD. And where is it you think we've come from?

TERENCE. I only refer to that particular part of the world where the mystic and the rational first conjoined forces in forming the roots of our civilisation.

HAROLD. So you returned from your travels a fan of the Eastern Mediterranean did you, young man? Did you especially admire their politics or their sewage systems?

TERENCE. It is true that when it comes to plumbing our role as world leaders in the field is incontestable.

VANESSA. Do we really need to discuss plumbing and sewage before dinner?

TERENCE. Not only plumbing mind you; our contribution to all aspects of technology – to science in all its forms is unmatched and admirable, no question about that. I am almost willing to bet that one day soon we will be flying to the Moon and planting a Union Jack on it, another far-fetched corner of the Empire.

GEOFFREY. Oh, the Americans will get there first, they're a pushy bunch.

VANESSA. And brash too like that awful Simpson creature.

TERENCE. But how sad it will be and pathetic if we do it all in the wrong order.

HAROLD. What 'wrong order'?

TERENCE. If we proudly land on the Moon and have all these machines announcing our prowess and the shining brilliance of human intelligence when we still live in a world that is scarred by inequality and riddled with poverty and ignorance.

HAROLD. Good God I was right, your son's a Red. I'm surprised you haven't packed your bags to join Orwell and all those other Commies in Spain yet.

VANESSA. He's an idealist that's all and a passionate one at that.

TERENCE. I simply think that somewhere along the way, as we were busy building machines we didn't notice that the world we were living in began to resemble those very machines.

GEOFFREY. Hold on, you've lost me, what machines?

TERENCE. And so the machines took over and meanwhile they had robbed us of some of the better things that made us human to begin with, the best of our natures and our imaginations. As well as our more mystical side.

HAROLD. Stuff and nonsense, young man. 'Mystical side' indeed – backward superstition and mumbo-jumbo.

GEOFFREY. Easy does it, old man, he's just young.

HAROLD. Well, I've never heard such a load of rubbish, is that the expansive education you picked up on your travels around the world? If it is God help us, I'm more worried about the next generation than I was to begin with. Is that what we fought the war for, Geoffrey?

He rings the bell again, more aggressively.

TERENCE. I'm not saying it's one without the other or a choice between the two. Machines are wonderful things that make our lives a whole lot better, you'd be an idiot to disagree.

HAROLD. My point exactly.

TERENCE. But why should we allow a machine, or an economic system that works like a machine to dictate everything to us at great cost to that strange thing we call the human soul?

HAROLD. Because there is no viable alternative.

TERENCE. I would suggest, sir, with some caution that that statement indicates a distinct lack of imagination.

GEOFFREY. Easy, Terence.

TERENCE. And surely this is the best opportunity – now that the machine seems to have temporarily broken down – to ask ourselves the most fundamental questions on whether it has been working to our best advantage and with our well-being as its priority. Otherwise I fear history will keep repeating itself and the results will eventually prove catastrophic.

HAROLD. And now you have become a prophet of doom.

TERENCE. No, rest assured, sir, I haven't such an important opinion of myself. It was just that you asked me what we could learn from the East and I suppose my answer is that perhaps humility would be a good quality for us to cultivate.

HAROLD. A few months away, Geoffrey, and your son's spouting a whole lot of dangerous hogwash, I'd keep an eye on him if I were you.

GEOFFREY. What do I know, I'm just a bloody shopkeeper.

VANESSA. Don't talk yourself down. You're an antiques dealer and the best one in London.

The door opens and EILEEN *enters in a state of distress.*

HAROLD. Where the hell have you been? I've been ringing for ages.

EILEEN. Oh, sir, madam, I do beg your pardon, the strangest thing.

ELIZABETH. What's wrong, Eileen? You look ashen.

EILEEN. I was up in… I was upstairs unpacking young Mr Avery's case –

TERENCE. You needn't do that, I can do it myself after dinner.

EILEEN. Oh, it's no trouble, sir, no trouble at all, but I had just finished and I'd put away all your shirts, sir, and everything else too, folded them all away in the little cupboard and placed the case under the bed so that it isn't in the way and I turned off the light and walked out into the corridor but then I remembered I'd forgotten the towels for the bathroom on the bed so I started to make my way back into the room and then… and then…

HAROLD. And then what?

EILEEN. I pushed the door and it was jammed, sir. I mean it wasn't locked or anything because it was ajar like so much, a couple of inches or so, but when I pushed to open it wouldn't budge, like someone else was standing on the other side and pushing it towards me and this went on and on and I thought perhaps someone was playing a joke on me or something but it still wouldn't open and then eventually, a whole minute later, all of a sudden the pressure from the other side stopped and it swung open and I nearly fell to the ground with the force of it.

HAROLD. So what's all the fuss about, you silly girl. It was a draft, you know what it's like up there.

EILEEN. Oh, but, sir, but it wasn't a draft, I could have sworn there was somebody pushing it on the other side.

HAROLD. For God's sake, we were all down here so it wasn't any of us and unless Cook suddenly decided to abandon preparing the lamb in order to terrorise you with a ridiculous prank the likelihood is it was a powerful gust of wind.

EILEEN. Oh, but, sir, I swear on my mother's –

HAROLD. Anyway, enough of that. Tell Cook we'll be having dinner at eight as planned.

EILEEN. Yes, sir.

She makes a move to go.

ELIZABETH. It's all right, Eileen. I know it wasn't a draft or a gust of wind. I understand.

EILEEN. Yes, ma'am. Thank you, ma'am.

She goes.

HAROLD. The girl's an hysteric, always has been.

Pause.

GEOFFREY. Now you two ladies will want to do some catching up. Ten years is a hell of a long time.

HAROLD. Tell you what, why don't we men go into my study for a cigar and leave you to do a little chatting on your own?

GEOFFREY. What a winning idea.

VANESSA. A cigar before dinner? Are you sure?

GEOFFREY. Of course we're sure.

HAROLD. And then we'll all convene for Cook's leg of lamb.

VANESSA. You don't have to. We can catch up later can't we, Elizabeth.

GEOFFREY. Now's a good time to start.

HAROLD. Only if your son promises to keep his progressive ideas to himself.

GEOFFREY. I can't make my son promise a thing.

TERENCE. As long as I'm not provoked you have my word, sir.

HAROLD. Come on then, follow me.

VANESSA. Off you go then.

The men leave the room and the women are left alone. For a few seconds there is an awkward silence.

So, here we are.

ELIZABETH. Yes, here we are.

VANESSA. Oh, my darling, I don't know where to start. Ten years is a lifetime.

ELIZABETH. A lifetime, yes.

VANESSA. But the most important thing is that here we are now and we can pick things up again as if nothing at all has happened.

ELIZABETH. As if nothing has happened?

VANESSA. What I mean is we can resume our friendship and slowly start to do things again and how wonderful it would be if you did get out of this place for a little while and you got onto that train and came down to London and we could all get together again, the whole pack of us and Milly Hughes and the Bedford sisters and all of us again like old times and we could go to the Café Royal and have those lethal cocktails, wouldn't that be fun?

ELIZABETH. Yes, maybe.

VANESSA. But here we are again, the two of us, the best of friends.

ELIZABETH. Yes.

Pause.

Only trouble is, my darling, I don't know how long I'll be around for.

VANESSA. You're not planning to emigrate are you?

ELIZABETH. You see I had to keep going didn't I? For Harold really. For better or worse, that sort of thing. But you know, I think he'll be fine. His work keeps him going, he doesn't dwell on things like I do. So he'll be all right when I'm gone, I'm sure of it.

VANESSA. Gone where, my sweet?

ELIZABETH. And now I think the time is coming.

VANESSA. What time? My darling, what are you talking about?

ELIZABETH. Do you know he's like a lover that I call every night?

VANESSA. Harold is?

ELIZABETH. No, darling, not Harold. I lie in bed at night and open myself up and I whisper, 'Come on, come on, I'm waiting for you,

come and take me away, my love, take me with you, I'm all yours.'
And so I call him every night into the stillness of my bedroom and
into the coldness of my sheets.

VANESSA. Darling, who on earth do you mean?

ELIZABETH. Death, of course.

VANESSA. Oh, my dear girl, what a terrible thing to say.

ELIZABETH. Is it?

VANESSA. What a dreadful, dreadful thing to say.

ELIZABETH. But surely being such good friends means being
honest with one another. Or is it just talking of trivial things that
constitutes a friendship?

VANESSA. Elizabeth.

ELIZABETH. Oh, don't worry I shan't kill myself, that would be too
cruel. No, I just know that soon my body will become host to
some illness, a cancer will grow in me like a black flower or
perhaps my lungs will fill up with fluid and slowly drown me but
whatever it is I know he'll carry me away because I've begged
him so.

Pause. VANESSA *suddenly stands.*

VANESSA. This really won't do. I won't tolerate it, I simply won't.

ELIZABETH. I do beg your pardon.

VANESSA. And of course you've been to hell and back, God knows
you have and I'm the first to feel that with you because I love you
so, to *commiserate* with you, to sympathise and feel with the
things you have –

ELIZABETH. Thank you, Vanessa.

VANESSA. But there's a time for mourning, my darling, and then
there's a time for returning and maybe that's what I'm here for.

ELIZABETH. For returning to what?

VANESSA. To life, Elizabeth, to *life*.

Pause.

ELIZABETH. All right then, you win, I'm beginning to get rather
excited. Tell me how it is you plan to return me to life, Vanessa.

VANESSA. Well, darling, I'm sorry but I do think the rooms one passes one's days in have such power and influence over our moods, wouldn't you say?

ELIZABETH. Most definitely.

VANESSA. The colours and shades and – well, the overall *atmosphere* really – and I'm sorry to say this and you'll think me insensitive but, my dear girl, this house of yours really does need some cheering up.

ELIZABETH. So you think we need new furniture?

VANESSA. Well, what I was going to suggest – dear me, Harold is going to want my head on a platter for coming up with this – but what I was going to suggest is that I send you someone.

ELIZABETH. Send me someone?

VANESSA. There's this man – he's a genius, he really is – and he's just done up the Sebagos' place in Eaton Square and you've never seen anything like it. I'm sure he's terribly booked up but a phone call won't do any harm at all and we did get on, I sat next to him when Clarissa had her fortieth. He calls himself Hubert De Carcasson though Clarissa says his real name is Reginald and he's from Northampton. But anyway, the things he does with colours and fabrics – the man's a magician. He found these curtains for the Sebagos' and – it sounds hideous I know but they're absolutely beautiful – well, they have pineapples on them.

ELIZABETH. Pineapples?

VANESSA. Yes, my darling, can you believe it, these massive, fat pineapples. And I know that sounds awfully vulgar but do you know they're completely gorgeous and the room is so much fun.

ELIZABETH. I'm sure it is. Do you think we should get pineapples on our curtains here as well?

VANESSA. Well, I wouldn't go that far but all I'm saying is you could do with a little of that up here. Reg De Carcasson could work wonders. Maybe not pineapples but butterflies or something and a more joyful colour like yellow or pink or even –

ELIZABETH. A bright, shining orange. Yes, that would be nice. And butterflies is a good idea. Or rainbows or palm trees or little white seashells, and we can fill the room with cushions too and Persian rugs and maybe in the corner there we can place a fountain and people can come up from London, all those foolish, empty people and we can stand in this room holding cocktails and saying witty things to each other and laughing at one another's jokes and reminding ourselves how brilliant our lives are and so full of mirth and meaning.

Pause.

My son died, Vanessa.

VANESSA. Oh, my darling sweet angel, I know that.

ELIZABETH. And you come here and talk to me of curtains and plans to return me to life. As if that were possible. My son died.

VANESSA. I know, my darling. Ten years ago.

ELIZABETH. Oh, as long ago as that is it? Silly me, I thought it was only a few weeks. I really should pull myself together.

VANESSA. That isn't what I meant. All I was trying –

ELIZABETH. I really should try and cheer up because it's been a whole ten years. I wonder if my difficulty in pasting a smile on my face and getting on with things in the appropriate way has less to do with the fact that he actually died and more to do with the manner in which he did so. Which do you think it is, Vanessa?

VANESSA. Oh, Elizabeth, don't.

ELIZABETH. The way in which he died is what I mean, Vanessa, the *manner* of his death.

VANESSA. I know how he died, my sweet.

ELIZABETH. Do you though? Because perhaps I need to tell you. Perhaps you haven't heard the details of my son's demise.

VANESSA. No, my darling, please.

ELIZABETH. Because there have been times when I've thought that if my boy had breathed his last in his warm bed with his mother – with me, his mother – holding his hand, whispering comforting words to see him on his way, well then yes, maybe things would be a trifle easier, and maybe after a whole ten years had passed I would be able to sit here with you and discuss various types of curtains and whether we should have pineapples or butterflies or God knows what on them –

VANESSA. Please, Elizabeth.

ELIZABETH. But the simple fact is, Vanessa, that he didn't die at home with his mother kissing his brow. He died at Bracken Moor.

VANESSA. I know. I know he did.

Pause.

ELIZABETH. He used to love roaming the whole area but we never thought he'd go as far as that. You see he always used to play these imaginary games and he'd get carried away.

VANESSA. I know he did. Sometimes with Terence.

ELIZABETH. Yes, when you'd come and visit us on holidays.

VANESSA. We'd only just left.

ELIZABETH. Only the day before. Maybe that's why he'd ventured a little further on that particular morning, he was feeling sad. Maybe that's what took him to Bracken Moor.

VANESSA. Oh, my dear.

ELIZABETH. There used to be a mine there. It's been closed for years and years, since the 1870s I think.

VANESSA. Yes.

ELIZABETH. And then I suppose the bracken grew and grew and some of it grew over that one shaft.

VANESSA. It's too terrible.

ELIZABETH. Harold had a theory that some of the boys from the village had been playing there and had removed the cover. Anyway, how it happened I suppose is irrelevant really. The point is my boy fell into that mine and it was there he died.

VANESSA. The angel.

The door opens and TERENCE *walks in. They don't notice him and he remains in the corner of the room without interrupting.*

ELIZABETH. It was a shallow mine and it wasn't the fall that killed him. He'd broken his legs you see. That's why he couldn't climb out again. I bet he'd tried and tried, they found so much earth under his nails and they said that it was because he'd been fighting his way out, clawing and scratching and digging his way out like some poor little animal in the dark. He was a fighter you know, our Edgar, tough and determined even though you wouldn't know it looking at him.

VANESSA. I know he was.

ELIZABETH. But I suppose there's only so much fighting a boy can do before despair sets in.

VANESSA. Yes.

ELIZABETH. He'd never gone into that direction. So we were busy scouring to the south and the west, with me at the front of the search party, the only woman, and my voice grew hoarse from all the shouting.

VANESSA. I'm sure.

ELIZABETH. 'Edgar, my Edgar, where are you?'

VANESSA. Don't, Elizabeth.

ELIZABETH. And then when we found him a few days later his little body was limp and cold and lifeless.

Pause.

Do you know, Vanessa, they say that it took our Lord Jesus Christ nine hours to die on the cross? Well, it took my Edgar longer than three days to die in that hole. And he was frightened of the dark even though his father chided him for it. Three days of terror and anguish and pain. Three days of wondering why his parents hadn't found him yet.

Pause.

So you see, my dear, I lie in bed at night and bid death come and find me.

TERENCE *coughs a little and moves into the room.*

TERENCE. I'm sorry.

VANESSA. Oh, darling, there you are, have you all smoked your cigars and put the world to rights?

TERENCE. I wouldn't go that far. We did touch on the subject of Mr Gandhi and I rather held back but I'm afraid Mr Pritchard wouldn't even meet me halfway. He branded the man a charlatan and a nuisance and even suggested assassination.

ELIZABETH. His opinions are very fixed.

TERENCE. Anyway, I've been asked to summon you both to dinner. The lamb is done apparently.

ELIZABETH. Thank you, Terence.

VANESSA. Do you know, I'm feeling rather a chill. I think I'll fetch my cardigan.

ELIZABETH. We can send Eileen to find it.

VANESSA. Oh, don't worry her, she'll be busy getting ready to serve dinner. It'll only take me a minute.

ELIZABETH. All right then, we'll see you in the dining room.

VANESSA. Yes, yes, all right.

She leaves.

ELIZABETH. You heard some of that didn't you?

TERENCE. Just a little.

ELIZABETH. It's fine, there's no reason why you shouldn't. After all, I think you're the only person in the house who'd ever really understand.

TERENCE. Yes.

ELIZABETH. The depth of loss, I mean. The infinite depth.

TERENCE. I know what you mean, Mrs Pritchard.

Pause.

ELIZABETH. Call me Elizabeth. You don't have to if you don't want to. Not in front of the others. Only when we're alone if you like. After all, we're both adults now.

TERENCE. All right.

ELIZABETH. And he loved you so.

TERENCE. And I loved him.

Pause.

I think of him often, Elizabeth. Perhaps I've forgotten the shape of his eyes, the sound of his voice – perhaps I've forgotten these things even though a part of me yearns to remember them. But he is a presence in my life, always somewhere near me. And I think of his spirit and I think of his suffering, Elizabeth.

Pause.

ELIZABETH. He calls me sometimes.

TERENCE. Calls you.

ELIZABETH. A small voice. Usually in the dark hours of the morning.

TERENCE. Yes.

ELIZABETH. Of course I'm not going to tell Harold. He thinks me mad enough as it is. But he calls me.

TERENCE. I believe you.

ELIZABETH. 'Mummy,' he cries. 'Where are you? Come and find me.'

Pause.

We'd better go in to dinner or they'll send a search party.

TERENCE. We'd better.

ELIZABETH. We don't want to alarm them.

TERENCE. Certainly not.

She stands to go but stops.

ELIZABETH. Terence, can I ask you a favour?

TERENCE. What is it, Elizabeth?

ELIZABETH. It'll sound ever so queer but I really need to.

TERENCE. Go on then.

ELIZABETH. Hold me. Put your arms around me like you used to put them round your mother when you were a little boy and hold me.

TERENCE. Of course. Of course I will.

Slowly, tentatively, he steps forward and carefully wraps his arms around her.

The lights fade to darkness.

Scene Two

*The middle of the night, a few days later. It is very windy, with a
storm raging outside and the windows rattling from time to time.*

All the lights are off and the stage is in darkness.

*Then suddenly, the silence is pierced by a loud, terrifying scream. A
few seconds pass and then* EILEEN *runs into the room in her nightie,
and in obvious distress at the sound of the scream. She nervously
tries to decide whether she should go upstairs to investigate or stay
in the room and away from the danger.*

*A few seconds later, there is a second scream, even more piercing
than the first.* EILEEN *is terrified and, crossing herself, she runs out
of the room, muttering inaudibly as she does so and closing the door
behind her.*

*Muffled voices are heard from upstairs, and footsteps too. The
footsteps are heard rushing down the stairs and the voices too, but
now they are audible. The hall light goes on outside the door.*

TERENCE (*offstage*). I'm so sorry, I really am, I don't know what
came over me.

ELIZABETH (*offstage*). Don't apologise, it isn't your fault, you
must have had a nightmare.

The door opens and TERENCE *bursts into the room, followed by*
ELIZABETH. *They are both in dressing gowns and slippers.*
TERENCE *is in a distressed state.*

TERENCE. There was this thing, not so much a nightmare, more a
feeling, unlike anything I've ever experienced before and then all
I remember is waking up in the pitch black and I didn't know *who*
I was any more, it was as if I was someone else. And then I felt
this overwhelming terror and I heard this stomach-churning
scream and it took me a few seconds to realise that the person
who was screaming was me.

Pause.

I'm so sorry, what an appalling house guest I am, waking you up
in the middle of the night like a raging lunatic.

ELIZABETH. Don't be foolish, Terence, you can't help it, these
things happen.

TERENCE. But I've never experienced anything like it.

ELIZABETH. You said it was as if you weren't yourself.

TERENCE. Yes, that's exactly what it felt like.

ELIZABETH. Well, who were you then?

TERENCE. I really don't know. But it was terrifying. As if the walls had collapsed.

ELIZABETH. What walls?

TERENCE. *My* walls. I don't know. The walls that keep me safe, that make me Terence. It was as if, in that second that I woke up, I wasn't Terence at all but some poor, desperate creature who had always lived and was doomed to live eternally in the darkness.

VANESSA *rushes in, closely followed by* GEOFFREY. *They too are in their dressing gowns.*

VANESSA. Oh, my dears, what was that terrible noise?

ELIZABETH. Terence woke up in a state of terror.

VANESSA. Darling, what happened?

TERENCE. I'm awfully embarrassed.

GEOFFREY. Some sort of a nightmare, my boy?

TERENCE. More than that, but yes, a nightmare is the most accurate word to describe it I suppose.

VANESSA. That's three nights in a row now.

GEOFFREY. What is?

VANESSA. Well, we got here on Tuesday and you've had some sort of nightmare every night. And at breakfast yesterday you mentioned that thing with the whispering.

ELIZABETH. What whispering?

TERENCE. It doesn't really matter.

VANESSA. He said that he woke up with a start because –

TERENCE. It's really not important, Mother, let's leave it.

ELIZABETH. No, tell me, what whispering, what happened?

GEOFFREY. Maybe it was all that Stilton after pudding.

TERENCE. Nothing really, I was half-asleep so I must have dreamt that as well.

ELIZABETH. Dreamt what?

VANESSA. He said he heard a voice whispering in the dark, didn't you, darling? My skin crawled when you told me about it at breakfast.

ELIZABETH. What did the whisper say?

TERENCE. I imagined it, that's all. But it wasn't really saying anything in particular, it was indiscernible really, like the whisper –

ELIZABETH. Of a child?

HAROLD *comes in, also in his dressing gown and slippers.*

HAROLD. What on earth is going on?

VANESSA. Everything's fine, we can go back to bed now.

HAROLD. What happened?

GEOFFREY. Our Terence had a bit of a turn I'm afraid.

HAROLD. What kind of a turn?

TERENCE. We really should go back to bed you know and I'm sorry about the theatrics. How very dramatic, I feel a right imbecile.

HAROLD. It's four o'clock in the morning.

TERENCE. All I can repeat is that it's never happened to me before and I can only wish it never does again.

HAROLD. What hasn't?

ELIZABETH. He said it was as if he wasn't himself. As if he had become someone else.

VANESSA. That's a little worrying.

GEOFFREY. I'd keep that to yourself if I were you, people have been sent to Bedlam for less than that.

HAROLD. Not himself?

TERENCE. Anyway, really, I insist we all return to bed. If I'd known I was going to cause this much commotion I'd have stayed in my room.

VANESSA. And then we would have thought you were murdered or something.

TERENCE. In the morning we'll have forgotten all about it.

GEOFFREY. And no more cheese for you after dinner.

VANESSA. Oh, Geoffrey, do stop going on about the cheese, it has nothing to do with it.

HAROLD. Off we go then. See if we can get a couple of hours more. Elizabeth.

ELIZABETH. Yes.

They start to move towards the door. ELIZABETH first, followed by HAROLD and then VANESSA and GEOFFREY. TERENCE hovers in the background.

TERENCE. Betsy.

They all stop, turn around, and look at him. ELIZABETH's face changes, as if she's seen a ghost.

That was it. That was the name. It's all coming back.

HAROLD. What is?

TERENCE. Before I screamed. When I had that feeling – that strange sensation – that I was somebody else, this name kept coming to me and I must have spoken it. 'Betsy.' I think I said it over and over again. 'Betsy, Betsy, Betsy.' I was calling someone called Betsy. I needed to talk to her. To let her know something. So I kept speaking her name. 'Betsy.'

ELIZABETH *reels, she sits down.*

ELIZABETH. What did you need to let her know?

TERENCE. I don't know, I can't remember. All I know is that there was this thing I felt – like an urge, I suppose, a powerful, persistent urge to speak to Betsy.

VANESSA. Who's Betsy?

ELIZABETH. I am.

VANESSA. Darling, you're Elizabeth, not Betsy. I mean it may be a common diminutive but I've known you for over thirty years and nobody has ever called you Betsy.

ELIZABETH. Only Edgar.

Pause.

Our secret names for each other. I was Betsy, he was Bob. It was a private thing, like a little game. The names we used for each other when we were alone. Nobody else knew them. Not even Harold.

HAROLD. Apart from his friend Terence of course. Boys share secrets. I think we should go to bed now. In the morning, in the clear light of day perhaps you can explain to us what all this is about, young man.

TERENCE. Explain?

HAROLD. What exactly it is you're playing at I mean.

TERENCE. I'm not playing at anything, sir.

HAROLD. Why it is that you've decided to play this cruel game on my wife.

ELIZABETH. Harold.

TERENCE. I assure you, sir, I am not playing any sort of game at all. I am not some kind of sadist.

VANESSA. Terence can't hurt a soul.

HAROLD. Well then, I'm sure there's another rational explanation. I look forward to hearing it in the morning otherwise you can pack your bags and be on your way.

GEOFFREY. Steady on, Harold.

TERENCE. Fry us an egg, Betsy.

ELIZABETH*'s hand comes to her mouth and she gasps in shock.*

VANESSA. Darling, what are you talking about?

GEOFFREY. Fry you *an egg*?

TERENCE. Yes, I think so. That's what he's saying. He keeps saying it, over and over. An egg. That's what he says.

HAROLD. That's what who says?

TERENCE. He's saying it now. Over and over again. He keeps saying it. In my head, in my head.

VANESSA. My dear boy, you're scaring me.

GEOFFREY. Are you feeling all right, old chap?

TERENCE. Fry us an egg. Fry us an egg. Fry us an egg, Betsy.

> TERENCE *suddenly falls to the ground and begins convulsing on the floor.* VANESSA *lets out a small scream and, with* GEOFFREY*, runs up to him and tries to grab hold of him. After shaking violently for a few seconds, he loses consciousness.*

VANESSA. Oh my dear God, what's wrong with him?

GEOFFREY. He's gone stone cold.

VANESSA. Terence my darling, my darling boy, wake up.

GEOFFREY. His whole body was shaking like a leaf.

HAROLD. Has this happened before?

GEOFFREY. No, never, never.

VANESSA. Terence my love, can you hear me?

HAROLD. The boy's obviously an epileptic.

GEOFFREY. Rubbish, I tell you nothing like this has ever happened before.

HAROLD. Maybe he's play-acting or something.

VANESSA. Why on earth would he do that?

HAROLD. You'd have to ask him.

GEOFFREY. Now look here, Harold, I understand this is all very upsetting but there's nothing to be gained by accusing my son of these outrageous –

> EILEEN *runs in.*

EILEEN. Oh Good Lord, sir, ma'am, what's been happening? I heard the scream and thought you were all being murdered in your beds and then I heard you all running downstairs and I've been hiding because I fancied there were intruders in the house and –

HAROLD. Nobody's been murdered and there are no intruders or ghosts or goblins, Eileen. Mr Avery has fallen ill that's all.

GEOFFREY. I think we ought to call a doctor.

VANESSA. Yes, Harold, please.

HAROLD. Eileen, I'd like you to call Dr Gibbons and tell him to come here as soon as he can. And on your way back bring a glass of cold water and a blanket.

EILEEN. Yes, sir.

She goes.

HAROLD (*indicating the sofa*). Let's sit him up here.

GEOFFREY. That's a good idea.

HAROLD. Grab him by the legs, Geoffrey, I'll get the arms.

VANESSA. Be careful.

They pick him up carefully and rest him on the sofa.

Put the cushion under his head.

GEOFFREY *does this.*

GEOFFREY. There. That's better.

Pause.

VANESSA. I've never had such a fright in my life.

GEOFFREY. The way he shook.

VANESSA. Salivating at the mouth like a rabid dog.

HAROLD. You say this has never happened before?

GEOFFREY. And what was he saying before it all happened?
Something about a voice telling him to say it. Something about an egg.

VANESSA. 'Fry us an egg, Betsy' is what he said. He kept saying it
again and again… 'Fry us an egg, fry us an egg.'

GEOFFREY. How very peculiar.

VANESSA. Oh, my poor boy.

Pause.

ELIZABETH. It's what he used to say to me. Edgar.

Pause.

Mocking me. Because he always used to say I couldn't. 'You
wouldn't know your way around a kitchen,' he used to say.
'Wouldn't know a grater from a whisk. What would happen if
your servants all went on strike?' he'd ask. 'You'd starve.' And
then, when we were alone and he wanted to tease me he'd say,
'Fry us an egg, Betsy. Go on, prove that you can do it. Fry us an
egg.' It always made me laugh.

HAROLD. I've never heard that.

ELIZABETH. Because we never shared it. There was a whole territory that wasn't yours, Harold. There are things that happen and are said between mothers and children and no one else.

VANESSA. But Terence must have known.

ELIZABETH. Must he?

HAROLD. Of course he must.

ELIZABETH. Why are you so sure of that?

HAROLD. Because, Elizabeth, I am not willing to entertain ludicrous notions of the supernatural. I will not stand here in my own house and allow you or anyone else for that matter to talk such mindless drivel.

VANESSA (*to* ELIZABETH). Perhaps, my darling, there's another explanation for it.

HAROLD. I'm almost certain that there is. I'm sure your Dr Freud and some of his Viennese colleagues would have quite a lot to say about what has driven your – about what has driven young Terence here – to behave in such a confounding way tonight. Perhaps our own Dr Gibbons, though not possessing as sophisticated a grasp on the subject of human psychology will nevertheless provide his own theory as to what has caused this evening's events. But I will not hear of the other stuff.

ELIZABETH. 'The other stuff.'

HAROLD. I'm sorry, Elizabeth, but we need to keep our heads about us.

EILEEN *returns with a glass of water and a blanket.*

EILEEN. Dr Gibbons said he'll be here in five minutes, sir, as long as he can get the motor started. It's been giving him problems lately, he said, especially in the cold.

GEOFFREY. Thank you, Eileen, why don't you give me that?

She gives him the blanket and he throws it over TERENCE.

VANESSA *takes the water from her.*

VANESSA. Darling, try and have a sip of water.

HAROLD. Maybe you should throw it in his face. That should bring him to his senses.

VANESSA. That's a good boy, just sip it gently.

TERENCE *begins to sip the water but then suddenly chokes on it a little. He sputters and coughs and regains consciousness.*

TERENCE. What happened?

GEOFFREY. Welcome back to reality, boy.

TERENCE. What's happening?

VANESSA. You gave us such a terrible fright you know. Writhing and twitching on the floor like a man possessed.

TERENCE. I felt as if I was.

GEOFFREY. Well, it's all over now, thank heavens.

VANESSA. Yes. And in the morning we can go for a long walk and get some fresh air.

HAROLD. Please don't take this the wrong way, Vanessa, but I do think that the best thing for you to do in the morning is to return to London. Terence is obviously under a great deal of strain and I'm not sure that Yorkshire is doing him much good.

ELIZABETH. I want him to stay.

HAROLD. And I think they should return to London. And sometimes, Elizabeth, what I say is the law of the land I'm afraid, whether you like it or not.

ELIZABETH. What did he want to say to me, Terence?

TERENCE. I beg your pardon?

ELIZABETH. You said he needed to talk to me. He needed to let me know something. And I'm asking you again if you remember what it was?

TERENCE. I can't. I wish, but the thing is –

ELIZABETH. What was it?

TERENCE. I can't remember, I'm sorry. My head is throbbing so.

VANESSA. The doctor will be here soon, darling, he'll give you something.

TERENCE. I'm sorry, I can't remember anything. It's all a bit of a fog I'm afraid.

ELIZABETH. It's all right, I understand.

Pause.

GEOFFREY. I don't know about you, Harold, but I rather need a shot of something.

HAROLD. I'll pour you a Scotch.

He walks over to the drinks cabinet and pours two glasses of Scotch, one for GEOFFREY *and one for himself.*

GEOFFREY. Maybe whilst we're waiting for the doctor we can change the subject and talk about something a little more cheerful.

VANESSA. Yes, maybe you can tell us a few jokes, Geoffrey, or perhaps we can play a game of bridge.

GEOFFREY. Well, I just think that things being as they are –

VANESSA. Don't be ridiculous, we've just had a very traumatic experience and there's no use pretending that none of it happened.

GEOFFREY. Well, there's no use dwelling on it either.

VANESSA. Nobody's dwelling on it, Geoffrey. We're just all trying to understand it.

HAROLD *hands* GEOFFREY *his drink.*

HAROLD. I apologise, young man, if I came across rather aggressively.

GEOFFREY. I must say, you did a little.

HAROLD. But you must understand that when one is confronted in the middle of the night by somebody pretending – by somebody speaking words and names that only one's son – one's *dead* son happened to know – it is rather difficult to keep one's rag. I think it's natural.

TERENCE. Please don't apologise. I think I would have probably reacted in a very similar way. I have never experienced anything quite like this and I too am very disturbed by it.

HAROLD. And it was hasty and ill-judged of me to accuse you of malicious motives.

VANESSA. Terence isn't like that.

HAROLD. No, of course.

Pause.

So perhaps what has happened has something to do with one's –
well, with Terence's – with that part of his mind that isn't fully
conscious. I won't proclaim myself an expert on the subject and
understand little of all that – but what I am suggesting is that maybe
returning here after all these years has stirred certain parts of your
mind – those parts that usually remain hidden in dark corners – into
some sort of overdrive shall we say. Perhaps there are things –
emotional things, God knows what, again this territory is one with
which I am not familiar – that have unleashed this reaction. The fact
that you are back in the house where you last saw my son and have
had a reunion with my wife and myself, well, perhaps you have
reacted to all that in this violent way because certain memories are
too painful to *consciously* acknowledge.

Pause.

Does that make any sense at all?

TERENCE. Yes, it does, it does.

GEOFFREY. Do you know, Harold, you're beginning to sound rather
like that Dr Freud yourself, I'm impressed.

TERENCE. Carry on, Mr Pritchard. You haven't finished have you?

HAROLD. Well, what I'm suggesting is that you did in fact know
these things as a boy – you knew for instance that Edgar's name
for his mother was Betsy and he had mentioned to you how he
used to tease her by saying 'fry us an egg, Betsy' and all that but
that you've simply forgotten it. But that that part of your mind
that I was talking about hadn't forgotten either of those things at
all.

TERENCE. Yes, yes.

HAROLD. And all that's happened is that these memories have now
released themselves from that dark corner and have forced you
into speaking them – albeit in a strange and disconcerting way.

ELIZABETH. Why can't you just accept that there are things you
will never fully understand, Harold? Does that make you feel
powerless?

The doorbell rings.

EILEEN. Oh, that'll be the doctor, sir.

HAROLD. Well, don't just stand there, go and open the door.

EILEEN. Yes, sir.

She goes.

TERENCE. I must say I rather agree with Mr Pritchard's analysis. And come to think of it I was apprehensive about returning here even though many years had passed. I've often thought about how terrible it was that poor Edgar died the day after we'd all left and also about the last few days we were here and how close the two of us were. And there's no question that he may well have mentioned those things to me in passing. So yes, I think I rather agree with you, Mr Pritchard.

HAROLD. I believe that's the most reasonable explanation for all this.

ELIZABETH. Reasonable, yes.

EILEEN *returns, followed by* DR GIBBONS, *who is carrying a bag and looks as if he has been battling the elements.*

EILEEN. Dr Gibbons, sir.

DR GIBBONS. That raging wind nearly blew my motor into a ditch. Mr Pritchard, sir, Mrs Pritchard.

HAROLD. Thank you for coming so swiftly, doctor, though it may have been in vain, young Terence here is looking a whole lot perkier than he was a few minutes ago.

TERENCE. Even more cause for embarrassment.

DR GIBBONS. What seems to be the problem?

VANESSA. Hello, doctor, I'm Vanessa Avery.

DR GIBBONS. How d'you do, Mrs Avery?

VANESSA. I've been better. My son here had some sort of fit a few minutes ago, he went into convulsions and was shaking on the floor in the most appalling way.

DR GIBBONS. Is there a history of any sort of –

GEOFFREY. No, nothing at all, no history of anything untoward, he's always been as fit as a fiddle.

DR GIBBONS. And how did it all start then?

TERENCE. Doctor, I really do feel rather ashamed to have got you out of bed in the middle of the night like this. I'm absolutely fine,

I think I just had something of an – let's see, how can I describe it – I think, loath as I am to admit it – that it was something of an emotional nature.

DR GIBBONS. Your mother said you had convulsions.

TERENCE. I did, yes, but I think that what brought it on was...

DR GIBBONS. Was what?

TERENCE. I think, if truth be told, that I just need a good rest, that's all.

DR GIBBONS. I'll still need to examine you, young man.

TERENCE. Yes, I do understand. Shall we...

DR GIBBONS. We'll need some privacy and you can tell me in your own words exactly what happened tonight.

TERENCE. Do you mind if I give myself a quick wash beforehand? I seem to have worked up quite a sweat.

DR GIBBONS. Of course.

GEOFFREY. Off you go then, Terence, and the doctor will join you in a few moments.

TERENCE (*slowly standing*). Thank you all for being so understanding and I apologise once again for the histrionics I forced you to watch.

VANESSA. No need to apologise, my darling, you haven't done a thing wrong.

TERENCE. I shall see you all in the morning.

He walks up to HAROLD.

And thank you, sir, for your thoughts on it. Do you know, I think they're rather accurate. It's quite ironic thinking of all the conversations we've been having since we got here. It's all very well saying that we need to reintroduce the mystical into our lives but it's not very pleasant when one feels that the mystical has marked one out for some special purpose. Quite the opposite.

DR GIBBONS. Mystical?

TERENCE. Goodnight, all.

HAROLD. Goodnight, Terence.

TERENCE. Doctor, I shall see you in a few minutes.

DR GIBBONS. You shall indeed.

TERENCE begins to leave but ELIZABETH's *voice stops him.*

ELIZABETH. Do you believe, Dr Gibbons, that the dead can contact us through the living?

They both stop.

HAROLD. For God's sake, Elizabeth, please.

VANESSA. Darling, I really think you ought to get to bed.

TERENCE. Yes.

DR GIBBONS. I'll be up soon, Mr Avery.

TERENCE. Of course. Thank you, doctor.

TERENCE leaves the room.

DR GIBBONS. That's an interesting question, Mrs Pritchard.

HAROLD. It's a ridiculous question, doctor, and I'm only sorry you've been asked it. You have to forgive my wife, the evening's events have unsettled her.

ELIZABETH. Do you, doctor?

Pause. He thinks about how to best respond.

DR GIBBONS. Well, I'm a man of science. So sceptical too.

Pause.

Any talk of the supernatural – of the metaphysical side of life has me usually rushing for the nearest door. It makes me uncomfortable. Not because it frightens me – no, far from it. Only because the subject seems to attract a somewhat – how shall I put it – slow-witted pool of admirers. Oh, please don't misunderstand me I'm not –

ELIZABETH. Don't worry, doctor, I won't take the remark personally.

DR GIBBONS. Heaven forbid. And perhaps slow-witted is the wrong word in this instance in any case. The less educated shall we say. Superstition and ignorance often go hand in hand.

HAROLD. My thoughts exactly.

DR GIBBONS. But that doesn't exclude things from happening from time to time, Mrs Pritchard, which completely confound our rational selves and for which we can find no discernible answers.

GEOFFREY. So true.

DR GIBBONS. A particular incident comes to mind. It happened a few years ago in one of the mining villages near Peterborough. The miners and their families – well, perhaps this has something to do with what I was just saying about a lack of education – but the miners and their families are often prone to believing things that the rest of us would be quick to dismiss as fantastical.

ELIZABETH. Maybe it's simply to do with the fact that their experience of life is so different to ours.

DR GIBBONS. They have a woman in one of the villages – 'the layer-on of hands' they call her and all I can say is she's good competition. It's not an exaggeration to say that with many ailments they rush to her for remedy long before they come knocking on my own door. The woman, they say, has hands that heal.

HAROLD. Hands that heal, eh?

DR GIBBONS. Well, a few years back this same woman who is also said by the miners and their families – some of them mind you, not all – to have some sort of what you would call *psychic* abilities was called to the house of one of the miners in which there'd been some sort of disturbance. There were six people living in the small house – the miner and his wife and their four children. Apparently objects had been seen flying around the house –

HAROLD. Insanity.

DR GIBBONS. – a frying pan or whatnot would suddenly fling itself across the kitchen say. I never witnessed this myself but spoke to a number of people who swore that they had. And then there was a persistent smell of rotting meat. But even though they searched everywhere to find the source of the stench, going so far as to pull up the floorboards to look for it, they never found a thing. And then this woman – the 'layer-on of hands' – spent a week in the house, sleeping on the kitchen floor and all of a sudden on the seventh day, she seemed to be taken over by some sort of – well, let me word it a different way – she began behaving very oddly, speaking in a voice which wasn't her own but belonged to a young girl and also making all sorts of terrible groaning noises as if she was in the most appalling pain. Eventually she started repeating the same words over and over again and it transpired to be an address three streets away. She kept repeating something along the lines of 'the third house down on Chapel Way'. Well, finally a number of people took the initiative to make their way to the house she kept describing. It was an old derelict place, unlived-in for some time. And in there – down in the small, dank cellar – they found the skeleton of a young woman who had been brutally murdered and dismembered.

VANESSA. How ghastly.

DR GIBBONS. And then – and this is the part that makes my skin crawl – they came to discover that the man who had murdered this poor woman was none other than the miner in whose house the strange happenings had first occurred.

HAROLD. A haunting tale, Dr Gibbons. But I must say I'm surprised by the fact that you entertain the possibility of it being anything other than fiction.

DR GIBBONS. Like you, Mr Pritchard, I'm sure, I am alarmed and made uncomfortable by the possibility that there are things I may never fully grasp or comprehend.

HAROLD. And there is a slight problem that I have with your story, doctor. Well, not so much a problem as a query.

DR GIBBONS. What is it?

HAROLD. Why did the miner let this 'layer-on of hands' into his house? Why did he allow her into his home if he believed it would be likely to lead to the discovery of his crime?

DR GIBBONS. A good question, Mr Pritchard. Perhaps he was just exhausted of carrying the guilt.

There's a loud clap of thunder and suddenly the electrics are affected – the lights momentarily fail and the room is plunged into darkness.

GEOFFREY. Good heavens.

VANESSA. What on earth…

HAROLD. That's all we bloody need.

Then, they suddenly switch on again. And, as if out of nowhere, TERENCE has appeared at the bottom of the stairs. He is only

half-dressed, his top half is bare, though he is still wearing his
pyjama bottoms. He has a strange expression on his face, not
quite his own.

ELIZABETH. Terence.

VANESSA *lets out a yelp of surprise.*

VANESSA. Dear God, darling, you gave me the fright of my life.

GEOFFREY. Why aren't you wearing your top, Terence?

VANESSA. Darling, you're only half-dressed. And what are you
doing here anyway? The doctor is coming up to you now, he was
just talking to us.

GEOFFREY. You'll catch a chill, my boy.

DR GIBBONS. I was just on my way, young man.

VANESSA. You gave me a terrible fright, just standing there.

GEOFFREY. Get back to bed, Terence, there's a good chap.

VANESSA. Did you hear what I said? You really shouldn't be down
here, not after what you've been through. Darling?

TERENCE *does not answer. Slowly, as if in a trance, he walks up*
to HAROLD. *When he speaks his voice has changed, he sounds*
like a young boy.

TERENCE. Thank you for the chocolates, Father.

HAROLD. I'm not your father so don't call me it.

TERENCE. It's very kind of you. And you know they're my
favourite.

HAROLD. Stop it. Do you hear what I'm saying to you? Stop it now,
otherwise I've a good mind to beat you to a hair's width of your
life.

VANESSA. Harold, please!

TERENCE. Mother, Father's bought me chocolates.

ELIZABETH. I know he has, my angel. From Leeds.

TERENCE. I know, Mother. He must have bought them yesterday.

ELIZABETH. He did, my darling, he did. Because he drove the
Averys to Leeds so that they could get their train back to London
and then he had a business meeting too and he stopped off at the

arcade after that and bought you those chocolates, the ones you like so much.

TERENCE. Thank you, Father.

HAROLD. Stop it!

VANESSA. Stop it, Terence, stop calling him 'Father', stop speaking in that voice, you're frightening me.

ELIZABETH. How could he know, Harold? How could he know these things?

GEOFFREY. Know what?

ELIZABETH. How could he know that on the morning he went missing, that very morning, his father gave him a box of chocolates that he'd bought him in Leeds the day before…

TERENCE. Thank you, Father.

ELIZABETH. How could he know?

HAROLD. This is madness, sheer madness I tell you.

DR GIBBONS. I've never seen the like.

ELIZABETH. How?

> TERENCE *walks up to* ELIZABETH *and mimes handing her something*.

TERENCE. And here's heather for you, Mother, because you love it so.

ELIZABETH. And that afterwards he went and gathered heather for me and gave me it tied in a little string? Just before, just before he left, it was the last thing he did.

TERENCE. Because you love it so.

ELIZABETH. I've never told a living soul, how could he know?

TERENCE. And now, Mother, there's something I need to tell you.

ELIZABETH. What is it, my love? What is it? What is it?

HAROLD. Stop this madness! Stop it now.

VANESSA. Terence, I beg you.

ELIZABETH. What is it?

TERENCE. Mother, Father, you must take me to Bracken Moor. I have to tell you what it was like. I have to tell you what happened in the dark. What happened at Bracken Moor.

EILEEN *lets out a spine-chilling scream and falls to her knees.*

Blackout.

End of Act One.

As at the beginning of the play, the actors who are on stage at the top of the act – in this instance those playing the parts of JOHN *and* EILEEN *– walk on while the house lights are still on. The actor playing* JOHN *puts on his coat while the actor playing* EILEEN *brings on a tray of tea things and rests it on a table. She rearranges her costume a little and gets into her position for the top of the act.*

Blackout.

ACT TWO

Scene One

Lights up.

The following afternoon. It continues to be stormy though the wind has abated a little. The windows, however, are being pelted with rain.

EILEEN *is standing in the middle of the room and preparing for tea. She has a tray of cups and saucers and is carefully placing them one by one onto the coffee table. But as she sees to the task her hands are slightly shaking.*

JOHN *is there in his coat, which is soaking wet.*

EILEEN. So you understand, Mr Bailey, this is not the time for any sort of business.

JOHN. I can see that now.

EILEEN. Perhaps it were best for you to return in the morning, sir.

JOHN. Yes.

EILEEN. Because I can not imagine that after all that's happened – oh, the horrible, horrible things, Mr Bailey, which I saw with my own two eyes – well, I don't imagine that after all that poor Mr Pritchard would have the head for any sort of business.

JOHN. I expect not.

EILEEN. He turned as white as the whitest sheet when we were there and poor Mrs Pritchard wailing like some sort of – well, like an animal, Mr Bailey, if you'll forgive me for saying, like a trapped deer or something and the boy – that strange, haunted Mr Avery, rolling on the floor down in the pit, his clothes covered in mud and his hair matted with it. They'd thrown down a rope ladder you see and they wanted me there so that I could help carry things and we all went down into the pit where the poor boy breathed his last all those years ago and it was as if we were descending into the bowels of the earth, as if we were entering Hell itself.

JOHN. That can't have been pleasant.

EILEEN. Oh, it wasn't, Mr Bailey, it wasn't, it wasn't and – (*Suddenly drops the cup and saucer she is holding and bursts into tears*.) and I don't know what to do with myself, Mr Bailey, I don't know what to do but I can't stay in this house any more even though I'd feel terrible for leaving them, especially poor Mrs Pritchard who's like a ghost herself, wandering the corridors like a sleepwalker these last ten years, but I can't stay, Mr Bailey, even though I have nowhere else to go and my mother and brothers to support but I can't stay, not after the things I've seen and heard and I haven't slept in three days and I think I'm losing my mind, I'm ever so frightened, Mr Bailey, ever so unhappy, but what can I do.

JOHN. But did the boy say anything?

EILEEN (*trying to pull herself together*). Oh, I do beg your pardon, sir, for making such a fuss and crying and all but I really am ever so unhappy.

JOHN. Of course you are.

Pause.

EILEEN. No, the boy didn't say a word, Mr Bailey, just rolled on the floor making these noises as if he were in the most terrible anguish and tearing his clothes off as if he was trying to escape his very own body, it makes me shiver just remembering it.

Pause.

So they've covered him in a blanket and are carrying him home now with Mrs Pritchard walking in their wake asking him all the time, 'What is that you need me to know, Edgar, what is it that you need me to know?' but the boy not saying a word just rolling his head around like someone who's lost their mind for good. But they sent me ahead so that I could light the fire and make some tea for them, God knows they'll need it after hours in that cold, damp place.

JOHN. What a terrible situation.

EILEEN. Oh, it is, Mr Bailey, it is. And it makes you think about all sorts of things.

JOHN. What sort of things, Miss Hannaway?

EILEEN. I mean about your own life, Mr Bailey, and about what it means to be a human being.

JOHN. How do you mean?

EILEEN. About what all the pain is about and the loss and the cruel things we do to each other and if there's any meaning to it at all or if we were just put on this earth to suffer and die. Oh Jesus, forgive me for even thinking this way.

JOHN. Miss Hannaway –

EILEEN. Oh, I'm sorry, Mr Bailey, I'm not making any sense at all.

JOHN. On the contrary, Miss Hannaway, I think you're making a whole lot of sense. It's a shame though that it takes such frightful things to happen before we question things the way we ought.

EILEEN (*crossing herself*). I'll be going to church in the morning and doing a whole lot of praying, that's for certain.

JOHN. Whatever brings you comfort, Miss Hannaway.

EILEEN. Oh God help us all, Mr Bailey, God help us all.

There is the sound of a door opening and voices entering the house.

Oh, there they are now.

JOHN. I'd better be on my way then.

EILEEN. And I need to get the pot of tea. Why don't you follow me, sir, and I'll let you out the back way.

JOHN. Thank you, Miss Hannaway.

EILEEN. And maybe you can come back at a better time.

JOHN. I shall.

EILEEN *leads* JOHN *out of the room.*

For a few seconds the room is empty. Then the door to the hallway opens and they all enter: HAROLD *and* GEOFFREY, *half-carrying* TERENCE *who is semi-conscious, and behind them* ELIZABETH *and* VANESSA. *The men carry* TERENCE *over to the sofa and lay him down on it. All of them are covered in mud and dirt, but especially* TERENCE *who is in a state of semi-dress, with a blanket thrown over him but with no shoes or socks on his feet.*

GEOFFREY. That'll do.

VANESSA. I really think we should take him upstairs instead, Geoffrey.

ELIZABETH. He can rest here for a little while.

VANESSA. And he'll need a wash, we need to wash him.

HAROLD. We all will, look at us, covered in grime and dirt, as if we've carried that damned place with us.

GEOFFREY. Those bloody rats.

ELIZABETH. Why don't you go upstairs and rest a little, I'll stay here with Terence and if he wakes in the meantime I'll be sure to call you.

GEOFFREY. And we can have a wash ourselves and get into a clean set of clothes.

VANESSA. I just don't think it's a good idea, I want him to come upstairs with us.

ELIZABETH. It's warm here, he'll be comfortable. Why don't you go and rest, I'll stay by his side.

VANESSA. I said I don't think it's a good idea.

ELIZABETH. You could even start pouring him a bath and Harold will help him up in no time.

VANESSA. My dear, you're not listening, I said I don't think it's a good idea.

ELIZABETH. Why ever not?

VANESSA. Because I don't, I don't, I DON'T!

Pause.

I'm sorry, Elizabeth, but I don't, I just don't like it at all, not one bit, all this that's been happening.

HAROLD. None of this is Elizabeth's doing, Vanessa.

VANESSA. And I'm sorry to have to say this –

GEOFFREY. Careful, darling.

VANESSA. But it's as if you want something from him.

ELIZABETH. Want something?

VANESSA. Yes, it's as if you do and I can't lie, I don't like it one bit. And I don't think we should have taken him there, to that horrible place, and I bitterly regret we did and that we had to witness what we did and I think that Harold's right and the best thing for us to do is to get on the next train out of here and head straight back to London.

ELIZABETH. He was the one who wanted us to go.

VANESSA. So I'd rather appreciate it, Harold, if you asked your man to drive us into Leeds in the next hour so that we can get on the train and leave you all in peace.

ELIZABETH. In peace, yes.

HAROLD. You won't make the evening train, you might as well leave in the morning.

VANESSA. Well then we can stay at an hotel or something.

GEOFFREY. Darling.

VANESSA. Because I really can't bear this any longer.

HAROLD. None of us can, Vanessa.

> TERENCE *makes a noise, as if he is in discomfort and shivers quite violently.*

VANESSA. He's cold, we need to put his sweater on again, I don't know why you took it off to begin with. Geoffrey, where have you put it?

ELIZABETH. He pulled it off himself as we made our way back and fought when I tried to put it on him again.

HAROLD (*handing* VANESSA *the sweater*). Here we are.

VANESSA. And his socks too, for Heaven's sake.

HAROLD. And the socks.

ELIZABETH *takes* TERENCE'*s socks from* HAROLD.

ELIZABETH. Those too, he pulled them off himself.

VANESSA. That's neither here nor there, Elizabeth, it was freezing cold and he didn't know what it was he was doing, he'll catch his death.

ELIZABETH *kneels down and starts to put his socks on.*

ELIZABETH. I'll put his socks on and he'll be warm again and you can go upstairs and pour him a bath and in less than ten minutes we'll be up and he'll be well once more, you'll see, Vanessa, your boy will be well again.

VANESSA. Geoffrey.

GEOFFREY. Yes, dear. Harold, I really think we need to draw a line here. The best thing to do is to let the boy come up with us.

HAROLD. Elizabeth.

ELIZABETH. He said he needs to speak to me. Five minutes that's all.

VANESSA *tries to move* ELIZABETH *out of the way as she starts putting the socks on* TERENCE'*s feet.*

VANESSA. Leave that, Elizabeth, I shall do it, it's fine.

ELIZABETH. It's all right, I'm nearly finished, let me.

VANESSA. I said please leave it, Elizabeth.

ELIZABETH. We need to be left alone for just a moment. Maybe that's why he hasn't spoken. He said he had something to tell me.

VANESSA. He may have said many things, Elizabeth, but the time has come to put an end to all of it.

ELIZABETH. He said he had something to say to his mother.

VANESSA. I am his mother, Elizabeth, *I am* his mother.

ELIZABETH. So let us be for just one minute, I beg you.

VANESSA *becomes more forceful in moving* ELIZABETH *out of the way.*

VANESSA. Leave him alone please, Elizabeth, put those down and leave him alone.

ELIZABETH. One minute is all I'm asking for.

VANESSA. And I'm sorry you lost your boy, Elizabeth, God only knows how sorry I am, but I'm not prepared to lose mine as well.

ELIZABETH. How do you mean?

VANESSA. To this madness that's gripped him since we got here. YOURS IS LOST ALREADY, MINE I WILL HOLD ON TO WITH ALL MY STRENGTH AND MIGHT!

She bursts into tears.

I'm so sorry, what a cruel, cruel thing to say.

ELIZABETH. It's all right, Vanessa, it's all right.

VANESSA. What a monstrous thing to say.

ELIZABETH. Really, it's all right. You're upset.

VANESSA. I'm so sorry, I'm so sorry, I'm so sorry.

ELIZABETH. Stay for the night and go tomorrow, I beg you.

VANESSA. I'm not sure it's for the best.

ELIZABETH. And in the morning we'll put everything behind us.

HAROLD. I asked the girl to make some tea. Why don't you go and change and then come downstairs and have a cup. We'll look after him, don't worry yourselves.

GEOFFREY. Good idea. A cup of tea smacks of a little sanity.

VANESSA. All right then.

VANESSA *walks up to* ELIZABETH *and kisses her.*

I'm sorry, my dear. My nerves.

ELIZABETH. You needn't apologise, Vanessa, I understand.

GEOFFREY. Come on, my girl.

VANESSA. Ten minutes, Elizabeth. And then upstairs.

ELIZABETH. Ten minutes, no longer.

VANESSA *and* GEOFFREY *leave.*

ELIZABETH *and* HAROLD *are left alone with* TERENCE. *Neither of them speak for some time.* ELIZABETH *sits on the floor by* TERENCE*'s side and picks up one of his hands.*

His nails are covered in dirt.

HAROLD. They would be, wouldn't they? The way he was scratching and clawing the earth.

EILEEN comes in with the pot of tea.

EILEEN. The tea's ready, ma'am.

ELIZABETH. Thank you, Eileen, put it there on the table.

EILEEN. Yes, ma'am.

ELIZABETH. And then I want you to bring me something.

EILEEN. What is it, ma'am?

ELIZABETH. Pour some of the boiling water from the kettle into a bowl and bring it to me with a bar of soap and a washrag.

EILEEN. Yes, ma'am.

She goes. HAROLD *goes over to the tea.*

HAROLD. Shall I pour you a cup?

ELIZABETH. In a little while.

He pours himself a cup and goes to stand by the window, looking out at the rain. ELIZABETH *remains by* TERENCE's *side.*

He looks more peaceful now. His breathing has quietened, and his pulse is a little slower.

HAROLD. That's a good thing.

ELIZABETH. It is, yes.

Pause.

Do you remember about three weeks before the… three weeks before we lost him, we spent that Sunday over towards Sheffield and had a picnic on that hillside.

HAROLD. I think so, yes.

ELIZABETH. It was a glorious day. And fun too. He sat on your knees in the motor and pretended he was driving it.

HAROLD. I remember. It was a pleasant Sunday.

ELIZABETH. But then your mood changed.

HAROLD. Did it?

ELIZABETH. He said something. Edgar did. And you disapproved.

HAROLD. I don't remember.

ELIZABETH. You said it was a girly thing to say and then you were in the foulest mood all afternoon.

HAROLD. I really don't remember.

ELIZABETH. But it wounded him and I remember noticing that his eyes were moist with tears around the edges. But of course he held back because if he had cried you would have become even angrier.

HAROLD. I was trying to instil in him some understanding of what the world expects of a man.

ELIZABETH. Is that what you were doing?

Pause.

I can't remember what it was he said. Something silly, innocuous, the way children talk. But you punished him for it.

HAROLD. I really don't recall it.

EILEEN *returns with a bowl of steaming water, a bar of soap and a washrag.*

EILEEN. Here you are, ma'am.

ELIZABETH. Thank you, Eileen, you can leave it here.

EILEEN *places the bowl, the soap and the washrag by* ELIZABETH's *side.*

That'll be all, thank you, Eileen.

EILEEN. Yes, ma'am.

She goes. ELIZABETH *begins to soak the washrag in the steaming water.*

ELIZABETH. I always felt, Harold, that what you wanted most from Edgar was for him to reflect something of yourself.

HAROLD. Why are you saying these things now?

ELIZABETH. Because I never have before.

Pause.

As if you wanted him to be an extension of yourself, not a person in his own right.

HAROLD. He was a child, Elizabeth.

ELIZABETH. And I wonder if we're all extensions. If you've ever really known how to see people for what they are.

Pause.

Harold, can you leave me alone with him for a minute? I want to... Could you? Not longer than a minute. I just want to wash the dirt from under his nails but I want to do it alone.

HAROLD. I shall be in my study. If he stirs, call me.

ELIZABETH. I shall, thank you.

HAROLD *leaves the room and goes to his study.*

ELIZABETH *picks up the washrag, squeezes it and begins to clean the areas around* TERENCE*'s nails. A few seconds pass like this and then, quietly, she begins to speak to him.*

I need to talk to you. I don't know if you can hear me or if you can understand me but there's something that I need to tell you.

Pause.

I love you. I love you with all my heart and my soul and from the very depth of my being.

I was so grateful because when I knew you I learnt the meaning of faith. How could I not believe in a good future when I held you in my arms and cradled you? How could I not believe that there was a beautiful plan of which we were both a part and which would lead us to some beckoning place where God's face would finally be revealed? So thank you for those years of faith, my angel.

Pause. She places the washrag into the bowl of water and picks up the boy's head in her hands and cradles him.

I ran, my love, and screamed and shouted and ran and ran and ran. Even in the night and all hours of the day, through the fields and the backs of houses, in the villages and on the hills and by the river too and as I ran all I kept doing was shouting your name. And I'm still running, and I'll be running till the day I die. But I'm sorry I didn't find you in time.

Suddenly, TERENCE *starts convulsing and gasping for air and his eyes open and are full of terror.* ELIZABETH *jumps back and lets out a small scream.*

Harold! Harold, come!

As TERENCE *writhes in terror on the floor,* HAROLD *runs back into the room.*

TERENCE. Rats, Mother, rats, rats in the dark, rats, rats, rats.

ELIZABETH. Where, darling, where?

TERENCE. Rats in the dark, Mother, here in the dark, scurrying to and fro over my legs, Mother, scurry, scurry, scurry.

ELIZABETH. I'm here, darling, here, I'm here.

TERENCE. On my own, Mother, Father, on my own in the dark and I can't move my legs and the rats are running over them.

ELIZABETH. Can you hear me, my love, we're looking for you, we're looking everywhere trying to find you.

TERENCE. Pain, pain, pain, pain in my legs, running through my spine, so much pain, so much pain.

ELIZABETH. I know, my love, I know.

TERENCE. You'll find me, you'll find me, I hope you'll find me, I pray you'll find me.

ELIZABETH. Oh, my angel, my sweet angel.

TERENCE. Though I walk through the valley of the shadow of death, I will fear no evil; for Thou art with me; Thy rod and Thy staff they comfort me.

HAROLD. He prays.

TERENCE. The Lord is my shepherd, the Lord is my shepherd, the Lord is my shepherd.

ELIZABETH. Yes, my darling, yes my darling.

TERENCE. Though I walk through the valley of the shadow of death, I will fear no evil; for Thou art with me; Thy rod and Thy staff they comfort me.

ELIZABETH. Oh, my child, my poor, poor child.

TERENCE. I pray, Mother, I pray, just like you taught me, just like we did at school, I pray, Mother, pray, I pray for the pain in my legs to

go away and for the rats to go, I pray, I pray, I pray. I pray for you
to come and find me and I pray to remind myself of who I am.

ELIZABETH. You're a boy, *my* boy, the most beautiful boy with a
soul as big as everything in the world and as infinite.

TERENCE. Where are you, Father, why aren't you here, where are
you, Father?

ELIZABETH. Talk to him, Harold, speak to him.

TERENCE. Frightened, Father, frightened, frightened that you'll
never find me.

ELIZABETH. We're looking for you, angel, looking everywhere.

TERENCE. Frightened that I'm all alone.

ELIZABETH. Harold, speak to him, I beg you, comfort him!

TERENCE. Mother, Father, I don't want to die.

ELIZABETH. Oh, my darling, we're looking for you, searching
everywhere, calling you.

TERENCE. I am alone, I am alone, I am alone. Alone in the dark,
forever alone.

ELIZABETH. No, my darling, no.

TERENCE. My God, my God, why hast Thou forsaken me?

ELIZABETH. Oh, my boy, my sweet boy.

TERENCE. Matter wins, matter, matter, matter.

ELIZABETH. No, my angel, no.

TERENCE. Death is coming, fear, fear, fear, death death, death.

ELIZABETH. I'm with you, my angel, I am with you, always with
you.

TERENCE. Always alone, forever alone, in the darkness and the fear
and the death forever.

ELIZABETH. No. No. No.

TERENCE *collapses onto the floor and* ELIZABETH *falls on
him, wraps her arms around him and sobs. For a few seconds
they remain like this on the ground, with* HAROLD *standing
nearby looking down at them. Then, slowly,* TERENCE *stands up.
He walks over to another corner of the room and kneels down
again.*

TERENCE. Mother, come here, give me your hand.

She goes to him and kneels beside him. He looks into her eyes and speaks softly, simply.

This is what I needed to tell you.

ELIZABETH. What is it, my angel?

TERENCE. I know that you ran and still run, Mother. But you need to stop now.

Pause.

I know that you called my name and that you still call it. But you need to stop.

ELIZABETH. No.

And then, almost as if the words are not his own but passing through him:

TERENCE. Death is birth Mother through the flesh into the eternal life through the darkest hour back into the light I am through now Mother I am the new blades of grass in the churchyard where you buried me and the same bird that returns to the steeple every morning and the ants that walk in the cracks outside your window Mother Mother I can see you through the window and I am the boy that picks the apples from the tree at the bottom of the garden Father Mother I am the owl of the night and the cockerel that announces the morning from the farm beneath our house and Father Father I am the miners working in the dark working working working working toiling toiling toiling toiling for the common good...

ELIZABETH. The common good.

TERENCE. And I am the daughters of the miners and I shall be their daughters too and their sons as well look after me Father look after me the walls are gone for ever and all is understood I am life Mother Father I am life forever here forever returning look after me Mother look after me Father we are One.

He closes his eyes and loses consciousness again.

ELIZABETH *lets out a noise, something like a wail, a guttural sound of release, as if she is letting go of something she has held onto for many years.*

Blackout.

Scene Two

The following morning. It is a sunny day outside and thick shafts of light flood into the room, brightening everything.

HAROLD *is reading the newspaper.*

EILEEN *enters. She is carrying a tray with a coffee pot and cups on it.*

EILEEN. Would you like your coffee in here, sir?

HAROLD. Yes, thank you, Eileen.

She places the tray on the coffee table and pours him a cup.

EILEEN. Cook is asking if you'd like your breakfast now, sir?

HAROLD. I won't be wanting any today, Eileen. But you best ask the Averys if they should like theirs.

EILEEN. They've already eaten breakfast, sir, they were up at the crack of dawn.

HAROLD. Did you tell Mr McLean to get the motor ready?

EILEEN. I did, sir, and I told him that Mr and Mrs Avery and young Mr Avery need to be at the train station by midday so he suggested leaving just after ten o'clock.

HAROLD. Can you notify them?

EILEEN. Oh, I have done already, sir, though young Mr Avery is still asleep. But his mother said she would wake him shortly and help him pack his bag.

HAROLD. Good.

EILEEN. Is there anything else, sir?

HAROLD. Not for the time being.

EILEEN. Thank you, sir. Do ring if you need me. I shall be upstairs helping Mrs Pritchard with her packing.

Pause.

HAROLD. Helping Mrs Pritchard with her packing?

EILEEN. Yes, sir.

HAROLD. Surely you mean Mrs Avery.

EILEEN. Oh, no, sir, I mean Mrs Pritchard. She said she needed some help packing her suitcase. She told me she's going to be visiting her sister in London for a few days.

HAROLD. Is she?

EILEEN. Oh, I thought you knew, sir.

HAROLD. I didn't.

EILEEN. Isn't that wonderful news, Mr Pritchard?

He doesn't answer. EILEEN *walks over to the window and pulls back one of the curtains to let the full force of the sun in.*

It's a beautiful day, sir.

HAROLD. Yes.

EILEEN. Nice to see the sun again, isn't it, sir?

HAROLD. Indeed.

She goes. He puts the paper down for a second, lost in thought.

GEOFFREY *walks in.*

GEOFFREY. Hello, old boy.

HAROLD. Morning, Geoffrey.

GEOFFREY. What's the news?

HAROLD. It looks as if Franco has secured the North.

GEOFFREY. Vanessa's waking the boy and then we said we'd go for a stroll in the garden.

HAROLD. Excellent idea.

GEOFFREY. Make the most of it, eh?

HAROLD. Definitely.

Pause.

Help yourself to coffee.

GEOFFREY. Do you know, I think I will.

GEOFFREY *pours himself a cup and sits down.*

What to say, eh? What to say.

HAROLD. Yes.

Pause.

GEOFFREY. I would think the most important thing for all of us now is to try and return to some kind of normality.

HAROLD. Essential, yes.

GEOFFREY. Easier said than done, of course.

HAROLD. Absolutely.

GEOFFREY. But one must make one's best effort.

HAROLD. One must.

GEOFFREY. Even though the world is changed for ever.

HAROLD. Is it?

GEOFFREY. Well, what I mean is, how can you not... I mean after... the *things*. You know.

HAROLD. The things, yes.

GEOFFREY. How can you not... review... not review, what's the word, *re-evaluate* I suppose is what I mean. Re-evaluate.

HAROLD. Re-evaluate what, Geoffrey?

GEOFFREY. Well, everything really. Life, I mean. One's perceptions at least, one's views. Nothing is what one thought it was, is it? As if one's been holding on to something concrete and then finds out that it isn't concrete at all but something entirely different. Almost as if –

HAROLD. When you walk around the garden you mustn't forget to stop off by the little wall behind the elm trees. There's a wonderful view of the meadow.

GEOFFREY. Won't you join us?

HAROLD. I'm going to have to start working I'm afraid.

GEOFFREY. Of course.

HAROLD. Lots to be getting on with.

Pause.

GEOFFREY. Take me for instance. I am surrounded by beautiful objects all day long, every day. And each object has its own unique personality and its own exclusive history. But I spend so much time either valuing these objects for their monetary worth or cataloguing them that sometimes I forget to really observe them, to *appreciate* them I suppose. The force of habit, isn't that what they say. You behave in a certain way and cease to really notice things. You forget their power and beauty and innate essence. I'm probably not making much sense –

HAROLD. Not a lot, Geoffrey.

GEOFFREY. But what I think I'm saying is that sometimes these extraordinary events occur which are so beyond one's own sphere of experience, so beyond everything one's known and recognised up till that point, well, that suddenly life seems to be new and full of infinite potential. As if your eyes have been opened for the very first time to its inexhaustible possibilities. I think most of us are walking around in a sort of slumber really.

VANESSA and ELIZABETH *walk in.*

VANESSA. Terence has risen at last, like Lazarus from the dead. Good morning, Harold.

HAROLD. Morning, Vanessa.

VANESSA. And Elizabeth's coming down with us and we'll drop her off at Charlotte's, isn't that marvellous?

HAROLD. I heard.

ELIZABETH. I was coming to tell you.

HAROLD. Of course.

ELIZABETH. Charlotte can't quite believe it. She's emptying the little spare room for me.

VANESSA. Are you quite sure you don't want to come and stay at ours?

ELIZABETH. No, it's fine, really, but thank you, Vanessa. It'll be nice to spend some time with my sister.

GEOFFREY. Of course.

ELIZABETH. After all it's been years and years.

VANESSA. She'll be happy to see you again. Well, everybody will. I'm already making plans to show you off to all and sundry.

ELIZABETH. Oh, Vanessa, I beg you.

VANESSA. Beg me what, darling?

ELIZABETH. I just need a little time. And then we'll see.

VANESSA. Of course. Of course, I understand, trust me.

ELIZABETH. I do.

GEOFFREY. Well then you need your head examined.

VANESSA. Shut up, Geoffrey, and drink your coffee.

Pause.

Terence says he's never felt better and do you know, I don't think he's ever looked it. The colour's back in his cheeks and the sparkle's in his eyes.

GEOFFREY. That's our boy.

VANESSA. And he says he doesn't remember a thing about yesterday.

ELIZABETH. I'd imagine that's a good thing.

VANESSA. I think so too. Who'd want to remember... well, who'd want to remember all the dreadful things that happened to him.

GEOFFREY. Who indeed.

VANESSA. But he's looking a whole lot better.

Pause.

Come on then, let's get that walk in.

GEOFFREY. Round the garden, yes.

VANESSA. Don't worry, you lazy sod, no further. We shan't be climbing any mountains.

GEOFFREY. What a shame.

ELIZABETH. I'll join you in just a minute.

VANESSA. All right, my darling.

ELIZABETH. And then we'll have the suitcases brought downstairs and loaded into the motor.

VANESSA. Come on then, Geoffrey, move those ancient, sagging limbs.

VANESSA *and* GEOFFREY *leave the room. A few seconds pass before* ELIZABETH *speaks.*

ELIZABETH. I don't know how long I'm going for, Harold.

HAROLD. I see.

Pause.

ELIZABETH. Or if I'm even coming back.

HAROLD. Funny that. I too must be something of a psychic. I was almost certain you were going to say that.

ELIZABETH. Something's happened.

HAROLD. That's a bit of an understatement isn't it?

Pause.

ELIZABETH. Charlotte said I can stay at hers for as long as I like.

HAROLD. Why don't you stay at ours? I'll speak to Mrs Greene and she can tidy the place up, it'll only take her a day or two.

ELIZABETH. I don't want to stay at your flat, Harold.

HAROLD. *Our* flat.

ELIZABETH. *Your* flat, Harold. It's yours. Everything is yours.

HAROLD. Anyway, your sister lives in two rooms and hasn't any money. You won't last a day.

ELIZABETH. I will.

HAROLD. In any case I'll speak to the man at Coutts and you can pass by later this week and take whatever money you need.

ELIZABETH. I shan't do that.

HAROLD. And then when you're feeling a little better I may come down myself for a few days, God knows it might do me some good.

ELIZABETH. You're not listening, Harold. You're not listening, you're not listening.

Pause.

I don't want the flat. I don't want the money. I *shall* manage, one way or another. Charlotte mentioned someone was looking for a French teacher.

HAROLD. Don't be absurd.

ELIZABETH. It's for young children, my French is good enough. And then we'll see. But I *shall* manage.

EILEEN *comes down the stairs carrying a couple of suitcases.*
She makes her way across the room and exits to the hallway.
ELIZABETH *only continues to speak when she is gone.*

Everything is yours. I sat in my room last night, after all that had
happened and I looked at the wall and do you know what I
thought?

HAROLD. What did you think, Elizabeth?

ELIZABETH. I thought, 'That wall is Harold's.' The bricks and
mortar that made this house. The fields beyond the window. The
way we are and the way we live. I sat there and I thought,
'*Everything is his.*' He has shaped this place in his image, has
stamped it with his mark. I stood up – I actually started walking
around the house – looking for myself. I thought maybe I would –
I *hoped* – that maybe I would find myself somewhere. In a
picture, an armchair, in the smallest room. Something. But even
when I looked in the mirror you stared back at me.

HAROLD. What are you saying?

ELIZABETH. I am complicit. Not a victim but an accomplice. It was
the easier life you see. And it was seductive too. In the beginning
I worshipped all those qualities one admires in a man.
Determination and leadership. You frightened me sometimes but
even the fear I felt excited me. And I gave myself to you and
found my place in your shade and felt some safety there. So I am
as much to blame as you. I see that now and I see something else
too.

HAROLD. And what is that?

ELIZABETH. That you cower in the corner at the thought of your
own extinction. That you're threatened by the whispers in the trees,
by the shapes and shadows that dance at your feet and more than
anything else, by the true meaning of love.

Pause.

So you see I have to leave, Harold. I don't know where to – oh, to
my sister's yes, but then what? – what the future is I do not know.
But I think that if I stay here we shall both go mad.

She goes.

HAROLD *is left alone. He does not move. A few seconds pass but*
he remains completely still.

Then TERENCE *enters*.

TERENCE. Good morning.

HAROLD. Hello.

TERENCE. At last when I woke up this morning and looked out of the window I could see for miles and miles and remembered what a glorious part of the world this is.

HAROLD. It is, yes.

TERENCE. Where are the others?

HAROLD. They're walking around the garden.

TERENCE. Getting a bit of fresh air before the journey home.

HAROLD. Yes, they are.

TERENCE *walks over to where the coffee is and pours himself a cup*.

So you slept well.

TERENCE. Like a baby, yes. And no dreams or visions or anything of the kind.

HAROLD. Good. I think we've had enough of those.

TERENCE. Yes, quite enough.

He walks over to the window and looks out.

Mrs Pritchard is a little transformed. She looks as if some weight has been lifted from her shoulders.

HAROLD. Does she?

TERENCE. And I think it's a good thing that she's coming to London.

HAROLD. Is that what you think?

TERENCE. Returning, I mean.

HAROLD. Returning, yes.

TERENCE. To life.

Pause.

I have a confession to make.

HAROLD. What sort of a confession?

TERENCE. The night we arrived I was coming down to meet you. I got to the door but you were in a business meeting.

HAROLD. With my chief collier, yes.

TERENCE. I didn't want to interrupt. So I stood outside that door and overheard the conversation.

HAROLD. So you're an eavesdropper then?

TERENCE. In that instance, yes, I must admit it. My feet were rooted to the ground.

Pause.

His arguments, as you effectively pointed out, were naive and unrealistic. Almost laughable really. He cajoled and begged, invoked pity, and then suggested a revolution of sorts. The ambition of the man was monumental even if his proposal was a little jejune.

HAROLD. Where are you going with this? I'm really not in the mood to discuss with you any of the dealings I have with my employees.

TERENCE. I do however think you misunderstood the gist of his point. I don't think he was denouncing technological advances, merely trying to suggest that the welfare of his colleagues – and their families – should be the driving motive.

HAROLD. Thank you for clarifying that.

TERENCE. Anyway, perhaps the unemployment is temporary. If we're lucky a little war and carnage will pick things up again. Isn't that what's necessary?

HAROLD. You're back to your normal self I see.

TERENCE. And then less than an hour after that I was witness to a different kind of pleading.

HAROLD. And what was that?

TERENCE. The pleading of your wife – her pleading for redemption.

He puts down his coffee cup.

I have something that I think you should have. It doesn't really belong to you but I think you should have it anyway.

He takes a small gold coin out of his pocket.

On my last morning on Mount Athos I swam to a tiny island a mile from the coast. Well, less of an island really, more of a rock with a little vegetation on it. I thought it was uninhabited but when I reached its shore I noticed there was a fire burning a few hundred feet inland, so fuelled by curiosity I made my way towards it. I came across a tiny wooden shack which was home to an alarming creature that bore a strong resemblance to a human being, only quite a bit more hirsute and shall we say malodorous.

HAROLD. Why are you telling me this?

TERENCE. At first I was a little frightened but then I realised that despite the mad glare in his eyes he was harmless, in fact completely benevolent. He was a monk who had been ejected from the monastery and labelled an apostate. His crime was to challenge those who mistake myth for reality. In somewhat fractured English he said to me, 'It is not the words of the story that matter, it is the meaning behind them.' Then he gave me this.

HAROLD. What is it?

TERENCE. A lucky coin. He said I was to always keep it on my person. He said it would help me make the right choices and lead me to them.

HAROLD. And you believed him.

TERENCE. Well, even though I thought he was a bit of a lunatic I rather liked him. So I took the coin and have had it ever since. Like a memory of my trip.

HAROLD. Good for you.

TERENCE. And as I was about to leave the island and swim back to the literalists he asked me a little about myself. I remember telling him that one day I would like to call myself an artist. And to that he said something that I shan't easily forget.

HAROLD. And what was that?

TERENCE. He said, 'When the world is separated into those who believe in nothing at all and those whose belief has made them blind it will be your duty to bridge the gap.'

Pause.

Anyway, the first night we arrived here, as I was undressing and getting ready for bed – well, wouldn't you know it – my lucky coin slipped out of my pocket and rolled to the edge of the room and disappeared under the carpet.

HAROLD. Did it?

TERENCE. That tiny slither of a gap between the edge of the carpet and the wall. Well, of course I couldn't let it disappear for ever without an effort to retrieve it and so I pulled up the carpet which surprisingly enough succumbed quite easily to my fingers, as if it had been lifted before, albeit many years ago.

HAROLD. Why are you telling me all this?

TERENCE. Do you know that the damn coin had gone one step further and fallen into the gap between the floorboards. Well, I wasn't going to give up that easily and so I tried to see if there was any way I could lift the floorboard and hey presto, it too surrendered to my attempt with hardly any resistance. I knew then that I wasn't the first.

HAROLD. So you got your coin back.

TERENCE. Yes, but more importantly it led me to this.

He takes out of his pocket a small, leather-bound book.

The handwriting I recognised immediately, that messy, childish scrawl that had written me many a letter. It brought tears to my eyes when I recognised it. This is the first page:

He reads from it.

'And so within these covers I offer you my secret thoughts, my secret hopes, my secret fears, my secret everythings in the hope that not only will you safeguard them but that in returning to your pages later on in life and reflecting on them you will help me to discover and understand something of where I've come from and suggest something of where I'm headed.' He's twelve years old, it's extraordinary.

And a few pages later: 'Betsy, God bless her, has bought a new hat that makes her look like a mad ostrich. "How are you going to fry us an egg in that?" I asked her and she laughed and laughed and laughed.'

And the very last entry: 'Father bought me chocolates from Leeds to cheer me up now that the Averys have gone – my favourite kind! Mother must have told him to because she knows I'm sad and I miss Terence already, he is the best friend I've ever known

and he understands me more than any other. I shall now go and
pick some heather for Mother because she loves it so and then set
off on an adventure. I shall head east for the first time, and go far,
maybe get as far as Bracken Moor.'

Pause. TERENCE *hands him the diary*.

Take it. You will learn things about your son and his indomitable,
courageous spirit.

HAROLD. A piece of theatre then. An artifice, a melodrama.

TERENCE. Performed with dedication though.

HAROLD *hits him hard across the face*. TERENCE *reels*.

Well, no surprises there. The language of force, the only one you
know.

HAROLD. What kind of an animal are you?

TERENCE. A human being, sir.

HAROLD. A lying dog, a charlatan.

TERENCE. Don't speak of lying and of lies, your life is made of them.

HAROLD. I warn you.

TERENCE. No doubt you've sat in smoke-filled rooms with men
that mirror you in every way, brandishing words like 'enterprise'
and 'meritocracy' with passionate conviction. These words ring
hollow in your mouth. Perhaps you've also invoked Darwin as an
excuse for everything you are, citing him as proof that your way
is the best. But now, for once, you listen to someone else.

HAROLD *takes him by the lapels and drags him across the room,
pinning him against the wall as if to silence him. But* TERENCE
will not be silenced.

You know nothing of the truth. This house is built on the sweat of
others and the way you think the coal your own is an affront to
God and every living being. The irrationality is yours: you can not
own the coal any more than you can own the waters that lap our
shores or the sky that rages above our heads. None of it is yours to
own and the people who have given their lives to wrench it from
the earth have more a right to it than you do.

HAROLD *throws him on the floor*.

Think on that before you throw them to the dogs.

He stands just as ELIZABETH, VANESSA *and* GEOFFREY *walk into the room.*

GEOFFREY. Damn cold out there.

VANESSA. I'm afraid our stroll has been cut short.

GEOFFREY. More's the pity.

ELIZABETH. Mr McLean thinks we should be heading off a little earlier than he first suggested. He said there's a possibility of snow this afternoon.

VANESSA. You wouldn't think so looking at that blue sky.

ELIZABETH. So he's helping Eileen load the car.

VANESSA. Oh, I do hope the trains will be on time.

GEOFFREY. Are you all right, old man? You look as if you've seen a ghost.

ELIZABETH. Harold?

VANESSA. Terence, what's the matter? Are you two all right?

TERENCE. We're fine. Aren't we, Mr Pritchard?

Pause.

HAROLD. Yes. Yes. Yes, we're fine.

ELIZABETH (*pointing to the diary*). What's that you're holding, Harold?

HAROLD. This?

Pause.

Oh, this. It's a book of… it's accounts. Nothing important.

He tries to conceal it from her, walks to the desk, places it in a drawer. But she has seen it, recognises it.

VANESSA. Well, Harold, now that Elizabeth has decided to make a journey south perhaps you should consider it as well. We look forward to having you for dinner at some point before the spring. You can't stay up here for ever, can you?

GEOFFREY. I'll take you to the club, old boy, and we can misbehave.

VANESSA. You're far too old to misbehave, you'll just look ridiculous.

GEOFFREY. Thank you for having us anyway. I wish I could say it's been a pleasure but I'd be lying through my teeth.

VANESSA. And don't you worry, we'll keep an eye on her and make sure no harm comes to her and send her back fresh as a daisy and with lots of beautiful new clothes. God knows, maybe even with pineapple curtains and Hubert De Carcasson in tow.

GEOFFREY. What on earth are you babbling on about?

VANESSA. Never you mind. Goodbye, Harold.

She kisses him.

HAROLD. Goodbye, Vanessa. Goodbye, Geoffrey.

TERENCE (*stretching his hand out for* HAROLD *to shake*). Goodbye, sir. And thank you for your kindness.

HAROLD *looks at his hand but does not take it for some time. Eventually, he shakes it.*

VANESSA, GEOFFREY *and* TERENCE *leave.*

ELIZABETH *walks over to the drawer that* HAROLD *placed the diary in, opens it, takes it out, begins to read it. Then, slowly, she understands everything. She looks at the door that* TERENCE *has just left through.*

Pause.

ELIZABETH. He's quite an extraordinary boy isn't he?

HAROLD. Extraordinary, yes.

ELIZABETH. And when he did what he did – lived those last, terrible moments of our Edgar something happened, didn't it. He went there, all the way, became him, felt his fear, his anguish.

Pause.

Perhaps that's what I mean by love. To be able to do that. To feel the pain of others as if it is your own. Maybe that's all it is. An act of imagination.

She kisses him. With difficulty, she decides to let him keep the diary, places it in his hands. She makes her way to the door but stops when he begins to speak. He speaks slowly and in a confused way, as if he is talking mostly to himself, trying to solve some half-forgotten problem.

HAROLD. Elizabeth. I am not. What I mean to say is. Not a bad man, Elizabeth, not a bad man. My father. His father before him. It isn't easy is what I think I'm trying to say. And everything we have, the roof above our head, the food on our table, the walls that keep us warm, Elizabeth – the ones you say are mine. Sometimes I feel as if the world will fall apart if I cease to carry it on my shoulders.

ELIZABETH. Will it, Harold?

She goes. He looks at the diary in his hands.

HAROLD. Edgar. My boy. My angel.

And suddenly, for a second, it looks as if he'll break. His body looks as if it might collapse under the weight of this new emotion, he begins to make a sound of unbearable pain. But just as quickly, he suppresses it.

EILEEN *enters.*

EILEEN. Excuse me, sir, Mr Bailey is here to see you.

HAROLD. Send him in.

EILEEN. Yes, sir. Will you be wanting any more coffee, sir?

HAROLD. No, thank you, Eileen.

EILEEN. Shall I clear it all away, sir?

HAROLD. Do that.

She starts to clear up the coffee cups.

EILEEN. Sir, it's my day off today.

HAROLD. Is it indeed?

EILEEN. I know things have changed, sir, what with Mrs Pritchard leaving for London so unexpectedly but will it be all right if I still go into the village to see my mother? I'll be back before dinner.

HAROLD. Do that.

EILEEN. So I shall tell Mr Bailey he can come through, sir, and then after that I'll be off. Are you sure you'll be all right on your own, sir?

HAROLD. We'll have to wait and see.

EILEEN is slightly confused by his answer but she shrugs it off and goes. HAROLD is left alone. He remains still. A few seconds later, JOHN enters.

JOHN. Good morning, sir.

HAROLD. Good morning, Mr Bailey.

JOHN. I dropped by yesterday but at the wrong time and so I've returned today.

HAROLD. What is it, Mr Bailey?

JOHN. The papers have come through, sir.

HAROLD. What papers?

JOHN. For you to sign, sir, for the purchase and delivery of the new machinery from America.

HAROLD. I see.

JOHN. Mr Milson asked me to tell you that if we send them off by tomorrow morning there's every likelihood the machines will get here before the end of the year.

HAROLD. That's good.

JOHN. That means that the installation can begin in the first week of January and that they'll be in full operation by the middle of the same month. The work shouldn't take longer than a couple of weeks at most if everything runs like clockwork.

HAROLD. Yes.

JOHN. But you need to sign them, sir.

HAROLD. Of course.

Pause.

Well, bring them here then and I'll sign.

JOHN. Yes, sir.

JOHN *takes the papers over to him.* HAROLD *puts down* EDGAR*'s diary, places the papers on the table and takes his pen out of his pocket. He starts skimming through the documents.*

And so Ramshaw Drift is to close, sir.

HAROLD. As arranged, yes.

JOHN. And those one hundred and forty men and their families –

HAROLD. Please refrain, Mr Bailey. Please.

JOHN. Yes, sir.

HAROLD *signs all the documents. He puts his pen back into his pocket and hands the papers back to* JOHN. *He takes them and starts to walk towards the door. But* HAROLD *stops him. He talks to* JOHN *but does not turn to look at him. Instead he is staring forwards.*

HAROLD. I am running a business, Mr Bailey. I am running a business.

JOHN *does not answer. He leaves the room, closing the door behind him.*

HAROLD *is left alone. He stares ahead. A few seconds pass like this. He walks back to where he has left* EDGAR's *diary and picks it up again. He opens it and begins to read.*

Then suddenly, EDGAR *appears out of nowhere behind him. He is covered in soil and dirt, as if he has been underground for a long time. When he speaks his voice is terrible, as if its source is down deep in the ground, miles below the surface, in the bowels of the earth.*

EDGAR. Father.

Blackout.

The End.

SUNSET AT THE VILLA THALIA

Sunset at the Villa Thalia was first performed in the Dorfman auditorium of the National Theatre, London, on 1 June 2016 (previews from 25 May). The cast was as follows:

THEO	Sam Crane
CHARLOTTE	Pippa Nixon
HARVEY	Ben Miles
JUNE	Elizabeth McGovern
MARIA	Glykeria Dimou
STAMATIS	Christos Callow
ADRIAN	Thomas Berry/Billy Marlow/ Ethan Rouse
ROSALIND	Sophia Ally/Dixie Egerickx/ Scarlett Nunes
AGAPE	Eve Polycarpou
Director	Simon Godwin
Designer	Hildegard Bechtler
Lighting Designer	Natasha Chivers
Music	Michael Bruce
Movement Director	Jonathan Goddard
Sound Designer	Tom Gibbons
Company Voice Work	Jeannette Nelson
Dialect Coach	Charmian Hoare
Staff Director	Caroline Williams

Characters

THEO, *English, in his thirties, then forties*
CHARLOTTE, *English, in her thirties, then forties*
HARVEY, *American, in his forties, then fifties*
JUNE, *American, in her forties, then fifties*
MARIA, *Greek, seventeen*
STAMATIS, *Greek, in his fifties*
ADRIAN, *English, eight years old*
ROSALIND, *English, seven years old*
AGAPE, *Greek, in her sixties or seventies*

Note on Play

The play takes place in two different time periods:

April, 1967
August, 1976

The play takes place entirely on the terrace of a small house on the island of Skiathos, Greece.

ACT ONE

The terrace of a simple peasant cottage in Greece, on the island of Skiathos. The few pieces of furniture which are scattered around the space are genuinely rustic, the furniture that a local Greek family would have used.

Somewhere on stage there is a small table with a chair in front of it. On the table there is an old Corona typewriter and a typed manuscript by its side, with a large stone placed on it to prevent the loose pages from blowing away.

It is early evening in April, 1967.

THEO *stands on the terrace, dressed casually in slacks and an open-neck shirt, sandals. He stares out at the sea, and the sunset.*

THEO *is a dreamer.*

CHARLOTTE (*offstage*). Theo!

> CHARLOTTE *emerges from the house. She is dressed in a simple but bohemian style of the period. She is carrying two small wooden chairs and seems slightly flustered.*

> There's only whisky and something Greek that smells lethal.

THEO. He seemed like the whisky type. And she'll drink lighter fluid. She got through that bottle of retsina on the port as if it were water.

CHARLOTTE. There's Greek folk music on the radio, it's quite pleasant in a plaintive sort of way. Why are you just standing there?

THEO. Oh, you know, trying to think where it should go next, that kind of thing.

CHARLOTTE. They can sit on these. I found them in the basement.

> THEO *notices she's carrying the chairs and goes to her, takes them from her.*

THEO. I could have fetched them.

CHARLOTTE. It's fine, they're light.

She walks over to a small table that has a bunch of wild flowers resting on it, and a vase of water. She starts to work on the flowers, cutting off the rougher bits, and the leaves, before inserting them one by one into the vase.

THEO *places the chairs down.*

THEO. Why did you invite them?

CHARLOTTE. I thought it would be fun.

THEO. Liar.

CHARLOTTE. They're interesting.

THEO. He inveigled himself. You were an easy target. (*Puts on an exaggerated American accent.*) 'I knew you were an actress, Charlotte. You have that thing. Like a kind of restlessness. Are you restless, Charlotte? Are you a searcher?'

CHARLOTTE. He's strange.

THEO. 'What are you searching for, Charlotte?'

CHARLOTTE. My flip-flops, usually.

He walks up to her, drags her playfully away from the flowers, they embrace.

They won't stay long.

THEO. The duration of their stay is entirely up to us. We have to be rude, make them feel unwanted and unloved.

CHARLOTTE. You've had a good day.

THEO. Another good day, yes.

CHARLOTTE. Tell me.

THEO. Seven pages. Strong ones, though. I haven't torn them up.

CHARLOTTE. It's flowing.

THEO. Maybe not quite flowing. But trickling with a little more ease than it does in Camberwell.

CHARLOTTE. It's this place. This magical place.

They kiss.

HARVEY *and* JUNE *walk on to the terrace but* CHARLOTTE *and* THEO *do not see them; they are still kissing.* HARVEY *and*

JUNE *are both dressed quite smartly but there is nothing stuffy about them –* HARVEY *has a loose, somewhat preppy style, and* JUNE *is elegant in an American way. They are a good-looking couple.*

HARVEY. Okay, that's not good, we need to start again.

CHARLOTTE. Hello!

HARVEY. We need to cough, or something. Coughing is always effective, a little clearing of the throat. It's the oldest trick in the book because it works! June, come with me.

He takes JUNE *by the hand and leads her off the terrace again, out of sight.*

JUNE. Oh, Harvey, please! Why can't we just make a normal appearance for once?

Out of sight he starts coughing very loudly, in an exaggerated fashion, almost as if he is choking. Then they reappear and JUNE *is laughing.*

Now you sound like you're contagious!

THEO. Or consumptive, or something.

HARVEY. You're in love!

JUNE. My God, this view!

HARVEY. I can tell, they're in love! They were kissing, June.

JUNE. I know, I saw them, they were.

THEO. Hello, Harvey.

HARVEY. I know what you're thinking. The Americans. Were you not having that conversation just before we emerged from the bushes?

THEO *and* CHARLOTTE *are flummoxed; they think they may have been overheard.*

THEO. No, we weren't, I wasn't…

HARVEY. Were you not saying – (*Puts on an exaggerated English accent.*) 'What were you thinking, darling, when you invited those blasted Americans? That man is an aberration.'

THEO. No, I promise, nothing like that.

HARVEY. I believe you, Theo.

CHARLOTTE. We're very happy you're here.

HARVEY. We'll grow on you. You'll see, we do that, don't we, June.

JUNE. He does. He grows on you.

There is a small pause.

HARVEY. Where is it?

THEO. Where's what?

HARVEY. Where do you write, Theo? I want to see where you write your plays.

THEO. Well, it varies. I don't really…

HARVEY *walks up to the table with the Corona on it.*

HARVEY. Is this it? This is it, isn't it? Oh my God, here it is.

THEO. There it is.

HARVEY *touches the typewriter.*

HARVEY. The evidence. June, this is it. This is where the man writes.

JUNE. It's a beautiful spot, Theo.

CHARLOTTE. It's his private little table.

HARVEY. With a view to the west. He sits here, on the very edge of the European Continent, a messenger and a guard, both at once. Staring out over the wine-dark sea and writing from the very depth of his soul. Sophocles, Euripides and Theodore…?

THEO. Manning.

HARVEY. This is the only place for you to write, Theodore Manning.

CHARLOTTE. He has been having a creative time, haven't you?

THEO. It's been fine.

And HARVEY *now sees the manuscript.*

HARVEY. Oh my dear Lord. And this… can I? May I? Can I?

THEO. I'd rather you didn't. I'm a little…

HARVEY. Superstitious. Of course you are, and you have every right to be. You are communing with the gods, my friend, make sure those sullied, mortal hands stay firmly tucked away.

He puts his hands in his pockets, like an admonished boy.

JUNE. He envies you.

HARVEY. I don't envy him, June, I admire him.

JUNE. The two often go together.

HARVEY. How can you not admire a man who does this for a living?

THEO. Tries to.

HARVEY. Even more worthy of my admiration. *Tries* to. Sweats it out. Excavates. Digs with his bare soul to make life a little more bearable for the rest of us even though he can hardly pay the bills.

CHARLOTTE. That last part is true.

THEO. You're getting carried away.

JUNE. He does that.

HARVEY. No, I'm not. And I know you're good.

THEO. How do you know?

HARVEY. I just know these things. You're both good. A fine playwright and a fine actress.

CHARLOTTE. Why are you flattering us, Harvey?

HARVEY. I'm not, Charlotte. That's my gift. Sniffing people out. Identifying. It's what I'm good at.

JUNE. He means it.

HARVEY. I do.

JUNE. After you left us on the port he said to me, 'Those two are talented. You can sense it. They have it.'

THEO. 'It'?

THEO *and* CHARLOTTE *feel awkward.* CHARLOTTE *breaks the moment with a clap of her hands.*

CHARLOTTE. What shall I get us to drink?

JUNE. Oh, thank God, I thought you'd never ask.

THEO. I'll get them.

CHARLOTTE. We're very low on provisions, I'm afraid, and didn't have a chance to get the bus into the village.

JUNE. And we've come empty-handed.

HARVEY. Siesta time. The shops were all closed. Or should I say, *the* shop.

CHARLOTTE. There's whisky. And something Greek.

JUNE. Something Greek sounds good.

HARVEY. I'll come with you.

THEO. Darling?

CHARLOTTE. A very small whisky.

> THEO *heads off, with* HARVEY *in tow.*

HARVEY. They gave the world civilisation, now they sleep all afternoon.

THEO. They've earned it, I suppose.

> *They go.* JUNE *is hovering by the table with the flowers, and notices them.*

JUNE. They're beautiful.

CHARLOTTE. From the garden. I was just arranging them when you arrived...

JUNE. Let's finish the job together.

> CHARLOTTE *joins* JUNE *at the table and together they continue pulling the leaves off the flowers and arranging them in the vase.*

> It's very kind of you to ask us over.

CHARLOTTE. We wanted to. It's been... we've been living in some isolation.

JUNE. That's romantic.

CHARLOTTE. I've been reading paperback novels and Theo's been writing his play.

JUNE. What's it about?

CHARLOTTE. Oh, he never tells me. But we've been spending so much time on our own so it's nice to talk to people.

JUNE. We forced ourselves onto you.

CHARLOTTE. You did no such thing.

JUNE. Well, Harvey did. It's what he does. He spots people he likes and then he goes for them like a torpedo.

CHARLOTTE. How can he like someone without knowing them?

JUNE. Well, appearances, you know. He liked how you were dressed and we saw the book you were reading, Truman Capote.

CHARLOTTE. Oh, that.

JUNE. And then we overheard some of the conversation you were having.

CHARLOTTE. You did?

JUNE. Oh, that sounds creepy. But you were sitting two tables away, we couldn't help it. You were talking about the theatre –

CHARLOTTE. I was talking about a friend of ours who's performing in a play in the West End, yes.

JUNE. Well, Harvey's *obsessed* with the theatre. When we're in London or New York, he drags me to everything. So he leaned forward and said to me, 'They're my kind of people.'

CHARLOTTE. Then he turned around and introduced himself.

JUNE. Yes.

CHARLOTTE. Well, it's lovely to meet you.

A pause.

JUNE. And it's part of his job, really.

CHARLOTTE. What is?

JUNE. Being able to make quick decisions about people, that sort of thing.

CHARLOTTE. I don't think he mentioned what his job is.

JUNE. Oh, Harvey works for the Government. The US Government, I mean.

CHARLOTTE. Of course.

JUNE. He's like a diplomat.

CHARLOTTE. 'Like'?

JUNE. Well, it's complicated. He works for the State Department. He's a floater.

CHARLOTTE. What's a floater?

JUNE. No, I mean, we travel. He gets around. My God, Charlotte, the places I've lived in.

CHARLOTTE. That's exciting, to see the world.

JUNE. I married him when we were both quite young. He'd just left Harvard, I was modelling in New York. Six months later, we're in Persia and I'm curtsying in front of the Shah.

CHARLOTTE. How glamorous.

JUNE. Sometimes it is. But I miss having a base, a home. We do have a little brownstone in Washington but we're hardly ever there.

CHARLOTTE. And you've been living in Athens?

JUNE. For the last few months, yes.

CHARLOTTE. Have you enjoyed it?

JUNE. It's okay. Harvey's always busy so I try to find my own things.

CHARLOTTE. What sort of things?

JUNE. Depends where we're at. So in Athens, for instance, I thought I'd learn something about the ancient history, that sort of thing. So I was taking a course at the American College. And then there's the embassy people too, cocktail parties, barbecues, you know.

CHARLOTTE. Of course.

JUNE. Sometimes it gets lonely but I can't complain.

Pause. They have finished with the flowers, and JUNE *moves away from the table.*

But we're moving back soon, things are coming to a close.

CHARLOTTE. What things?

JUNE. I'm not mad about Athens but the islands are divine. Not the arid ones to the south but these northern ones are beautiful and green.

CHARLOTTE. So you're here for a short holiday?

JUNE. Harvey said we should get out of Athens for a few days. His job is nearly done, and things are heating up a little.

THEO and HARVEY *come out of the house. They are holding two glasses each.*

HARVEY. What's heating up? You're not talking politics again, are you?

THEO gives one to CHARLOTTE, HARVEY *gives one to* JUNE.

CHARLOTTE. Thank you, darling.

JUNE. Would I ever?

HARVEY. Don't bore Charlotte with the boring stuff.

CHARLOTTE. So, darling, June was saying that Harvey works for the Government.

THEO. Oh, right.

HARVEY. That's what I mean by the boring stuff.

CHARLOTTE. June said you were a floater, Harvey.

JUNE. Geographically, I meant, not in any other way.

CHARLOTTE. Not ideologically, or anything.

JUNE. No, I meant, as in we travel a lot.

HARVEY. We do, we do, we do.

THEO. How wonderful for you.

Pause. HARVEY *decides to change the subject and he does it with a burst of new energy.*

HARVEY. So what's the play about? I will not touch it with my grubby claws but give me something, for God's sake.

JUNE. He doesn't say, Harvey, so don't push him.

HARVEY. Not a word, not a syllable?

CHARLOTTE. No, not a word.

HARVEY. Not a crumb? I don't know, something like, 'pain'. Or 'innocence', or, maybe, if you're feeling generous 'my mother's fondness for gin' or 'the day Uncle Desmond rubbed up against me for just a minute too long'.

JUNE. Harvey Parker.

HARVEY. What was the inception? The trigger?

CHARLOTTE. He really doesn't like telling people.

THEO. I just don't talk about it. When I'm working on it, I mean.
And I don't think it's superstitious. It's something else. I'm
nervous of...

HARVEY. Dissipation.

THEO. Well, yes, I suppose...

HARVEY. And so you should. It's sacred. Keep it close, Theo.

THEO. I'll try.

HARVEY. But the most important thing is, you have been working.
The *only* important thing. The Muse is sitting here, on this terrace.
We can not see her, but her presence is felt.

JUNE. I feel her, I feel her!

THEO. She was having a siesta this afternoon, along with everyone
else, but the morning was good.

HARVEY. And tomorrow she will be with you again.

THEO. Here's hoping.

HARVEY. To the Muse!

> *They toast –* HARVEY *and* JUNE *with enthusiasm,* THEO *and*
> CHARLOTTE *with slight bemusement.*

> Because you see, Theo, Charlotte – I love the theatre.

CHARLOTTE. June said.

HARVEY. No, I mean, I *love* the theatre. I love all art – well, most
art – but more than any other art form I love the theatre. Do you
know why I love the theatre?

THEO. Why do you love the theatre, Harvey?

HARVEY. I love the theatre because she's democracy's twin.

JUNE. And Harvey loves democracy.

HARVEY. They were born together, were they not?

THEO. They were indeed.

HARVEY. Just, what – less than one hundred miles away from here, and together they came spitting and crying into this savage world and together they crawled, and together they learnt to walk, and talk, and gave us everything we hold dear.

THEO. He likes the theatre.

HARVEY. But I mean seriously, have you thought of that? How they both just, *emerged*, just morphed into being, at pretty much exactly the same time? That the two of them just appeared simultaneously? Have you thought of that?

THEO. Just a little.

JUNE. I told you he's passionate about it.

HARVEY. People in a space telling other people a story and then asking them, 'What would you do, little man? What would you do if you were in my place? What would you do if you found out you'd been fucking your mother'…

JUNE. Language, Harvey!

THEO. It's the passion talking.

HARVEY. Or some knuckle-head leader barred you from burying your own brother in the rightful way or God knows what, what would you do, little man? Because that's what theatre is, *was*, and the Greeks knew that – that's what *tragedy* is, that point, after the debate, when the audience, have to make a choice. And that choice will make a difference to the state, you know, the *demos*, the community, whatever, the way they all live.

THEO. Wow.

They think it's over. And he's off again.

HARVEY. And the playwright – and Theo, you know what the playwright, what *you*, are called, what the word in Greek is?

THEO. *Didaskalos?*

HARVEY. Thank you, which means…

THEO. Teacher?

HARVEY. Someone who shows you the way, takes you by the hand and leads you to a place where you might have a broader perspective of yourself and the world you live in.

THEO. I'd be a little nervous to describe myself in that particular way.

CHARLOTTE. Theo's modest.

HARVEY. But the point being that these guys – these *didaskaloi*, these teachers, whatever you want to call them, were part of the system. They were questioning things, they were making people uncomfortable, they were rocking the boat – but they were doing it from *within*. Christ, Sophocles was made a general, Aeschylus fought the Persians at Marathon, they were part of the world they were interrogating, they were shaking it from inside, but they were *loyal to it*.

THEO. Loyal.

HARVEY. You and I need each other, Theo, we're a pair. Bread and butter, whisky and soda.

THEO. Cheese and pickle.

HARVEY. Stay loyal, Theo, stay loyal.

THEO. I'll do my best.

JUNE. Sweetheart, take a break. You need to breathe.

Suddenly, MARIA *and* STAMATIS *appear from the pathway. They are local Greeks, simply dressed. They edge their way forward tentatively.* MARIA *speaks English with quite a heavy Greek accent.*

MARIA. *Yia sas.*

CHARLOTTE. Hello.

HARVEY. Enter the Greeks.

MARIA. Good evening. It is Friday.

CHARLOTTE. Friday, yes.

MARIA. We have come for the taking of the furniture.

CHARLOTTE. The furniture?

Suddenly, CHARLOTTE *remembers.*

Good God, yes, of course, I'm so sorry.

HARVEY. They're taking your furniture?

CHARLOTTE. I'm so sorry, I completely forgot. Darling, it's Friday.

THEO. Friday, yes?

CHARLOTTE. Do you remember, I told you that Maria and her father were coming by to pick up that furniture from the basement?

THEO. Of course.

CHARLOTTE. Maria, this is, these are our friends.

JUNE. Hi, Maria.

CHARLOTTE. This is Maria, everyone, and her father, Mr... Mr...

MARIA. Mr Stamatis, he does not speak English.

STAMATIS *bows his head in greeting*.

HARVEY. But you do it for the both of you, and you do it well.

CHARLOTTE. Maria and her family are the owners of this beautiful house, we are renting it from them.

HARVEY. Maria, you've been uprooted.

CHARLOTTE. Maria and her family are about to move. I mean more than move...

THEO. They're emigrating.

MARIA. To Australia, yes. To the Sydney.

HARVEY. The Sydney. How exciting.

CHARLOTTE. They've kindly moved out of the house while we're here...

HARVEY. Kindness has nothing to do with it, Charlotte, it's economic necessity.

MARIA. We are staying with my uncle in the village.

CHARLOTTE. And they're here to pick up some furniture of theirs from the basement.

MARIA. We will try and sell it.

HARVEY. Of course.

CHARLOTTE. Well, you know the way in. And do let us know, if there's anything you need, we're more than happy to help.

MARIA. Thank you, Mrs Manning.

She turns to her father.

Έλα Πατέρα. [Come on, Father.]

They enter the house.

JUNE. What a lovely girl.

CHARLOTTE. She's a darling, yes.

JUNE. Have you met the whole family?

CHARLOTTE. I get the feeling it's just the two of them.

THEO. No sign of the mother.

JUNE. And how did you find them and their beautiful house?

THEO. Plain good luck.

CHARLOTTE. Yes, luck really. We came to the island blindly, we'd
    been told we would easily find somewhere to stay, especially
    since it's this time of year.

JUNE. Off season.

CHARLOTTE. But we were expecting a room, or something, you
    know, a bed and breakfast.

HARVEY. And then you found Maria.

THEO. We asked in the port, that little tobacconist place near where
    you step off the ferry and the man happened to be Maria's uncle,
    the father's brother.

CHARLOTTE. Next thing you know we were being driven here in
    one of those things, the open cars with three wheels. We were like
    a couple of goats.

THEO. We arrived here and we fell in love.

HARVEY. How lucky.

Slight pause.

JUNE. Can I? Is there any more of this Greek stuff?

CHARLOTTE. Of course, I'm so sorry, I'll fetch the bottle.

THEO. We thought you'd like it.

JUNE. It works.

CHARLOTTE. And I'll fetch the whisky, too.

JUNE. Can I take a peek? At the house, I mean. Can I look inside?
    I'm so curious.

CHARLOTTE. Of course you can, it's lovely. Come with me, I'll give you the tour.

The women enter the house. HARVEY *watches them go, and the men are left alone.*

HARVEY. She protects you.

He starts to wander around the space, taking it all in, but he gravitates back towards the table with the typewriter and the manuscript on it.

Okay, Theo, so humour me, will you.

THEO. I'll do my best.

HARVEY. So I understand that you'd rather not talk about what it is you're writing.

THEO. Correct.

HARVEY. But could you talk to me about the process a little. I mean what it's like. What it *feels* like. To sit down at this place and create stories, debates, myths, whatever it is you create. What does that feel like, Theo?

Pause.

It's all I ask.

Pause. THEO *thinks for a little.*

THEO. Okay, I'll try.

He thinks a little more.

You have a sketch, maybe. Well, I mean I do. A plan. And something you feel you want to explore.

HARVEY. A road map and a terrain.

THEO. And then you set off into – yes, into this *terrain*, I suppose – and then you realise that the road map is not quite accurate. But as you come to realise that you also start to think that perhaps it's not even necessary. What I mean is…

HARVEY. That once you're in the terrain, the road map becomes a little redundant?

THEO. But you needed it to begin with. Maybe just for confidence, I don't know. And then this other thing takes over, and it's the intelligence, I don't know…

HARVEY. Of the terrain itself, Theo. The intelligence of
the world.

THEO. Something like that.

Pause.

HARVEY. Maybe June's right. Maybe I am a little envious of you.
Because I don't have access to that intelligence. I only have my
own.

THEO. Your own?

HARVEY. My own intelligence, I mean. It's all I have.

Pause.

And do you know, I think I'm falling a little in love with you.

Pause.

Oh, don't get nervous, I'm not a pansy, I'm not a queer. I don't
want to mount you.

THEO. That's a relief.

HARVEY. I'm just falling a little in love with you, is all.

Pause.

These are exciting times to be alive, aren't they?

THEO. Are there ever dull ones?

HARVEY. Change, I mean. It's everywhere. In the air, and on the
ground and in the smell of my wife's hair.

THEO. What sort of change?

HARVEY. Those girls – I mean Charlotte and June. The world is
opening for them. In the next ten years, things are going to change
for them. It's going to be different. I think of my mother, you
know, corseted into submission, a forced silence – and then I see
June, and I'm excited for her. Because the opportunities – you
know, for self-expression, for freedom, that sort of thing.

THEO. Yes.

HARVEY. And other things, too. I mean in the States, in my country,
major things are happening to the coloured community. Civil
rights, and now, a constant effort to question what the role of that
race is within the society, and we are allowing them, the *system* is

allowing them to forge their way forward and ask those all-important questions.

THEO. Allowing them?

HARVEY. So that they too can play their part in this great democracy.

THEO. I see.

HARVEY. So it's an exciting time to be alive. And especially to be a *didaskalos*.

Pause.

THEO. It's funny.

HARVEY. What is, Theo?

THEO. It's just a coincidence, that's all.

HARVEY. Because you happen to be writing something about coloured people?

THEO. Good God, no, I wouldn't dare. I mean, it's not quite within my sphere of experience.

HARVEY. But you're writing something similar?

THEO. Well, I mean, not really, but it's a coincidence.

HARVEY. Is it?

Pause.

THEO. A very dear friend of mine was arrested for, what they call in England, importuning, for, it's like… indecent…

HARVEY. He's a queer.

THEO. Well, in a word, yes. And he is the nicest man, and a good friend, intelligent, a profound thinker…

HARVEY. Why shouldn't he be?

THEO. And he has no way of meeting other people, and there is much hatred aimed towards him, and it feels unjust, and it needs to be…

HARVEY. Explored. Interrogated. Put in front of an audience.

THEO. Well, yes. I suppose.

HARVEY. You're right, it does, I agree.

Pause. When HARVEY *speaks it is genuine, with affection, and sincerity. But he touches the manuscript gently with his hand.*

Thank you for telling me.

And only then does THEO *realise what he's done.*

There is a commotion and CHARLOTTE, JUNE, MARIA *and* STAMATIS *emerge from the house, all of them carrying a large chest of drawers.*

JUNE. Look what we found, Harvey.

HARVEY. Jesus.

JUNE. Isn't it wonderful?

CHARLOTTE. It's quite heavy, we had to give them a hand.

They put it down; rest.

MARIA. Thank you very much.

CHARLOTTE. Leave it here for the minute and once you've got the chairs and the sideboard we can carry them all down the path to the driveway. Then the truck can pick it all up from there.

JUNE. Isn't it gorgeous, Harvey? It's from the 1920s. Made by a man in the village, the carpenter. It has this beautiful design on the surface, come see.

CHARLOTTE. Oh, the drinks!

CHARLOTTE *runs back into the house.*

HARVEY *and* THEO *both approach the chest of drawers. They all congregate around it, start to explore it, opening drawers, running their hands across the surface of it, admiring it.*

HARVEY. Oh, that's pretty, what is it? Are those goats?

JUNE. It's like a pastoral thing, you know a pastoral scene or whatever you want to call it, all done with such detail and care. Look at those little things, like little cottages, aren't they adorable?

THEO. They look like this one.

MARIA. It was the property of my grandmother.

JUNE. Well, your grandmother had great taste, Maria.

CHARLOTTE *returns with a tray. On it are two bottles – the whisky and the Greek stuff. She rests it somewhere, then picks up the bottles and goes around refreshing the glasses that people are holding. The whisky bottle is nearly empty.*

JUNE *opens one of the drawers.*

And look, Harvey, it's deceptive. So much space in those drawers. So it's practical, too.

HARVEY. Yes, very.

JUNE. Isn't it just divine, Harvey?

HARVEY. It is, June, it is.

JUNE. It's beautiful and practical, both at once.

HARVEY. But I'm not having it shipped to Washington, sweetheart, so you can forget it.

JUNE. Killjoy.

THEO. It's a very special piece of furniture, Maria.

MARIA. Thank you.

HARVEY. And now you have to sell it.

MARIA. We will try.

JUNE. That's sad.

HARVEY. You need money for the move to Australia, right?

MARIA. We have already the tickets, but yes, we need more money.

HARVEY. So you're all set to sail?

MARIA. In two weeks we take the boat from Piraeus.

HARVEY. That's a long journey.

MARIA. Yes, very.

HARVEY. I wish you nothing but the best.

Pause. He runs his hand across the surface of the chest of drawers.

And what about the house?

MARIA. The house?

HARVEY. Are you selling the house as well?

JUNE. Why are you asking, Harvey?

HARVEY. I just want to know, that's all.

MARIA. The house?

JUNE. But why?

HARVEY. Yes. Are you selling the house?

There is a pause. STAMATIS *speaks in Greek.*

STAMATIS. *Τι λέει;* [What's he saying?]

MARIA. *Ρωτάει άμα πουλάμε το σπίτι.* [He's asking if we're selling the house.]

STAMATIS. *Το σπίτι;* [The house?]

MARIA. *Ναι, ρωτάει άμα το πουλάμε.* [Yes, he's asking if we're selling the house.]

HARVEY. Well, are you?

THEO. Why do you want to know if they're selling the house, Harvey?

HARVEY. I'm just asking. Can't a man ask a question without being pounced on?

STAMATIS. *Γιατί ρωτάει άμα πουλάμε το σπίτι;* [Why is he asking if we want to sell the house?]

MARIA. *Δεν ξέρω πατέρα.* [I don't know, Dad.]

STAMATIS. *Θέλει να το αγοράσει;* [Does he want to buy it?]

MARIA. He is asking do you want to buy it?

HARVEY. Well, I'm just asking, but yes, well, maybe, yes, maybe we do want to buy it. But I'm just asking.

JUNE. Harvey, where are you going with this?

CHARLOTTE. We? Who's we?

HARVEY. Depending of course on what kind of arrangement we can come to.

THEO. He means we as in 'me and June', darling.

CHARLOTTE. I hope so.

HARVEY. But I'm open to negotiation. And you can throw the furniture in, saves you from carrying it down that path.

STAMATIS. *Τι λέει;* [What's he saying?]

HARVEY. Maria, let's not get carried away. Why don't you and your dad continue with what you were doing and then, depending on how things evolve here between the four of us, we can resume the conversation?

MARIA *seems a little confused.*

MARIA. I don't understand.

HARVEY. I mean just carry on with what you were doing.

MARIA. Yes.

She turns to STAMATIS.

Έλα πατέρα, πάμε να μαζέψουμε τις καρέκλες. [Come, Dad, let's go get the chairs.]

MARIA *leads a bemused* STAMATIS *back into the house.*

HARVEY. Hello, can I speak to Theodore Manning, please?

THEO. Speaking.

HARVEY. Theo Manning, this is your Destiny calling.

CHARLOTTE. I knew it.

THEO. Hello, Destiny?

HARVEY. Okay, so now, listen, I need you both to listen to me, and listen to me carefully –

JUNE. What are you doing, Harvey?

CHARLOTTE. I think I know what he's doing.

HARVEY. And I'm feeling the resistance already, Charlotte, but you really need to listen to me because this is important, maybe the most important moment of your lives.

THEO. We're listening.

CHARLOTTE. Oh, for God's sake.

HARVEY. Because, Charlotte, when I saw you here, when I walked onto this terrace earlier this evening and saw you kissing your husband the playwright right here on this spot, I *knew* this was your house.

THEO. Our house?

HARVEY. And maybe now you have to also entertain the notion that I too have come into your lives for a particular reason.

He walks up to the table with the typewriter and manuscript on it.
He goes full throttle, giving a performance.

Because it is here, my friend, at this table, with this glorious view
of the sea that you will write your greatest plays. And write a part
for Charlotte, too, the kind of part she deserves, and yearns for,
am I right, Charlotte?

CHARLOTTE. That's cheap.

HARVEY. Maybe it's cheap, yes, I'm working hard, too hard, but it's
true, Charlotte, he will, and you want that, don't you, so he *will*,
and as he writes it your children will be playing at your feet and
you will walk them down to the beach every morning and swim in
that blessed sea. This is your house, Theo, Charlotte. I knew it
from the moment I saw you here. This is your house, the house of
your dreams.

CHARLOTTE. And why do you care so much?

HARVEY. You really want to know?

CHARLOTTE. Yes, I do, I want to know.

THEO. Why are you so keen for us to buy it, Harvey?

CHARLOTTE. Yes, why?

HARVEY. BECAUSE I WANT YOU TO BE HAPPY!

Pause.

THEO. He's persuasive, isn't he?

JUNE. I married the man.

CHARLOTTE. But it's ridiculous.

HARVEY. Why is it ridiculous?

CHARLOTTE. Because even if we did, I mean even if we loved the
house…

HARVEY. You do love the house, Charlotte, that part's not
hypothetical.

CHARLOTTE. But even if we do, we could never buy it.

HARVEY. Why not?

CHARLOTTE. Because we can't afford it.

HARVEY. Yes, you can, you can afford it.

THEO. How can we afford it?

HARVEY. You can afford it because it's very, very cheap.

Pause.

Maria and her family are moving to Australia.

THEO. I know that.

HARVEY. You know why they're moving to Australia?

CHARLOTTE. Because they need to.

HARVEY. Yes, that's right, because they need to, they desperately need to.

JUNE. I hope Maria succeeds, she's a nice girl.

HARVEY. So do I, June, so do I. But the point is that in order to begin this new life and give his daughter the opportunities she deserves, her father is having to sell their furniture. That is how much they need the money. My suspicion is that the only reason he hasn't put the house on the market – apart from sentimental reasons – is that he hasn't thought anyone would want to buy it. Most people are not like you, they don't appreciate, how shall I put it, rustic peasant dwellings, and property's not moving here anyway, it's undiscovered.

THEO. So what you're saying is…

HARVEY. What I'm saying is that Maria and her father need the money so bad that they'll sell you the house of your dreams for close to nothing.

Pause.

CHARLOTTE. But that's immoral.

HARVEY. Why is it immoral, Charlotte?

CHARLOTTE. It's exploitative.

HARVEY. Why?

CHARLOTTE. Because you are taking advantage of the fact that they are in need, that they are down.

HARVEY. So give them triple what they ask for, Charlotte. If you have the money and you really care for them, give them triple what they ask for.

Pause.

THEO. How much do you think…

CHARLOTTE. Theo!

HARVEY. I don't know, all we have to do is ask. I mean if it's crazy, well, then obviously, it's a non-starter and this conversation is a waste of time. But if it's the price of a jar of peanut butter, which I suspect it may well be, you'd be foolish not to consider it. You love this place.

THEO. It's true, but…

CHARLOTTE. Theo, can I talk to you?

HARVEY. Of course.

CHARLOTTE. Oh, thank you, Harvey, but I mean in private.

HARVEY. So June and I will take our drinks and stroll for a short while down in those pine trees and we will join you again presently. Come on, sweetheart.

He leads the way.

JUNE. Sometimes you really go too far, Harvey Parker.

They go; CHARLOTTE and THEO are left alone. CHARLOTTE starts pacing.

CHARLOTTE. Theo, what are you doing?

THEO. What am I doing, I haven't done anything.

CHARLOTTE. How can you even be serious about it? We've only just met him.

THEO. It's not about him, it's about the house.

CHARLOTTE. But he's directing it all.

THEO. But what if he wasn't here? I mean, what if we had the idea ourselves? Does it matter that it's come from him?

She checks to see she's not being overheard.

CHARLOTTE. I don't like him.

THEO. Why not?

CHARLOTTE. Why is he deciding things for us? And then talking to that poor girl about it, on our behalf? As if he owns us all.

THEO. I don't see it like that.

CHARLOTTE. And then saying, 'Buy it while it's cheap. Rob them in broad daylight.' I mean this house has probably been theirs for generations.

THEO. But he's also right when he says we might be doing them a favour. That we'll be helping them, Charlotte, that we'll be giving them a helping hand.

CHARLOTTE. Oh, Theo, don't be so naive.

THEO. Anyway, for just one moment let's keep him out of the equation. Just for a minute, Charlotte, let's keep him out.

Pause.

I do love it here, Charlotte. I've never written like this, it's true. He's right.

CHARLOTTE. I thought you said we'd keep him out of the equation.

THEO. We knew it from the first minute we got here. That first evening, do you remember? We sat here, the two of us, looking at that sunset and do you remember what we said to each other?

CHARLOTTE. That we'd never been to such a beautiful place.

THEO. And we do have that money from my aunt which we've put aside. I mean it may not be enough but...

CHARLOTTE. That money's for when we have children, Theo, we said we wouldn't touch it.

THEO. Well, this place would be for our children too. And I think we could be so happy. And we could rent it out on the side. I mean if things got tough. It's cheap to run and our summers would be... our summers would be blissful, Charlotte.

CHARLOTTE. I know.

THEO. So all I'm saying is let's consider it, that's all.

Pause.

And I don't think he's that bad. I mean he's full of himself, and yes, a bit of a bully, and bullish and all those things but he's also charming and there's something else...

He thinks for a minute as if trying to come up with the right word but then gives up.

It's more complicated is what I mean. But anyway, we're getting carried away. They probably don't even want to sell the place.

MARIA *emerges from the house with* STAMATIS *in tow. They approach* CHARLOTTE *and* THEO *a little sheepishly.*

MARIA. Mrs Manning, Mr Manning.

CHARLOTTE. Hello, Maria.

STAMATIS. *Πες τους, μίλα τους.* [Tell them, talk to them.]

MARIA. My father wants me to speak with you and with also the American man.

THEO. He's gone for a little walk, you can tell us, Maria.

STAMATIS. *Που είναι ο Αμερικάνος;* [Where is the American?]

MARIA. *Λένε να μιλήσουμε μ' αυτούς.* [They say we can talk to them.]

STAMATIS. *Πες τους ό,τι είπα, όπως τα είπα.* [Tell them exactly what I said, the way I said it.]

THEO. What is it, Maria? What do you want to tell us?

MARIA *starts to speak but she is finding it hard to conceal her emotion and her voice quivers with it a little.*

MARIA. My father wants me to say to you that we will be very happy if the man will buy the house.

THEO. It's not for him, Maria, it's for us, we're the ones who might be interested in buying the house. Who are considering it, I mean.

STAMATIS. *Εκατό σαράντα χιλιάδες, αλλά σε Αυστραλέζικα δολάρια, όπως είπαμε.* [One hundred and forty thousand, but in Australian dollars, like we said.]

MARIA. The cost will be one hundred and forty thousand drachmas.

THEO. One hundred and forty?

MARIA. But my father is saying that you must pay all the monies in the bank in Australia.

THEO. In Australian dollars, yes, of course, that makes sense, that wouldn't be difficult.

STAMATIS. *Τι λέει;* [What's he saying?]

THEO *turns to* CHARLOTTE.

THEO. One hundred and forty thousand, eighty-three drachmas to the pound, that's under one thousand seven hundred pounds.

CHARLOTTE. That can't be right.

STAMATIS. *Να τα βάλουμε στο λογαριασμό στο Sydney.* [They put it in a bank in Sydney.]

MARIA. My father says you place the monies in the bank in the Sydney.

CHARLOTTE. The thing is, Maria, we're not really sure that…

STAMATIS. *Και πες τους για τα στρέμματα.* [And tell them about the acres.]

MARIA. *Δεν ξέρω πως λέγονται τα στρέμματα στα Αγγλικά.* [I don't know what the word for acres is.]

STAMATIS. *Τότε πες τους για το κτήμα. Τι θα πάρουν με τα λεφτά τους!* [Tell them about the land then. What they get for their money!]

CHARLOTTE. I mean it's a big decision, Maria, and we need a little time to think. That man, the American I mean, was being a little hasty.

STAMATIS. *Πες τους για το κτήμα, πες τους για τα δέντρα!* [Tell them about the land, tell them about the trees!]

THEO. That's less than half of my aunt's money, Charlotte.

CHARLOTTE. And Mr Manning and I are not rich people, you understand.

STAMATIS. *Πες τους, Πες τους!* [Tell them, tell them!]

MARIA. My father is wanting me also to tell you that with it comes the trees.

THEO. Trees, what trees?

CHARLOTTE. The pine forest.

STAMATIS. *Τα δέντρα, τους είπες για τα δέντρα;* [The trees, did you tell them about the trees?]

MARIA. *Ναι πατέρα, ναι πατέρα, τους το'πα!* [Yes, Dad, yes, Dad, I told them!]

THEO. So you mean there's land, Maria, that comes with the house?

CHARLOTTE. That's what she's saying, Theo.

THEO. And what's the land, Maria? I mean where does it start and where does it end?

STAMATIS (*increasingly forceful*). Και για την παραλία! Ψυχή δεν πατάει! Σαν ιδιωτική παραλία είναι, πες τους το! [And the beach! No one ever comes to that beach! It's like a private beach, tell them!]

MARIA. And the beach!

THEO. What beach?

CHARLOTTE. Theo!

STAMATIS. Πες τους το! Για όνομα του Θεού, πες τους το! [Tell them! For God's sake, tell them!]

MARIA. The house, and the trees, and the sea!

And she suddenly bursts into tears.

STAMATIS. Τρελάθηκες; Τι έβαλες τα κλάματα; [Have you lost your mind? What are you crying for?]

MARIA. Το δάσος πατέρα, το δάσος! [The forest, Dad, the forest.]

CHARLOTTE. Maria, what's wrong?

THEO. God.

CHARLOTTE. Why are you so upset, we don't want to upset you.

STAMATIS (*screaming at the top of his voice now*). Για συμμαζέψου λιγάκι! Για σένα τα᾽χουμε ανάγκη τα χρήματα! [Pull yourself together! It's you we need the money for!]

MARIA (*through tears*). Είναι το σπίτι της γιαγιάς πατέρα, είναι το σπίτι της γιαγιάς! [It's Yia-yia's house, Dad, it's Yia-yia's house.]

STAMATIS. Το σπίτι δικό μας είναι και τα λεφτά τα᾽χουμε ανάγκη! [The house is ours and we need the money!]

THEO. You really don't need to shout at her, we don't want to upset anyone.

CHARLOTTE. What's happening, Maria? Why are you so upset?

STAMATIS. *Θα με τρελάνεις!* [You'll drive me crazy!]

> *But* MARIA *keeps crying.* HARVEY *and* JUNE *return, glasses in hand.*

HARVEY. Decision time. Have you chosen hope or fear?

> *They notice* MARIA.

Dear Lord, what have you done to her?

THEO. We haven't done a thing, I promise.

STAMATIS (*still shouting at the top of his voice*). *Σταμάτα να κλαίς σαν μωρό και συμμαζέψου!* [Stop crying like a baby and pull yourself together!]

JUNE. Why is he screaming at her?

THEO. Please don't shout at her, it was just a question.

CHARLOTTE. What's wrong, Maria, tell me what's wrong.

JUNE. Don't cry, little girl.

> *Still through tears,* MARIA *starts to speak.*

MARIA. It's my yia-yia's house, Mrs Manning, my yia-yia's.

CHARLOTTE. Yia-yia's?

HARVEY. Her grandmother's.

STAMATIS. *Μην μου τα χαλάσεις τώρα, θα σε σφάξω!* [Don't go ruining things now, I'll kill you!]

CHARLOTTE. Oh, I see, of course.

MARIA. When my yia-yia was still living she sit with me here – here, exactly here, where you are standing, Mrs Manning, and she says to me, 'One day, when you are a lady, Maria, this house will be yours, promise me, Maria, you will always look after this house' and now Mrs Manning, we go to Australia, I hope that one day I will be possible to come back to the island, and this house, my yia-yia's house.

CHARLOTTE. Of course, I understand, Maria. But listen to me, you needn't worry, we're not going to take the house away from you, and we won't make you break the promise you made your yia-yia, we'd never do that. So you can stop crying now.

MARIA *pulls herself together, stops crying*. CHARLOTTE *hands her a handkerchief*.

MARIA. Thank you, Mrs Manning.

CHARLOTTE. There's nothing to thank me for.

HARVEY. I go away five minutes and the whole thing falls apart.

CHARLOTTE *and* JUNE *both give him a look*. STAMATIS *suddenly surprises them by speaking in English*.

STAMATIS. One hundred forty thousand!

THEO. That's what they're asking for it.

HARVEY. What did I tell you? Peanut butter.

CHARLOTTE. *He's* asking for it, Theo, she isn't.

THEO. It's his house, darling.

CHARLOTTE. It's theirs.

STAMATIS. One hundred forty!

THEO. In Australian dollars, yes.

HARVEY. I mean, that's like, you know, that's cheap.

CHARLOTTE. We know it's cheap, Harvey, we know that.

STAMATIS. One hundred forty!

THEO. He's very keen to sell it, Charlotte.

HARVEY. He's more than keen, he's going to take a chunk out of your leg.

CHARLOTTE. We can see that.

STAMATIS. One hundred thirty!

THEO. No, no, keep it at one hundred and forty, one hundred and forty is fine, we just need a little time to think about it.

HARVEY. You'd be keen if you were moving to a strange part of the world with close to nothing and had your family to protect.

MARIA (*quietly, almost to herself*). I make promise to my yia-yia.

HARVEY *suddenly beckons to* MARIA.

HARVEY. Maria, can I talk to you for a short while?

MARIA *slowly steps forward.* HARVEY *takes her aside but the others can still hear what they're saying. He speaks to her gently, comfortingly.*

Okay, Maria, listen to me. There's no reason to be upset any more. We don't like to see you upset. So let me tell you what will happen.

CHARLOTTE. How do you know what will happen?

HARVEY. Let me tell you what I *think* will happen, Maria, what I *hope* will happen. But first let me try and understand why you are so upset.

Pause.

You love this house. You love it because it is full of memories of happy times. And sad ones, too. Sometimes the sad ones mean even more than the happy ones. They go deeper.

CHARLOTTE. God Almighty.

HARVEY (*with a little anger aimed at* CHARLOTTE *in his voice*). They do.

Pause.

You grew up here.

MARIA. Yes.

HARVEY. And you would run though those trees in the mornings and down to the sea.

MARIA. Yes, with no shoes on.

HARVEY. With no shoes on. And I imagine your yia-yia would cook things here for you, because they do that, don't they? Yia-yias do that.

MARIA. Yes, she was a very good cook.

HARVEY. And she taught you. Did she make fig jam?

CHARLOTTE. Fig jam!

MARIA. Yes, how did you know?

CHARLOTTE. He knows things.

HARVEY. And those little things, those round little potato-cake things.

MARIA. *Πατατοκεφτέδες!* [Patatokeftethes!]

HARVEY. Patatoke… whatever.

Pause. MARIA smiles, she thinks it's amusing that he can't pronounce it.

So listen to me now, Maria. If your father decides to sell the house – either to Theo and Charlotte, or to anybody else –

MARIA. There is nobody else who will buy the house.

HARVEY. But if he does, you take those memories – of your yia-yia and the pine trees, of the sea and the fig jam and the potato thingies…

JUNE. Patatokeftethes.

HARVEY. And you take those precious memories and you move on. Because I know something else about you, Maria.

CHARLOTTE. Of course you do.

MARIA throws a quick look at CHARLOTTE.

HARVEY. Listen to me now, Maria, don't listen to Charlotte.

She turns back to him. Again his voice goes quieter and he speaks with a slow-burning intent, and feeling too.

You speak good English, you've worked hard at it. I like the way you speak for your father. You represent him, you take responsibility. Five years from now your English will be very fine indeed. Read as much as you can in Sydney and always be curious. Every morning when you wake, set your mind to the task at hand. Pray – to whoever or whatever you pray to – for strength and reassurance. Or if you're not the praying kind then just be focused, that's all you need. Challenge your father when you do not agree with what he is saying. Don't be frightened of him, his bark is definitely worse than his bite.

CHARLOTTE. Another risky guess.

HARVEY. And whatever you do, do not be discouraged by those who want to stop you dreaming and achieving. The only reason they will try and do so – sometimes to great effect – is because they haven't found a way of doing it themselves and they resent you for it.

Pause.

So take this place in your heart and move forward. This is a good time to leave Greece, Maria, your father has made an intelligent decision. Things are difficult here but in a few years they will be better again. And one day, you will come back and buy another house here, and start new memories for your children and your children's children. Because what your yia-yia wanted more than anything else, was for you to be happy, and for her house to be loved. And Theo and Charlotte will love her house and honour her memory. So you won't have broken the promise.

CHARLOTTE. Incredible.

Pause. MARIA *thinks a little, then walks up to* CHARLOTTE.

MARIA. I would like you to have my yia-yia's house, Mrs Manning. You are a very nice woman and Mr Manning too he is nice man.

HARVEY. They are.

MARIA. You will look over it, yes?

CHARLOTTE (*not quite believing what she's saying*). Look after it, yes, yes we shall.

MARIA. The garden and the house...

CHARLOTTE. And the pine forest that runs down to the sea, yes.

MARIA. Thank you.

She leans forward and gives CHARLOTTE *a small kiss on the cheek. She then starts moving back towards the chest of drawers and her father. But she stops, and turns.*

And you will have the furniture, too, Mrs Manning.

CHARLOTTE. If that's what you want, Maria.

MARIA. For just another ten thousand drachmas.

HARVEY. Good girl.

And she goes to her father.

STAMATIS. *Τι έγινε; Θα μου πεις τι στο διάολο έγινε;* [What happened? Will you tell me what the hell has happened?]

MARIA. *Το πουλήσαμε πατέρα. Και τα έπιπλα, για δέκα χιλιάδες.* [We sold it, Dad. And the furniture. For ten thousand.]

STAMATIS. *Δέκα χιλιάδες;* [Ten thousand?]

MARIA. *Ναι. Εκατόν σαράντα χιλιάδες για το σπίτι και δέκα χιλιάδες για τα έπιπλα.* [Yes. One hundred and forty thousand for the house and ten thousand for all the furniture.]

STAMATIS *walks up to her, grabs her head in his hands, and plants a big kiss on her forehead.*

STAMATIS. *Κορίτσι μου, Θησαυρέ μου! Θα προκόψεις!* [My girl, my treasure! You'll go far!]

He turns to the others.

Whisky! Whisky!

HARVEY. Yes! Whisky! Definitely whisky!

THEO (*holding up the whisky bottle*). This one is finished.

CHARLOTTE. There's another one in the kitchen.

STAMATIS *runs towards the house.*

STAMATIS. *Έλα Μαρία! Πάμε να βρούμε το Ουίσκι! Να το γλεντήσουμε μαζί τους!* [Come, Maria! Come and find the whisky! We celebrate with them!]

MARIA. He wants us to get the whisky. He wants everyone to have the whisky.

HARVEY. What a fine idea.

THEO. I'll come and show you where it is.

MARIA. It is fine, Mr Manning, I will find it.

CHARLOTTE. It's on the kitchen counter, Maria.

MARIA *and* STAMATIS *head towards the house.*

HARVEY. And, Maria…

MARIA. Yes, Mr?

HARVEY. Tell your father that tomorrow morning at eleven we'll meet him in town, by his brother's tobacco shop.

MARIA. I will say to him.

HARVEY. And then Mr Manning and myself will take him to a lawyer's so that we can get the whole thing sorted quickly and efficiently.

THEO. You don't need to come.

HARVEY. Greek lawyers, Theo, Greek bureaucracy, trust me, you
    need me there. And I know the lingo.

MARIA smiles at HARVEY.

MARIA. Thank you, Mr.

HARVEY. You're very welcome.

She turns to STAMATIS.

MARIA. *Έλα πατέρα, πάμε για το Ουίσκι!* [Come, Dad, let's get
    the whisky.]

And they run into the house.

For a second, nobody says a word. Then JUNE *shrieks.*

JUNE. Oh my God, you own this house! You own this house! You
    own this house!

THEO *too is suddenly overwhelmed.*

THEO. We do, it's true, we do. Charlotte, we own this house!

He kisses her. She attempts to partake, for him, but it's difficult.

CHARLOTTE. I know we do, I know we do.

THEO. It's good, Charlotte, it's good. Whatever you're feeling now,
    I know it's good!

CHARLOTTE. Maybe, yes, probably.

HARVEY. It is, Charlotte, for God's sake, lighten up and live this
    glorious moment!

JUNE. Oh, Charlotte, it's wonderful! So wonderful!

CHARLOTTE. Yes.

JUNE. Can I kiss you, can I kiss you both?

THEO. I've been waiting all evening, June.

She kisses them.

JUNE. Just think, all the summers you'll have here.

HARVEY. To rest, and play, and *work*, Theo.

THEO. To work, yes!

HARVEY *hugs him. He goes up to* CHARLOTTE, *opens
    his arms.*

HARVEY. May I?

She doesn't reply, just looks at him.

Jesus, woman, put down your defences for just one moment.

She lets him, he hugs her. At first she resists and it's awkward but then she gives in and the moment is sexually charged. JUNE *notices;* THEO *is oblivious. Then* HARVEY *ends the embrace. When he speaks, it is with some feeling.*

Blessed be this house and all that live in it.

Then MARIA *comes running out of the house, in a state of some excitement.*

MARIA. Mr Manning, Mrs Manning!

CHARLOTTE. What is it, Maria? Is everything all right?

MARIA. It's the radio!

CHARLOTTE. What about the radio?

MARIA. It's the... how you call it, the *nea.*

HARVEY. The news.

MARIA. There has been in Athens this morning a big thing. With tanks.

THEO. Tanks? What kind of tanks?

MARIA. With the Government. They have thrown them out with tanks. There has been, I don't know how you say in English...

HARVEY. It's a French word, Maria, well, technically three.

MARIA. Come, come and listen. Please, come.

JUNE. Okay, sweetheart, we'll come and listen to the news.

THEO. Jesus. A bloody coup is what she means!

THEO *and* JUNE *follow an excited* MARIA *into the house,* JUNE *throwing a slightly worried look over her shoulder at leaving* HARVEY *alone with* CHARLOTTE. CHARLOTTE *begins to make her way towards the house too, as the penny starts to drop.* HARVEY *hovers, knowing what's coming.*

Eventually, she stops, and turns to him.

CHARLOTTE. I thought you were a fan of democracy.

HARVEY. I am, Charlotte, more than you'll ever know.

Pause.

But democracy is a work in progress.

CHARLOTTE *lets out a little laugh.*

I don't like the means any more than you do but they *will* be justified one day, mark my words.

CHARLOTTE. Keep saying that to yourself, otherwise how do you look in the mirror every morning?

HARVEY. With great difficulty, Charlotte, so please don't be glib.

Pause.

Have you ever heard a man screaming under extreme and devastating physical pain?

CHARLOTTE. I can't say I have.

HARVEY. I'm happy for you, I hope you never have to.

Pause.

It's high-pitched and insistent, something like an animal in the middle of the dark night.

Pause.

I have heard those screams walking down subterranean corridors in strange small countries that you would have some difficulty finding on a map. I have heard them and taken them with me, ringing in my ears and my soul, so that you will never have to.

CHARLOTTE. Why?

HARVEY. Because, Charlotte, whether you are aware of it or not, we are at war for the soul of the world, and I, for one, care about the outcome.

CHARLOTTE. That fills me with hope. The outcome you plan to bring about.

HARVEY *talks slowly and with a quiet, dangerous steel in his voice.*

HARVEY. I am up to my elbows in dirt, and blood, and grime, Charlotte, so that you and Theo and people like you can carry on living the way you are. So that Theo can write his plays and you can act in them and then the two of you can stand on this terrace at the end of a day of clean work and bask in the feeling that you are good people. So please, as a token of your appreciation, try at least to give me a little due respect.

CHARLOTTE. And how can I do that?

HARVEY. Begin by using your imagination and refusing to think in a lazy and convenient way. It's lazy and convenient for you to consider me some sort of sociopath just as it's lazy and convenient for you to believe that all the fine things you have in your life do not come with a very hefty price. But I am the one, Charlotte, who will defend you and the way you live. And I ask you only one favour.

CHARLOTTE. Which is?

HARVEY. That you remember this. I too am a good man. A good man who has done – and does – certain things for which he feels a terrible remorse. Things which will revisit me over and over again in both my waking and my sleeping hours, and will continue to do so until my dying breath.

CHARLOTTE. So why do you do these things?

HARVEY. Because I believe in something.

When CHARLOTTE *speaks, it is with sarcasm.*

CHARLOTTE. What do you believe in, Harvey? Democracy?

HARVEY. I believe in never capitulating my will, my reason, or my imagination, to any authority – neither so-called sacred or temporal – which expects me to stop thinking, questioning, *demanding* answers. It's who I am, Charlotte.

Pause.

What do you believe in, Charlotte? Unicorns?

He walks up to her. For a few seconds they just stand there, dangerously close to each other, neither of them moves.

Why did I turn around to you at that café on the port and start the conversation yesterday morning?

CHARLOTTE. I don't know, why did you?

HARVEY. Because, Charlotte, I was attracted to you. Quite overwhelmingly, the force of it took me by surprise.

Pause.

And why did you then ask me and my wife over for drinks at your house?

CHARLOTTE. Why?

HARVEY. Because you felt exactly the same way.

Pause.

So we are attracted to each other and nothing will ever come of it because we will not permit it. You love Theo and I think I'm beginning to love him as well and we do not want to hurt him. He is too precious. And I don't want to hurt June either, because she has been loyal to me through thick and thin and has comforted me when I have woken her with my own screams in the middle of the night, soaked in a pool of sweat. So nothing will ever come of it – that's where the will part comes in handy.

Pause.

You are a good woman, Charlotte, and I am a good man.

Pause.

So now it has been named, we can put it away for ever and all of us can be friends.

THEO *comes running out,* HARVEY *and* CHARLOTTE *automatically move apart.*

THEO. It's true, it's on the World Service, there's been some sort of a right-wing coup, some colonels or something have taken over. Charlotte, come, Harvey, come and listen!

CHARLOTTE *makes her way towards the house, shaken.* HARVEY *stands where he is, he does not move.*

Harvey, don't you want to listen to the news?

CHARLOTTE. I think Harvey may know the news already, darling.

And she enters the house.

HARVEY *still doesn't move, he is lost in thought.* THEO *starts to make his way towards him.*

THEO. Harvey, there's been some sort of a coup, the military has taken over.

HARVEY. Was there bloodletting, violence? Were many killed?

THEO. Doesn't sound like it, not much resistance at all, they just marched in, unchallenged.

HARVEY. Good. I mean good that there wasn't much blood.

THEO. Still, Christ. A coup.

HARVEY. Yes.

Pause.

THEO. Puts a bit of a damper on buying this house.

HARVEY. Does it?

THEO. Well, what I mean is, who wants to own a house in a military dictatorship?

HARVEY. The island won't be affected. Nothing will change here. Life will go on as usual.

THEO. I know, but still, as *a feeling*. It doesn't feel right.

HARVEY *smiles to himself.*

HARVEY. Ah, yes, as *a feeling.*

Pause.

Anyway, don't worry, it won't last for ever. It's transitional. A few years maybe. Just until things settle down. And compared to your South Americans, they're a little lightweight this lot, bordering on the ridiculous. I wouldn't worry too much about it.

THEO. How do you know these things?

HARVEY. Just guessing.

Pause.

So what are you going to call the house?

THEO. Call it?

HARVEY. This house needs a name.

THEO. It does?

HARVEY. Every house needs a name, Theo.

THEO. If you say so.

Pause.

HARVEY. I know.

THEO. What?

HARVEY. Your Muse, name it after your Muse.

THEO. My Muse?

HARVEY. Yes, Theo. Make her feel wanted, welcome, cherished and appreciated.

THEO. I like that.

HARVEY. Put a chair in the corner, there for her, and name the house after her so she will always feel at home by your side.

THEO. Okay, the Muse, yes. So I just call the house 'Muse', do I? That sounds a little strange.

HARVEY. No, you call the house Villa Thalia.

THEO. That's even stranger.

HARVEY. Why is it stranger?

THEO. Well, for a start, it's not really a villa, it's more of a peasant shack.

HARVEY. You're a writer, Charlotte's an actress and once you stock up the bar and offer people dry Martinis and whisky sours, it will be a villa.

THEO. And then, of course, Thalia…

HARVEY. Is the Muse of Comedy, yes.

THEO. But I don't really write comedies, or aspire to.

HARVEY. But you should, Theo. A fine comedy is an exquisite thing. I don't mean a farce, adulterous English folk running around with their pants around their ankles…

THEO. No, that's not really my style.

HARVEY. But something satirical, Theo, and provocative, and funny.

Pause. THEO *considers it for a minute. Then looks at the house over his shoulder, almost as if to check that* CHARLOTTE *isn't listening.*

THEO. Okay then, Villa Thalia. For you. In honour of the man who made it happen.

HARVEY *smiles, with bittersweet irony.*

HARVEY. Thank you.

THEO. Come, we need to listen to the news, we need to know what's happening.

And he makes his way towards the house.

HARVEY. In a moment.

THEO *goes back into the house.*

But HARVEY *remains where he is, staring out at the sunset, and the sea.*

Lights fade to darkness.

End of Act One.

ACT TWO

The scene is now nine years later and there have been some alterations to the terrace – an awning, a painted door, an outside light, a splashing of tiles. And the furniture that is scattered across the space – a couple of tables, some sunloungers, are all new too. Even though underneath the more Europeanised feel of the place one can still discern the rustic quality that the house once had, it can now be categorised quite easily as a 1970s holiday villa, albeit of a slightly bohemian quality.

And there is nothing luxurious or ordered about this villa – at this moment in time, it appears very lived in, almost messy. The terrace is scattered with the usual summer-holiday paraphernalia – beach towels, random flip-flops, two rackets and a ball, a beach umbrella leaning precariously against a wall. There is a clothes horse in a corner with lots of summer clothes drying on it. And somewhere on the edge, there is also a cassette recorder too, and a box of cassettes by it.

And on a small table somewhere, THEO*'s Corona, and next to it, pages under a large stone.*

It is a late afternoon in August, 1976.

ADRIAN *and* ROSALIND *are stretched out on the ground in swimsuits and T-shirts, reading children's books.*

JUNE *walks on. Her clothes and hair are of a very different style to when we last saw her – very seventies now, and casual, summery. But whatever it is she is wearing, her shoulders are bare. She is holding a small bottle of nail varnish in one hand and a glass of Bacardi in the other.*

JUNE. Hello, sweetnesses.

The children look up.

ADRIAN. Hello, Mrs Parker.

JUNE. Honey, how many times have I told you to call me June, I'm not a schoolteacher, I'm your friend.

ADRIAN. Hello, June.

JUNE. That's better. Look at you both reading your books, aren't you just the most adorable things! What's that, what are you reading, honey?

ADRIAN *shows her the cover of the book.*

ADRIAN. *Five Have a Mystery to Solve,* I told you earlier.

JUNE. Oh, that's right, you did, but you know, sweetheart, you have to be told things more than once when you're my age and you like Bacardi.

She positions one of the sunloungers so that it faces the sun, aims for the right angle, moves it around a bit.

Just ignore me, I'm going to do my nails, God knows they need it.

ADRIAN. All right, we'll ignore you.

JUNE sits down, unscrews the bottle of nail varnish, rests one of her feet on the edge of the sunlounger and begins working on her toenails.

CHARLOTTE strolls on, holding an empty basket. She is there to take the dry clothes off the clothes horse – for the next few minutes and as she chats, she takes the items off one by one, folds them on the table, and places them all into the basket.

THEO follows her on, but he carries a tray with a large jug of something red and some floating fruit in it, and a few glasses. He rests the tray on the table.

CHARLOTTE. Children, time to get out of your swimsuits and get dressed for supper.

ADRIAN. But Harvey promised he'd take us for a swim, Mummy!

JUNE. Well, maybe you should go remind him, sweetheart, he needs a nudge.

ROSALIND. Can we go, Mummy?

CHARLOTTE. Maybe Harvey's changed his mind, darling.

JUNE. A promise is a promise, go get him, kids.

CHARLOTTE. Are you sure?

JUNE. I'm positive, he needs to be dragged out of that room, he's being morose.

CHARLOTTE. All right then, but it will be a quick one, five minutes, it's gone six o'clock.

ADRIAN. Yes, Mummy!

The children start to run off in a state of some excitement,
ROSALIND *grabs a pair of armbands as she goes and hands*
them to THEO.

ROSALIND. Blow them up for me, Daddy!

THEO. Please, yes I may.

ROSALIND. Please! Thank you!

And the children run off. THEO *starts to blow up the armbands.*
CHARLOTTE *continues to fold the clean clothes.* JUNE *is*
concentrating avidly on her toenails.

THEO. I've made some of that fruit punch you like so much, June.

JUNE. Oh, Theo, I love that stuff, thank you, all punch and
no fruit.

CHARLOTTE. I don't know why you call it fruit punch. More of a
sangria really, half a gallon of red wine in there.

THEO. And a pint of rum.

JUNE. Yummy.

CHARLOTTE. Did you manage a siesta?

JUNE. Not really, I had to finish the packing, then Harvey seems
tense, pacing up and down like a predatory animal, he was
making me nervous, you try snoozing with that in the room.

THEO. Why is he tense?

JUNE. Why is it hot in Greece, Theo? Why do those cicada things
never shut up?

CHARLOTTE. I noticed he hardly said a word at lunch.

JUNE. I think something happened last night.

THEO. Happened, what happened?

JUNE. I wish I knew, Theo. When we went into the port to get the
newspapers and some cigarettes, he left me in a bar for half an
hour, then when he came back again he was being weird, sullen,
and just plain moody.

CHARLOTTE. How strange.

JUNE. Maybe something he read in the papers, God knows, or some depressing thought he had. And then that phone call this morning didn't help.

THEO. Bad news?

JUNE. They want him in Kinshasa next week, can you imagine? His heart sank when he heard. The Congo, for God's sake, or Zaire or whatever its name is these days. He hates that place.

CHARLOTTE. Duty calls.

THEO. But you've had a good holiday? Restful, at least.

JUNE. Oh, God, we've loved it, Theo, even if it was just a few days. Just being here with you and Charlotte, and those gorgeous children of yours, I could eat them!

CHARLOTTE. I'd rather you didn't.

JUNE stops with the nails for a second, touches her right shoulder with her left hand.

JUNE. My shoulders are burnt, I should have listened to you, Charlotte.

And then she's back at the toenails again.

THEO has finished with the armbands, he puts them down, and stands.

THEO. Right, before I start indulging, I'm going to do my exercises. Just ignore me, ladies.

He starts doing some squats.

CHARLOTTE. Why do you insist on doing those in public every evening?

THEO. Because I need to exhibit my virile manhood.

JUNE. I can't see it, Theo. I keep looking for it when you're doing those squats but I can never see it.

CHARLOTTE. When he does them in his briefs, it pops out from time to time.

JUNE. How wonderful.

CHARLOTTE. But you need to get quite close. It's like a cheeky little goldfish.

THEO. Don't listen to her, June, it's a barracuda.

ADRIAN *and* ROSALIND *drag* HARVEY *on. He's in shorts and a T-shirt, looking more haggard than when we last saw him. He too has had a couple of drinks and there's a bit of an edge to him. He comes on with a slightly forced joviality.*

ROSALIND. We found him!

HARVEY. They found me!

JUNE. There you are.

ADRIAN. He was hiding!

HARVEY. But your agents are effective.

JUNE. Have you packed your bags yet, Harvey?

HARVEY. Yes, dear. So this is where the party is. Nice to see you working on those quadriceps, Theo, they need a little firming, I noticed that earlier.

THEO. I am a man of steel.

HARVEY. I've been coerced into joining you. Well, physically forced.

JUNE. Stops you brooding, mister.

HARVEY. I expect it's a good thing. I grew sick of arguing with myself, I need external stimuli if only for amusement.

CHARLOTTE. We'll do our best.

THEO *has finished his squats and now throws himself into push-ups.*

THEO. What were you arguing about?

HARVEY. This place seems to have that effect on me, it makes me introspective.

CHARLOTTE. That can't be a bad thing.

JUNE. Well, at least you're a little livelier now than you were last night and this morning.

HARVEY. I'm doing my best, June.

JUNE (*watching* THEO *doing his push-ups*). You look very sexy when you're doing those, Theo.

THEO. Thank you, June, I believe I do.

HARVEY *pours himself a glass of the punch and raises his glass.*

HARVEY. And so the time is fast approaching when we shall say goodbye, it breaks my heart.

THEO. We've liked having you, Harvey.

HARVEY. Thank you, Theo, that's kind of you to say.

THEO. I mean it.

JUNE. Harvey, the kids are waiting for that swim you promised them.

THEO*'s push-ups are over. He jumps up.*

THEO. Right, and a few sit-ups and we're done.

He's down again, doing the sit-ups.

HARVEY. I know you mean it, Theo, I'd never doubt it. At least we offer novelty value, if nothing else. I mean from what you have pointed out a few times over the last few days, Charlotte, most of your friends are artists like yourselves, well, actors, writers, directors, *theatre folk*, June, theatricals if you like, that sort of thing.

JUNE. Well, that makes sense, it's their world.

HARVEY. So to have us two under your roof must be an exception, we're different animals altogether, aren't we, June?

JUNE. Speak for yourself, I'm a human being, not a hyena. Did you see that after-sun cream in the room, Harvey? I need some for my shoulders.

HARVEY *claps his hands.*

HARVEY. Right, is it time to head to the beach, kiddos?

ROSALIND/ADRIAN. Yes! Yes, it is!

HARVEY *and the children start to make their way towards the path that leads to the beach. But on his way,* HARVEY *passes by the pages of* THEO*'s new play sitting next to the typewriter. He places his hand on it.*

HARVEY. A good day's work, Theo?

THEO *has finished his sit-ups, the exercises are over. He walks over to the punch, and pours himself a glass.*

THEO. Not bad. Done some rewrites on the second scene and started on Act Two.

HARVEY. I'm happy to hear it.

CHARLOTTE. He was up at five with the cockerels.

THEO. I got a couple of hours in. And then a little more when you all went off to the taverna for lunch.

HARVEY. Good man.

JUNE. You're so industrious, Theo, it's admirable.

HARVEY. He has a vocation, June, a calling.

THEO. I don't know if it's that.

JUNE. I have a vocation too.

CHARLOTTE. For what, June?

JUNE. For breathing. I have a calling towards inhaling oxygen, I can't help it, I do.

HARVEY. But seriously, can I just have a moment here?

Suddenly inspired, HARVEY *pulls out a chair and jumps onto it.*

JUNE. Why are you standing on the chair, sweetheart?

HARVEY. In order to create an atmosphere of awe and ceremony. I need you to listen to me now with some attention and just a little reverence. This is serious, folks.

ADRIAN. Harvey, come on, let's go swimming!

HARVEY. One minute, kids, one minute, that's all, I promise you.

He takes a moment to find the right words and when he does he speaks with sincerity and some emotion.

Isn't it extraordinary how things worked out for you? Was I right or was I right about you, Theo?

THEO. Right about what?

HARVEY. This place, Theo, this house.

THEO. What about it, Harvey?

HARVEY. Nine years ago, Theo, in 1967, when we were younger and just a little less tired, we all stood where we are now, and do you remember what I said to you?

JUNE. You said many things, sweetheart, you always do.

HARVEY. But do you remember what I said more than anything else?

THEO. What did you say, Harvey?

HARVEY (*with some passion*). I said that you were going to be a successful and important writer. I said that somehow, buying this house, making it your own, writing here – *here*, Theo, here, at this exact spot – was going to help you become the writer you were always destined to be.

THEO. You did.

HARVEY. Thank you. And then it happened.

THEO. Did it?

HARVEY. And I am proud of that. I mean, of the very small part I played in that process, in making that come to be.

CHARLOTTE. Harvey, could you get off that chair, please? They're quite delicate, those chairs, fragile.

HARVEY. You even wrote a comedy, Theo. You said you never would but you did.

THEO. It was a critical catastrophe, thank you for the suggestion. *The Times* said, and I quote, that 'the play came into its own at the curtain call'.

HARVEY. But the public queued around the block and sometimes the public know a thing or two.

THEO. It was the coldest winter on record, the Criterion is famously warm.

HARVEY. And you have grown, as a writer, Theo and expanded, and your voice has become stronger and more confident, and it *has* changed things, damn it.

THEO. 'Changed things'? What things?

CHARLOTTE. Please get off the chair, Harvey.

HARVEY. Your plays are quietly political, Theo, and even though their politics may lean a little too much to the left for my liking,

well, damn it, you have a way of coaxing people towards
broadening their sympathies and that, my friend, can only be a
good thing in this screwed-up world of ours.

THEO. Thank you, Harvey, enough now.

JUNE. He's right, Theo, your plays are always moving.

CHARLOTTE (*still about the chair*). Harvey, please.

HARVEY. Well, it's interesting you use that word, June, because you
know I was thinking the other day that to *move* someone, well,
yes it means, you make them feel something, you inspire some
sort of emotional response in them, you elicit sympathy, I don't
know, *empathy*, but it also means that you *reposition* them, they
have a new perspective, a new angle, they have been *moved*.

JUNE. God, you're right, Harvey, I'd never thought of it like that.

HARVEY. And you have done that, Theo. Writing here. In *this* place.
You have repositioned us.

Pause.

So I was right. That's all.

THEO. If you say so.

HARVEY *jumps off the chair.*

HARVEY. And that chair is doing just fine, Charlotte.

Turns to the children.

Come on, kids, let's have that swim.

JUNE. That was beautiful, honey, if a little strange.

CHARLOTTE *has finished folding the clothes.*

CHARLOTTE. It's true what you say about Theo's work.

THEO. Thank you, darling.

CHARLOTTE. But you exaggerate the role this house has played.

*She picks up the basket of folded clothes and starts to move
towards the house.*

Don't get me wrong, we have loved it here…

HARVEY. *Have* loved it?

CHARLOTTE. But if it hadn't been this place, it would have been
somewhere else.

HARVEY. I don't think so, Charlotte.

CHARLOTTE. Well, I do.

And she enters the house with the basket. HARVEY *is riled but does his best to conceal it.* ROSALIND *is now pulling him by the hand,* ADRIAN *joins her at it.*

ROSALIND/ADRIAN. Harvey! Come on, Harvey!

JUNE. Well, either way, it's a wonderful holiday home and that's all that matters.

HARVEY. It's more than that. Did you not listen to what I said, June?

ROSALIND. Come on, Harvey!

ADRIAN. Harvey, it's going to be too late to swim!

JUNE. If you're going to take the kids swimming, Harvey, you better do it now.

ROSALIND. Harvey, you promised!

HARVEY. Okay then, come on, kids, let's go and have that final swim.

THEO. A quick one, kids, five minutes, that's all!

They start to go.

Armbands!

ROSALIND *goes and grabs them, then follows* HARVEY *and* ADRIAN *as they head towards the beach. But* HARVEY *stops for a second, looks at* THEO.

HARVEY. You understand me, though, Theo, don't you?

THEO. I'm trying, Harvey.

JUNE. Sweetheart, before you disappear, can you fetch me that bottle of after-sun cream from the room?

But they've gone.

I think that's a no.

She stands.

I need some of that stuff on my shoulders.

She starts to wander off to get the cream.

You see, what I mean, he's being so weird, I don't know what it is.

And she goes.

THEO *is left alone.*

He walks over to the table and picks up a Polaroid camera that is resting on it, next to a sheet of paper and a tape measure. He starts moving around the terrace, taking photographs of it, and of the house, from every angle.

CHARLOTTE *returns. She goes to the clothes horse and starts to fold it away.*

CHARLOTTE. Where is everyone?

THEO. Harvey's taken the kids for that swim. And June's getting something from her room.

CHARLOTTE *approaches* THEO, *speaks quietly and with urgency, looking over her shoulder to make sure she isn't being heard.*

CHARLOTTE. I can't do this again.

THEO *keeps taking photographs.*

THEO. You invited them.

CHARLOTTE. They didn't give me a choice. She said, 'We're in Athens for a few weeks, we'll take the ferry and come see you.' They invited themselves, Theo, you know that.

THEO. I believe you.

CHARLOTTE. Why are we their friends? What have we got in common?

THEO. Not a lot. But is that a bad thing?

CHARLOTTE. Never again.

She looks at him taking the photographs.

Why are you taking photos?

THEO. For the Bauers. Gustav said they'd like some to show their architects in Hamburg. A few changes they want to make. And I measured everything this morning, it's on that sheet of paper over there.

He points over to the piece of paper.

CHARLOTTE. Don't do that now, do it tomorrow.

THEO. I want to post it off in the morning. Gustav said the architect needs them by next week. I can stop at the post office on the way back from the port.

CHARLOTTE. It can wait, Theo. I don't want them to know.

THEO. Know what?

CHARLOTTE. About the house, about the Bauers. I don't want them to know.

THEO. It's fine, I'm not going to tell them, we said we wouldn't.

CHARLOTTE. You saw what he's like about it. Sentimental.

THEO. Some of what he said was true, I think.

CHARLOTTE. Just put them away somewhere. And the measurements.

THEO places the photos and measurements under a flower pot so that they won't blow away.

JUNE comes back, after-sun cream in hand.

JUNE. I'm sore all over but at least I'm grilled and ready for the fall.

THEO. What fall?

JUNE. I mean the autumn, Theo, not my personal decline.

THEO stands in front of her with the camera.

THEO. Smile!

JUNE. Wait! Give a woman a chance.

She touches up her hair a bit, poses.

Ready!

He takes the photo.

THEO. Something to remember you by.

JUNE. You make it sound like I'm about to die. Oh, wait, and I want one with my friend Charlotte.

She beckons CHARLOTTE.

Come on, Charlotte, stand here, next to me!

CHARLOTTE joins her reluctantly. JUNE puts her arm around CHARLOTTE's shoulder, there is a slight awkwardness to the moment.

Me and my friend Charlotte.

CHARLOTTE. Go on, Theo. Take the photograph.

THEO takes it. CHARLOTTE moves quickly, releasing herself from the pose.

I should go take that stew thing off the hob.

THEO. I'll do it.

CHARLOTTE is annoyed – she wanted an escape. But THEO, who also doesn't want to be left alone with JUNE, has already put the camera and the photos down on the table and is moving towards the house. CHARLOTTE gives him an accusing look as he goes.

JUNE pours herself a glass of punch, then moves back towards sunlounger, perches on it, takes the lid off the after-sun cream.

JUNE. Can you do my shoulders for me, Charlotte?

CHARLOTTE. Of course.

But she's not that effective at hiding the fact she'd rather not.

CHARLOTTE walks over to where JUNE is and takes the bottle from her. She pours some cream into her hand and starts to apply it onto JUNE's shoulders.

JUNE. That bit is sore, serves me right.

For a few seconds, they continue like this, CHARLOTTE rubbing cream into JUNE, JUNE sipping her punch.

We haven't really had any girl time, have we?

CHARLOTTE. I suppose not.

JUNE. What with those men around, and the kids. I mean, don't get me wrong, I love their company, but the two of us haven't had a chance, have we?

CHARLOTTE doesn't say anything, just keeps applying the cream.

I know we could have gone for a walk or something, but I felt that maybe you didn't want to…

CHARLOTTE. It isn't that, it's just, well, you know…

JUNE. Of course, I understand.

For a few seconds they continue in silence, CHARLOTTE *applying the cream onto* JUNE*'s back.*

I'm frightened of him. And frightened *for* him. I don't know which. Both.

She waits for something from CHARLOTTE *but doesn't get it. So she perseveres.*

You don't know the half of it, Charlotte. You don't know how bad it is.

And suddenly JUNE *stands up, and steps away from her, overcome by a sudden burst of emotion.*

Oh, God.

She puts her hand to her mouth, lets out a little sob. Then turns back to CHARLOTTE, *pulls herself together.*

I'm sorry.

CHARLOTTE *is disconcerted, doesn't how to respond.* JUNE *begins to talk with some urgency, knowing she hasn't much time.*

Certain things… I couldn't even tell my mother, Charlotte, *especially* my mother, and my friends, the girls back home, they wouldn't understand, oh God, I'm scared.

CHARLOTTE (*tentatively, knowing she's opening a can of worms*). What are you scared of?

JUNE. But you're different, you and Theo are *different*, you'd understand.

Again, JUNE *checks to see nobody is listening, as if about to impart a terrible secret. She comes back to the sunlounger, sits next to* CHARLOTTE.

You know we're not together, any more.

CHARLOTTE. Not together?

JUNE. Not *sexually*, I mean, Charlotte, he hasn't fucked me in six months and before that it was like… well, it wasn't fun, not like he wanted to is what I mean, it's been like that for a very long time.

CHARLOTTE. I see.

JUNE. I mean even after we found out we couldn't… we weren't going to have children, well, even then for some time, there was some enjoyment, we were still, you know…

CHARLOTTE. June, I really –

JUNE. But then it all stopped, after Chile.

CHARLOTTE. Chile?

JUNE. After our time in Santiago. That's when it happened, Charlotte, that's when he changed.

THEO *comes out.*

THEO. It needs a bit longer, but I've put it on a low heat.

There is an awkward moment.

CHARLOTTE. Theo, could you slice those tomatoes. The ones on the counter. For the salad, I mean. And then put them in the fridge.

THEO. Now? Surely we can do that later.

CHARLOTTE. No, *now*, Theo.

And he gets it.

THEO. Oh, yes. Of course.

He goes back into the house. JUNE *stands, moves to the table, grabs her Virginia Slims, lights one.*

JUNE. The situation was very bad, I'm sure you read about it, everything fell apart, the whole place was in chaos and then there was the coup, and then all the other stuff.

CHARLOTTE. Other stuff?

JUNE. But we were there for the whole thing, I mean Harvey was living through it every day –

CHARLOTTE. He was a part of it.

JUNE. So they put us up in this apartment in this fancy area of Santiago, and it was perfectly nice, I mean it was a middle-class neighbourhood, there were parks nearby, a couple of cafés, and the apartment itself was elegant, tall ceilings, beautiful parquet floors, that sort of thing.

CHARLOTTE. How lovely.

JUNE. And there was this woman who lived next door with her son. So we got to know her, well, both of them really, they even came over for dinner one night. She was a music teacher, she taught music at a local girls' school and he was... the son, well he was in his twenties and he was a pianist, Charlotte, he was training to be a concert pianist. He was a beautiful boy, black curly hair, and strong too, but his hands were the hands of a pianist.

CHARLOTTE. All right.

JUNE. Sometimes we'd hear him practise through the walls, Bach, Mozart, Chopin, you name it, and he played so beautifully and the walls were thin, so you could hear it, but it never disturbed us, because he was *good*, and you know Harvey would actually put his chair near the wall so that he could hear it even better. So it never bothered us is what I mean, because he played so well.

CHARLOTTE. Why are you telling me all this?

JUNE. Well, then he went missing. The boy went missing, Charlotte.

Pause.

It was madness, you have to understand. Because even if you read about it in the papers you will never comprehend what was going on there. It was pandemonium, and things had to be done to save the country, it was that bad.

CHARLOTTE. Things were bad after the coup you mean?

JUNE. No, I mean *before* the coup, Charlotte, the country was in free fall, economically, socially, every which way, that man Allende was a Marxist and he was taking the country to hell in a hand basket. But anyway, in the few days after the coup, things happened, people were gathered up, you know, *communists*, I mean, people who were trying to destroy... well, people who were dangerous, Charlotte, a lot of them were anarchists and worse, but there's no denying that in that effort to quash... in that effort to return the country to safety, mistakes were made, because there was chaos, and the Chileans themselves, well, they can be disorganised, impulsive, like children, it's in their blood. So terrible things happened, there's no denying.

CHARLOTTE. What happened to the boy?

JUNE. There was a football stadium, Charlotte, the army gathered people in it, and then afterwards, many went missing. And he was one of them.

CHARLOTTE. And then what?

JUNE. Well, the mother, she went crazy, wouldn't you have done? She'd shuffle around in her slippers all day and all night calling his name, like she was looking for him, expecting him to pop out, I don't know, from behind the wardrobe or something, and we could hear it, she'd be calling his name all day and all night, '*Gabriel, Gabriel, dónde estás?*'

CHARLOTTE. Where are you?

JUNE. Harvey started playing records so that we wouldn't have to listen to her. Jazz, for Christ's sake, and Burt Bacharach and God knows what else, so that we wouldn't have to listen to this woman calling her son's name.

Pause.

And the thing is, Charlotte, he wasn't even a communist. He was young, that's all, idealistic, I suppose, a *kind* boy, sensitive. He got caught up in it all, I expect, took a few bad turns, was in the wrong place at the wrong time.

And JUNE *realises she's gone too far, decides to pull back a little.*

But at least the country was saved, that's the one good thing.

CHARLOTTE. Was it?

JUNE. So that's when it all started falling apart. And that's when the paranoia started.

CHARLOTTE. What paranoia, June?

JUNE. He just started getting these weird ideas, like he was being followed all the time, every time he got in the car his eyes would be glued to the rear-view mirror and then he'd get jumpy in restaurants or walking down the street, like he was expecting someone to leap out from behind a bush or something and put a bullet to his head. And the last few weeks it's been unbearable, of course.

CHARLOTTE. Why's that?

JUNE. Well, remember he said he got called back to Athens because they assassinated that guy from the Embassy in December?

CHARLOTTE. He's investigating it, yes.

JUNE. Well, the more he's been working on all that, the more nervous he's become, like an animal being hunted. He even asked the security guys at the Embassy for a gun, it's horrible.

CHARLOTTE. A gun?

JUNE. He carries it with him everywhere now. But it's crazy, I mean, we're coming here, and I'm like, 'We're going to stay with friends on an island, Harvey, you don't need that thing with you, it's crazy.'

CHARLOTTE *is in shock; she stands.*

CHARLOTTE. He has a gun here? In this house?

JUNE. Don't worry, it doesn't mean anything, it's like a state of mind.

CHARLOTTE. 'A state of mind'?

She moves towards the house, begins to shout THEO*'s name.*

Theo, Theo!

JUNE. Charlotte, please!

CHARLOTTE. I don't want a gun in this house!

JUNE. For God's sake, Charlotte, we're leaving in the morning.

CHARLOTTE. Theo!

JUNE. It doesn't mean a thing.

CHARLOTTE. So why does he have it then, and why did you tell me?

THEO *emerges from the house. He's wearing an apron, holds a tomato in one hand, a sharp knife in the other.*

THEO. What's wrong?

JUNE. Charlotte, please, I told you in confidence!

CHARLOTTE. I'm sorry, June, but I don't like it, I don't like it one bit.

THEO. Don't like what, what's happening?

JUNE. Charlotte, please.

CHARLOTTE. Not in this house, not with children here, you should have told us.

THEO. Told us what?

CHARLOTTE. I just don't like it!

JUNE points at THEO who is standing there with a knife in his hand.

JUNE. I mean, look at Theo, he's holding a knife, he's not going to use it to kill someone.

CHARLOTTE. That's not the same, June.

JUNE. Why isn't it the same?

CHARLOTTE. Because he's slicing tomatoes with it.

THEO. Who's going to kill someone?

JUNE. No, but what I mean is, he's not going to use it any more than Theo is going to use that knife.

THEO. I am using the knife.

JUNE. Not to kill someone is what I mean.

THEO. Kill who?

CHARLOTTE. Oh, for God's sake! This is my house and there are children here. I'm sorry, June, for what's happened, and I'm sorry that Harvey is paranoid or whatever you want to call it, but I do not want a gun in this house.

THEO. Harvey's got a gun?

And HARVEY suddenly runs on with ADRIAN and ROSALIND in tow. He jumps up behind THEO, THEO turns and HARVEY sees the knife in THEO's hand. He screams, hamming it up.

HARVEY. No! No, please don't kill me! I'm sorry I insulted your quadriceps! Please don't kill me with that tomato!

JUNE. Harvey!

Pause. JUNE looks at CHARLOTTE, pleadingly.

Charlotte, I beg you.

HARVEY. Beg her what?

JUNE. We're leaving in the morning, we'll be out of your hair for good.

HARVEY. Are you sick of having us?

Pause. CHARLOTTE decides to keep quiet.

CHARLOTTE. Right, Theo, you better get back to those tomatoes and let's forget it all.

THEO. Do I have to?

HARVEY. Oh, that's what the knife is for, what a relief!

CHARLOTTE *goes to the table, pours herself a glass of punch.* THEO *hovers.*

JUNE. That was a quick swim.

HARVEY. Well, we got excited about something else, didn't we, kids?

ADRIAN. Harvey's going to teach us how to Greek dance!

JUNE. Oh, for God's sake, Harvey.

HARVEY. I think it's appropriate, on our last day here, to do something in celebration of the spirit of this beautiful country. Where's that tape you were listening to the other night, Theo? You know, the Greek one.

THEO. Should be there, by the cassette recorder.

HARVEY *makes his way over to where the recorder is, starts to shuffle through all the different cassettes.*

HARVEY. Because that's another thing we've not discussed, let alone celebrated.

THEO. What's that?

HARVEY (*still rummaging through the tapes*). When we first met on this island, all those many years ago, it happened to be on the unfortunate day that the colonels came to power, remember, Charlotte? And here we are, ten years later, and those very same colonels are rotting in jail somewhere, they served their purpose, the communist threat was averted, and we are now holidaying in what this country was always destined to be – a shining beacon of modern democracy. Isn't that a wonderful thing?

He has found the tape he's looking for.

Ah, here it is, I believe this is the one.

He takes whatever tape is in the recorder out, and replaces it with the Greek one. He presses play. The music begins and it is a rebetiko *song, 'Fragosiriani', plaintive and beautiful.*

So, kids, in honour of the resilient spirit of this nation and its people and their return to civilisation, I am going to teach you the rudiments of Greek dancing.

JUNE. When did you learn anything about Greek dancing?

HARVEY. Maybe not so much the technical aspects of the footwork but more the spirit of the thing, the emotional commitment it demands.

JUNE. God help us.

HARVEY. Theo, I think you should join us. You need a little loosening up.

THEO. I don't really…

HARVEY. I insist, Theo.

ADRIAN. Yes, Daddy!

HARVEY. But put that knife down first, we don't want you dancing with a carving knife in your hand.

HARVEY moves to the centre of the terrace and stretches out his arms, crossing his legs and clicking his fingers Greek-style.

JUNE. You look ridiculous.

HARVEY. Come on, kids, get into place, Theo, you too, stand behind me and do what I do.

ADRIAN and ROSALIND run and get into position behind him. THEO puts the knife down and joins them too, a little sheepishly. CHARLOTTE is annoyed by his participation.

CHARLOTTE. Theo, what are you doing?

HARVEY. Stretch your arms out like this and click your fingers in tune to the music but do it with some feeling!

They all do as instructed. The dance begins.

The main thing is to keep your head up high! You're survivors, you've been through four hundred years of Turkish occupation, and you need the world to know that nothing will ever get you down again!

As he dances he turns and looks at what the kids are doing.

Jesus, Adrian, higher, that's four hundred years, not a weekend! Rosalind, bend those knees a little, and get the fire in the eyes, you need the fire, you look like you're from Surrey, England, not this troubled land!

JUNE. I think she's doing well, she looks Greek.

HARVEY. Feel the pain and pride in the music and let it sweep through every part of your body like an electric current!

Adrian, I won't say it again, stick that head up in the air, that's good, Theo, get those hips moving, it's that Middle Eastern influence coming through!

THEO (*gyrating his hips quite suggestively*). Like this?

HARVEY. More, Theo, more, think Egypt, it's not that far away, just across the Med there, think Cleopatra, Theo, think belly dancing, you can do it!

CHARLOTTE *suddenly and quickly moves to the cassette recorder, switches it off. The abrupt action shocks them all into silence for a few seconds.*

ADRIAN/ROSALIND. Mummy! Why did you switch it off!

CHARLOTTE. You're still in your swimsuits, and they're wet, I want you to get dressed for dinner.

ADRIAN. Mummy, please!

ROSALIND. Mummy!

CHARLOTTE. Children, please do as I say.

HARVEY. You don't like our dancing, Charlotte?

ADRIAN. Why can't we dance with Harvey, Mummy?

CHARLOTTE. Children, please.

THEO. It's just fun, Charlotte.

HARVEY. You don't like our dancing? You don't like watching your husband shaking his hips like that?

CHARLOTTE. Honestly? No, I don't like it, Harvey, I don't like your dancing.

THEO. It's just fun, Charlotte.

She ejects the tape out of the cassette recorder, takes it in her hand.

CHARLOTTE. I'm sorry, it's this music, this tape.

HARVEY. What about it?

CHARLOTTE. I'm not going to say it again, children. I want you to go and get out of your wet clothes and into your dry ones.

ADRIAN *storms off, into the house*.

ADRIAN. You're horrible!

ROSALIND *follows him off, both in a tantrum*.

CHARLOTTE. I'm sorry, I bought this cassette in town, from that little shop behind the church.

THEO. So what, Charlotte?

CHARLOTTE. And the young woman in the shop told me something about it. I mean, I said I wanted to buy something Greek and she recommended it to me, and she talked to me about it, I mean about this particular type of music.

HARVEY. Jesus.

THEO. Why does that mean we can't have fun with it?

CHARLOTTE. It's called *rebetiko*, Theo, it's a type of music, and it's called *rebetiko*…

THEO. So what?

HARVEY. I think I know where this is going.

HARVEY *goes and pours himself a glass of the punch*.

CHARLOTTE. It's originally from Asia Minor across the sea there, from the small Greek towns of Asia Minor, and people brought it to Greece when they were forced to migrate here after the war with the Turks and the population exchange that ensued.

JUNE. The cassette, they brought the cassette?

HARVEY. She means the music, June.

CHARLOTTE. Its history is rooted in this part of the world – the Eastern Aegean – and its *soul* – I mean, the place it comes from, Harvey, its *source*, its flame, its ignition, is in people who have little power or money trying to express experiences such as alienation, subjugation, poverty, migration, that sort of thing, you know.

THEO. Like Greek blues?

CHARLOTTE. Yes, Theo, exactly, like Greek blues.

HARVEY. Please tell me you are joking about this.

CHARLOTTE. So I'd rather my children weren't taught to trivialise
the experiences of other people, especially those they know
nothing about and whose pain they can't begin
to fathom.

Pause.

That's all.

JUNE. Charlotte, I'm sorry, I think that's overreacting. I mean it was
just a joke, and the kids were having fun.

THEO. I do think that's a bit over the top, love.

HARVEY. I wasn't trivialising, or mocking.

Pause.

I said to you – well, not to you personally, but to everyone here –
that I thought it was fitting to celebrate the fact that Greece is now
a democracy and I suggested we do so in a light-hearted and
entertaining way. Your response is ridiculous, Charlotte, and
melodramatic.

CHARLOTTE. Well, I'm sorry, yes, maybe I am being a little
melodramatic but there's something I find innately distasteful
about people from one culture appropriating things from another
one, and then imposing things onto it which are not even native to
its character.

HARVEY. You mean the way Theo was moving his hips?

CHARLOTTE. Anglo-Saxons or whatever we are, sitting here, on
this terrace, in this country we don't know all that much about,
ridiculing their dancing, and imposing things on them, making
them live the way we want them to live, forcing them to be like
us.

JUNE. Actually, Charlotte, my ancestors are Swedish.

THEO. Charlotte, I've lost you, what were we forcing them to do,
what are you talking about?

CHARLOTTE. And before we start celebrating democracy, Harvey,
maybe we should ask if this particular kind of democracy is the
one the Greek people had in mind.

HARVEY. Go on.

CHARLOTTE. I'm sure that a handful of Greek families are appreciative of this new democracy, of the way it benefits their Swiss bank accounts, but the real people of Greece – oh, I mean teachers, Harvey, and nurses, and workers, and I don't know, people on the streets, people in the fields –

HARVEY. 'Fields'? Did you actually say '*fields*'?

CHARLOTTE. I wonder if they have as much reason to celebrate as you do, Harvey. Time will tell, I suppose.

Pause.

Yes, Harvey, I said fields. It's an agricultural country after all, that much I do know.

HARVEY. You're amazing. She's amazing, Theo.

CHARLOTTE. Thank you, Harvey. But anyway, yes, let's try and imagine what's best for the majority of people, not just a small and favoured elite. Both here, and in Chile.

She throws the last word at HARVEY *and it lands effectively. She exits.* HARVEY *stares daggers at* JUNE.

JUNE. Speaking of chilly, I need my cardigan, always a tiny bite in the air when the sun goes down.

JUNE *stands, starts to move towards the table a little unsteadily. She picks up the jug of punch but accidentally drops it and the punch spills everywhere.*

Oh, shit, oh, no! Fuck, shit, fuck!

HARVEY. Jesus, June.

THEO *makes a move.*

THEO. I'll get something to clean that up.

JUNE. No, I'll do it, I'll do it, I made the mess so I'll clean it up, Theo, that beautiful wooden table, and the stone floor. You stay here with Harvey, I'll sort it out, it's all under control.

And she totters off into the house, almost tripping as she does so.

HARVEY. She's hammered.

THEO. This place is a mess.

He starts to tidy up – picking scattered things up from around the terrace and placing them in a corner. HARVEY *grabs a lighter from the table and walks around the space, lighting the candles.*

HARVEY. God, Charlotte is angry, Theo.

THEO. Well, she's passionate.

HARVEY. Are you guys okay together? I mean in every way?

THEO. Every way?

HARVEY. Is there anything you feel you want to say to me?

THEO. About what?

HARVEY. You know what.

THEO. Not really.

HARVEY. 'Not really' you don't know what or 'not really' you don't have anything to say to me.

THEO. Both, I think.

HARVEY. Are you sure?

THEO. Yes, I think so.

HARVEY. *Think* so?

THEO. Yes, I do.

HARVEY. Okay.

Pause.

It's just I'm trying to figure out why your wife is so angry, you know, wound up all the time.

THEO. Maybe she's just a little confused, Harvey.

HARVEY. Maybe.

THEO. Most of us are, aren't we?

There's a pause and they stare at each other, holding it for a few seconds.

Thank you for that eulogy a little earlier, though I didn't recognise the man you were talking about.

HARVEY. Don't say that, Theo.

THEO. You say my work is quietly political but I suspect that's a little like saying something is moderately excellent. A bit of an oxymoron, isn't it?

HARVEY. Is it?

THEO. I'm not quite the same man you met all those years ago. Slowly, imperceptibly, drip, drip, drip, I have made... I make choices which are the easier ones. The ones that demand less of me.

HARVEY. I don't think...

THEO. Oh, I'm successful I suppose, yes, you were accurate in that. And I enjoy that success a little too much. But *important*... I'm not saying I don't have that gift... the one you mentioned... the gift of being able to imagine myself into other people's shoes.

He thinks about it a little, and it is as if, when he speaks, he is articulating something for the first time, and for his own benefit.

But what is the point of being able to imagine what it is like being other people, if we never, ever act on it? Oh, you may be repositioned, Harvey, but the view is always the same, just from a different angle. Nothing really changes, does it?

Pause.

Do you know, I feel as if I don't quite remember who I am. And that only a strong, sharp shock will be able to remind me.

CHARLOTTE *returns with* JUNE *in tow.* CHARLOTTE *is carrying a bowl of water and a washrag.*

JUNE. I'm so sorry, Charlotte, I'm a klutz, I just knocked it over and it went everywhere, I'm such a klutz.

CHARLOTTE. It's fine.

JUNE. Let me do it, give me the washrag, let me do it.

CHARLOTTE *starts trying to clean up the mess, but* JUNE *gets in* CHARLOTTE*'s way.*

CHARLOTTE. I think I'll just mop it up with water first.

JUNE. It's only fair that I should clean it up, I was the one who did it.

CHARLOTTE. It's fine, June, it doesn't matter who cleans it up.

JUNE. Oh, and it's on the floor too. Please, I insist, give me that, let me do it.

CHARLOTTE *snaps*.

CHARLOTTE. It's fine, I'm fine! Just let me do it my way, June, please!

HARVEY. She doesn't want your help, June, just let her do it, you've done enough already.

JUNE. It was an accident, Harvey.

HARVEY. Leave it, June. Pour yourself another glass of punch and watch the sun go down.

JUNE. I want to help.

CHARLOTTE. Tell you what, June, why don't you go and get the plates, we can start setting the table for dinner.

HARVEY. Is that a good idea?

JUNE. It's a great idea, I'll do that, thank you, Charlotte.

HARVEY. I know it's a Greek tradition, but try not to break any, sweetheart.

JUNE *goes back into the house*. CHARLOTTE *is wiping the table*. THEO *hovers*.

THEO. Do you want… should I?

CHARLOTTE. No, I'm fine, Theo, it's fine.

THEO. Okay.

There is a slight pause as she keeps cleaning up.

HARVEY. I feel I need to apologise on behalf of my wife.

CHARLOTTE. You don't need to do that.

HARVEY. She's clumsy after she's had a few.

CHARLOTTE. She's unhappy, that's all.

HARVEY. Wow. You girls have been talking, haven't you?

CHARLOTTE *hands the bowl of water to* THEO *but holds onto the washrag*.

CHARLOTTE. Theo, can you take this back inside?

He takes the bowl from her.

Thank you.

He takes the bowl inside, leaving CHARLOTTE *alone with* HARVEY. *For a few seconds they don't talk.*

CHARLOTTE *takes a look at the floor, notices the stain that the punch has left. She kneels down, scrubs a little.* HARVEY *watches her a while before he speaks.*

HARVEY. You don't know anything about Chile, Charlotte.

CHARLOTTE. I know enough.

HARVEY. What you read in your left-wing papers?

CHARLOTTE. Oh, Harvey, come on, you can do better than that.

HARVEY. So what do you know?

CHARLOTTE *stops scrubbing. She stands and looks at him, speaks with precision, and intent, head-on.*

CHARLOTTE. I know that there was a democratically elected government, Harvey, that was aiming to improve the lives and livelihoods of the majority of Chileans including the very poorest, and that those aims were sabotaged by your own government and by big-business interests. I know that your government was instrumental in bringing about the eventual downfall of the democratically elected Chilean one. I know that many people were tortured and killed in the process. And that many disappeared, Harvey.

She holds his stare. She holds it for a few seconds, but it's enough.

I know that your definition of democracy is quite a selective and unique one and that you've been very effective at convincing a large number of people in the world that it's also honourable. I know that it's useful to have an enemy like the Soviet Union – a bogeyman – because you can use that enemy to justify a whole lot of what you do whilst diverting attention from your own crimes and misdeeds and I know that if it wasn't for the Soviet Union, that bogeyman would be someone else.

She looks him straight in the eye again.

And I know that at some point soon, you're going to have to stop lying to yourself.

He moves away from her, goes to the cigarettes, takes one out of the packet, lights it.

HARVEY. Are you angry with me because I never fucked you, Charlotte?

CHARLOTTE. Don't do this. To yourself, I mean. Hold on to something. If dignity is out of reach, then I'd settle for decorum.

ADRIAN and ROSALIND run on to the terrace, dressed for supper.

ADRIAN. Mummy, we're ready for supper!

ROSALIND. We're ready, Mummy!

She kisses them.

CHARLOTTE. Well done, darlings, we'll be eating in a few minutes.

ADRIAN. Please, Mummy, now that we're in our dry clothes, can we dance with Harvey again?

ROSALIND. Yes, please, Mummy.

CHARLOTTE. No, darling, no more dancing with Harvey.

JUNE returns from the kitchen, holding a tray with a stack of plates on it, and cutlery. THEO follows her, carrying a plate with some small spinach triangles on it.

JUNE. Oh my God, look at you two, all dressed for dinner, don't you look adorable, like you're going to church or something.

THEO. That thing's going to take some time to heat up so I brought these spinach thingies to snack on.

He places them on the table, the kids take one each. JUNE puts the tray down, fills up her glass. CHARLOTTE takes the cutlery off the tray, starts placing it around the table.

JUNE. I wanna make a little speech now, why should I always be the one left out?

THEO. When do we ever leave you out, June?

JUNE. Adrian, Rosalind, come here.

The children go up to her. She kneels down to them.

Auntie June wants to say thank you so much for having us and we love you very much.

She kisses them, then stands again.

There, that's my speech.

She looks across at HARVEY.

Look at my husband, isn't he a handsome man? A little tired, but still a handsome devil, isn't he, Charlotte?

CHARLOTTE. Very, yes.

JUNE. And I know he's not perfect, but I love him to bits and he's all mine.

She returns to the plates, starts to place them around the table.

ADRIAN. Mummy, where are the papers and the crayons?

CHARLOTTE. Wherever you left them, darling.

ROSALIND. In the box!

She runs over to a box by the edge of the terrace and brings out some paper and crayons. ADRIAN *follows her, gets some too.*

ADRIAN. We're going to draw the sunset, like we did the other day.

They run to a spot on the terrace and sit down with their papers and crayons.

CHARLOTTE. What a good idea.

JUNE (*looking up at the sky*). I hope you've got lots of orange crayons, sweetie, you'll need them. And purple, and lilac, and a pale, pale blue.

She puts the plates down for a minute, leans over and has a spinach triangle.

These spinach thingies are so good, they're so yummy.

THEO. They're good, aren't they?

JUNE. They're delicious. Feta cheese, you see, Harvey, say what you like but it works.

She picks up the plates again, continues to place them around the table.

These are such beautiful plates, Charlotte.

CHARLOTTE. Yes, you said you liked them the other night, June.

JUNE. They're so special, I just can't get over it. The pattern, and the colours are just so lovely.

THEO. They came with the house.

JUNE. They're beautiful.

THEO. Yes, we were lucky, weren't we. We got all the stuff with the house, the furniture and everything, the plates, and cutlery…

CHARLOTTE. Theo, can you bring the chairs over?

THEO. And those beautiful old iron beds. They all belonged to the grandmother.

JUNE. Well, we were here when it all happened, Harvey, don't forget, we were standing right there.

HARVEY. We were, June, how could I ever forget?

CHARLOTTE. I'll go get the food.

THEO starts to gather the chairs around the table, CHARLOTTE goes back into the house. HARVEY drifts over to the area where the Polaroid photos are and spots them under the flowerpot. He moves the pot, picks the photos and pages of measurements up, starts looking through them. THEO notices.

THEO. Oh, that's… em… could you…

JUNE. I'm going to do some Greek cooking back at home, Harvey. I'll try a moussaka, and maybe that macaroni-pie thing we had on the beach. And those little potato cakes you like so much.

THEO. Doubt they'll taste the same in Washington, June.

JUNE. We'll have a Greek night, ouzo on tap.

HARVEY (*holding the photos*). This is a nice one of you, June.

JUNE. Let me see it.

She walks up, takes it off him. THEO comes and looks at it too.

Oh, it's awful, I look horrible, like a sad, ugly, old woman.

THEO. You don't look sad.

JUNE. Oh, you brute!

And she playfully pummels him on the arm.

HARVEY is looking through the other photos.

HARVEY. Why have you taken all these photographs of the house, Theo?

THEO immediately tenses up.

THEO. Oh, them, they're nothing.

HARVEY. What do you need them for?

THEO. Oh, nothing… they're just, em, they're just for a friend.

HARVEY. A friend?

HARVEY *now looks at the paper with all the measurements of the house on it.*

And the measurements. You've measured everything.

He reads from the paper.

'Square footage of front terrace.' 'Wall between door and kitchen window.' 'East-facing side wall.' What's it for?

THEO. Some work that will be done to the house.

HARVEY. You're renovating?

THEO. Well, yes, I mean, not really… but it's more complicated.

HARVEY. What is?

THEO. The thing is…

He pauses. Throws a quick look towards the house to check that CHARLOTTE *is out of earshot.*

HARVEY. Go on.

THEO. It's not important.

HARVEY. Tell me, Theo.

Pause.

THEO. We have loved it here, Harvey.

HARVEY. That's what your wife said earlier. You *have* loved it.

THEO. But the time has come to move on.

Pause as this information sinks in.

HARVEY. You're selling the house?

THEO. Well, kind of.

HARVEY. Kind of?

THEO. Well, yes. We are. We're selling the house.

Pause. JUNE *looks up.*

Not to *anyone*, though, not to strangers. To some people we know.
A German couple. They visited last July and fell in love with it.
They've made an offer we can't refuse.

HARVEY. I see.

JUNE. You're selling the house, Theo?

HARVEY. That's what he said, June.

JUNE. Oh, that makes me sad.

THEO. Me too, June. But our needs have changed.

HARVEY. Your *needs*.

THEO. It's not easy. With the children, I mean, up and down to
Greece. And life is expensive.

JUNE. But you're doing so well, Theo.

THEO. We spent Easter in Cornwall. We happened to find this little
cottage at the end of a dirt track, near the cliffs. We rented it but
it's up for sale.

HARVEY. How lovely.

THEO. So it's about convenience, really.

HARVEY. Convenience.

THEO. Maintaining this place is difficult. And then, as I say, with the
kids. I suppose it's easier to just get in the car…

HARVEY. And zoom it down to Cornwall.

THEO. But it won't be easy. We've spent some of our happiest times
here.

JUNE. Of course you have.

THEO. And we can't turn the offer down. It's a lot of money, it will
pay for the place in Cornwall and there'll be quite a bit left over.

HARVEY. How much are they offering?

THEO *is taken aback by the abruptness of the question, seems
suddenly embarrassed.*

THEO. Best not to talk about it with Charlotte. It's a sore point,
she'd rather I hadn't told you.

HARVEY. I'm sure.

JUNE. Of course, we understand, our lips are sealed.

THEO. So maybe let's just change the subject.

HARVEY. Yes, fine.

THEO. Anyway, we were very lucky when we found this place.

HARVEY. Best day of your lives.

> CHARLOTTE *returns with a large bowl of salad. She places it in the middle of the table.*

CHARLOTTE. We can start with this and then I'll get the stew after, it still needs a few minutes, that hob is acting up again.

> *They all start to sit down.*

JUNE. That salad looks beautiful, Charlotte.

CHARLOTTE. Same as usual. Children, put away the drawing things and come and sit at the table, supper's ready.

ADRIAN. In a minute, Mummy.

JUNE. Our last meal together.

THEO. Indeed.

JUNE. You've been so kind and hospitable. You've made us feel loved. I'd make another speech, but I think I might just start to cry. I don't know why, but I think I might. I feel very sad all of a sudden.

THEO. Let's try not to cry, June.

JUNE. I'm such a softie, especially when I've had a few drinks.

CHARLOTTE. Help yourselves to the salad.

> *They all start to help themselves to the food.*

HARVEY. So you're selling the house, Charlotte.

> CHARLOTTE *throws* THEO *a look, who in turn stares at* HARVEY.

THEO. Harvey…

HARVEY. I know, I'm sorry, Theo, but no more secrets. No more secrets between friends.

CHARLOTTE. Yes, Harvey, we are. We're buying a house in Cornwall.

We love it down there and it will be good for Theo. It's the perfect spot to write in.

HARVEY. Well, Cornwall's beautiful.

*He moves over to the punch, pours himself a glass. There is a
pause as the others continue to serve themselves the food.*

Did you ever enquire about Maria and her father, Theo? I mean
about how things turned out for them in Australia?

THEO. Not really, no, I mean the uncle was the only one left on the
island but then about three or four years ago he too must have
moved away because suddenly he disappeared.

HARVEY. No, he didn't move away, Theo. He died of pancreatic
cancer.

THEO *stops what he's doing, as does* JUNE. CHARLOTTE
looks up.

That's when all those words come in handy – I mean the English
words which come from ancient Greek, you realise how many
words share that root and it really helps when you're having a
conversation with the man on the street. Because, yesterday when
we went to the port to get the *Tribune*, I left June in a bar and
stopped by the tobacconist's to buy her cigarettes and I asked the
guy, I said, 'Where was the man who used to own this shop,' and
then he told me what had happened to him but his English was so-
so, and every so often he'd say something in Greek and when he
said that the guy had died of '*pankreatikos karkinos*', well,
I figured, that's pancreatic cancer.

Pause.

And then I asked him about Maria and her father too, and if
he knew what had happened to them. And as it turned out, he did.
His mother knew the family quite well, it's a small community,
it's natural. So he told me what happened to them.

THEO. Why didn't you tell us?

HARVEY. Because I didn't want to upset you, Theo. I didn't even
tell June, did I, sweetheart?

JUNE. Tell me what?

HARVEY. But now I think that you should know. I think it only right
that you should know.

Pause.

JUNE. What happened, Harvey?

HARVEY. Well, June, he told me that in the beginning everything had started out okay. Maria and her dad had arrived in Sydney, the father had a job waitering in a Greek restaurant and they were renting a small apartment but that then the father – well, the father had joined up with two other Greek guys and had invested whatever money he had in setting up his own taverna, but they'd got it wrong because the only area they could afford to rent the premises in was – well, it just wasn't the right neighbourhood for that kind of venture, it was full of Oriental people or something, Chinese, I don't know. And then he fell out with one of the guys he'd opened it with, and he was swindled, and from what I understood, he just lost all his savings, and remember he didn't have all that much to begin with, I mean he was quite desperate when he left Greece in the first place, he had to sell the skin off his back for next to nothing.

JUNE. I remember, that poor man.

HARVEY. So then this young tobacconist guy tells me that eventually all this took its toll on his health – well, it does, doesn't it – and that he died – Maria's father died a few years after they arrived in Australia, of some heart thing.

THEO. What happened to Maria?

HARVEY. Well, Maria was alone now, Theo, because by that point her uncle over here had died as well. So she was in Australia, and she was on her own. Apparently, she found a job in a hotel, cleaning rooms or whatever, but she was finding it hard to make ends meet.

THEO. Then what?

HARVEY. Well, then, one day, a couple of years later, the tobacconist's mother got a letter from a cousin of hers in Australia who bumped into Maria one night on a street somewhere in the rougher outskirts of the city. But that was the last time anybody ever saw her so nobody from the island knows what happened to her after that.

Pause.

This cousin wrote that on that occasion when she saw Maria for the last time she seemed a little strange, I don't know, lost or something, confused, and that she had said something that the tobacconist's mother had never been able to forget.

THEO. And what was that?

HARVEY. That when her father had died all she had wanted was to return to Greece. It's natural. To come home.

Pause.

But that she didn't have a house to return to.

Pause.

It's sad. Life doesn't always turn out the way we hope it will.

There is a pause, and suddenly JUNE *starts crying.*

JUNE. Oh, God, that girl, that poor baby girl.

CHARLOTTE *turns to the children. She speaks calmly, but resolutely.*

CHARLOTTE. Adrian, take your sister inside, darling. Go into your room, and Daddy or I will bring your supper there.

ROSALIND. We're drawing, Mummy.

CHARLOTTE. Adrian, Rosalind, will you please do as I say.

ADRIAN. But Mummy, we want to eat with –

CHARLOTTE. Don't argue, Adrian. Do it now!

ADRIAN *grabs* ROSALIND *by the hand and angrily leads her into the house, shouting as he goes.*

ADRIAN. What's wrong with you today?

They go. CHARLOTTE *turns to* HARVEY *and* JUNE.

CHARLOTTE. I'm sorry, June, but I'd like you and Harvey to leave the house, please. I mean, I'd rather you didn't stay here tonight, I'd rather you left.

THEO. Darling…

JUNE (*through tears*). What did you say?

HARVEY. We're being kicked out, June. I'll go get the cases but you'll need your handbag, where have you put it?

JUNE. Being kicked out?

THEO. Charlotte…

HARVEY. It's August, I imagine most of the hotels are full, but we'll find something and if the worse comes to the worst we'll settle on a bench at the port, it's just the one night.

CHARLOTTE. Get out of this house.

HARVEY. So I'll get those cases now, June, but it would help me a great deal if you could look for your handbag and gather any other things you may have lying around and then we'll call a taxi and get out of your way.

THEO. Harvey, wait, let's just talk…

CHARLOTTE. THEO, NO!

HARVEY. Come on, June, get into gear.

JUNE *stands, but is unsteady on her feet, and emotional.*

JUNE. Why are you kicking us out, Charlotte? What have we done?

CHARLOTTE. I'm sorry, June.

HARVEY. Come on, sweetheart.

HARVEY *makes his way towards the house, then stops, turns to* CHARLOTTE *and* THEO.

It may come as a surprise to you to learn this, but when I heard that news yesterday I had to take a five-minute walk through the backstreets of the port, on my own. You see, I remembered that girl, and all the hope she had, and I…

But he is suddenly overcome with emotion, his voice breaks and he stops. He takes a few seconds, then continues.

I didn't want to tell you, Theo, Charlotte, and that's the honest truth. But you haven't given me a choice, Charlotte.

Pause.

I will carry that boy on my shoulders – the Chilean one, his music, the way it ended so abruptly. I will carry him – the full weight of him – and many more like him. But you should carry Maria.

Pause.

You see, Charlotte, if we're going to stop lying, I think it only fair that we do so together.

And he walks into the house.

JUNE *walks unsteadily towards the small bottle of nail varnish, and picks it up.*

JUNE. I'm sorry, I don't know any more, I just don't understand.

And she follows HARVEY *into the house.* CHARLOTTE *breaks, falling into* THEO*'s arms, then pushing him away. She is hysterical.*

CHARLOTTE. Oh, God, why did we do it, why did we do it? Why did we do it, Theo?

THEO. We weren't to know.

CHARLOTTE. She said... she had a sense... she tried to stop us, Theo, she tried to stop us!

THEO. I know, I know she did.

CHARLOTTE. But we didn't listen, we didn't listen, Theo!

THEO. It was my fault, Charlotte, I wanted it so much.

CHARLOTTE. It wasn't ours, it wasn't ours to have!

THEO. We didn't think we were doing anything wrong.

CHARLOTTE. But we were, Theo, we were. We bought the house for nothing.

THEO. I know, Charlotte, I know we did.

CHARLOTTE. Because they needed it so much, they *needed* it so much!

THEO. We're not bad people, Charlotte.

CHARLOTTE. And I didn't ask, I never asked.

THEO. Asked what?

CHARLOTTE. About them. About what had happened to them. In Australia, or afterwards. I didn't want to know, I didn't want to know, Theo.

THEO. It's all right, Charlotte, it's all right.

CHARLOTTE. I never went near that tobacconist's because I didn't want to know!

THEO. Okay.

CHARLOTTE. She tried to warn us but we didn't listen!

And she falls into his arms, and weeps.

HARVEY *returns, carrying two suitcases and a backpack.*

CHARLOTTE *immediately separates from* THEO, *not wanting to show* HARVEY *her vulnerability.*

HARVEY. June's make-up is all over the place, she's going to take a few minutes gathering her stuff up.

THEO. That's fine.

HARVEY. But we'll need to order a taxi.

THEO. I'll do it.

He checks to see if that's all right with CHARLOTTE; *she assents.*

THEO *goes into the house.* CHARLOTTE *walks to the front of the terrace, stares out at the sunset.*

A few seconds pass before she speaks.

CHARLOTTE. You know that first evening when you came here, you said that I'd asked you over because I was attracted to you.

HARVEY. I did.

CHARLOTTE. Well, you were right, I was. And I kept asking you back. Even this year, I wanted to see you, I couldn't help myself. I didn't understand it, and I resented it, but I did.

Pause.

Now I think it's because I believed what you said that night on this terrace – that you were a good man. And that those things you talked about – those ideals, those values – reason, imagination, questioning, democracy – that all those things you spoke about with such conviction, well, that you were doing what you could to defend them, at great cost to yourself. I believed you, I felt the gratitude you wanted me to feel, and yes, I felt that attraction.

Pause.

But not any more. You have forfeited the right to use those words.

She turns and looks at him.

And there is nothing else left.

She walks into the house, HARVEY *is left alone.*

For a minute, he does nothing, just stands there, as if allowing the peremptory blows of the words she has just spoken to land on him.

Then, slowly, he moves towards the cassette recorder. He looks and finds the Greek tape – picks it up and puts it into the recorder, presses play.

The rebetiko *music comes on and fills the air: mournful, plangent.*

HARVEY *stands straight for a second or two, and listens to the powerful music.*

Then something happens – his body starts to move a little as if responding to it – his neck, his arm. A tiny movement, but awkward and faltering. It is an instinctive response to the music and the way he moves expresses a profound sense of alienation and despair.

THEO *comes out.* HARVEY *sees him and immediately switches off the music.*

HARVEY. Still trying to perfect that fucking dance. It isn't easy.

THEO *is terse, unyielding.*

THEO. The taxi will be here in five minutes. And I found you a room in a hotel near the port.

HARVEY. That's kind, Theo.

HARVEY *approaches* THEO *and reaches for him.* THEO *doesn't move. But* HARVEY *perseveres, moving closer to him. He stretches out his arms again, as if inviting* THEO *to embrace him.* THEO *continues to resist. Then, of course, he relents, opens his arms.* HARVEY *falls into them, and sobs.*

Then, he kisses THEO *on the mouth. But it is less of a sexual thing, something more ineffable, one person's desperate need for another.*

Don't worry, I'm not a queer. I just love you, is all.

THEO *doesn't know how to reply, so he doesn't.* HARVEY *holds* THEO*'s face in his hands, looks him in the eyes.*

And thank you, Theo.

THEO. What for?

HARVEY. For being loyal.

THEO. Cheese and pickle.

> HARVEY *points at the chair, the one he pointed at the end of Act One.*

HARVEY. There she is, in that chair, overlooking her terrain.

THEO. Thalia.

HARVEY. No, not Thalia. Not the Muse of Comedy, Theo. The other one.

THEO. The other one?

HARVEY. Melpomene.

> THEO *hovers for a minute, then goes into the house again.*

> HARVEY *is left alone. He just stands there, looking at the sunset, his eyes fixed into the distance. He does not move again until the end of the play.*

> *A few seconds pass.*

> *Then* AGAPE *walks on. She is an elderly Greek woman and she is wearing simple peasant clothes. She is carrying a bowl of string beans. She is* MARIA's *grandmother.*

> *She comes up to the table and pulls a chair up, sits.*

> *She starts stringing the beans, but after she's done a couple she stops, and shouts.*

AGAPE. *Μαρία, Μαρία, που είσαι;* [Maria! Maria, where are you?]

> *She carries on stringing the beans.*

> *A few seconds later,* MARIA *comes out of the house. She looks a couple of years younger than when we last saw her, maybe her hair is in a ponytail, maybe she's wearing a school uniform. She is carrying an English textbook, something from school.*

MARIA. *Γεια σου γιαγιά.* [Hello, yia-yia.]

AGAPE. *Που κρύβεσαι;* [Where have you been?]

MARIA. *Τ' Αγγλικά μου κάνω.* [I've been doing my English.]

AGAPE. *Κάτσε να με βοηθήσεις λίγο.* [Sit down and help me for a while.]

MARIA *sits down and starts stringing beans with her grandmother. She speaks to her in English.*

MARIA. I am doing the English homework, Yia-yia.

AGAPE. *Τι λες;* [What are you going on about?]

MARIA. *T' Αγγλικά μου.* [My English.]

AGAPE. *Τι τα θέλεις;* [What do you need it for?]

MARIA. My father is saying it is very useful for me to speak the English.

AGAPE. *Τι είναι αυτά που μου λες βρε!* [Listen to you!]

For a few seconds, they string the beans in silence. Then, AGAPE puts down the beans, and looks out. She is looking in the same direction that HARVEY is, out towards the sunset, and the sea. MARIA keeps stringing the beans, and looking at her English textbook.

Maria?

MARIA *looks up.*

MARIA. *Τι;* [What is it?]

AGAPE. *T'αγαπάς αυτό το σπίτι;* [Do you love this house?]

MARIA. *Το ξέρεις ότι το αγαπάω.* [You know I do.]

AGAPE *strokes the side of* MARIA*'s face.*

AGAPE. *Μια μέρα δικό σου θα'ναι. Θα το προσέχεις, μου το υπόσχεσαι;* [One day it will be yours. You'll look after it, you promise?]

MARIA. *Στο υπόσχομαι.* [I promise.]

AGAPE. *To σπίτι.* [The house.]

Pause.

Και τα δέντρα. [And the trees.]

Pause.

Και την θάλασσα. [And the sea.]

The End.

Other Titles in this Series

Mike Bartlett
BULL
GAME
AN INTERVENTION
KING CHARLES III
WILD

Jez Butterworth
THE FERRYMAN
JERUSALEM
JEZ BUTTERWORTH PLAYS: ONE
MOJO
THE NIGHT HERON
PARLOUR SONG
THE RIVER
THE WINTERLING

Alexi Kaye Campbell
ALEXI KAYE CAMPBELL
    PLAYS: ONE
BRACKEN MOOR
THE FAITH MACHINE
THE PRIDE
SUNSET AT THE VILLA THALIA

Caryl Churchill
BLUE HEART
CHURCHILL PLAYS: THREE
CHURCHILL PLAYS: FOUR
CHURCHILL: SHORTS
CLOUD NINE
DING DONG THE WICKED
A DREAM PLAY *after* Strindberg
DRUNK ENOUGH TO SAY
    I LOVE YOU?
ESCAPED ALONE
FAR AWAY
HERE WE GO
HOTEL
ICECREAM
LIGHT SHINING IN BUCKINGHAMSHIRE
LOVE AND INFORMATION
MAD FOREST
A NUMBER
PIGS AND DOGS
SEVEN JEWISH CHILDREN
THE SKRIKER
THIS IS A CHAIR
THYESTES *after* Seneca
TRAPS

Kevin Elyot
COMING CLEAN
THE DAY I STOOD STILL
FORTY WINKS
KEVIN ELYOT: FOUR PLAYS
MOUTH TO MOUTH
MY NIGHT WITH REG
TWILIGHT SONG

debbie tucker green
BORN BAD
DIRTY BUTTERFLY
HANG
NUT
A PROFOUNDLY AFFECTIONATE,
    PASSIONATE DEVOTION TO
    SOMEONE (– *NOUN*)
RANDOM
STONING MARY
TRADE & GENERATIONS
TRUTH AND RECONCILIATION

Lucy Kirkwood
BEAUTY AND THE BEAST
    with Katie Mitchell
BLOODY WIMMIN
THE CHILDREN
CHIMERICA
HEDDA *after* Ibsen
IT FELT EMPTY WHEN THE HEART WENT
    AT FIRST BUT IT IS ALRIGHT NOW
LUCY KIRKWOOD PLAYS: ONE
MOSQUITOES
NSFW
TINDERBOX

Conor McPherson
DUBLIN CAROL
GIRL FROM THE NORTH COUNTRY
    with Bob Dylan
McPHERSON PLAYS: ONE
McPHERSON PLAYS: TWO
McPHERSON PLAYS: THREE
THE NIGHT ALIVE
PORT AUTHORITY
THE SEAFARER
SHINING CITY
THE VEIL
THE WEIR

Stef Smith
GIRL IN THE MACHINE
HUMAN ANIMALS
REMOTE
SWALLOW

Jack Thorne
2ND MAY 1997
BUNNY
BURYING YOUR BROTHER IN THE
    PAVEMENT
HOPE
JACK THORNE PLAYS: ONE
JUNKYARD
LET THE RIGHT ONE IN
    after John Ajvide Lindqvist
MYDIDAE
STACY & FANNY AND FAGGOT
WHEN YOU CURE ME
WOYZECK *after* Büchner

Enda Walsh
ARLINGTON
BALLYTURK
BEDBOUND & MISTERMAN
DELIRIUM
DISCO PIGS & SUCKING DUBLIN
ENDA WALSH PLAYS: ONE
ENDA WALSH PLAYS: TWO
MISTERMAN
THE NEW ELECTRIC BALLROOM
ONCE
PENELOPE
THE SMALL THINGS
ROALD DAHL'S THE TWITS
THE WALWORTH FARCE

Tom Wells
BROKEN BISCUITS
FOLK
JUMPERS FOR GOALPOSTS
THE KITCHEN SINK
ME, AS A PENGUIN

'A great published script makes you understand what the play is, at its heart' *Slate Magazine*

Enjoyed this book? Choose from hundreds more classic and contemporary plays from Nick Hern Books, the UK's leading independent theatre publisher.

Our full range is available to browse online now, including:

Award-winning plays from leading contemporary dramatists, including *King Charles III* by Mike Bartlett, *Anne Boleyn* by Howard Brenton, *Jerusalem* by Jez Butterworth, *A Breakfast of Eels* by Robert Holman, *Chimerica* by Lucy Kirkwood, *The Night Alive* by Conor McPherson, *The James Plays* by Rona Munro, *Nell Gwynn* by Jessica Swale, and many more…

Ground-breaking drama from the most exciting up-and-coming playwrights, including Vivienne Franzmann, James Fritz, Ella Hickson, Anna Jordan, Jack Thorne, Phoebe Waller-Bridge, Tom Wells, and many more…

Twentieth-century classics, including *Cloud Nine* by Caryl Churchill, *Death and the Maiden* by Ariel Dorfman, *Pentecost* by David Edgar, *Angels in America* by Tony Kushner, *Long Day's Journey into Night* by Eugene O'Neill, *The Deep Blue Sea* by Terence Rattigan, *Machinal* by Sophie Treadwell, and many more…

Timeless masterpieces from playwrights throughout the ages, including Anton Chekhov, Euripides, Henrik Ibsen, Federico García Lorca, Christopher Marlowe, Molière, William Shakespeare, Richard Brinsley Sheridan, Oscar Wilde, and many more…

Every playscript is a world waiting to be explored. Find yours at **www.nickhernbooks.co.uk** – you'll receive a 20% discount, plus free UK postage & packaging for orders over £30.

'Publishing plays gives permanent form to an evanescent art, and allows many more people to have some kind of experience of a play than could ever see it in the theatre' *Nick Hern, publisher*

www.nickhernbooks.co.uk

www.nickhernbooks.co.uk

facebook.com/nickhernbooks

twitter.com/nickhernbooks